Lecture Notes in Computer Science   13960

Founding Editors

Gerhard Goos
Juris Hartmanis

Editorial Board Members

The series Lecture Notes in Computer Science (LNCS), including its subseries Lecture Notes in Artificial Intelligence (LNAI) and Lecture Notes in Bioinformatics (LNBI), has established itself as a medium for the publication of new developments in computer science and information technology research, teaching, and education.

LNCS enjoys close cooperation with the computer science R & D community, the series counts many renowned academics among its volume editors and paper authors, and collaborates with prestigious societies. Its mission is to serve this international community by providing an invaluable service, mainly focused on the publication of conference and workshop proceedings and postproceedings. LNCS commenced publication in 1973.

Martin Kutrib · Uwe Meyer

Editors

Reversible Computation

15th International Conference, RC 2023
Giessen, Germany, July 18–19, 2023
Proceedings

 Springer

Editors
Martin Kutrib ⓘD
Universität Giessen
Giessen, Germany

Uwe Meyer ⓘD
Technische Hochschule Mittelhessen
Giessen, Germany

ISSN 0302-9743   ISSN 1611-3349 (electronic)
Lecture Notes in Computer Science
ISBN 978-3-031-38099-0   ISBN 978-3-031-38100-3 (eBook)
https://doi.org/10.1007/978-3-031-38100-3

This Springer imprint is published by the registered company Springer Nature Switzerland AG
The registered company address is: Gewerbestrasse 11, 6330 Cham, Switzerland

Preface

This volume contains the papers presented at the 15th Conference on Reversible Computation (RC 2023), held from July 18th to 19th, 2023. The conference was jointly organized by the Universität Giessen and the Technische Hochschule Mittelhessen in Giessen, Germany. It took place on the main campus of the Technische Hochschule Mittelhessen. After two years of holding the conference online because of the COVID-19 pandemic situation, last year's edition in Urbino returned to normal. Fortunately, this situation persisted and we could continue with an on-site, in-person event.

The Reversible Computation conference brings together researchers from computer science, mathematics, engineering, and physics to discuss new developments and directions for future research in the emerging area of Reversible Computation. This includes, for example, reversible formal models, reversible programming languages, reversible circuits, and quantum computing. The conference series is a major international venue for the dissemination of new results in reversible computations. The previous 14 conferences were held in the following locations: Urbino, Italy (2022), Nagoya, Japan (2021), Oslo, Norway (2020), Lausanne, Switzerland (2019), Leicester, UK (2018), Kolkata, India (2017), Bologna, Italy (2016), Grenoble, France (2015), Kyoto, Japan (2014), Victoria, Canada (2013), Copenhagen, Denmark (2012), Gent, Belgium (2011), Bremen, Germany (2010), York, UK (2009).

This year, the conference received 19 submissions from authors in 17 countries. Each submission was reviewed by at least three reviewers, who provided detailed evaluations as well as constructive comments and recommendations. For this purpose, an intensive single-blind review process was conducted. After extensive discussions, the Program Committee accepted 11 full papers and 3 short papers for presentation at the conference (leading to an acceptance rate of 74%). In addition to these papers, this volume contains the invited paper "Energy Complexity of Computation" by Cem Say (Boğaziçi Üniversitesi, Turkey) and an abstract of the invited talk "The Quantum Effect: A Recipe for Quantum Π" by Robin Kaarsgaard (University of Southern Denmark, Denmark).

We are very grateful to the invited speakers and all authors of the submitted papers, as well as the members of the Program Committee for their excellent work in making this selection. We also thank the additional external reviewers for their careful evaluation. Special thanks go to Markus Holzer, Claudio Mezzina, Claudio Moraga, and Mariusz Rawski, who helped the PC in a very short time with reviews and well-founded opinions. All these efforts were the basis for the success of the conference. We are indebted to all participants for attending the conference. Last, but not least, the collaboration with Springer in preparing this volume was very efficient and pleasant.

   Support from the Universität Giessen and the Technische Hochschule Mittelhessen is
gratefully acknowledged. Also, we would like to thank Rodolfo Rossini and his company
Vaire for having partially supported RC 2023.

July 2023   Martin Kutrib
                                                               Uwe Meyer

Organization

Program Committee Chairs

Martin Kutrib	Universität Giessen, Germany
Uwe Meyer	Technische Hochschule Mittelhessen, Germany

Steering Committee

Rolf Drechsler	University of Bremen, Germany
Robert Glück	University of Copenhagen, Denmark
Ivan Lanese	University of Bologna/Inria, Italy
Irek Ulidowski	University of Leicester, UK
Robert Wille	Technical University of Munich, Germany, and SCCH GmbH, Austria

Program Committee

Clément Aubert	Augusta University, USA
Kamalika Datta	German Research Centre for Artificial Intelligence, Germany
Robert Glück	University of Copenhagen, Denmark
James Hoey	University of Leicester, UK
Ivan Lanese	University of Bologna/Inria, Italy
Sylvain Lombardy	Université de Bordeaux, France
Andreas Malcher	Universität Giessen, Germany
Claudio Antares Mezzina	Universitá di Urbino, Italy
Torben Ægidius Mogensen	University of Copenhagen, Denmark
Iain Phillips	Imperial College London, UK
Giovanni Pighizzini	Universitá di Milano, Italy
Himanshu Thapliyal	University of Tennessee, USA
Irek Ulidowski	University of Leicester, UK
Shigeru Yamashita	Ritsumeikan University, Japan
Tetsuo Yokoyama	Nanzan University, Japan
Shoji Yuen	Nagoya University, Japan

Additional Reviewers

Niklas Deworetzki
Markus Holzer
Jarkko Kari
Pietro Lami
Pierre McKenzie
Carlo Mereghetti

Claudio Mezzina
Claudio Moraga
Krzysztof Podlaski
Luca Prigioniero
Mariusz Rawski
Claudio Sacerdoti Coen

The Quantum Effect: A Recipe for Quantum Π (Abstract of Invited Talk)

Robin Kaarsgaard (iD)

Department of Mathematics and Computer Science, University of Southern Denmark,
Campusvej 55, 5230 Odense, Denmark
kaarsgaard@imada.sdu.dk

Abstract. The prevalent view of quantum computing characterises it as an extension of reversible classical computing with constructs for managing superpositions. Adding native syntactic support for superpositions has disadvantages, however. It requires the addition of scalars with an associated algebra and imposes a low-level matrix-oriented perspective on the resulting model. We use free categorical constructions to characterise quantum computing as the combination of two copies of a reversible classical language, glued by the complementarity equations of classical structures. We apply this recipe to construct an approximately universal quantum programming language from two copies of Π, the classical language internal to rig groupoids. The construction takes the form of a series of arrows giving a positive answer to the question of the existence of a quantum effect, allowing the addition of measurement by layering a further effect on top, and permitting reasoning about quantum programs (with or without measurement) through a combination of classical reasoning and reasoning about complementarity.

Contents

Invited Paper

Energy Complexity of Computation

Ahmet Celal Cem Say[✉][iD]

Department of Computer Engineering, Boğaziçi University, İstanbul, Turkey
say@boun.edu.tr

Abstract. Computational complexity theory is the study of the fundamental resource requirements associated with the solutions of different problems. Time, space (memory) and randomness (number of coin tosses) are some of the resource types that have been examined both independently, and in terms of tradeoffs between each other, in this context. Since it is well known that each bit of information "forgotten" by a device is linked to an unavoidable increase in entropy and an associated energy cost, one can also view energy as a computational resource. Constant-memory machines that are only allowed to access their input strings in a single left-to-right pass provide a good framework for the study of energy complexity. There exists a natural hierarchy of regular languages based on energy complexity, with the class of reversible languages forming the lowest level. When the machines are allowed to make errors with small nonzero probability, some problems can be solved with lower energy cost. Tradeoffs between energy and other complexity measures can be studied in the framework of Turing machines or two-way finite automata, which can be rewritten to work reversibly if one increases their space and time usage.

Keywords: Thermodynamic complexity · Reversible computation · Energy complexity · Finite automata

1 Introduction

Computational complexity theory is the study of the fundamental resource requirements associated with the solutions of different problems. Time, space (memory) and randomness (number of coin tosses) are some of the resource types that have been examined both independently, and in terms of tradeoffs between each other, in this context. The fact [9] that each bit of information that is "forgotten" (in the sense that the machine's logical state in the previous step is not determined uniquely by its present state) by a computational device is linked to an unavoidable increase in entropy and an associated energy cost forces one to view energy as a computational resource as well.

Bennett [1] showed that every computation that can be carried out by a standard Turing machine (TM) can also be performed by a reversible TM (i.e., one where no configuration has more than one predecessor) that leaves no "garbage" information (which would have to be erased sooner or later for reusing the computer) in memory except the input and output strings at the completion of

M. Kutrib and U. Meyer (Eds.): RC 2023, LNCS 13960, pp. 3–11, 2023.
https://doi.org/10.1007/978-3-031-38100-3_1

its execution.[1] This result establishes that machines which possess the (time and space) resources and architectural flexibility to implement Bennett's construction in [1] can in principle operate with no lower bound on their energy cost, which naturally begs the question about what happens when those other resources are constrained. In this context, Lange et al. [10] showed that one can build "time-hungry" vs. "space-hungry" reversible machines for solving the same problem, where constraining one of those two resources leads to a high demand for the other one if one wishes to preserve reversibility.

The finite automaton, which is one of the oldest models in theoretical computer science, provides a good framework for the study of energy complexity, because the extemely constrained case of real-time deterministic constant-space machines enables us to identify subclasses of regular languages characterized by the energy requirements for their recognition, i.e. to actually talk about how much energy is required to solve a specific problem (at a specific temperature). In this paper, we will give an overview of recent work in this context. The rest of this manuscript is structured as follows. Section 2 lays the groundwork. Section 3 summarizes what is known about the intrinsic energy requirements associated by various regular languages, when one considers bounds on the total number of bits that have to be forgotten during the computation of any automaton recognizing the language as a function of the length of the input string. Section 4 summarizes the results of Yılmaz et al. [16] on the classification of regular languages according to the "peak energy load" required for their recognition by real-time finite automata. Quantum versions of such machines are also considered, and a tradeoff between the allowed error level and energy cost is demonstrated in this context. Section 5 looks at other tradeoffs with allowed time and memory budgets and input access modes, and Sect. 6 covers the notion of energy complexity of proof verification systems. We conclude with a list of open questions.

2   Preliminaries

We assume that the reader is familiar with the definitions of basic computational models like the deterministic finite automaton and the (single-tape) Turing machine [14]. Specifically, we model the input as being read from a tape that contains a special end-marker symbol on its leftmost cell. A *real-time* deterministic finite automaton (rtDFA) moves the input tape head to the right at each move. Some results are sensitive to whether a real-time machine is allowed to halt and announce its verdict about the input before it consumes all of the input string or not. In the following, we use the variant where the entire input is consumed, unless otherwise indicated.

For the study of time-space-energy tradeoffs, we will consider finite-state machines with more control on their input heads. A *one-way* deterministic finite automaton (1DFA) is allowed to pause its head for one or more computational

---

[1] Li and Vitanyi [11] extended this analysis to consider anything other than the input and output strings (for example, the code of the program computing the transformation) as a potential cause of energy cost.

steps on the same tape cell during its left-to-right walk. A *two-way* deterministic finite automaton (2DFA) can move its head to the left as well. These more flexible machines can enter infinite loops. We adopt the convention that any input string for such a machine is flanked on both sides by end-markers. These devices are best thought of as single-tape Turing machines operating on a read-only tape segment, and they halt only when they enter designated accept or reject states, or when they attempt to move the head beyond an end-marker.

A general real-time quantum finite automaton (rtQFA) model [12] will be used to examine the "peak load" requirements of regular language recognition by such machines for both the zero-error and bounded-error cases. Formally, a rtQFA is a 5-tuple $(Q, \Sigma, \{\mathcal{E}_\sigma | \sigma \in \Sigma_\triangleright\}, q_1, F)$, where

1. $Q = \{q_1, \ldots, q_n\}$ is the finite set of machine states,
2. Σ is the finite input alphabet,
3. $q_1 \in Q$ is the initial state,
4. $F \subseteq Q$ is the set of accepting states, and
5. $\Sigma_\triangleright = \Sigma \cup \{\triangleright\}$, where $\triangleright \notin \Sigma$ is the left end-marker symbol, and for each $\sigma \in \Sigma_\triangleright$, $\mathcal{E}_\sigma$ is the superoperator describing the transformation on the current configuration of the machine associated with the consumption of the symbol σ. For some $l \geq 1$, each $\mathcal{E}_\sigma$ consists of l operation elements $\{E_{\sigma,1}, \ldots, E_{\sigma,l}\}$, where each operation element is a complex-valued $n \times n$ matrix.

The operation of these machines is discussed in detail in [16]. The following is an overview of the important aspects: It has been realized [5,12] that quantum finite automaton models have to support both unitary transformations and partial measurements in order to be able to match the computational power of classical finite automata, since early rtQFA models that restricted the machine to unitary evolution throughout its execution can only recognize some, but not all regular languages. Essentially, a classical finite automaton forgets information (about its previous configuration) every time it consumes an input symbol σ to transition into a state that has more than one such incoming σ-transitions. The execution of a "modern" rtQFA consists of alternating stages of unitary evolutions and measurements. Since the machine's memory is limited, it has to "forget" past measurement results as new observations come in during the execution. The number l in the definition above plays the same role as the maximum number of simultaneous σ-transitions in a classical machine: $\log_2 l$ corresponds to the amount of information associated with each such measurement, which corresponds to the energy cost that will have to be paid for that step in the execution of the rtQFA.

3 Energy Complexity of Language Recognition by Real-Time Machines

Two main sources of computational energy cost have been studied in the previous work mentioned in Sect. 1. The first of these is associated with the entropy increase caused by individual computational steps which map multiple configurations into a single one. The second corresponds to "garbage", i.e. the erasure cost of resetting the device's configuration to its initial state for the subsequent execution. When the model in question is a real-time finite automaton that consumes all of its input, the only thing that may need resetting is the final state of the machine, which corresponds to $\log_2 k$ bits of deleted information, where k is the number of states of the minimal automaton. This is a constant, whereas the total cost incurred by the computational steps can of course be an increasing function of the length of the input, which is more in line with the other resources considered in complexity theory.

We define the *energy complexity* of a real-time finite automaton as the maximum number of bits of information that it forgets while running on any input of some length n. Group languages, [2] which have rtDFAs that contain no states with more than one incoming transition with the same input symbol, can be recognized with zero energy energy complexity. The following results regarding the energy requirements of the remaining class of "irreversible" regular languages according to this metric are from [7]:

Theorem 1. *Every irreversible regular language has linear energy complexity.*

The lower bound in Theorem 1 can be established by considering that any rtDFA that recognizes an irreversible language running on inputs of the form $w\sigma^*$ must be "trapped" in a loop of at least $U \geq 1$ states, and at least one of those states must have at least two incoming σ-transitions. It is clear that the repeated state will have to be visited once every U steps for long input strings, leading to an energy complexity that is proportional to at least $\frac{n}{U}$.

As for the upper bound, Kıyak and Say [7] present a template that can be used to build energy-efficient rtDFA's for any irreversible regular language. Given any rtDFA recognizing some language L on alphabet Σ and any desired positive real number ϵ, their method can be used to construct a finite automaton with energy complexity at most $(\log_2 |\Sigma| + \epsilon)n$ for L. The construction involves a space-energy tradeoff, where one uses more states in the machine to let it run "reversibly" (by storing, rather than forgetting information about its past configurations) for, say, k steps, and then forgetting that stored information wholesale at the end of each such run of k steps. Increasing the value of k increases the number of states, but it also allows the machine to "compress" the information to be forgotten more efficiently.

But do some irreversible languages really require more energy to recognize than some others? The answer is yes. We can, in fact, define the following sets of regular languages on a binary alphabet Σ:

- An irreversible language L is said to be *minimally expensive* if, for every positive real number ϵ, L can be recognized by some finite automaton M with energy complexity $c_M n$, where $c_M < \epsilon$.
- An irreversible language L is said to be *maximally expensive* if any rtDFA M recognizing L has energy complexity at least $(1 + \epsilon)n$ for some positive real number ϵ.

The language $L_1 = \{w \mid w \in \Sigma^*, |w| \geq 1\}$ is shown to be minimally expensive in [7].

Let $L_{bb} = \{w \mid w$ contains the substring bb and ends with a $b\}$.

The main result in [7] is the demonstration of the fact that L_{bb} is maximally expensive. The proof uses information theoretic arguments and the probabilistic method. Interestingly, any rtDFA recognizing L_{bb} has to forget more information than is contained in the input string while processing some inputs.

4   Peak Energy Requirements of Regular Languages

In this section, we summarize the results in [16] on "peak" energy requirements associated with the recognition of regular languages. Different computational steps (into states receiving different numbers of incoming σ-transitions) contribute differently to the energy cost. For any machine M, let k_M be the smallest number such that, for any symbol σ, no state of M has more than k incoming σ-transitions. Minimizing the cost that any individual machine step can incur during the recognition of L corresponds to finding a machine M^* such that $k_{M^*} \leq k_M$ for all machines M that recognize L.

Yılmaz et al. have shown that regular languages can be classified according to this metric:

Theorem 2. *Every regular language on an alphabet Σ can be recognized by a rtDFA M such that $k_M \leq |\Sigma| + 1$.*

We now describe a language family. The first member of this family, L_1, was defined in Sect. 3. For $j > 1$, define the "successor" function F on $\{1, ..., j\}$ by $F(i) = (i \bmod j) + 1$. On the alphabet $\Sigma_j = \{\sigma_1, ..., \sigma_j\}$, define

$$L_j = \{w \mid w \text{ ends with } \sigma_i \sigma_{F(i)} \text{ for some } 1 \leq i \leq j\}.$$

Theorem 3. *For every $j \geq 1$, any rtDFA M that recognizes L_j has the property that $k_M \geq j + 1$.*

Another language with maximal peak energy requirement is L_{bb}, which was also defined in Sect. 3: Any rtDFA M recognizing L_{bb} must have at least one reachable state with at least three incoming transitions labeled with the same symbol, and must (for some input strings) forget at least $\log_2 3$ bits in at least one computational step.

The celebrated additional features of quantum computers (like superposition and interference) provide no advantage in this regard: Recall from Sect. 2 that each rtQFA has a parameter l that corresponds to the number of operation elements in its superoperators. Yılmaz et al. proved the following theorem in [16]:

Theorem 4. *For any $n, l > 0$, if a language is recognized with zero error by a rtQFA with n machine states and l operation elements per superoperator, then the same language is also recognized by a rtDFA M with n states, such that $k_M \leq l$.*

So if one does not allow one's rtQFA to commit any errors, and excepts it to accept or reject every input correctly with probability 1, the peak energy requirements on individual steps of the rtQFA are no better than those on some rtDFA for the same job.

When one makes the problem easier by allowing the machine to give wrong answers with probability not exceeding some positive bound less than $\frac{1}{2}$, the peak loads described above decrease:

Theorem 5. *There exists a rtQFA with just two operating elements per super-operator that recognizes the language L_2 with error probability $\frac{1}{3}$.*

Theorem 6. *For all $j \geq 3$, there exists a rtQFA M_j with just three operating elements per superoperator that recognizes the language L_j with error probability $\frac{j-1}{2j-1}$.*

5   Time-Space-Energy Tradeoffs

The following facts are known about the costs to be paid in other resources when one wishes to reduce the energy expenditure of a finite automaton.[2]

Theorem 7. *Every regular language which can be recognized by a rtDFA with k states can also be recognized by a reversible[3] 2DFA with $2k + 6$ states. [6]*

In addition to the space overhead, the two-way machines of Theorem 7 pay the price of a longer runtime for attaining zero energy cost. Every two-way finite automaton that enters no infinite loop has, of course, a linear time bound, but the construction in the proof of the theorem is interesting in the sense that "more irreversible" real-time computations (i.e. those on inputs which require a rtDFA to go through more "energy-hungry" steps) are simulated by the reversible 2DFAs in correspondingly longer time.

Machines that can move their reading head in only one direction on the input string pose an interesting intermediate regime. Consider a Turing machine (with arbitrarily large time and space budgets) which is restricted to read each symbol of the input only once. It has been proven [8] that any such machine recognizing the set of all strings containing the letter a (on the alphabet $\{a, b\}$) must leave some unrecycled garbage which is at least $\log_2 n$ bits long when it terminates after processing an n-bit input. Another result by Fırat Kıyak[4] states that any rtDFA on any alphabet can be simulated by a 1DFA that has at most two transitions labeled with the same symbol entering the same state; i.e. the "peak energy load" of any step of any 1DFA need not be greater than the cost of forgetting just one bit.

---

[2] For the classical result on space-time tradeoffs ignoring energy complexity, see [13].
[3] A *reversible* automaton is one with the property that none of its configurations can have more than one predecessor.
[4] Personal communication.

6 Energy Complexity of Proof Verification

The setup of a "weak" machine (called a *verifier*) checking a claim made by a powerful but possibly deceitful agent called the *prover* has been studied at great length in theoretical computer science. In the general case of interactive proof systems, the communication between these two agents can be two-way, with the prover responding to questions posed by the verifier based on the common input string, an internal source of randomness, and a record of previous communications. The special case where the verifier says nothing corresponds to the prover sending a string called the "certificate", which is essentially a (possibly erroneous) proof of the prover's claim that the common input string is a member of the language under consideration. It is well known that the complexity class NP is the collection of languages whose members have such certificates that can be verified successfully by polynomial time Turing machines. When one changes the resource budgets of the verifiers, the class of verifiable languages seem to change accordingly [14].

To our knowledge, Villagra and Yamakami [15] were the first to consider the power of reversible constant-space machines as verifiers. They showed that the class of verifiable languages depends on the precise model of real-time finite memory computation that one adopts: If we require the verifier to scan the input string to completion (as is standard for finite automata) before it announces its decision, only a proper subset of the regular languages can be verified. If, on the other hand, one allows the verifier to halt (by entering an accepting or rejecting state, as is standard for Turing machines) at any point during the computation (i.e. not necessarily waiting for the entire input to be scanned), all and only the regular languages are verifiable: Even the naturally costly languages identified in Sect. 3 can be verified with zero energy cost for all steps of the computation.[5]

7 Conclusion

Several interesting questions remain open about the energy complexity of finite memory computations.

- In Sect. 3, we identified three mutually exclusive classes of regular languages, namely, those which can be decided (with zero computation cost) by reversible automata, minimally expensive irreversible languages, and maximally expensive irreversible languages. Recent work by Bilal Aytekin shows that there exist infinitely many "intermediate" classes corresponding to different values of the coefficient c, where each member of each such class can be recognized

---

[5] Interactive proof systems provide a natural model for *delegated computation* [4], where the weak verifier buys the help of the powerful prover to carry out a computation that it cannot carry out itself with its meager time resources. This result of Villagra and Yamakami shows that an analogous application, where the verifier is aided by the prover to reach a conclusion about the input without spending any energy is also theoretically possible.

by some machine with energy complexity cn, but not by any machine with complexity $c'n$ for any $c' < c$.

- The only results we currently have about a tradeoff between the error bound and energy requirements of real-time finite automata are about peak loads, discussed in Sect. 4. It would be interesting to learn whether probabilistic or quantum finite automata can use their ability to make errors to save energy, e.g. recognize the maximally expensive language L_{bb} by forgetting less than n bits for any input string of length n.

- Probabilistic versions of the finite memory verifiers described in Sect. 6 are known [3] to be able to verify membership in some nonregular languages with bounded error, when the zero-energy condition is not imposed on them. Do these machines lose some power when one imposes a limit on the number of predecessors of their configurations? Does the answer to this question change when the verifiers are allowed to carry out a two-way interaction with the provers?

Acknowledgements. Some of the results reported in this manuscript are from unpublished work by Fırat Kıyak. I thank him, Nevzat Ersoy and Özdeniz Dolu for many helpful discussions. This research was partially supported by Boğaziçi University Research Fund Grant Number 22A01P1.

References

1. Bennett, C.H.: Logical reversibility of computation. IBM J. Res. Dev. **17**(6), 525–532 (1973)
2. Brodsky, A., Pippenger, N.: Characterizations of 1-way quantum finite automata. SIAM J. Comput. **31**, 1456–1478 (2002)
3. Dolu, Ö., Ersoy, N., Gezer, M.U., Say, A.C.C.: Real-time, constant-space, constant-randomness verifiers. In: Caron, P., Mignot, L. (eds.) Implementation Appl. Automata, pp. 212–224. Springer International Publishing, Cham (2022)
4. Goldwasser, S., Kalai, Y.T., Rothblum, G.N.: Delegating computation: Interactive proofs for muggles. J. ACM **62**(4) (Sep 2015)
5. Hirvensalo, M.: Quantum automata with open time evolution. Int. J. Natural Comput. **1**, 70–85 (2010)
6. Kondacs, A., Watrous, J.: On the power of quantum finite state automata. In: Proceedings 38th Annual Symposium on Foundations of Computer Science, pp. 66–75 (1997)
7. Kıyak, F., Say, A.C.C.: Energy complexity of regular languages (2023). https://arxiv.org/abs/2204.06025
8. Kıyak, F., Say, A.C.C.: Read-once machines and the thermodynamic complexity of Maxwell's demons (2023). https://arxiv.org/abs/2304.11452
9. Landauer, R.: Irreversibility and heat generation in the computing process. IBM J. Res. Dev. **5**(3), 183–191 (1961)
10. Lange, K.J., McKenzie, P., Tapp, A.: Reversible space equals deterministic space. J. Comput. Syst. Sci. **60**, 354–367 (2000)
11. Li, M., Vitányi, P.: Reversibility and adiabatic computation: Trading time and space for energy. In: Proceedings of the Royal Society of London, Series A 152, pp. 769–789 (1996)

12. Say, A.C.C., Yakaryılmaz, A.: Quantum finite automata: A modern introduction. In: Calude, C.S., Freivalds, R., Kazuo, I. (eds.) Computing with New Resources. LNCS, vol. 8808, pp. 208–222. Springer, Cham (2014). https://doi.org/10.1007/978-3-319-13350-8_16
13. Shepherdson, J.C.: The reduction of two-way automata to one-way automata. IBM J. Res. Dev., 198–200 (1959)
14. Sipser, M.: Introduction to the Theory of Computation. Cengage Learning (2012)
15. Villagra, M., Yamakami, T.: Quantum and reversible verification of proofs using constant memory space. In: Dediu, A.H., Lozano, M., Martín-Vide, C. (eds.) Theory and Practice of Natural Computing, pp. 144–156. Springer International Publishing, Cham (2014)
16. Yılmaz, Ö., Kıyak, F., Üngör, M., Say, A.C.C.: Energy complexity of regular language recognition. In: Implementation and Application of Automata: 26th International Conference, CIAA 2022, pp. 200–211 (2022)

Foundations

Replications in Reversible Concurrent Calculi

Clément Aubert[✉] [iD]

School of Computer and Cyber Sciences, Augusta University, Augusta, USA
caubert@augusta.edu
https://spots.augusta.edu/caubert/

Abstract. Process calculi such as CCSor the π-calculus provide specification languages for the study and correctness of communication protocols. They also served in detailing subtle differences between formalisms to represent infinite behaviors, notably in expressiveness [7, 16]. To our knowledge, such results were never investigated from a reversible perspective. One question we would like to answer is how recursion, replication and iteration compare in the reversible setting. Of course, comparing them requires to define them first, and this short note highlights some of the difficulties in defining replication for reversible concurrent calculi.

Keywords: Formal semantics · Process algebras and calculi · Reversible Computation · Concurrency · Replication

1 What Makes a Good Reversible Calculus?

A specification language for protocols should itself have strong, desirable properties, and presenting it as a labeled transition system (LTS) often makes it amenable to mathematical reasoning. Quite often, for reversible systems, causal consistency is seen as a "must-have": this property informally states that an action cannot be undone unless all of its consequences has been undone as well. Thanks to the axiomatic approach to reversible computation [14], it is known that causal consistency can be derived from three axioms: the square property (SP), the fact that backward transitions are independent (BTI), and well-foundedness (WF).

As a consequence, endowing reversible LTSes with infinite behaviors should preserve those axioms. Representing infinite behaviors is of interest for multiple reasons, notably mathematical curiosity (what *is* infinity when you can go back?) and expressivity, since it allows to represent the spawning of new threads and non-terminating programs such as servers. This short note offers to look at the reference process calculus for reversible systems—CCSK [13,17]—endowed with an original definition of concurrency [1,2], and to highlight some of the difficulties arising from the addition of a replication operator.

© The Author(s), under exclusive license to Springer Nature Switzerland AG 2023
M. Kutrib and U. Meyer (Eds.): RC 2023, LNCS 13960, pp. 15–23, 2023.
https://doi.org/10.1007/978-3-031-38100-3_2

2   Reminders on Reversible Concurrent Calculi

We very briefly restate the syntax and semantics of CCSK, using our definition of concurrency [1,2] inspired by proved transition systems [9,10]–a variation on LTSes that eases the syntactical definition of concurrency. The reader curious to interact with CCSKprocesses can experiment with an existing implementation [3,4].

Definition 1 ((Co-)names, labels and keys). *Let* $N = \{a, b, c, \dots\}$ *be a set of* names *and* $\overline{N} = \{\overline{a}, \overline{b}, \overline{c}, \dots\}$ *its set of* co-names. *The set of* labels L *is* $N \cup \overline{N} \cup \{\tau\}$, *and we use* α, β *(resp.λ) to range over* L *(resp.$L \backslash \{\tau\}$). A bijection* $\overline{\cdot} : N \to \overline{N}$, *whose inverse is written* $\overline{\cdot}$, *gives the* complement *of a name, and we let* $\overline{\tau} = \tau$. *Finally, we let* $K = \{m, n, \dots\}$ *be a set of* keys, *and let* k *range over them.*

Definition 2 (Operators). *CCSK processes are defined as usual:*

$$
\begin{array}{llll}
X, Y := & 0 & \text{(Inactive process)} & X \backslash \alpha & \text{(Restriction)} \\
& \alpha.X & \text{(Prefix)} & X + Y & \text{(Sum)} \\
& \alpha[k].X & \text{(Keyed prefix)} & X \mid Y & \text{(Parallel composition)}
\end{array}
$$

The inactive process 0 *is omitted when preceded by a (keyed) prefix, we write* $key(X)$ *for the set of keys in* X, *and* $std(X)$ *iff* $key(X) = \emptyset$, *i.e., if* X *is* standard.

Definition 3 (Enhanced keyed labels). *Let* υ, υ_1 *and* υ_2 *range over strings in* $\{|_L, |_R, +_L, +_R\}^*$, enhanced keyed labels *are defined as*

$$\theta := \upsilon \alpha[k] \parallel \upsilon \langle |_L \upsilon_1 \alpha[k], |_R \upsilon_2 \overline{\alpha}[k] \rangle$$

We write E *the set of enhanced keyed labels, and define* $\ell : E \to L$ *and* $k : E \to K$:

$$
\begin{array}{ll}
\ell(\upsilon \alpha[k]) = \alpha & \ell(\upsilon \langle |_L \upsilon_1 \alpha[k], |_R \upsilon_2 \overline{\alpha}[k] \rangle) = \tau \\
k(\upsilon \alpha[k]) = k & k(\upsilon \langle |_L \upsilon_1 \alpha[k], |_R \upsilon_2 \overline{\alpha}[k] \rangle) = k
\end{array}
$$

We present in Fig. 1 the rules for the *proved* forward and backward LTS for CCSK, let $\twoheadrightarrow = \to \cup \rightsquigarrow$, and $\cdot^*$ be the transitive closure of any of those three relations. The rules $|_R$, $|_R^{\bullet}$, $+_R$ and $+_R^{\bullet}$ are omitted but can easily be inferred.

Definition 4 (Dependency and concurrency). *The* dependency relation $\lessdot$ *on enhanced keyed labels is induced by the axioms of Fig. 2. Two enhanced keyed labels* θ_1 *and* θ_2 *are* concurrent, $\theta_1 \smile \theta_2$, *iff neither* $\theta_1 \lessdot \theta_2$ *nor* $\theta_2 \lessdot \theta_1$.

Our dependency relation, contrary to what the symbol $\lessdot$ suggests, it is not a pre-order but a conflict relation, as it is reflexive [2, Claim 1]. The symbol comes from a study of forward-only dependency [9, Definition 2] that inspired this work—but whose dependency was used to construct a causality partial order.

Definition 5 (Concurrencies). *A transition* $t_1 : X \xrightarrow{\theta_1} Y_1$ *is concurrent - with* $t_2 : Y_1 \xrightarrow{\theta_2} Y_2$ *or with* $t_2 : X \xrightarrow{\theta_2} Y_3$, $t_1 \smile t_2$, *iff* $\theta_1 \smile \theta_2$.

We refer the reader to our recent articles [1,2] for an in-depth discussion of the benefits and correctness of this definition, and for examples.

Action, Prefix and Restriction

Forward

$$\mathrm{std}(X)\dfrac{}{\alpha.X \xrightarrow{\alpha[k]} \alpha[k].X}\text{act.}$$

$$\Bbbk(\theta) \neq k \dfrac{X \xrightarrow{\theta} X'}{\alpha[k].X \xrightarrow{\theta} \alpha[k].X'}\text{pre.}$$

$$\ell(\theta) \notin \{a,\overline{a}\} \dfrac{X \xrightarrow{\theta} X'}{X\backslash a \xrightarrow{\theta} X'\backslash a}\text{res.}$$

Backward

$$\mathrm{std}(X)\dfrac{}{\alpha[k].X \overset{\alpha[k]}{\rightsquigarrow} \alpha.X}\text{act.}^{\bullet}$$

$$\Bbbk(\theta) \neq k \dfrac{X' \overset{\theta}{\rightsquigarrow} X}{\alpha[k].X' \overset{\theta}{\rightsquigarrow} \alpha[k].X}\text{pre.}^{\bullet}$$

$$\ell(\theta) \notin \{a,\overline{a}\} \dfrac{X' \overset{\theta}{\rightsquigarrow} X}{X'\backslash a \overset{\theta}{\rightsquigarrow} X\backslash a}\text{res.}^{\bullet}$$

Parallel Group

Forward

$$\Bbbk(\theta) \notin \mathrm{key}(Y)\dfrac{X \xrightarrow{\theta} X'}{X \mid Y \xrightarrow{\mid_{\mathrm{L}}\theta} X' \mid Y}\mid_{\mathrm{L}}$$

$$\dfrac{X \xrightarrow{\upsilon_1 \lambda[k]} X' \quad Y \xrightarrow{\upsilon_2 \overline{\lambda}[k]} Y'}{X \mid Y \xrightarrow{\langle \mid_{\mathrm{L}}\upsilon_1\lambda[k],\mid_{\mathrm{R}}\upsilon_2\overline{\lambda}[k]\rangle} X' \mid Y'}\text{syn.}$$

Backward

$$\Bbbk(\theta) \notin \mathrm{key}(Y)\dfrac{X' \overset{\theta}{\rightsquigarrow} X}{X' \mid Y \overset{\mid_{\mathrm{L}}\theta}{\rightsquigarrow} X \mid Y}\mid_{\mathrm{L}}^{\bullet}$$

$$\dfrac{X' \overset{\upsilon_1 \lambda[k]}{\rightsquigarrow} X \quad Y' \overset{\upsilon_2 \overline{\lambda}[k]}{\rightsquigarrow} Y}{X' \mid Y' \overset{\langle \mid_{\mathrm{L}}\upsilon_1\lambda[k],\mid_{\mathrm{R}}\upsilon_2\overline{\lambda}[k]\rangle}{\rightsquigarrow} X \mid Y}\text{syn.}^{\bullet}$$

Sum Group

Forward

$$\mathrm{std}(Y)\dfrac{X \xrightarrow{\theta} X'}{X + Y \xrightarrow{+_{\mathrm{L}}\theta} X' + Y}+_{\mathrm{L}}$$

Backward

$$\mathrm{std}(Y)\dfrac{X' \overset{\theta}{\rightsquigarrow} X}{X' + Y \overset{+_{\mathrm{L}}\theta}{\rightsquigarrow} X + Y}+_{\mathrm{L}}^{\bullet}$$

Fig. 1. Rules of the *proved* LTS for CCSK

Action

$$\alpha[k] \lessdot \theta \quad \forall \alpha, k, \theta$$

Sum Group

$$+_{\mathrm{L}}\theta \lessdot +_{\mathrm{R}}\theta'$$
$$+_{\mathrm{R}}\theta \lessdot +_{\mathrm{L}}\theta'$$
$$+_d\theta \lessdot +_d\theta' \quad \text{if } \theta \lessdot \theta'$$

Parallel Group

$$\mid_d\theta \lessdot \mid_d\theta' \qquad\qquad \text{if } \theta \lessdot \theta'$$
$$\langle \theta_{\mathrm{L}}, \theta_{\mathrm{R}}\rangle \lessdot \theta \qquad \text{if } \exists d \text{ s.t.} \theta_d \lessdot \theta$$
$$\theta \lessdot \langle \theta_{\mathrm{L}}, \theta_{\mathrm{R}}\rangle \qquad \text{if } \exists d \text{ s.t.} \theta \lessdot \theta_d$$
$$\cdot\langle \theta_{\mathrm{L}}, \theta_{\mathrm{R}}\rangle \lessdot \langle \theta_{\mathrm{L}}', \theta_{\mathrm{R}}'\rangle \quad \text{if } \exists d \text{ s.t.} \theta_d \lessdot \theta_d'$$

For $d \in \{\mathrm{L}, \mathrm{R}\}$.

Fig. 2. Dependency Relation on Enhanced Keyed Labels

3   Replication and Reversibility

Two different sets of rules for replications have been considered for CCSand π-calculi. Their benefits and drawbacks have been discussed in detail [18, pp. 42–43] for forward-only systems, but, to our knowledge, never in a reversible setting. We briefly discuss the elements needed to define them, and then how they behave.

3.1   Preamble – How to Make My LTS Infinite?

Adding replication to CCSKrequires to

1. Add $!X$ to the set of operators (Definition 2),
2. Add $!$ to the set of strings over which υ, υ_1 and υ_2 can range in Definition 3,
3. Add rules for the $!$ operator in the proved LTS (Fig. 1),
4. Fine-tune the definition of the dependency relation (Definition 4).

Then, proving that it is "correct" requires to prove SP^1, BTI and WF:

$$\forall t_1 : X \xrightarrow{\theta_1} X_1, t_2 : X \xrightarrow{\theta_2} X_2 \text{ with } t_1 \smile t_2, \exists t_1' : X_1 \xrightarrow{\theta_2} Y, t_2' : X_2 \xrightarrow{\theta_1} Y \quad (\text{SP})$$

$$\forall t_1 : X \overset{\theta_1}{\rightsquigarrow} X_1, t_2 : X \overset{\theta_2}{\rightsquigarrow} X_2, t_1 \neq t_2 \implies t_1 \smile t_2 \quad\quad\quad (\text{BTI})$$

$$\forall X, \exists X_0, \ldots, X_n \text{ with } std(X_0) \text{ s.t. } X \rightsquigarrow X_n \rightsquigarrow \cdots \rightsquigarrow X_1 \rightsquigarrow X_0 \quad\quad (\text{WF})$$

Below, we will assume that the first and second steps described above have been completed (they are straightforward), and compare two different sets of rules for the semantics of the $!$ operator, and how they impact the possibility of preserving those properties.

3.2   Replication – First Version

The first set of rules we consider is the following:

Infinite Group

Forward

$$\frac{X \xrightarrow{\theta} X'}{!X \xrightarrow{!\theta} !X \mid X'}\text{repl.}_1 \qquad \frac{X \xrightarrow{\theta_L \lambda[k]} X' \quad X \xrightarrow{\theta_R \overline{\lambda}[k]} X''}{!X \xrightarrow{!\langle|_L \theta_L \lambda[k], |_R \theta_R \overline{\lambda}[k]\rangle} !X \mid (X' \mid X'')}\text{repl.}_2$$

Backward

$$\frac{X' \overset{\theta}{\rightsquigarrow} X}{!X \mid X' \overset{!\theta}{\rightsquigarrow} !X}\text{repl.}^{\bullet}_1 \qquad \frac{X' \overset{\theta_L \lambda[k]}{\rightsquigarrow} X \quad X'' \overset{\theta_R \overline{\lambda}[k]}{\rightsquigarrow} X}{!X \mid (X' \mid X'') \overset{!\langle|_L \theta_L \lambda[k], |_R \theta_R \overline{\lambda}[k]\rangle}{\rightsquigarrow} !X}\text{repl.}^{\bullet}_2$$

---

[1] This version of SP is a slight generalization, as motivated in our related work [2].

Let us now reason about how we should extend the dependency relation (Definition 4)[2]. First, one would want the following two co-initial transitions to be concurrent:

$$!(a+b) \xrightarrow{!+_La[m]} !(a+b) \mid (a[m]+b) \qquad !(a+b) \xrightarrow{!+_Rb[m]} !(a+b) \mid (a+b[m]).$$

Hence, one may be tempted to decide that we should not have for axiom $!\theta \lessdot !\theta'$. However, the following two should be dependent:

$$!(a.b) \xrightarrow{!a[m]} !(a.b) \mid (a[m].b) \rightsquigarrow !(a.b)$$

As $+_La[m] \lessdot +_Rb[m]$, one cannot simply solve this dilemma by requesting $!\theta \lessdot !\theta'$ iff $\theta \lessdot \theta'$. Let us try to approach this question from "easier" axioms.

The $!\theta \lessdot._{\mid R}\theta'$ and $!\theta \lessdot._{\mid L}\theta'$ axioms seem straightforward: the $\mid$ parallel operator "does not exist" until the !-transition is fired, so the existence of further transitions on either side of it should depend on the !-transition that "created" it. Those axioms seem to keep track of the fact that a newly-spawned thread has a source, and their presence seem critical, e.g., to make the following transitions dependent:

$$!(a.b) \xrightarrow{!a[m]} !(a.b) \mid (a[m].b) \xrightarrow{\mid_Rb[n]} !(a.b) \mid (a[m].b[n])$$

However, both axioms are questionable, as we discuss now, starting with $!\theta \lessdot._{\mid R}\theta'$.
Letting $X = a \mid (\overline{a} + b)$, we have

$$X \cdot \xrightarrow{\mid_La[m]} a[m] \mid (\overline{a}+b) \xrightarrow{\mid_R+_Rb[n]} a[m] \mid (\overline{a}+b[n])$$
$$X \xrightarrow{\mid_R+_L\overline{a}[m]} a \mid (\overline{a}[m]+b)$$

and hence

$$!X \xrightarrow{!\langle\mid_L\mid_La[m],\mid_R\mid_R+_L\overline{a}[m]\rangle} !X \mid ((a[m] \mid (\overline{a}+b)) \mid (a \mid (\overline{a}[m]+b)))$$
$$\xrightarrow{\mid_R\mid_L\mid_R+_Rb[n]} !X \mid ((a[m] \mid (\overline{a}+b[n])) \mid (a \mid (\overline{a}[m]+b))) \quad = X_1$$

It would seem intuitive to let those two transitions be concurrent, since $!X$ can act on b first, and then synchronize a and $\overline{a}$. Indeed, since we have

$$X \xrightarrow{\mid_R+_Rb[n]} a \mid (\overline{a}+b[n]) \xrightarrow{\mid_La[m]} a[m] \mid (\overline{a}+b[n])$$

The resulting transitions would be:

$$!X \xrightarrow{!\mid_R+_Rb[n]} !X \mid (a \mid (\overline{a}+b[n]))$$
$$\xrightarrow{\langle\mid_L!\mid_R+_L\overline{a}[m],\mid_R\mid_La[m]\rangle} (!X \mid (a \mid (\overline{a}[m]+b))) \mid (a[m] \mid (\overline{a}+b[n])) \quad = X_2$$

---

[2] This discussion was greatly improved thanks to a reviewer's comment.

This advocates for *not* including the $!\theta < |_{\mathrm{R}} \ \theta'$ axiom, or at least including it only with conditions on θ and θ'. *However*, X_1 and X_2 are not identical, a condition required to obtain (SP), and making them equivalent up to a congruence relation is challenging: in a nutshell, adding e.g., $P \mid Q \equiv Q \mid P$ makes $|_{\mathrm{L}}$ and $|_{\mathrm{R}}$ indistinguishable, which completely defeats the purpose of proved transition systems. The original system for forward-only transition had the same flaw [9, Definition 2], and it is not clear what would be the best way to make those transitions concurrent while preserving (SP).

The $!\theta < |_{\mathrm{L}}\theta'$ axiom also raises questions. In the following transitions,

$$!(a.P) \xrightarrow{!a[m]} !(a.P) \mid (a[m].P) \xrightarrow{|_{\mathrm{L}}!a[n]} (!(a.P) \mid (a[n].P)) \mid a[m].P \qquad (1)$$

one would want to be able to backtrack on the two transitions independently. Indeed, $!(a.P)$ can spawn as many threads as needed to interact with different processes, but if the process that interacted using the m key wants to backtrack, the process that interacted using the n key should not have to. Our repl.$_1$ rule does not permit to rewind the prefix keyed m unless the one keyed n has been undone first. The following transition, however, could be performed:

$$(!(a.P) \mid (a[n].P)) \mid a[m].P \overset{|_{\mathrm{R}}a[m]}{\rightsquigarrow} (!(a.P) \mid (a[n].P)) \mid a.P$$

but it decorrelates the creation of the new thread with its first interaction, while the repl.$_1$ rule precisely suggests that both events should be intertwined.

Leaving the $!\theta < |_{\mathrm{L}}\theta'$ and $!\theta < !\theta'$ axioms status unspecified, let us finally assume that we want to include the $!\theta < |_{\mathrm{R}}\theta'$ axiom as an approximation, and reason about the required properties. Then, one can immediately prove that our system does not enjoy (BTI). Indeed, looking back at $!(a.P) \mid (a[m].P)$, we have

$$t_1 : !(a.P) \mid (a[m].P) \overset{!a[m]}{\rightsquigarrow} !(a.P) \qquad t_2 : !(a.P) \mid (a[m].P) \overset{|_{\mathrm{R}}a[m]}{\rightsquigarrow} !(a.P) \mid (a.P),$$

and since $!a[m] < |_{\mathrm{R}}a[m]$, t_1 and t_2 are *not* concurrent.

There are at least three options that could be explored to restore (BTI) while potentially settling the question of the remaining axioms:

1. One could argue that t_1 and t_2 are the same up to the structural congruence $!P \mid P \equiv !P$ [7, Definition 12] (which, again, will introduce many additional complications in our proved transition system since it allows a parallel operator to "vanish"),
2. One could "mark" the key m so that it cannot backtrack independently, thus forbidding the $|_{\mathrm{R}}a[m]$-transition (but then this prevents to backtrack independently on $a[m]$ and $a[n]$ in Eq. (1)),
3. One could decide that rep.$_1$ and rep.$_2$ are irreversible rules (which sounds like a defeat).

Before exploring those options in more details, we thought it would be preferable to explore the alternative formalism for replication, as we discuss now.

3.3   Replication – Second Version

The second set we consider is actually older [15], and made of the following rules:

Infinite Group	
Forward	Backward

$$\frac{!X \mid X \xrightarrow{\theta} X'}{!X \xrightarrow{!\theta} X'}\text{rep.} \qquad\qquad \frac{X' \xrightarrow{\theta} !X \mid X}{X' \xrightarrow{!\theta} !X}\text{rep}^\bullet$$

We extend the dependency relation (Definition 4) with
$$\begin{array}{l} !\theta < \mid_L \theta' \\ !\theta < \mid_R \theta' \quad \text{if } \theta < \theta'. \end{array}$$

This version seems to behave more nicely w.r.t.(BTI): e.g., we have

$$!a.X \mid a[m].P \xrightarrow{\mid_R a[m]} !a.X \mid a.X \quad \text{and} \quad !a.X \mid a[m].P \xrightarrow{!\mid_R a[m]} !a.X$$

but as $\mid_R a[m] \smile !\mid_R a[m]$, both transitions *are* independent. However, obtaining (SP) would require to find backward transitions from $!a.X \mid a.X$ and $!a.X$ converging to the same process, which is impossible since they are both standard.

In addition, this formalism "make[s] it difficult to obtain any result concerning causality in our approach, which is based on enhanced labels, hence it relies on proofs by structural induction"[9, p. 310]. Those types of proofs are really difficult to carry on with the possibility offered by those rules to (de)activate a copy of X at any depth, and all our attempts at proving (SP) have failed so far (even setting aside the case we discussed above). The impossibility to carry on proofs by induction with this rule has been known for a long time [18, p. 43], and it does not seem that adding reversibility allows to sidestep any of it.

4   Concluding Notes

Two interesting features of those two versions are first that we do not need to worry about memory duplication, since $!X$ is reachable iff X is standard. This contrasts with RCCS [8], where a process $m \triangleright !a.P$ needs to decide how the memory m is split when transitioning to $!a.P \mid P$ [6, Section 4].

Second, we can note that with our current LTS, every process reachable from $!X$ has infinitely many origins: if $!X \rightarrow^* Y$, then $Y \rightsquigarrow^* !X$, $Y \rightsquigarrow^* !X \mid X$, $Y \rightsquigarrow^* (!X \mid X) \mid X$, etc. Obtaining a well-behaved system with replication could require adopting a powerful structural equivalence, but this is a difficult task, both for proved transition systems and for reversible systems. Indeed, the "usual" structural congruence is missing from all the proved transition systems [10], or missing the associativity and commutativity of the parallel composition [11, p. 242]. While adding such a congruence would benefit the expressiveness, making it interact nicely with the derived proof system *and* reversibility [13, Section 4]

[5] is a challenge that may not even grant the required properties to define a replication satisfying the desired properties we discussed in this short note.

Two possible ways forward emerge. One would be to consider how reduction systems fare w.r.t.this question, using e.g., a reduction rule [12, Figure 4.1]

$$!(a.P)|\overline{a}.Q \xrightarrow{\langle_{L}!a[m],|_{R}\overline{a}[m]\rangle} !(a.P)|(a[m].P|\overline{a}[m].Q)$$

that "bundles" the thread created with the process that requested it. Another, more adventurous, path is to look for another set of rules to formalize replications in the LTS.

Acknowledgments. I am very grateful to the reviewers, Alexis Ghyselen, Ivan Lanese and Gianluigi Zavattaro for their observations and suggestions. This material is based upon work supported by the National Science Foundation under Grant No. 2242786 (SHF:Small:Concurrency In Reversible Computations).

References

1. Aubert, C.: Concurrencies in reversible concurrent calculi. In: Mezzina, C.A., Podlaski, K. (eds.) RC 2022. LNCS, vol. 13354, pp. 146–163. Springer (2022). https://doi.org/10.1007/978-3-031-09005-9_10
2. Aubert, C.: The correctness of concurrencies in (Reversible) concurrent calculi (Jan 2023). https://hal.science/hal-03950347, under revision for JLAMP
3. Aubert, C., Browning, P.: Implementation of reversible distributed calculus. In: Kutrib, M., Meyer, U. (eds.) RC 2023. LNCS, Springer (2023). https://hal.science/hal-04035458v1, to appear
4. Aubert, C., Browning, P.: IRDC-CCSK (5 2023). https://github.com/CinRC/IRDC-CCSK
5. Aubert, C., Cristescu, I.: Structural equivalences for reversible calculi of communicating systems (2020). https://hal.science/hal-02571597, research report
6. Aubert, C., Medić, D.: Enabling replications and contexts in reversible concurrent calculus (May 2021). https://hal.science/hal-03183053, research report
7. Busi, N., Gabbrielli, M., Zavattaro, G.: On the expressive power of recursion, replication and iteration in process calculi. MSCS **19**(6), 1191–1222 (2009). https://doi.org/10.1017/S096012950999017X
8. Danos, V., Krivine, J.: Reversible communicating systems. In: Gardner, P., Yoshida, N. (eds.) CONCUR 2004. LNCS, vol. 3170, pp. 292–307. Springer, Heidelberg (2004). https://doi.org/10.1007/978-3-540-28644-8_19
9. Degano, P., Gadducci, F., Priami, C.: Causality and replication in concurrent processes. In: Broy, M., Zamulin, A.V. (eds.) PSI 2003. LNCS, vol. 2890, pp. 307–318. Springer, Heidelberg (2004). https://doi.org/10.1007/978-3-540-39866-0_30
10. Degano, P., Priami, C.: Proved trees. In: Kuich, W. (ed.) ICALP 1992. LNCS, vol. 623, pp. 629–640. Springer, Heidelberg (1992). https://doi.org/10.1007/3-540-55719-9_110
11. Degano, P., Priami, C.: Non-interleaving semantics for mobile processes. Theor. Comput. Sci. **216**(1–2), 237–270 (1999). https://doi.org/10.1016/S0304-3975(99)80003-6

12. Ghyselen, A.: Sized types methods and their applications to complexity analysis in Pi-calculus. Ph.D. thesis, University of Lyon (2021). https://tel.archives-ouvertes.fr/tel-03405961

13. Lanese, I., Phillips, I.: Forward-reverse observational equivalences in CCSK. In: Yamashita, S., Yokoyama, T. (eds.) RC 2021. LNCS, vol. 12805, pp. 126–143. Springer, Cham (2021). https://doi.org/10.1007/978-3-030-79837-6_8

14. Lanese, I., Phillips, I., Ulidowski, I.: An axiomatic approach to reversible computation. In: FoSSaCS 2020. LNCS, vol. 12077, pp. 442–461. Springer, Cham (2020). https://doi.org/10.1007/978-3-030-45231-5_23

15. Milner, R.: Functions as processes. In: Paterson, M.S. (ed.) ICALP 1990. LNCS, vol. 443, pp. 167–180. Springer, Heidelberg (1990). https://doi.org/10.1007/BFb0032030

16. Palamidessi, C., Valencia, F.D.: Recursion vs replication in process calculi: expressiveness. Bull. EATCS 87, 105–125 (2005). http://eatcs.org/images/bulletin/beatcs87.pdf

17. Phillips, I., Ulidowski, I.: Reversing algebraic process calculi. J. Log. Algebr. Program. **73**(1–2), 70–96 (2007). https://doi.org/10.1016/j.jlap.2006.11.002

18. Sangiorgi, D., Walker, D.: The Pi-calculus. CUP (2001)

Towards a Taxonomy for Reversible Computation Approaches

Robert Glück[1] , Ivan Lanese[2](✉) , Claudio Antares Mezzina[3] ,
Jarosław Adam Miszczak[4] , Iain Phillips[5] , Irek Ulidowski[6,7] ,
and Germán Vidal[8]

[1] DIKU, Department of Computer Science, University of Copenhagen,
Copenhagen, Denmark
[2] Focus Team, University of Bologna/INRIA, Bologna, Italy
ivan.lanese@gmail.com
[3] Dipartimento di Scienze Pure e Applicate, Università di Urbino, Urbino, Italy
[4] Institute of Theoretical and Applied Informatics, Polish Academy of Sciences,
Gliwice, Poland
[5] Imperial College London, London, England
[6] Department of Applied Informatics, AGH, Kraków, Poland
[7] SCMS, University of Leicester, Leicester, England
[8] MIST, VRAIN, Universitat Politècnica de València, Valencia, Spain

Abstract. Reversible computation is a paradigm allowing computation
to proceed not only in the usual, forward direction, but also backwards.
Reversible computation has been studied in a variety of models, including sequential and concurrent programming languages, automata, process calculi, Turing machines, circuits, Petri nets, event structures, term
rewriting, quantum computing, and others. Also, it has found applications in areas as different as low-power computing, debugging, simulation, robotics, database design, and biochemical modeling. Thus, while
the broad idea of reversible computation is the same in all the areas, it
has been interpreted and adapted to fit the various settings. The existing notions of reversible computation however have never been compared and categorized in detail. This work aims at being a first stepping
stone towards a taxonomy of the approaches that co-exist under the term
reversible computation. We hope that such a work will shed light on the
relation among the various approaches.

Keywords: Reversible computing · Taxonomy · Models and languages

I. Lanese has been partially supported by French ANR project DCore ANR-18-
CE25-0007 and INdAM-GNCS Project CUP_E55F22000270001 "Proprietà qualitative
e quantitative di sistemi reversibili". I. Ulidowski has been partially supported by JSPS
Fellowship grant S21050. G. Vidal has been partially supported by grant PID2019-
104735RB-C41 funded by MCIN/AEI/ 10.13039/501100011033. J.A. Miszczak has
been partially supported by NCN grant 2019/33/B/ST6/02011.

© The Author(s), under exclusive license to Springer Nature Switzerland AG 2023
M. Kutrib and U. Meyer (Eds.): RC 2023, LNCS 13960, pp. 24–39, 2023.
https://doi.org/10.1007/978-3-031-38100-3_3

1   Introduction

Reversible computation is a paradigm considering computation to proceed not only in the usual, forward direction, but also backwards [22,68,76]. Reversible computation has been studied in a variety of models, including sequential programming languages (both imperative [30,31,96,97], functional [38,43,88,95], and object-oriented [35,36,85]), concurrent programming languages [37,53, 54], process calculi [18,19,51,83], universal logic elements [28,67,90], Turing machines [3,8,67,70], automata [46,68], cellular automata [40,66,69,91], modal logics [80], Petri nets [6,60,62], event structures [79], term rewriting [1,72], Markov chains [41], circuits [23,27], and others. Also, it has found applications in areas as different as low-power computing [27,47], debugging [59,93], bidirectional transformations [58,73], database design [11], simulation [84], robotics [56, 86], quantum computing [65,74], and biochemical modeling [16,44,45,82]. In some of those applications, including quantum computing, the reversibility of the computational process is enforced by the very nature of the physical process of computation. In some other areas, the reversibility is treated as a crucial feature, implemented, for example, by database transactions. Thus, while the broad idea of reversible computation is the same in all the areas, it has been interpreted and adapted to fit the various settings. The existing notions of reversible computation however have never been compared and categorized in detail. This work aims at being a first stepping stone towards a taxonomy of the approaches that co-exist under the term reversible computation.

We remark that defining a taxonomy for a field as heterogeneous as reversible computation is a very difficult task, and as far as we are aware this is the first effort in this direction. As such, we provide a *possible* classification, with the aim to start the discussion. We do not claim that our taxonomy is the final word on the subject, and indeed other dimensions may be worth considering, in addition to or instead of some of the ones that we propose (cf. Sect. 2), and of course we do not claim to be complete on our coverage of models[1] and languages (cf. Sect. 3). Indeed, our examples are concentrated in the area of formal methods and programming languages, which are the main expertise of most of the authors, and we may have missed very significant examples from other areas.

2   Taxonomy

In this section we present our taxonomy for approaches in the area of reversible computation. The taxonomy includes six *dimensions*, and for each dimension we describe different *positions* that a given approach may fit. In many cases, positions on a dimension are ordered, in the sense that one generalizes the other. Hence, of course, if an approach fits a position it fits also all the more general

---

[1] In the following we mainly use the term model to refer to the instances of reversible computation that we consider. Indeed, many of our examples are (formal) models. However, we think that our taxonomy can be applied also to more concrete entities, such as languages, applications or systems.

ones. We write (dim, pos) to refer to position pos in dimension dim. We write
(d1, p1) $\Longrightarrow$ (d2, p2) to say that pair (d1, p1) implies (d2, p2), and dually the
latter is a generalization of the former.

We note that the same approach may fit different positions, depending on the
level of abstraction. Vice versa, very different models may fit the same position
in the classification. This is the case for instance of the reversible imperative
language Janus [97] and of reversible logic elements [28]. This is partially by
construction, in the sense that we tried to focus in the taxonomy on the features
of the reversibility mechanisms, abstracting away as far as possible from the
features of the underlying model.

We describe below each dimension, by explaining the different positions, with
examples of approaches that fit each of them. We refer to Sect. 3 for a more
comprehensive description about where models from the literature fit in our
taxonomy.

Reversibility focus (FOC): This is the main dimension in the proposed taxonomy. It refers to which aspects of a model are looked at to check whether
it is reversible. It features three positions, listed below.

    Functional behavior (FUN): In this case a system is said to be reversible
if it computes an injective function. Indeed, injectivity ensures that there
is a single input which can result in a given output, hence from the output
one can recompute the input. As examples, reversible Turing machines,
Janus programs, reversible circuits, quantum circuits, and the biorthogonal automata of [1] all define injective functions, hence they fit this
position. The functional behavior can be computationally as powerful as
reversible Turing machines (r-Turing-complete) [3], or subuniversal [70]
and total (always terminating) such as in reversible primitive recursive
programs [75] and reversible circuits [28]. Reversible circuits compute
exactly the bijective Boolean functions, which are a proper subset of
the partial injective functions that are computable by reversible Turing
machines and r-Turing complete reversible languages, like Janus.

    Reachable states (STA): In this case a system is said to be reversible if it
can go back to past states. Checkpointing and SVN are real world techniques fitting this position. Some notions of reversibility in Petri nets [25],
requiring that the initial state is reachable from any state, fit this dimension too. Notably, this class of approaches does not consider how past
states are reachable, allowing one to reach them via transitions unrelated
to the ones used in the past of the computation. Actually, approaches such
as rollback directly restore past states, without taking a step-by-step approach to reach them. Notably, not all past states may be reachable, or
they may be reachable only with some approximation.

    Undoing steps (UND): In this case a system is said to be reversible if it
can undo previous steps. This may require or not using special memory or
history information. Reversible process calculi [10,12,19,51,83], cellular
automata [91] and Janus [97] fit in this position. Note that Janus fits the
FUN position too: the position depends on the level of abstraction. If

we consider a small step semantics, then Janus fits position **UND**; if we abstract away execution details and just look at the functional behavior, then Janus fits position **FUN**.

Note that, if one is able to undo steps, then by undoing steps one can reach past states. Hence, we have the relation (FOC, UND) $\implies$ (FOC, STA).

Also, if a functional behavior can be defined, by undoing steps one can compute the unique inverse function. Hence, the computed function is injective (keeping into account additional memory if present), and we have the implication (FOC, UND) $\implies$ (FOC, FUN).

Resources for reversibility (RES): This dimension refers to whether a model is directly reversible, or whether additional resources (e.g., memory) are needed to enable backward execution.

None (NON): The model is directly reversible, without needing additional memory. Janus, reversible Turing machines and reversible cellular automata fit here. Janus [97] is the standard representative of the class of *clean* (without garbage) reversible programming languages, which all fit this position [32]. This class includes imperative [30,31], functional [38, 43,88,95], and object-oriented [35,36,85] languages; reversible flowchart languages [96] to model the high-level structured languages, as well as low-level machine code for reversible von Neumann machines [4,89].
We remark that models designed without reversibility in mind (e.g., mainstream programming languages) in most of the cases do not fit this position (quantum circuits are an exception to this observation though). In order for models to fit this position, one normally restricts a general class of models. For example, the reversible Turing machines [8] are a forward- and backward-deterministic subset of the Turing machines.

Inside the model (INS): In order to enable reversibility some history information is needed. This information is represented in the same formalism as the original system. This happens, e.g., for some Petri nets [60], where additional places and tokens can be used to keep such history information. This is also the case for reversible rewrite systems [72], where some additional terms are added to make a function injective, an approach which is similar to the addition of a *complement* in the bidirectionalization of functional programs [58,73]. Another example is the Reverse C Compiler [76] that instruments C programs with statements that trace the computation history. Earlier work that trace at the source level are for Pascal programs [13] and for irreversible Turing machines [8].

Outside the model (OUT): In order to enable reversibility some history information is needed, but to represent this information the model needs to be extended. This happens normally in process calculi [19,51,83] and when mainstream programming languages are made reversible: RCCS processes [19] are not CCS processes, and reversible Erlang [53] is not plain Erlang (since the interpreter is instrumented to additionally store history information).

In reversible event structures, additional relations on events such as precedence or direct causation are used to work out how to reverse events [92].

It is easy to note that no history information is a particular case of history
information, and history information outside the model can mimic history information inside the model. Thus, (RES, NON) $\implies$ (RES, INS) and (RES, INS)
$\implies$ (RES, OUT).

Moreover, the classification in this dimension depends on the definition of the
model. Notably, by considering a model together with the additional memory
needed to make it reversible, one moves from position OUT to INS, or even
to NON if one considers history information as part of the normal runtime
information of the system. Notably, a model of category NON is able to run
backwards without having first run forwards, while for models in category IN or
OUT one first needs to run forward to generate and store history information.
However, if one looks at history information as part of the state, then one can
imagine running backwards directly, just by providing history information as
part of the starting state. In practice, the history is often difficult to construct
without running a program because it depends on the operational internals of
the program.

To summarize this discussion, the categorization of a model inside this dimension critically relies on a clear definition of which is the basic model and which is
the history information. This distinction comes out naturally when a reversible
model is obtained by extending a non-reversible one: in this case what is added
to the non-reversible model can be considered as history information kept to
enable reversibility. This is the case of, e.g., RCCS [19], which extends CCS with
reversibility by equipping each process with a dedicated memory, and in general
of Landauer embedding [47].

When reversibility is enabled (WHE): This dimension considers whether
reversibility is always enabled or not.

> **Always (ALW):** Reversibility is always enabled, one can take any state and
> compute backwards. This happens, e.g., in Janus. Process calculi require
> history information to compute backwards, but we fit them here if they
> can always go backwards provided that history information is available.
> The distinction between the Janus case and the process calculi case can
> be made by looking at dimension RES.

> **Sometimes (SOM):** Reversibility is not always enabled, i.e. there are irre-
> versible steps or other conditions that need to be satisfied for enabling
> reversibility. Some of the examples include RCCS with irreversible
> actions [20] (and in general models or languages featuring control mech-
> anisms for reversibility [50]), robotics [56], where some actions (e.g., glu-
> ing objects together and drilling holes) cannot be physically reversed, or
> hybrid quantum-classical algorithms, where only part of the calculation
> is executed using a reversible quantum circuit.

In this dimension we have (WHE, ALW) $\implies$ (WHE, SOM). Notably, we
stated above that Janus fits position ALW, since one can execute backwards from

any state, however Janus also has mechanisms to change the direction of execution, in particular the *uncall* of a function computes its inverse function, which can be seen as a control mechanism to decide when reversibility is enabled. Clean reversible programming languages, including reversible machine code, typically include mechanisms that allow to change the computation direction at run time. However, no such mechanism is available in reversible Turing machines [2].

Order of undoing (ORD): This dimension is a sub-dimension of the location (FOC, UND), and refers to which transitions can be reversed at a given point in the execution.

    Reverse order (REV): This requires actions to be undone in reverse order of completion. This is the typical notion of reversibility in sequential systems (e.g., reversible Turing machines, Janus), and backtracking in concurrent systems [9] is also an example of REV. Notably, REV ensures that at any point in time a single backward action is enabled, hence the model is backward deterministic.

    Causal order (CAU): This requires actions to be undone only if their consequences, if any, are undone beforehand. Equivalently, causal dependent actions need to be undone in reverse order, while independent actions can be undone in any order. This approach, born in the area of process calculi, is known as causal-consistent reversibility [19,52]. This is the typical notion of reversibility in concurrent process calculi and languages (e.g., RCCS [19], reversible Erlang [53,54], ...). It has also been used in reversible event structures [92], and reversible Occurrence Nets [62]. In this position the notion of backward determinism from position REV is weakened into backward confluence.

    Out of causal order (OCO): This position does not prescribe any constraint on when actions can be undone. This has been used, e.g., in biological systems and models for them (in some process calculi [45,82], some Petri nets [61,77]) and in modeling distributed antenna selection for massive MIMO [87] systems.

We have (ORD, REV) $\implies$ (ORD, CAU) and (ORD, CAU) $\implies$ (ORD, OCO). Some Petri net models [77] can be tuned so as to cover all three positions in this dimension.

State reachability (STR): This dimension is a sub-dimension of (FOC, STA), and roughly corresponds to the dimension ORD above. This describes which states can be reached by backward execution.

    Only past states (PAS): In this position only past states can be reached. This is typical of sequential models (e.g., Janus) or concurrent models when backtracking is used.

    Only past states up-to concurrency (CON): Only states that could have been reached in the past by swapping the order of concurrent actions can be reached. This is the typical behavior of concurrent systems based on the causal-consistent approach, such as concurrent process calculi and languages (e.g., RCCS [19], reversible Erlang [53]).

States reachable by going forward (FOR): In this case backward execution does not introduce new states, but may allow to reach states in different ways. This happens for instance in Petri nets [6], where one would like to avoid introducing new states, but it does not matter whether the states were in the past of the computation or not.

Also states not reachable by going forward (NOT): In this case backward execution allows computation to reach new states. This behavior may happen in the presence of out of causal order reversibility (ORD, OCO), hence typically in biological systems. In Petri nets there is a line of work [6] trying to understand whether the specific net falls under location NOT or under location FOR.

For state reachability, we have (STR, PAS) $\implies$ (STR, CON), (STR, CON) $\implies$ (STR, FOR) and (STR, FOR) $\implies$ (STR, NOT). This dimension is clearly related to dimension ORD: if a system can be looked at both from the point of view of undoing actions and from the point of view of reachable states, (ORD, REV) corresponds to (STR, PAS), (ORD, CAU) to (STR, CON), and (ORD, OCO) to either (STR, FOR) or (STR, NOT). It would be interesting to find a position in classification ORD corresponding to (STR, FOR), but it is not clear whether any such position exists.

Preciseness of reversibility (PRE): This dimension refers to whether by going backwards one perfectly undoes the effect of forward moves or not.

Precise (PRC): Going forwards and then backwards exactly restores the original state. This happens in most of the models (e.g., Janus, process calculi). This has been captured in causal-consistency theory by the Loop Lemma [19].

With additional information (ADD): When going backwards one keeps some information on the undone computation, e.g., that an unsuccessful try has been performed (to avoid doing the same try again), or that a possible solution of the problem has been found (but one would like to find all the solutions). This approach has been partially explored in the area of reversible process calculi using alternatives [48] (which allow one to select a different computation upon rollback) or predictions [94] (which are not involved in backward computation, hence keep trace of what happened). It has also been studied in the field of session types [17], where branches of a choice are discarded upon rollback, and of reversible contracts [5], where different alternatives are explored looking for a compatible behavior with another process.

Approximate (APP): By going forwards and backwards one can reach a state which is close in some sense to the starting one, but not exactly the same. This happens typically in long-running transactions with compensations [14,15], where the compensation does an approximate undo, and in robotics [56], where perfect reversibility is not possible due to small imprecisions in physical actions. Similarly, in reversible neural networks when inputs are recalculated from outputs (not using precise arithmetic), one only gets inputs equal to the original ones up to some small error [7,33].

We have (PRE, PRC) $\implies$ (PRE, ADD) and (PRE, ADD) $\implies$ (PRE, APP).

Another possible dimension concerns control of reversibility, namely whether there is any policy to decide which action to take when more than one (forward or backward) action is enabled. Possible positions include uncontrolled (no such policy), semantic control (policy hardwired in the language definition), internal control (there are specific constructs in the model to specify the policy) and external control (the policy comes from outside the program, e.g., from the user or from another program). This dimension has been discussed in [50]. We note that frequently uncontrolled reversibility corresponds to (WHE, ALW) while forms of control correspond to (WHE, SOM), since the policy may disallow backward actions under some conditions.

3   Application of the Taxonomy

While in the previous section we discussed the different dimensions of the taxonomy, here we focus on which approach fits which position in the taxonomy. While there is a partial overlap with the examples given in the previous section, this dual view provides interesting insights as well. The results of this section are captured in Table 1.

Research on reversible computing first tackled sequential models of computation, such as finite state automata and Turing machines. The basic idea was to take the original models and restrict to those instances which were reversible. This naturally led to approaches focused on undoing actions at the small step level, computing injective functions at the global level. Actions were undone in reverse order, as natural for sequential systems, leading back to past states in a precise way. This is the case, e.g., of the language Janus and the biorthogonal automata of [1]. In turn, some sequential models were extended in order to become reversible by introducing a so-called Landauer embedding [47]. Here, we find, e.g., reversible rewrite systems [72] and the *bidirectionalization* of functional programs in [58].

Such an approach was less suitable for concurrent systems, where reverse order of undoing was too strict in many cases, and one would like to be able to undo independent actions in any order, while undoing dependent actions in reverse order. This was first argued in [19], which introduced the notion of causal-consistent reversibility. Instead of restricting calculi to their injective part, memories were added to keep track of past execution (thus fitting position (RES, OUT)), and enable backward computation. Given that in concurrency functional behavior is of limited interest, since interaction with the environment is important, the focus is mainly on undoing actions. A similar approach has been applied to programming languages for concurrency, in particular Erlang [53,54], where causal consistency is ensured for both forward (replay) and backward computations during debugging [29,55].

While the first approaches considered precise reversibility which was always enabled, further studies introduced control mechanisms [20,49] as well as forms

Table 1. Application of the taxonomy to sample approaches from the literature

Formalism	Approach	FOCus	RESource	WHEn	ORDer	STate R.	PREcis.
Reversible Turing machines	[8,67]	FUN UND	NON	ALW	REV	PAS	PRC
Janus	[97]	FUN UND	NON	ALW	REV	PAS	PRC
Biorthogonal automata	[1]	FUN UND	NON	ALW	REV	PAS	PRC
Reversible cellular automata	[66,91]	FUN UND	NON	ALW	REV	PAS	PRC
Reversible logic elements	[28,67]	FUN UND	NON	ALW	REV	PAS	PRC
Reversible rewriting	[72]	UND	INS OUT	ALW	REV	PAS	PRC
Causal-consistent calculi	[19,83] [18,51] [10,12]	UND	OUT	ALW	CAU	CON	PRC
Calculi + control	[20,49]	UND	OUT	SOM	CAU	CON	PRC
Calculi + predictions	[94]	UND	OUT	ALW	CAU	NOT	ADD
Reversible Erlang	[53,54]	UND	OUT	ALW SOM	CAU	CON	PRC
Petri nets	[6]	STA	NON	ALW	OCO	FOR NOT	PRC
Reversing Petri nets	[77,78]	UND	INS	ALW	CAU OCO	CON FOR NOT	PRC
Occurrence nets	[62]	UND	NON	ALW	CAU	CON	PRC
Petri nets	[60]	UND	INS	ALW	CAU	CON	PRC
Biological models	[45,82]	UND	OUT	SOM	OCO	NOT	PRC
Event structures	[81,92]	UND	OUT	SOM	CAU OCO	CON FOR NOT	PRC
Quantum circuits	[24,26]	FUN UND	NON	ALW	REV	PAS	PRC
Quantum programming languages	[42,74]	UND	INS	SOM	REV	PAS	PRC
Reversible neural networks	[33]	UND	NON OUT	SOM	REV	NOT	APP
Reversible Markov chains	[41]	STA	NON	ALW	REV	PAS	PRC
Sagas	[14]	UND	INT	SOM	CAU	X	APP
SVN	[63]	STA	INT	ALW	X	PAS	PRC

of reversibility which were not precise [94]. Some applications, most notably in the biochemical setting, triggered the need for weakening causal order, thus introducing out of causal order reversibility [45,82]. We note that CCSK [83], with the addition of a control mechanism in the form of a rollback operator inspired by [49], has been modeled using reversible event structures exploiting out of causal order reversibility [34].

Petri nets, while being a model for concurrency like process calculi, resulted in a number of different approaches. The fact that Petri nets have a clear representation of state (in terms of tokens inside places), triggered approaches [25] focusing on state reachability more than on action undoing. Approaches based on action undoing were also considered and contrasted with the ones based on state reachability [6]. Other works [62] considered the causal-consistent approach, thus matching the one of process calculi. Further work tailored Petri nets for biological applications [77], allowing one to explore different forms of reversibility, most notably the out of causal order one.

In the quantum circuit model [24,26] used for developing most quantum mechanical algorithms, the set of allowed operations is represented by unitary matrices or unitary gates. Such matrices act on an isolated physical system and, in this scenario, one is always able to undo the last action. Hence, the term reversible is, in quantum computer science, synonymous with the term 'unitary'. Compared with classical reversible gates, unitary matrices provide us with a larger set of operations. However, to read out the result of the computation, one needs to translate the final state into the classical result. Such a process requires a measurement which is achieved through interaction with the system executing the computation. The main feature of such a process is its irreversibility. Thus, reversibility is lost at the moment of 'interfacing' with a classical machine or with the readout procedure. Architecture-specific limitations of current quantum hardware lead to the problem of optimizing quantum circuits [71], most importantly taking into account the hardware topology [21]. Such optimization is part of the process of transpilation – translation of quantum circuits to the form suitable for the target quantum computer.

This need of interfacing between the reversible and the irreversible elements motivated the development of quantum programming languages [42,64,74]. Also, many quantum algorithms (NISQ algorithms in particular) use classical subroutines. Quantum programming languages include a specialized type system for handling quantum structures used in purely quantum, reversible computation. Additionally, they also include an irreversible subsystem, suitable for dealing with classical – which in this case means irreversible – computation.

Reversibility is used in *Convolutional Neural Networks* [57] (CNNs) to undo computation of the networks' layers. This removes the need to store, retrieve and delete layers' inputs and outputs, which can be recomputed instead. Some layers perform transformations (of inputs to outputs) which have inverses, such as multiplication by a matrix, so are directly reversible. Other transformations, such as applying a convolution or max pooling, lose data so can only be reversed by enriching the network with additional components. A *Reversible Residual*

Network [33] (ResNet) is a form of CNN that adds *shortcuts* between layers. This makes it possible to undo computation of most layers. Calculation is not in precise arithmetic, so only approximate values of inputs can be uncomputed from outputs (up to an agreed precision), and thus new states can be reached.

In the field of performance evaluation, a Markov chain is (time) reversible [41] if it has the same behavior as its inverse, in terms of probabilistic distribution. Hence the focus is on states, and, since the approach restricts attention to Markov chains which naturally satisfy the reversibility property, no additional resources are required. Reversible transitions are always enabled, though they are subject to a probabilistic distribution, and the order of reversing is the inverse of the forward one. An initial work relating causal-consistent reversibility with reversible Markov chains in the setting of a stochastic process algebra is described in [10].

We conclude the table with a few approaches which are at the boundary of reversible computation, namely Sagas [14], used to model long-running transactions with compensation, and the well-known tool SVN for version control [39,63]. Given the distance from classical reversible computation, it is not clear whether some of the dimensions make sense in these cases. We put 'X' in the cells which we believe are not interesting.

4   Conclusion, Related and Future Work

We have presented a first proposal of taxonomy for reversible computation approaches, and discussed how various models fit in it. We focused on approaches from programming languages and concurrency theory, hence in future work it would be good to put our taxonomy at work also on other kinds of models.

We are not aware of other works putting forward proposals of taxonomies for reversible computing. A partial analysis in this direction is the classification of control mechanisms in [50] and an account of reversible computing from a programming language perspective [32]. Also, a few works in the context of Petri nets contrast different approaches [6,77], taking advantage of the existence of many such approaches.

Table 1, while not covering all the literature, highlights some holes which are interesting targets for future work. For instance, a large part of the approaches concern precise reversibility, and indeed this is the main focus of the reversible computing community. Approaches where reversibility is not perfect are however of interest as well, motivated, e.g., by applications in robotics and neural networks, and are an interesting research direction for the reversible computation community. Another interesting point is that most of the approaches focus on undoing actions, while a focus on functional behavior and on states has been adopted only in a few cases. From a theoretical perspective, it would also be interesting to investigate the computational power and inherent complexity of reversible computing models.

Acknowledgements. This work refines and extends the results of discussions that occurred during the meetings of the COST Action IC1405 on Reversible Computation – Extending Horizons of Computing. We thank all the participants to such discussions. The authors were partially supported by the COST Action IC1405. We thank the anonymous referees for their helpful comments.

References

1. Abramsky, S.: A structural approach to reversible computation. Theor. Comput. Sci. **347**(3), 441–464 (2005)
2. Axelsen, H.B., Glück, R.: A simple and efficient universal reversible Turing machine. In: Dediu, A.-H., Inenaga, S., Martín-Vide, C. (eds.) LATA 2011. LNCS, vol. 6638, pp. 117–128. Springer, Heidelberg (2011). https://doi.org/10.1007/978-3-642-21254-3_8
3. Axelsen, H.B., Glück, R.: On reversible Turing machines and their function universality. Acta Informatica **53**(5), 509–543 (2016). https://doi.org/10.1007/s00236-015-0253-y
4. Axelsen, H.B., Glück, R., Yokoyama, T.: Reversible machine code and its abstract processor architecture. In: Diekert, V., Volkov, M.V., Voronkov, A. (eds.) CSR 2007. LNCS, vol. 4649, pp. 56–69. Springer, Heidelberg (2007). https://doi.org/10.1007/978-3-540-74510-5_9
5. Barbanera, F., Lanese, I., de'Liguoro, U.: A theory of retractable and speculative contracts. Sci. Comput. Program. **167**, 25–50 (2018)
6. Barylska, K., Koutny, M., Mikulski, Ł., Piątkowski, M.: Reversible computation vs. reversibility in Petri nets. Sci. Comput. Program. **151**, 48–60 (2018)
7. Behrmann, J., Vicol, P., Wang, K.-C., Grosse, R.B., Jacobsen, J.-H.: Understanding and mitigating exploding inverses in invertible neural networks. In: AISTATS 2021, volume 130 of Proceedings of Machine Learning Research, pp. 1792–1800. PMLR (2021)
8. Bennett, C.H.: Logical reversibility of computation. IBM J. Res. Dev. **17**(6), 525–532 (1973)
9. Bergstra, J.A., Ponse, A., van Wamel, J.J.: Process algebra with backtracking. In: de Bakker, J.W., de Roever, W.-P., Rozenberg, G. (eds.) REX 1993. LNCS, vol. 803, pp. 46–91. Springer, Heidelberg (1994). https://doi.org/10.1007/3-540-58043-3_17
10. Bernardo, M., Mezzina, C.A.: Towards bridging time and causal reversibility. In: Gotsman, A., Sokolova, A. (eds.) FORTE 2020. LNCS, vol. 12136, pp. 22–38. Springer, Cham (2020). https://doi.org/10.1007/978-3-030-50086-3_2
11. Bernstein, A.P., Newcomer, E.: Principles of Transaction Processing, 2nd edn. Morgan Kaufmann Publishers Inc., Burlington (2009)
12. Bocchi, L., Lanese, I., Mezzina, C.A., Yuen, S.: The reversible temporal process language. In: Mousavi, M.R., Philippou, A. (eds.) FORTE 2022. LNCS, vol. 13273, pp. 31–49. Springer, Cham (2022). https://doi.org/10.1007/978-3-031-08679-3_3
13. Briggs, J.S.: Generating reversible programs. Softw. Pract. Exper. **17**(7), 439–453 (1987)
14. Bruni, R., Melgratti, H.C., Montanari, U.: Theoretical foundations for compensations in flow composition languages. In: POPL 2005, pp. 209–220. ACM (2005)
15. Caires, L., Ferreira, C., Vieira, H.: A process calculus analysis of compensations. In: Kaklamanis, C., Nielson, F. (eds.) TGC 2008. LNCS, vol. 5474, pp. 87–103. Springer, Heidelberg (2009). https://doi.org/10.1007/978-3-642-00945-7_6

36   R. Glück et al.

16. Cardelli, L., Laneve, C.: Reversibility in massive concurrent systems. Sci. Ann. Comput. Sci. **21**(2), 175–198 (2011)
17. Castellani, I., Dezani-Ciancaglini, M., Giannini, P.: Reversible sessions with flexible choices. Acta Inform. **56**(7–8), 553–583 (2019)
18. Cristescu, I., Krivine, J., Varacca, D.: A compositional semantics for the reversible π-calculus. In: LICS 2013, pp. 388–397. IEEE Computer Society (2013)
19. Danos, V., Krivine, J.: Reversible communicating systems. In: Gardner, P., Yoshida, N. (eds.) CONCUR 2004. LNCS, vol. 3170, pp. 292–307. Springer, Heidelberg (2004). https://doi.org/10.1007/978-3-540-28644-8_19
20. Danos, V., Krivine, J.: Transactions in RCCS. In: Abadi, M., de Alfaro, L. (eds.) CONCUR 2005. LNCS, vol. 3653, pp. 398–412. Springer, Heidelberg (2005). https://doi.org/10.1007/11539452_31
21. Davis, M.G., Smith, E., Tudor, A., Sen, K., Siddiqi, I., Iancu, C.: Towards optimal topology aware quantum circuit synthesis. In: QCE 2020, pp. 223–234. IEEE (2020)
22. De Vos, A.: Reversible Computing: Fundamentals, Quantum Computing, and Applications. Wiley, Hoboken (2010)
23. De Vos, A., De Baerdemacker, S., Van Rentergem, Y., Synthesis of quantum circuits vs. synthesis of classical reversible circuits. In: Synthesis Lectures on Digital Circuits and Systems. Morgan & Claypool Publishers (2018)
24. Deutsch, D.: Quantum theory, the Church-Turing principle and the universal quantum computer. Proc. Roy. Soc. Lond. A. Math. Phys. Sci. **400**(1818), 97–117 (1985)
25. Esparza, J., Nielsen, M.: Decidability issues for Petri nets. BRICS Rep. Ser. **1**(8), 1994
26. Feynman, P.R.: Quantum mechanical computers. Found. Phys. **16**(6), 507–531 (1986)
27. Frank, M.P.: Reversibility for efficient computing. Ph.D. thesis, Massachusetts Institute of Technology, Cambridge, MA, USA (1999)
28. Fredkin, E., Toffoli, T.: Quantum mechanical computers. Int. J. Theor. Phys. **21**(3–4), 219–253 (1982)
29. Giachino, E., Lanese, I., Mezzina, C.A.: Causal-consistent reversible debugging. In: Gnesi, S., Rensink, A. (eds.) FASE 2014. LNCS, vol. 8411, pp. 370–384. Springer, Heidelberg (2014). https://doi.org/10.1007/978-3-642-54804-8_26
30. Glück, R., Yokoyama, T.: A linear-time self-interpreter of a reversible imperative language. Comput. Softw. **33**(3), 108–128 (2016)
31. Glück, R., Yokoyama, T.: A minimalist's reversible while language. IEICE Trans. Inf. Syst. **E100-D**(5), 1026–1034 (2017)
32. Glück, R., Yokoyama, T.: Reversible computing from a programming language perspective. Theor. Comput. Sci. **953**, Article 113429 (2023)
33. Gomez, A.N., Ren, M., Urtasun, R., Grosse, R.B.: The reversible residual network: backpropagation without storing activations. In: Advances in Neural Information Processing Systems. NIPS 2017, vol. 30, pp. 2214–2224. Curran Associates Inc. (2017)
34. Graversen, E., Phillips, I.C.C., Yoshida, N.: Event structure semantics of (controlled) reversible CCS. J. Log. Algebraic Methods Program. **121**, 100686 (2021)
35. Haulund, T., Mogensen, T.Æ., Glück, R.: Implementing reversible object-oriented language features on reversible machines. In: Phillips, I., Rahaman, H. (eds.) RC 2017. LNCS, vol. 10301, pp. 66–73. Springer, Cham (2017). https://doi.org/10.1007/978-3-319-59936-6_5
36. Hay-Schmidt, L., Glück, R., Cservenka, M.H., Haulund, T.: Towards a unified language architecture for reversible object-oriented programming. In: Yamashita,

S., Yokoyama, T. (eds.) RC 2021. LNCS, vol. 12805, pp. 96–106. Springer, Cham (2021). https://doi.org/10.1007/978-3-030-79837-6_6

37. Hoey, J., Ulidowski, I.: Reversing an imperative concurrent programming language. Sci. Comput. Program. **223**, 102873 (2022)

38. Jacobsen, P.A.H., Kaarsgaard, R., Thomsen, M.K.: CoreFun: a typed functional reversible core language. In: Kari, J., Ulidowski, I. (eds.) RC 2018. LNCS, vol. 11106, pp. 304–321. Springer, Cham (2018). https://doi.org/10.1007/978-3-319-99498-7_21

39. Jacobson, J.: A formalization of DARCs patch theory using inverse semigroups. Technical report, UCLA (2009)

40. Kari, J.: Reversible cellular automata: from fundamental classical results to recent developments. New Gener. Comput. **36**(3), 145–172 (2018)

41. Kelly, F.P.: Reversibility and Stochastic Networks. Wiley, Hoboken (1979)

42. Knill, E.: Conventions for quantum pseudocode. Technical report LAUR-96-2724, Los Alamos National Lab (1996)

43. Kristensen, J.T., Kaarsgaard, R., Thomsen, M.K.: Jeopardy: an invertible functional programming language. CoRR, arXiv:2209.02422 (2022)

44. Kuhn, S., Ulidowski, I.: Local reversibility in a calculus of covalent bonding. Sci. Comput. Program. **151**, 18–47 (2018)

45. Kuhn, S., Ulidowski, I.: Modelling of DNA mismatch repair with a reversible process calculus. Theor. Comput. Sci. **925**, 68–86 (2022)

46. Kutrib, M., Malcher, A.: Reversible pushdown automata. J. Comput. Syst. Sci. **78**(6), 1814–1827 (2012)

47. Landauer, R.: Irreversibility and heat generation in the computing process. IBM J. Res. Dev. **5**(3), 183–191 (1961)

48. Lanese, I., Lienhardt, M., Mezzina, C.A., Schmitt, A., Stefani, J.-B.: Concurrent flexible reversibility. In: Felleisen, M., Gardner, P. (eds.) ESOP 2013. LNCS, vol. 7792, pp. 370–390. Springer, Heidelberg (2013). https://doi.org/10.1007/978-3-642-37036-6_21

49. Lanese, I., Mezzina, C.A., Schmitt, A., Stefani, J.-B.: Controlling reversibility in higher-order Pi. In: Katoen, J.-P., König, B. (eds.) CONCUR 2011. LNCS, vol. 6901, pp. 297–311. Springer, Heidelberg (2011). https://doi.org/10.1007/978-3-642-23217-6_20

50. Lanese, I., Mezzina, C.A., Stefani, J.-B.: Controlled reversibility and compensations. In: Glück, R., Yokoyama, T. (eds.) RC 2012. LNCS, vol. 7581, pp. 233–240. Springer, Heidelberg (2013). https://doi.org/10.1007/978-3-642-36315-3_19

51. Lanese, I., Mezzina, C.A., Stefani, J.-B.: Reversibility in the higher-order π-calculus. Theor. Comput. Sci. **625**, 25–84 (2016)

52. Lanese, I., Mezzina, C.A., Tiezzi, F.: Causal-consistent reversibility. Bull. EATCS **114** (2014)

53. Lanese, I., Nishida, N., Palacios, A., Vidal, G.: A theory of reversibility for Erlang. J. Log. Algebr. Meth. Program. **100**, 71–97 (2018)

54. Lanese, I., Palacios, A., Vidal, G.: Causal-consistent replay reversible semantics for message passing concurrent programs. Fundam. Informaticae **178**(3), 229–266 (2021)

55. Lanese, I., Schultz, U.P., Ulidowski, I.: Reversible computing in debugging of Erlang programs. IT Prof. **24**(1), 74–80 (2022)

56. Laursen, J.S., Ellekilde, L.-P., Schultz, U.P.: Modelling reversible execution of robotic assembly. Robotica **36**(5), 625–654 (2018)

57. LeCun, Y., Bottou, L., Bengio, Y., Haffner, P.: Gradient-based learning applied to document recognition. Proc. IEEE **86**(11), 2278–2324 (1998)

58. Matsuda, K., Hu, Z., Nakano, K., Hamana, M., Takeichi, M.: Bidirectionalization transformation based on automatic derivation of view complement functions. In: ICFP 2007, PP. 47–58. ACM (2007)
59. McNellis, J., Mola, J., Sykes, K.: Time travel debugging: root causing bugs in commercial scale software. CppCon talk (2017). https://www.youtube.com/watch?v=l1YJTg_A914
60. Melgratti, H., Mezzina, C.A., Pinna, G.M.: Towards a truly concurrent semantics for reversible CCS. In: Yamashita, S., Yokoyama, T. (eds.) RC 2021. LNCS, vol. 12805, pp. 109–125. Springer, Cham (2021). https://doi.org/10.1007/978-3-030-79837-6_7
61. Melgratti, H.C., Mezzina, C.A., Pinna, G.M.: A Petri net view of covalent bonds. Theor. Comput. Sci. **908**, 89–119 (2022)
62. Melgratti, H.C., Mezzina, C.A., Ulidowski, I.: Reversing place transition nets. Log. Methods Comput. Sci. **16**(4) (2020)
63. Mimram, S., Di Giusto, C.: A categorical theory of patches. In: MFPS XXIX. Electronic Notes in Theoretical Computer Science, vol. 298, PP. 283–307. Elsevier (2013)
64. Miszczak, J.: Models of quantum computation and quantum programming languages. Bull. Polish Acad. Sci. Tech. Sci. **59**(3), 305–324 (2011)
65. Miszczak, J.: High Level Structures for Quantum Computing. Springer, Cham (2012). https://doi.org/10.1007/978-3-031-02516-7
66. Morita, K.: Computation-universality of one-dimensional one-way reversible cellular automata. Inf. Process. Lett. **42**(6), 325–329 (1992)
67. Morita, K.: Reversible computing and cellular automata–a survey. Theor. Comput. Sci. **395**(1), 101–131 (2008)
68. Morita, K.: Theory of Reversible Computing. Monographs in Theoretical Computer Science. An EATCS Series. Springer, Tokyo (2017). https://doi.org/10.1007/978-4-431-56606-9
69. Morrison, D., Ulidowski, I.: Direction-reversible self-timed cellular automata for delay-insensitive circuits. J. Cell. Autom. **12**(1–2), 101–120 (2016)
70. Nakano, K.: Time-symmetric Turing machines for computable involutions. Sci. Comput. Program. **215**, 102748 (2022)
71. Nash, B., Gheorghiu, V., Mosca, M.: Quantum circuit optimizations for NISQ architectures. Quantum Sci. Technol. **5**(2), 025010 (2020)
72. Nishida, N., Palacios, A., Vidal, G.: Reversible computation in term rewriting. J. Log. Algebr. Methods Program. **94**, 128–149 (2018)
73. Nishida, N., Vidal, G.: Characterizing compatible view updates in syntactic bidirectionalization. In: Thomsen, M.K., Soeken, M. (eds.) RC 2019. LNCS, vol. 11497, pp. 67–83. Springer, Cham (2019). https://doi.org/10.1007/978-3-030-21500-2_5
74. Ömer, B.: Structured Quantum Programming. Ph.D. thesis, Vienna University of Technology (2003)
75. Paolini, L., Piccolo, M., Roversi, L.: On a class of reversible primitive recursive functions and its Turing-complete extensions. New Gener. Comput. **36**(3), 233–256 (2018)
76. Perumalla, K.S.:Introduction to Reversible Computing. CRC Press/Taylor & Francis Group (2014)
77. Philippou, A., Psara, K.: Reversible computation in Petri nets. In: Kari, J., Ulidowski, I. (eds.) RC 2018. LNCS, vol. 11106, pp. 84–101. Springer, Cham (2018). https://doi.org/10.1007/978-3-319-99498-7_6
78. Philippou, A., Psara, K.: A collective interpretation semantics for reversing Petri nets. Theor. Comput. Sci. **924**, 148–170 (2022)

79. Phillips, I., Ulidowski, I.: Reversibility and asymmetric conflict in event structures. In: D'Argenio, P.R., Melgratti, H. (eds.) CONCUR 2013. LNCS, vol. 8052, pp. 303–318. Springer, Heidelberg (2013). https://doi.org/10.1007/978-3-642-40184-8_22

80. Phillips, I., Ulidowski, I.: Event identifier logic. Math. Struct. Comput. Sci. **24**(2) (2014)

81. Phillips, I., Ulidowski, I.: Reversibility and asymmetric conflict in event structures. J. Log. Algebr. Methods Program. **84**(6), 781–805 (2015)

82. Phillips, I., Ulidowski, I., Yuen, S.: A reversible process calculus and the modelling of the ERK signaling pathway. In: Glück, R., Yokoyama, T. (eds.) RC 2012. LNCS, vol. 7581, pp. 218–232. Springer, Heidelberg (2013). https://doi.org/10.1007/978-3-642-36315-3_18

83. Phillips, I.C.C., Ulidowski, I.: Reversing algebraic process calculi. J. Log. Algebr. Program. **73**(1–2), 70–96 (2007)

84. Schordan, M., Oppelstrup, T., Jefferson, D.R., Barnes Jr., P.D.: Generation of reversible C++ code for optimistic parallel discrete event simulation. New Gener. Comput. **36**(3), 257–280 (2018)

85. Schultz, U.P., Axelsen, H.B.: Elements of a reversible object-oriented language. In: Devitt, S., Lanese, I. (eds.) RC 2016. LNCS, vol. 9720, pp. 153–159. Springer, Cham (2016). https://doi.org/10.1007/978-3-319-40578-0_10

86. Schultz, U.P., Bordignon, M., Støy, K.: Robust and reversible execution of self-reconfiguration sequences. Robotica **29**(1), 35–57 (2011)

87. Siljak, H., Psara, K., Philippou, A.: Distributed antenna selection for massive MIMO using reversing Petri nets. IEEE Wirel. Commun. Lett. **8**(5), 1427–1430 (2019)

88. Thomsen, M.K., Axelsen, H.B.: Interpretation and programming of the reversible functional language RFUN. In: IFL 2015, pp. 8:1–8:13. ACM (2015)

89. Thomsen, M.K., Axelsen, H.B., Glück, R.: A reversible processor architecture and its reversible logic design. In: De Vos, A., Wille, R. (eds.) RC 2011. LNCS, vol. 7165, pp. 30–42. Springer, Heidelberg (2012). https://doi.org/10.1007/978-3-642-29517-1_3

90. Toffoli, T.: Reversible computing. In: de Bakker, J., van Leeuwen, J. (eds.) ICALP 1980. LNCS, vol. 85, pp. 632–644. Springer, Heidelberg (1980). https://doi.org/10.1007/3-540-10003-2_104

91. Toffoli, T., Margolus, N.: Cellular Automata Machines. A New Environment for Modeling. MIT Press, Cambridge (1987)

92. Ulidowski, I., Phillips, I., Yuen, S.: Reversing event structures. New Gener. Comput. **36**(3), 281–306 (2018)

93. Undo, UDB - reverse debugger for C/C++ (2020). https://undo.io

94. Vassor, M.: Reversibility and predictions. In: Yamashita, S., Yokoyama, T. (eds.) RC 2021. LNCS, vol. 12805, pp. 163–181. Springer, Cham (2021). https://doi.org/10.1007/978-3-030-79837-6_10

95. Yokoyama, T., Axelsen, H.B., Glück, R.: Towards a reversible functional language. In: De Vos, A., Wille, R. (eds.) RC 2011. LNCS, vol. 7165, pp. 14–29. Springer, Heidelberg (2012). https://doi.org/10.1007/978-3-642-29517-1_2

96. Yokoyama, T., Axelsen, H.B., Glück, R.: Fundamentals of reversible flowchart languages. Theor. Comput. Sci. **611**, 87–115 (2016)

97. Yokoyama, T., Glück, R.: A reversible programming language and its invertible self-interpreter. In: PEPM 2007, pp. 144–153. ACM (2007)

Computational Complexity of Reversible Reaction Systems

Markus Holzer[(✉)] [iD] and Christian Rauch

Institut für Informatik, Universität Giessen, Arndtstr. 2, 35392 Giessen, Germany
{holzer,christian.rauch}@informatik.uni-giessen.de

Abstract. The computational complexity of problems related to reaction systems (RSs) such as, e.g., reachability, simulation, etc., are well understood. We investigate the complexity of some of these problems for reversible RSs. Since some of the computational complexity (lower bound) proofs in the general case rely on reductions from Turing machine problems here the main challenge is to present constructions that ensure the reversibility of the RS that encodes Turing machine configurations by sets, which allows ambiguous representation. For the problems under consideration we can show that there is no difference in complexity for reversible RSs compared to the general case. One exception is the question of the existence of a reversible subcomputation.

Keywords: Reaction system · reversibility · computational complexity · completeness · decision problems

1 Introduction

The apparent irreversibility of events in the macroscopic world contrasts with the fundamental nature of physics, as represented by its laws, which have been shown to exhibit reversibility. Physical processes abstractly represented as states and transitions between states enable the formulation of computational models, which are amenable to the study in the field of computer science. It is therefore of interest to examine whether the principles of reversibility, fundamental to physics, can also be obeyed in abstract computational models. In [7] the very simple biologically inspired computational model of reaction systems (RSs) was introduced, which is based on the idea of interactions on biochemical reactions, whose underlying mechanism is that of facilitation and inhibition. A reaction consists of a set of reactants needed for the reaction to take place, a set of inhibitors which forbids the reaction to take place and a set of products produced by the reaction. Here it is assumed that reactions do not compete with each other, because whenever a resource is available, then it is present in sufficient amounts. Then the dynamical behaviour of a RS is given by the product of all reactions that are applicable to a certain state of the system. Recently also variants of reversible RSs were studied in, e.g., [2,3], mostly from a structural perspective. Up to our knowledge the computational complexity of standard problems such

© The Author(s), under exclusive license to Springer Nature Switzerland AG 2023
M. Kutrib and U. Meyer (Eds.): RC 2023, LNCS 13960, pp. 40–54, 2023.
https://doi.org/10.1007/978-3-031-38100-3_4

as, e.g., reachability, simulation, equivalence, etc., for reversible RSs was not
investigated so far, while for the general unrestricted case the computational
complexity of most of these standard problems are known to be either tractable,
coNP-, or PSPACE-complete; see, e.g., [1,4,5,9,13]. A careful inspection of the
proofs of these results reveals that throughout the literature non-reversible RSs
are used for the lower bounds or hardness constructions. Can some of these lower
bound results be shown with reversible RSs?

For reachability and multi-step simulation we can show that this is the case.
The main challenge here is to enforce the global property of reversibility while
using a Turing machine configuration encoding that inherently allows no bijective
correspondence of configurations and RS states—there are RS states that do not
encode any Turing machine configuration at all. Tedious encoding constructions
allow us to overcome this obstacle. Hence we can show that the reachability problem for reversible RSs is of same complexity as for RSs in general by using the
construction of a reversible Turing machine as described in [10] together with our
reversible Turing machine simulation by RSs. For multi-step simulation problem
of RSs a PSPACE lower and a EXPSPACE := DSPACE(2^{poly}) = NSPACE(2^{poly})
upper bound was shown in [9]. Here we prove that the lower bound turns over
to the multi-step simulation problem of reversible RSs. Obviously the upper
bound also applies to the reversible setting. Here we can improve this bound to
NEXPTIME := NTIME(2^{poly}) even for the general case. Then we study the problem whether a state in a RS belongs to a reversible subcomputation of the whole
system. Obviously, for reversible RSs this problem is trivial, but it turns out that
for RSs without any restriction this problem is PSPACE-complete. This is the
first problem that we come across which has a different computational complexity when considering reversible RSs and RSs without any restriction. Finally,
we consider the problem whether a given RS contains a non-trivial reversible
computation. There we show that this problem is coNP-hard and is solvable in
PSPACE.

The paper is organized as follows: in the next section we introduce the necessary definitions and complexity classes and RSs. An illustrative example explains
how a binary counter can be implemented by a RS. Later this example is a basic
build block on one of our constructions. Then the result section follows. There we
consider the problems of reachability, multi-step simulation, and reversible sub-
computations. Detailed definitions of these problems are given there. Finally, we
end up with a conclusion, where we also discuss future research on the reversible
RSs.

2   Preliminaries

We assume the reader to be familiar with the basics in computational complexity theory [12]. In particular we recall the inclusion chain: $P \subseteq NP \subseteq PSPACE$.
Here P (NP, respectively) denotes the class of problems solvable by deterministic (nondeterministic, respectively) Turing machines in polytime, and PSPACE
refers to the class of languages accepted by deterministic or nondeterministic

Turing machines in polynomial space [14]. As usual, the prefix co refers to the complement class. For instance, coNP is the class of problems that are complements of NP problems. Completeness and hardness are always meant with respect to deterministic many-one logspace reducibilities ($\leq_m^{\log}$) unless otherwise stated. Throughout the paper we assume that the input given to the Turing machine is encoded by a function $\langle \cdot \rangle$, such that the necessary parameters can be decoded in reasonable time and space.

Let S be a finite set. A *reaction over S* is a triple $a = (R_a, I_a, P_a)$, where R_a, I_a, and P_a are subsets of S such that $R_a \cap I_a = \emptyset$. We call R_a (I_a, P_a, respectively) the set of *reactants* (*inhibitors*, *products*, respectively). If both R_a and I_a are nonempty we refer to a as a *strict* reaction. In case only R_a (I_a, respectively) is nonempty the reaction is said to be *reactant-strict* (*inhibitor-strict*, respectively). A subset T of S, i.e., $T \subseteq S$, is said to be a *state*. For any state T and any reaction a, we say that reaction a is *enabled* in T, if $R_a \subseteq T$ and $I_a \cap T = \emptyset$. The *T-activity of a set of reactions A*, referred to as

$$en_A(T) = \{\, a \in A \mid a \text{ is enabled in } T \,\},$$

is the set of all reactions of A enabled by T. The *result $res_a(T)$ of a reaction a on a set $T \subseteq S$* is defined as

$$res_a(T) = \begin{cases} P_a, & \text{if } a \text{ is enabled by } T, \\ \emptyset, & \text{otherwise.} \end{cases}$$

This notion naturally extends to sets of reactions. The *result of a set of reactions A on $T \subseteq S$* is

$$res_A(T) = \bigcup_{a \in A} res_a(T).$$

Now we are ready to define reactions systems. A *reaction system* (RS) is a pair $\mathcal{A} = (S, A)$, where S is a finite set of symbols, called the *background* set, and A consists of a finite number of reactions over S. The *result function $res_\mathcal{A}$* of the RS $\mathcal{A}$ is res_A. Hence, the *result of $\mathcal{A}$ on a state $T \subseteq S$* is $res_\mathcal{A}(T) = res_A(T)$. In case all reactions in A are strict, we call the RS $\mathcal{A}$ a *strict* reaction system.

In order to clarify the notation we give a small example, which we literally take with slight adaptions from [7].

Example 1. Let $\mathcal{A} = (S, A)$ be a RS defined as follows: set $S = \{x_1, x_2, \ldots, x_n\}$ and let A contain the following four different types of reactions:

$$(\emptyset, S, \{x_1\}),$$
$$(\{x_i\}, \{x_1\}, \{x_1\}) \qquad\qquad \text{for } 2 \leq i \leq n,$$
$$(\{x_1, x_2, \ldots, x_{i-1}\}, \{x_i\}, \{x_i\}) \qquad\qquad \text{for } 2 \leq i \leq n,$$

and

$$(\{x_j\}, \{x_i\}, \{x_j\}) \qquad\qquad \text{for } 1 \leq i < j \leq n.$$

Then $\mathcal{A}$ implements a binary counter, where the subsets T of S define binary numbers: if $x_i \in T$, for $1 \leq i \leq n$, then the binary number represented by T has a 1 on position $i - 1$; otherwise it has a 0. For instance, in case $n = 4$, the subset $T = \{x_1, x_3\}$ represents the binary number 0101.

The behaviour of the RS is seen as follows: the first reaction starts the counting from number zero, the reactions of the second type (third type, respectively) perform adding 1 to an even (odd, resp) number, while the reactions of the last type sustain the bits x_j that are not affected by carry over results by the addition, and finally the counting process restarts with the smallest number 0 whenever the largest binary number with n times 1 is reached because all reactions are disabled. The reader may easily verify that $res_{\mathcal{A}}(T) = \{x_2, x_3\}$ and $res_{\mathcal{A}}^2(T) = \{x_1, x_2, x_3\}$, where $res_{\mathcal{A}}^2$ refers to the 2-times application of the result function. Hence the k-folded application of the result function runs through all states of the RS in the natural order of binary numbers and restarts the counting with 0 after reaching the largest value.   □

3   Results

We investigate the computational complexity of problems related to reversible RSs. Before we define reversible RSs let us recall how reversible Turing machines are defined. First, a Turing machine M is *deterministic*, if each node in M's (infinite) configuration graph has outdegree at most one. A deterministic Turing machine is *reversible* if this restriction also holds for the indegree. More precisely, a Turing machine is *reversible* if and only if the (infinite) configuration graph of M, in which an arc (C, C') indicates that M can go from configuration C to configuration C' in a single transition, has indegree and outdegree at most one—see, e.g., [10]. This definition can be directly applied to RSs as follows: a RS $\mathcal{A} = (S, A)$ is *reversible* if the state graph $G_{\mathcal{A}}$ induced by $\mathcal{A}$ w.r.t. the reactions A has indegree and outdegree at most one, where $G_{\mathcal{A}} = (V, E)$ with $V = 2^S$ and $E = \{ (T, res_{\mathcal{A}}(T)) \mid T \subseteq S \}$. Relaxing this global property results in the following definition: a RS $\mathcal{A} = (S, A)$ is *partially reversible* if the state graph $G_{\mathcal{A}}$ induced by $\mathcal{A}$ w.r.t. the reactions in A contains a non-trivial subgraph that has indegree and outdegree at most one. Here a graph is *trivial* if it is a single node graph.

First we show that every reversible RS is bijective and *vice versa*. Here a RS $\mathcal{A} = (S, A)$ is bijective if the function $2^S \rightarrow 2^S$ induced by A is bijective.

Lemma 1. *Let $\mathcal{A} = (S, A)$ be a RS. Then $\mathcal{A}$ is reversible if and only if $\mathcal{A}$ is bijective.*

Proof. Obviously, if $\mathcal{A}$ is bijective, then the state graph has indegree and outdegree exactly one. Hence $\mathcal{A}$ is reversible. Conversely, if $\mathcal{A}$ is reversible, then by definition the indegree and outdegree is at most one. Since a RS cannot be forced to hold, since $res_A(T)$ is defined for every state T, the outdegree is exactly one. Therefore there are 2^S edges in the state graph and every node has one outgoing edge. Without violating the condition that the indegree is at most one, all the edges must be connected to different states. Therefore the indegree is exactly one. In summary both the indegree and the outdegree are exactly one, which implies that the induced function $2^S \to 2^S$ on the state set of the RS is a bijection. Thus, the RS $\mathcal{A}$ is bijective, which proves the stated claim.   □

Bijective RSs were already subject to computational complexity research. In [5] the coNP-completeness on the complexity of the decidability on the bijectivity of RSs was shown—since by the previous lemma the notations on reversibility and bijectivity are equivalent for RSs the following holds.

Theorem 1. *The problem for a given RS to decide whether it is reversible (or equivalently bijective) is* coNP*-complete.*   □

What concerns the computational complexity of standard problems for RSs if restricted to reversible systems like, e.g., the reachability problem, which is PSPACE-complete for RSs in general. We show that this also holds true for reversible RSs. One might think that this is obvious, because deterministic space bounded computations can be simulated reversible [10], i.e.,

$$\mathsf{RSPACE}(s(n)) = \mathsf{DSPACE}(s(n)), \quad \text{for } s(n) \geq \log n,$$

where $\mathsf{RSPACE}(s(n))$ refers to the class of languages that are accepted by $s(n)$-space bounded reversible Turing machines, and the fact that polynomial space bounded Turing machines, regardless whether the machine is operating deterministically or reversible can be simulated by a RS [5]. However, there are subtle problems with the argumentation. For instance, Turing machines halt for acceptance but as mentioned already above, RSs cannot halt the computation. Moreover, due to the encoding of configuration of Turing machines in the form of sets for reaction systems, the simulation device has to correctly deal with sets that do not encode any configuration at all. The problem of non-valid encoding of configurations seems to be inherent for RSs reversible simulations of (space bounded) Turing machines computations—see also, e.g. [3], where in the simulation the RS is only partially reversible in our sense. Nevertheless, we overcome this problems and show the following theorem:

Theorem 2. *The problem for a given reversible RS $\mathcal{A} = (S, A)$ and two states T and U with $T, U \subseteq S$ to decide whether T leads to U in $\mathcal{A}$ is* PSPACE*-complete.*

Proof. The PSPACE upper bound follows from the corresponding result on the reachability problem for RSs presented in [5]. It remains to show PSPACE-hardness for the problem under consideration for reversible RSs. To this end we argue as follows: consider a polynomial space bounded single-tape deterministic Turing machine M that never falls off the tape. Moreover, without loss of generality we may assume that the input alphabet of M contains a neutral symbol $\diamond$. Here *neutral* is meant in the following sense: this symbol can be part of any configuration and cannot be rewritten. Additionally, if the tape head enters a tape cell containing $\diamond$ from the left (right, respectively) the input head continues the left (right, respectively) movement to the next cell. Later we will use this symbol in order to enforce reversibility on certain states of the RS.

From M we construct a reversible Turing machine working within the same space constraints as M by applying the construction given in [10] that relies on an Euler tour through the configuration graph starting in the unique accepting configuration running the computation of M backwards until the initial configuration is reached. Normally, in this situation the computation halts and accepts; compare with [15]. We alter this behaviour such that instead of halting and accepting the machine continues with the Euler tour computation until the unique accepting configuration is reached and the whole computation restarts again—see left drawing of Fig. 1. In this way, the constructed Turing machine becomes reversible. Moreover, the Turing machine is even bijective, i.e., indegree and outdegree of every configuration in the configuration graph is exactly one. It is worth mentioning that the initial (accepting, respectively) configuration of the reversible Turing machine corresponds to the unique accepting (initial, respectively) configuration of the deterministic Turing machine where our construction started from.

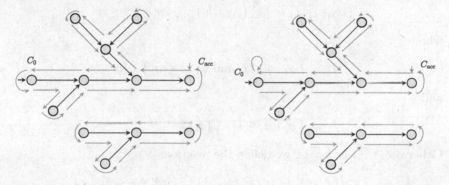

Fig. 1. (Left) Euler tour on the sample configuration graph of a deterministic Turing machine. (Right) Modified Euler tour construction where the computation loops on C_0. Here C_0 refers to the initial configuration and C_{acc} denotes the unique accepting configuration.

Now we are ready to simulate the bijective Turing machine with state set Q, tape alphabet Γ, blank symbol $\sqcup \notin \Gamma$, transition function $\delta : Q \times (\Gamma \cup \{\sqcup\}) \rightarrow Q \times (\Gamma \cup \{\sqcup\}) \times \{L, N, R\}$, initial state q_0, and accepting state q_f (that is non-halting). Recall that Γ contains the neutral symbol $\diamond$. Let m be the length of the polynomial size tape. We closely follow the lines of the proof on the simulation of an ordinary deterministic Turing machine given in [5]. A configuration of the reversible Turing machine is in state q and reads the ith symbol, for $1 \leq i \leq m$, of the tape content $a_1 a_2 \ldots a_m$, for $a_i \in \Gamma \cup \{\sqcup\}$ and $1 \leq i \leq m$. Such a configuration is encoded by a set

$$ T = \{q_i\} \cup \{\, (a_i)_i \mid a_i \in \Gamma \text{ and } 1 \leq i \leq m \,\}. $$

Observe, that we require $a_i \in \Gamma$ and *not* $a_i \in \Gamma \cup \{\sqcup\}$. For instance, the configuration where the machine is in state q reading the third letter of the tape description $aba \sqcup b \diamond a$ is described by the state set $\{a_1, b_2, q_3, a_3, b_5, \diamond_6, a_7\}$. Hence we will use the background set

$$S = \{\, a_i \mid a \in \Gamma \text{ and } 1 \leq i \leq m \,\} \cup \{\, q_i \mid q \in Q \text{ and } 1 \leq i \leq m \,\}.$$

For a_i (q_i, respectively) we will simply speak of letter a (state q, respectively) at position i. Observe, that there are also sets such as, e.g., $\{a_1, b_1, q_3\}$ or $\{a_1, q_3, p_2\}$, that do not describe any legal configuration at all. Even for these sets we have to ensure a reversible computation in the RS.

It remains to specify the reaction set A of the system. Every transition $\delta(q, a) = (p, b, D)$, for $q, p \in Q$, $a, b \in \Gamma \cup \{\sqcup\}$, and $D \in \{L, N, R\}$ gives rise to the following reactions—for $D \in \{L, N, R\}$ let $d = -1$, if $D = L$, $d = 0$, if $D = N$, and $d = 1$, if $D = R$. We distinguish three cases:

1. Let $a \in \Gamma$. For b we further distinguish two subcases. If $b \neq \sqcup$, then we have the reactions

$$(\{q_i, a_i\}, I_{q_i} \cup I_{a_i}, \{q_{i+d}, b_i\}), \quad \text{for } 1 \leq i \leq m,$$

where

$$I_{q_i} = \{\, q'_j \mid q' \in Q \text{ and } 1 \leq j \leq m \,\} \setminus \{q_i\}$$

and

$$I_{a_i} = \{\, a'_i \mid a' \in \Gamma \,\} \setminus \{a_i\}.$$

Otherwise, that is, $b = \sqcup$, we define the reactions

$$(\{q_i, a_i\}, I_{q_i} \cup I_{a_i}, \{p_{i+d}\}), \quad \text{for } 1 \leq i \leq m.$$

2. Assume $a = \sqcup$. We distinguish two subcases again. If $b \neq \sqcup$, then we add the reactions

$$(\{q_i\}, I_{q_i} \cup \{\, a'_i \mid a' \in \Gamma \,\}, \{p_{i+d}, b_i\}), \quad \text{for } 1 \leq i \leq m$$

and

$$(\{q_i\}, I_{q_i} \cup \{\, a'_i \mid a' \in \Gamma \,\}, \{p_{i+d}\}), \quad \text{for } 1 \leq i \leq m,$$

in case $b = \sqcup$. The set I_{q_i} is defined as above.

In order to maintain all the symbols that are not read by the read/write head we use the reactions

$$(\{a_i\}, \{\, q_i \mid q \in Q \,\}, \{a_i\}),$$

for $a \in \Gamma$ and $1 \leq i \leq m$.

The up to this point defined reactions simulate the reversible Turing machine and therefore all state sets that induce valid configurations have indegree and outdegree one. Even if the set contains two or more symbols on a certain position and the read/write head is not located on this position, a reversible computation is simulated. The case where the read/write head is located on a position with at least two symbols is treated below. Moreover, also the state sets that do not contain any state of the Turing machine belong to a trivial reversible computation in the RS, because all these sets map to itself.

What about the state sets that contain at least one state of the Turing machine and do not induce a valid configuration of the reversible Turing machine? Here we distinguish two cases (that are not disjoint):

1. If the encoding contains at least two states from the reversible Turing machine the following reactions are used: for the states $q, p \in Q$ and $a \in \Gamma$ define

$$(\{q_i, p_j\}, \emptyset, \{q_i, p_j\}),$$
$$(\{q_i, p_j, a_i\}, \emptyset, \{q_i, p_j, a_i\}),$$

and

$$(\{q_i, p_j, a_j\}, \emptyset, \{q_i, p_j, a_j\}),$$

for $1 \le i < j \le m$. The above defined reactions, together with the reactions that copy symbols that are not read, can be applied to the RS that contain at least two states form the reversible Turing machine. These reactions leave the state unchanged, i.e., the application of the rules of A induce a self-loop on such state sets.

2. Finally, if two symbols reside in the same position, then the $\diamond$-transition of the reversible Turing machine (that is defined for every state) comes into play. For $q, p \in Q$, $a, b \in \Gamma$ with $a \ne b$, and the transition $\delta(q, \diamond) = (p, \diamond, D)$ define the reactions

$$(\{q_i, a_i, b_i\}, \emptyset, \{p_{i+d}, a_i, b_i\}), \quad \text{for } 1 \le i \le m.$$

Here we take care of the situation that the read/write head is located on a position with at least two symbols. In this case we interpret this situation as seeing the $\diamond$-symbol for the computation step, while copying the actual tape symbols on that position. This means, that whenever we have at least two symbols on a position they cannot change at all. Therefore we can treat this situation as if we would see the $\diamond$-symbol. Hence we mimic a computation with $\diamond$-symbols on these particular positions, which is reversible by construction of the reversible Turing machine.

This completes the description of the RS A. The construction of A is computable by a deterministic logspace bounded Turing machine. By the discussion above the RS A is reversible and hence bijective.

For given input w taking an encoding T of the initial configuration and an encoding U of the unique accepting configuration of the reversible Turing machine, we obtain that T leads to U in the reversible RS A if and only if the word w is accepted by the reversible Turing machine. This proves the stated claim. □

The reachability problem for reversible RSs can be used to prove some further problems to be PSPACE-complete such as the multi-step simulation problem, which is defined as follows [11]: let $\mathcal{A} = (S_A, A)$ and $\mathcal{B} = (S_B, B)$ be two RSs with $S_A \subseteq S_B$. The RS $\mathcal{A}$ is k-*simulated by* $\mathcal{B}$, if for every $T \subseteq S_A$ we have

$$res_{\mathcal{A}}(T) = res_{\mathcal{B}}^k(T) \cap S_A.$$

In this case we simply write $\mathcal{A} \preceq_k \mathcal{B}$. This means that when considering the sequence of states of $\mathcal{A}$ and $\mathcal{B}$ starting from T, then the successor of T in $\mathcal{A}$ coincides with the kth successor of T in $\mathcal{B}$ w.r.t. the elements of S_A, where auxiliary elements of $S_B \setminus S_A$ may also occur. Finally, we say $\mathcal{A}$ is *simulated* by $\mathcal{B}$, for short $\mathcal{A} \preceq \mathcal{B}$, if there is a k such that $\mathcal{A} \preceq_k \mathcal{B}$. In [9] it is shown that it is PSPACE-hard to determine whether for two given RSs a number k exists such that the first RS can be k-simulated by the second one. We will show that this also holds if the given RSs are reversible.

Theorem 3. *The problem for two given reversible RSs $\mathcal{A}$ and $\mathcal{B}$, to decide whether $\mathcal{A} \preceq \mathcal{B}$, asking for the existence of a k with $k \geq 1$ such that $\mathcal{A} \preceq_k \mathcal{B}$, is* PSPACE-*hard.*

Proof. We reduce the PSPACE-complete reachability problem for reversible RSs from Theorem 2 to the problem in question. Let the reversible RS $\mathcal{C} = (S, C)$ and two states T' and U' with $T', U' \subseteq S$ be an instance of the reachability problem, i.e., the question whether T' leads to U' in $\mathcal{C}$. Let s, t be two symbols not contained in S.

Define the RS $\mathcal{A} = (\{s, t\}, \{((\{s\}, \emptyset, \{t\}), (\{t\}, \emptyset, \{s\}))\})$ that induces a permutation on its states $\{s\}$ and $\{t\}$ while its other states $\{s, t\}$ and $\emptyset$ are mapped onto itself.

In reversible RSs a state T' leads to U' if and only if $res(T')$ leads to $res(U')$. Since the calculation of $res(T')$ and $res(U')$ can be done in deterministic logspace then we can reduce this problem to the question whether $res(T')$ leads to $res(U')$ while we know T' and U'. For simplicity we define $T^{-1} := T'$ and $T := res_{\mathcal{C}}(T')$ just like $U^{-1} := U'$ and $U := res_{\mathcal{C}}(U')$. If T^{-1} or T would be equal to U then we know that T leads to U in $\mathcal{C}$ since $\mathcal{C}$ is reversible. Hence, we assume without loss of generality that $U \notin \{T, T^{-1}\}$.

The idea behind the construction of the RS $\mathcal{B}$ is that when it is started on the state $\{s\}$ it then verifies the reachability question of T to U for the RS $\mathcal{C}$. In case the answer is "yes," it generates the symbol t; otherwise it loops back to the state $\{s\}$ without producing the letter t. The analogue will be done for the state $\{t\}$. In the next step the original symbol is created while the computation continues. Obviously the constructed cycles will be very similar to the according cycle of T except that we change the transitions of T^{-1} and $\emptyset$ such that $T^{-1} \cup \{s\}$ is mapped onto $\emptyset \cup \{s\}$ which is mapped onto $T \cup \{s\}$ while the analogue applies for the sets $T^{-1} \cup \{t\}$, $\emptyset \cup \{t\}$, and $T \cup \{t\}$. Therefore we need that $U \neq \emptyset$. This can be achieved, since we can choose $\mathcal{B}$ as a reversible reaction system that is obtained through the construction in Theorem 2 and there we have that the empty set is mapped onto itself.

To this end let $\mathcal{B} = (\{s, t\} \cup S, B)$, and the set of reactions B contains the following reactions that implement the above described idea: to start the simulation of the reachability one of the reactions

$$(\{s\}, S \cup \{t\}, T), \qquad \text{and} \qquad (\{t\}, S \cup \{s\}, T),$$

is used, which introduces the elements of T to the state, respectively for the starting state $\{s\}$ and $\{t\}$. Then the actual computation takes place *via* the reactions

$$(R_a \cup \{z\}, I_a \cup \{z'\}, P_a), \qquad\qquad \text{for } z, z' \in \{s, t\} \text{ and all } R_a \supset T^{-1},$$
$$(R_a \cup \{z\}, I_a \cup \{x_i, z'\}, P_a), \qquad \text{for } z, z' \in \{s, t\}, \text{all}, x_i \in T^{-1} \text{ and all } R_a \subset T^{-1},$$

and

$$(R_a \cup \{x_i, z\}, I_a \cup \{z'\}, P_a), \qquad \text{for } z, z' \in \{s, t\}, \text{all } x_i \in S \text{ and all } R_a = T^{-1},$$

while the symbols s and t remain in each image state that is not equal to U and not equal to U^{-1} by applying the reactions

$$(\{x_i, z\}, \{x_j, x_j'\}, \{z\}), \quad \text{for } z \in \{s, t\}, \text{all } x_i \in S, x_j \in U^{-1}, x_j' \in U$$
$$(U^{-1} \cup \{x_i\} \cup \{z\}, \{x_j'\}, \{z\}), \qquad \text{for } z \in \{s, t\}, \text{all } x_i \in S \setminus (U^{-1}), x_j' \in U,$$
$$(U \cup \{x_i\} \cup \{z\}, \{x_j\}, \{z\}), \qquad \text{for } z \in \{s, t\}, \text{all } x_i \in S \setminus U, x_j \in U^{-1},$$

and

$$(U \cup U^{-1} \cup \{x_i\} \cup \{z\}, \emptyset, \{z\}), \qquad \text{for } z \in \{s, t\}, \text{all } x_i \in S \setminus (U \cup U^{-1}).$$

Then eventually the state $U^{-1} \cup \{s\}$ ($U^{-1} \cup \{t\}$, respectively) is reached for which exactly one of the reactions

$$(U^{-1} \cup \{s\}, S \setminus U^{-1}, \{t\}),$$

and

$$(U^{-1} \cup \{t\}, S \setminus U^{-1}, \{s\}),$$

and some of the previously defined reactions are applicable. Therefore $U^{-1} \cup \{s\}$ is mapped onto $U \cup \{t\}$ and $U^{-1} \cup \{t\}$ is mapped onto $U \cup \{s\}$. Therefore we have proceeded with the computation of $\mathcal{C}$ while exchanging the symbols s and t. This is also done in the next step *via* one of the reactions

$$(U \cup \{s\}, S \setminus U, \{t\}),$$

and

$$(U \cup \{t\}, S \setminus U, \{s\}).$$

Afterwards the computation continues without changing the letters s and t until the state $T^{-1} \cup \{s\}$ ($T^{-1} \cup \{t\}$, respectively) is reached. For this state the symbol s (t, respectively) will be preserved but none of the other reactions are applicable, which proves that $T^{-1} \cup \{s\}$ is mapped onto $\{s\}$ again. With the same arguments $T^{-1} \cup \{t\}$ is mapped onto $\{t\}$. Observe that no other state can mapped onto $\{s\}$ or $\{t\}$, because $res_{\mathcal{C}}(\emptyset) = \emptyset$, which implies that $res_{\mathcal{B}}(X \cup \{z, z'\}) = \{z''\}$ for $X \subseteq S$ and $z, z', z'' \in \{s, t\}$ can only be true for $z = z' = z''$ and $X = T^{-1}$. Additionally, every reaction producing a symbol in $\{s, t\}$ has a symbol in $\{s, t\}$ in its reactant set which implies that the preimages of $\{s\}$ and $\{t\}$ are unique.

We map the state $\{s, t\}$ onto itself by

$$(\{s, t\}, \emptyset, \{s, t\}).$$

For handling the sets which are not involved in the computation we define the reactions

$$(\{x_i, s, t\}, \emptyset, \{x_i, s, t\}), \qquad\qquad \text{for all } x_i \in S,$$

and

$$(\{x_i\}, \{s, t\}, \{x_i\}), \qquad\qquad \text{for all } x_i \in S,$$

which provide that each set that is unequal to $\{s, t\}$ and does not contain exactly one of the symbols s and t is mapped onto itself.

So it remains to prove that in the case that T does not lead to U in $\mathcal{C}$ the state $\{s\}$ does not lead to a state containing t and not containing s. Afterwards we have to show that $\mathcal{C}$ is reversible in both cases.

If T does not lead to U we observe that $\{s\}$ does not lead to $U \cup \{s\}$ which implies that neither $U^{-1} \cup \{s\}$ nor to $U^{-1} \cup \{t\}$ can be reached from $\{s\}$. The analogue is true for $\{t\}$. Therefore $\{s\}$ only leads to states

$$T \cup \{s\}, res_{\mathcal{B}}(T) \cup \{s\}, res_{\mathcal{B}}^2(T) \cup \{s\}, \ldots, T^{-1} \cup \{s\}$$

where $T^{-1} \cup \{s\}$ is mapped onto $\{s\}$ again. Like before the analogue is true for the state $\{t\}$.

It is not hard to see that for all sets $X \cup \{z\}$ for $X \subseteq S$ and $z \in \{s, t\}$ we have that $res_{\mathcal{C}}(X \cup \{z\}) = res_{\mathcal{B}}(X) \cup \{z\}$ which proves with the previously shown arguments that $\mathcal{C}$ is reversible.

Thus, by construction, state T leads to U in $\mathcal{C}$ if and only if state set $\{s\}$ leads to the state $X \cup \{t\}$ and the state $\{t\}$ leads to the state $X \cup \{s\}$ for $X \subseteq S$. Since the only other state of $\mathcal{A}$, namely $\{s, t\}$, is mapped onto itself in $\mathcal{A}$ and $\mathcal{B}$ we have that $\mathcal{A}$ is k-simulated by $\mathcal{B}$, for some k, if and only if the input $\langle \mathcal{C}, T, U \rangle$ is a positive instance of reachability. Note, that in both RSs $\mathcal{A}$ and $\mathcal{B}$ the empty state set is mapped to itself and has no effect on the k-simulation. This proves PSPACE-hardness, because the RSs $\mathcal{A}$ and $\mathcal{B}$ can be constructed in deterministic logspace from $\mathcal{C}$, T', and U'. $\qquad\qquad\qquad\qquad\qquad\qquad\qquad\qquad\qquad\qquad\qquad$ □

In [9] an $\mathsf{EXPSPACE} := \mathsf{DSPACE}(2^{\mathsf{poly}}) = \mathsf{NSPACE}(2^{\mathsf{poly}})$ upper bound on the $\preceq$-simulation problem by an involved argument that uses basic algebraic properties on the least common multiple function lcm was given. Here we present a much simpler argument and in passing improve the upper bound to the complexity class $\mathsf{NEXPTIME} := \mathsf{NTIME}(2^{\mathsf{poly}})$.

Theorem 4. *The problem for two given (reversible) RSs $\mathcal{A}$ and $\mathcal{B}$, to decide whether $\mathcal{A} \preceq \mathcal{B}$, that is, asking for the existence of a k with $k \geq 1$ such that $\mathcal{A} \preceq_k \mathcal{B}$, belongs to $\mathsf{NEXPTIME}$.*

Proof. Let $\mathcal{A} = (S_A, A)$ and $\mathcal{B} = (S_B, B)$. For every state $T \subseteq S_A$ we define a unary deterministic finite automaton $A_T = (Q, \{a\}, \delta, T, F)$ with state set $Q = \{ U \mid U \subseteq S_B \}$, the transition function $\delta(U, a) = res_B(U)$, for $U \subseteq S_B$, and the set of final states $F = \{ U \mid U \subseteq S_B$ and $res_A(T) = U \cap S_A \}$. By construction it is easy to see that if the word a^k belongs to the language accepted by $L(A_T)$, then $res_A(T) = res_B^k(T) \cap S_A$. Hence if

$$\bigcap_{T \subseteq S_A} L(A_T) \neq \emptyset$$

then there is word a^k that is accepted by all automata A_T and thus $\mathcal{A}$ can be k-simulated by $\mathcal{B}$. Then the containment of the $\preceq$-simulation problem for RSs in $\mathsf{NEXPTIME}$ follows because the intersection non-emptiness problem for unary finite automata, regardless whether they are deterministic or nondeterministic, is NP complete [8,16] and the problem instance $\langle A_T \mid T \subseteq S_A \rangle$ for this is of exponential size. $\square$

Next, let us have a look on the following problem: given a RS $\mathcal{A} = (S, A)$ and a state $T \subseteq S$, is T part of a reversible subgraph of the computation graph of $\mathcal{A}$? Obviously, for reversible RSs this problem is trivial. For RSs in general this problem is PSPACE-complete, which is shown in the next theorem. This is a significant difference between reversible RSs and RSs in general.

Theorem 5. *The problem for a given RS $\mathcal{A} = (S, A)$ and a state $T \subseteq S$ to decide whether T is part of a reversible subgraph of the state graph of $\mathcal{A}$ is PSPACE-complete.*

Proof. The containment in PSPACE is seen as follows: in the algorithm we cycle through all states U and check whether T leads to U in $\mathcal{A}$. If this is *not* the case, then we continue with the next U in the cycle computation. Otherwise, we verify whether U has two predecessor states in $\mathcal{A}$. This is done with a subroutine, which is described below. If the predecessor question is answered "yes," i.e., there are two predecessors, then we halt and reject; otherwise we continue with the next U in the cycle computation. If the U enumeration cycle finishes, then we halt and accept. The subroutine that verifies whether a state U has two predecessors first guesses two different states T_1 and T_2 and computes $res_A(T_1)$ and $res_A(T_2)$. If these sets are the same, then the subroutine answers yes; otherwise no. It is easy to see that the subroutine runs on a nondeterministic Turing machine in polynomial space, hence belongs to PSPACE. A careful inspection shows that the main algorithm with the enumeration cycle also runs on a nondeterministic polynomial space bounded Turing machine. Therefore, the problem in question is contained in PSPACE as claimed.

It remains to show PSPACE-hardness. Recall the proof of Theorem 2. For a given deterministic Turing machine we have constructed according to [10] a reversible Turing machine working within the same space bound by running the computation backwards towards the initial configuration of the original deterministic machine. Here we do the same but instead of continuing the computation whenever the initial configuration of the original machine is reached, we start cycling in this configuration—see the right drawing of Fig. 1. Hence the constructed machine M is almost everywhere reversible, except for this particular configuration, which is the unique accepting configuration of M. For M we construct a RS $\mathcal{A}$ as described in the proof of Theorem 2 and ask the question whether for the state T in $\mathcal{A}$ that represents the initial configuration of M belongs to a reversible subgraph of the computation graph of $\mathcal{A}$. If the initial configuration of M leads to the accepting configuration of M, then the initial configuration is not part of a reversible computation, since M loops on the accepting configuration. Otherwise, if the initial configuration does not lead to the accepting one, then it belongs to a reversible computation by construction. This argumentation carries over to the RS $\mathcal{A}$ and proves the PSPACE-hardness, because $\mathcal{A}$ can be constructed by a deterministic logspace bounded Turing machine.   □

Finally, we want to mention the following result:

Theorem 6. *The problem for a given RS $\mathcal{A} = (S, A)$ to decide whether it is partially reversible is* coNP-*hard and contained in* PSPACE.

Proof. The containment in PSPACE is seen as follows: for the given RS $\mathcal{A}$ a Turing machine guess a state $T \subseteq S$ and verifies (i) that $T \neq res_A(T)$ and (ii) that T belongs to a reversible subgraph of the state graph of $\mathcal{A}$. Both conditions can be verified in PSPACE—see Theorem 5 for the second condition. Thus the problem under consideration belongs to PSPACE.

We prove coNP-hardness by a reduction from the tautology problem for Boolean formulas in disjunctive normal-form. Given a formula

$$\varphi = C_1 \vee C_2 \vee \cdots \vee C_m$$

over the variables $X = \{x_1, x_2, \ldots x_n\}$, we construct a RS $\mathcal{A} = (S, A)$, where $S = X \cup \{s, t\}$ and the reactions are

$$(pos(C_j) \cup \{s\}, neg(C_j) \cup \{t\}, \{t\}), \qquad \text{for } 1 \leq j \leq m,$$

and

$$(\{x_i\} \cup \{s\}, \{t\}, \{x_i\}), \qquad \text{for } 1 \leq i \leq n,$$

where $neg(C)$ ($pos(C)$, respectively) denotes the set of variables from X that negatively (positively, respectively) appear in the clause C as literals, together with reactions for counting—see Example 1—with the variables

$$(\{t\}, X \cup \{s\}, \{x_1\} \cup \{s\}),$$
$$(\{x_i\} \cup \{t\}, \{x_1\} \cup \{s\}, \{x_1\} \cup \{s\}), \qquad \text{for } 2 \le i \le n,$$
$$(\{x_1, x_2, \dots, x_{i-1}\} \cup \{t\}, \{x_i\} \cup \{s\}, \{x_i\} \cup \{s\}), \qquad \text{for } 2 \le i \le n,$$

and

$$(\{x_j\} \cup \{t\}, \{x_i\} \cup \{s\}, \{x_j\} \cup \{s\}), \qquad \text{for } 1 \le i < j \le n.$$

This completes the description of the RS $\mathcal{A}$. For the analysis of the state graph $G_{\mathcal{A}}$ we need some further notation. Let $\text{BIN}(i)$ denote the set $T \subseteq X$ with $i = \sum_{k=0}^{n-1}[x_{k+1} \in T] \cdot 2^k$, where $[x \in T] = 1$, if $x \in T$, and $[x \in T] = 0$, otherwise. Moreover, for states U and T with $U = res_{\mathcal{A}}(T)$ we simply write $T \to U$. We find

$$\text{BIN}(i) \cup \{s\} \to \text{BIN}(i) \cup \{t\} \to \begin{cases} \text{BIN}(i+1) \cup \{s\} & \text{if } 0 \le i < 2^n - 1, \\ \text{BIN}(0) \cup \{s\} & \text{otherwise,} \end{cases}$$

if φ is satisfied by the assignment induced by $\text{BIN}(i)$, and

$$\text{BIN}(i) \cup \{s\} \to \text{BIN}(i) \to \emptyset$$

otherwise. Every state set that does *not* contain s nor t is mapped to $\emptyset$; in particular $\emptyset$ is mapped to $\emptyset$ by the RS $\mathcal{A}$. Moreover, this is also true for the state $\{s, t\}$. Thus, we get that φ is a tautology if and only if the state graph of $\mathcal{A}$ contains a non-trivial reversible subgraph that checks for all assignments in sequence whether they all satisfy φ. This proves the stated claim. □

We have to leave open the exact complexity of the partial reversibility problem, but we conjecture it to be PSPACE-complete. It is worth mentioning that problems related to cycle structures in the RS's state graph were already considered in [5] and vary from P- over NP- and coNP- to PSPACE-completeness. Note that a cycle structure is not necessarily a reversible computation since other states may lead into a cycle state.

4 Conclusions

We have studied the computational complexity of certain problems for reversible RSs. Although the state graph of a reversible RS is very simple and consists of cycles only, they are still complicated enough to even encode PSPACE computations of Turing machines. In fact, as in the case of unrestricted RSs, the complexity of the problems considered in this paper vary from coNP- to PSPACE-completeness in most cases. For some problems only non-matching upper and lower bounds are given. Reversible and in particular partially reversible RSs are a natural host for further investigations of other problems such as, special properties on RSs such as, e.g., isotonicity, antitonicity, etc., and minimality problems [6,17], and threshold properties [4].

References

1. Azimi, S., Iancu, B., Petre, I.: Reaction system models for the heat shock response. Fund. Inform. **131**(3–4), 299–312 (2014)
2. Bagossy, A., Vaszil, G.: Simulating reversible computation with reaction systems. J. Membrane Comput. **2**, 179–193 (2020)
3. Cienciala, L., Ciencialová, L., Csuhaj-Varjú, E.: About reversibility in SP colonies and reaction systems. Natural Comput., October (2022)
4. Dennunzio, A., Formenti, E., Manzoni, L.: Reaction systems and extremal combinatorics properties. Theor. Comput. Sci. **598**, 138–149 (2015)
5. Dennunzio, A., Formenti, E., Manzoni, L., Porreca, A.E.: Complexity of the dynamics of reaction systems. Inf. Comput. **267**, 96–109 (2019)
6. Ehrenfeucht, A., Kleijn, J., Koutny, M., Rozenberg, G.: Minimal reaction systems. In: Priami, C., Petre, I., de Vink, E. (eds.) Transactions on Computational Systems Biology XIV. LNCS, vol. 7625, pp. 102–122. Springer, Heidelberg (2012). https://doi.org/10.1007/978-3-642-35524-0_5
7. Ehrenfeucht, A., Rozenberg, G.: Reaction systems. Fund. Inform. **75**, 263–280 (2007)
8. Galil, Z.: Hierarchies of complete problems. Acta Informatica **6**(1), 77–88 (1976). https://doi.org/10.1007/BF00263744
9. Holzer, M., Rauch, C.: On the computational complexity of reaction systems, revisited. In: Santhanam, R., Musatov, D. (eds.) CSR 2021. LNCS, vol. 12730, pp. 170–185. Springer, Cham (2021). https://doi.org/10.1007/978-3-030-79416-3_10
10. Lange, K.-J., McKenzie, P., Tapp, A.: Reversible space equals deterministic space. J. Comput. Syst. Sci. **60**(2), 354–367 (2000)
11. Manzoni, L., Poças, D., Porreca, A.E.: Simple reaction systems and their classification. Int. J. Found. Comput. Sci. **25**(4), 441–457 (2014)
12. Papadimitriou, C.H.: Computational Complexity. Addison-Wesley (1994)
13. Salomaa, A.: Functions and sequences generated by reaction systems. Theor. Comput. Sci. **466**, 87–96 (2012)
14. Savitch, W.J.: Relationships between nondeterministic and deterministic tape complexities. J. Comput. Syst. Sci. **4**(2), 177–192 (1970)
15. Sipser, M.: Halting space-bounded computations. Theor. Comput. Sci. **10**, 335–338 (1980)
16. Stockmeyer, L.J., Meyer, A.R.: Word problems requiring exponential time. In: Proceedings of the 5th Symposium on Theory of Computing, pp. 1–9 (1973)
17. Teh, W.C., Atanasiu, A.: Minimal reaction system revisited and reaction system rank. Int. J. Found. Comput. Sci. **28**(3), 247–261 (2017)

Reversible Programming

Optimization of Reversible Control Flow Graphs

Niklas Deworetzki[✉][iD] and Lukas Gail[✉][iD]

Technische Hochschule Mittelhessen, Wiesenstr. 14, 35390 Giessen, Germany
{niklas.deworetzki,lukas.gail}@mni.thm.de

Abstract. Growing interest in reversible computation has led to an accelerated development of reversible programming languages and software, which reinforces the need for optimizing compilers. In this paper, we report on our recent progress on optimizing reversible intraprocedural control flow. Like previous work on the optimization of reversible programs, the techniques in this paper are based on the reversible intermediate language RSSA. A formalization of RSSA's control flow as an extended directed multigraph is introduced. This serves as a basis for three analysis and optimization techniques for reversible control flow, which enable the identification and removal of a) unreachable code, b) branches between strictly consecutive code sequences, and c) immediately redirected branches. To our knowledge, this is the first work being done to investigate the optimization of reversible control flow.

Keywords: reversible computation · reversible programming languages · compiler optimizations · control flow

1 Introduction

Reversible computation as an area of research is concerned with computational models where steps of computation are reversible. At the heart of this area lies Landauer's principle, which states that reversible computations can be made free of inherent energy loss [11] and represents a major opportunity for the development of low-energy computing [7]. In 1973 Bennet demonstrated the computational powers of reversible systems by developing the reversible turing machine [4]. Since then, research has spread across the subfields of hardware design (e.g. [13,14]), language design (e.g. [8,15,16]), and compiler implementations (e.g. [6,9]).

An important part of compiler construction is program analysis and optimization, as optimizing compilers play an important role in the runtime efficiency of computer systems [1]. While there has been ongoing work to transfer the knowledge about the optimization of conventional programs into the reversible world, reversible program optimization is still a young but promising area of research. Recent advancements include common subexpression elimination, constant propagation, procedure inlining, and dead code elimination for reversible programs [5,6], all of which are done on RSSA code [12].

© The Author(s), under exclusive license to Springer Nature Switzerland AG 2023
M. Kutrib and U. Meyer (Eds.): RC 2023, LNCS 13960, pp. 57–72, 2023.
https://doi.org/10.1007/978-3-031-38100-3_5

Control flow optimizations are a yet unexplored area of optimization for reversible programs. They are a class of optimizations in which the structure of possible execution paths in a program is modified or simplified. A common case of simplification of control flow is the removal of code that is not reachable, for example due to a condition that can never be fulfilled. On their own, control flow optimizations contribute to the reduction of code size. Additionally, they can also act as enabling optimizations, as the simplification of control flow also benefits other analysis such as constant propagation.

This paper is organized into the following sections: In Sect. 2 we present a formalization and visualization of reversible control flow in RSSA as a directed multigraph. In Sect. 3 we present three possible simplification techniques for reversible control flow:

1. Removal of unreachable code.
2. Merging strictly consecutive program sections that are separated by a jump.
3. Eliminating redundant jumps immediately followed by another jump.

The techniques are also discussed under the lens of a lesser safety requirement. Section 4 concludes the presented optimizations and discusses future work.

2   Reversible Control Flow in RSSA

The optimizations presented in this paper act on the control flow of a reversible program's procedures. The goal is the simplification of control flow and removal of redundant control flow constructs to speed up execution and reduce the program overhead and size.

Just as in previous work in the area of reversible compiler optimizations, we perform both analysis and program transformation on RSSA code. RSSA is a reversible intermediate programming language designed by T. Æ. Mogensen in 2015 [12]. Conceptually it can be placed between high-level reversible programming languages which often employ structured reversible control flow [15,16] and low-level reversible machine languages which describe control flow as changes on a machine's state (for example by modifying registers) [3]. This position of RSSA in between different reversible technologies increases the applicability and reusability of the presented optimizations. Furthermore, RSSA has proven to be a suitable platform for optimizations during our recent work on reversible program optimizations in the *rc3* compiler [5].

In general, control flow can be separated into two categories: Interprocedural control flow describes how routines interact with each other. Intraprocedural (also called local) control flow is concerned with control flow inside of a specific procedure [1]. This paper focuses on local, intraprocedural control flow.

RSSA provides symmetrical constructs for both execution directions in order to implement bidirectionally deterministic control flow, which can be divided into entry and exit points. Exit points compare to a classical jump in forwards direction and come in two variants: Unconditional exit points contain a single label and always cause a jump to it at runtime. Conditional exit points contain

$$L\,(as) \leftarrow \quad \rightleftharpoons \quad \rightarrow L\,(as)$$
$$L_1\,(as)\,L_2 \leftarrow c \quad \rightleftharpoons \quad c \rightarrow L_1\,(as)\,L_2$$

Fig. 1. Intraprocedural entry (left) and exit instructions (right) in RSSA.

two labels and a condition. At runtime, the condition is evaluated to determine which of the two labels is the jump's target (left label if true, right label if false). The symmetrical mirror-image of exit points are entry points which act as the target of a jump and also come in two variants. An unconditional entry point contains a single label and is the instruction from which execution continues after a jump to that label occurs. A conditional entry point, just like its counterpart, contains two labels and a condition. Here, the condition is evaluated and acts as an assertion in order to verify that control flow can be reconstructed during backwards execution. Depending on which label was used to reach a conditional entry point, its condition is required to be true or false. Figure 1 shows the syntactic representation of entry and exit points. In both conditional variants, the left label is associated with a condition evaluating to true and the right label is associated with a condition evaluating to false. Entry and exit points contain a list of atoms (variables or constants) that are passed from exit point to entry point. These lists of atoms are written as as in Fig. 1.

A sequence of instructions can be grouped into a collection of basic blocks, each encompassing the maximal sequence of instructions that are always executed sequentially without incoming or outgoing branches interrupting them [1, p. 525]. In RSSA, basic blocks always start with an entry point and include all subsequent instructions up to and including the next exit point. As entry and exit points are the only means of intraprocedural control flow, these instructions must be executed strictly in that order without interruption. Basic blocks constitute nodes in control flow graphs, with jumps connecting them as edges.

Two properties in RSSA ensure that local control flow is deterministic in both execution directions and therefore reversible:

1. Labels appear exactly twice in an RSSA program: Once in an entry point and once in an exit point. This way, the origin of a jump can always be uniquely identified, unlike in non-reversible computing where a label can be the target of many different jumps.
2. Assertions in conditional entry points ensure that an execution path can be reconstructed during backwards execution.

Assertions play a major role in RSSA. They act as proof that information can be reconstructed (i.e. is not lost) if execution is reversed and therefore ensure reversibility. Invalid data, unexpected program states or simply programming mistakes can cause an assertion to fail. We call these failures *runtime reversibility violations* and expect a runtime environment to detect and report these. There is no point in continuing a program's execution after a violation occurred, as reversibility is no longer guaranteed.

$$\text{begin } L\,(as) \quad \rightleftharpoons \quad \text{end } \dot{L}\,(as)$$
$$(as_1) \;\coloneqq\; \text{call } L\,(as_2) \quad \rightleftharpoons \quad (as_2) \;\coloneqq\; \text{uncall } L\,(as_1)$$

Fig. 2. Interprocedural control flow instructions in RSSA.

RSSA provides two instructions which define the boundaries of a routine. The `begin` instruction is the entry point of a routine's first basic block and the `end` instruction is the exit point of a routine's last basic block. The simplest routines only consist of a single basic block containing both. The name of a routine can only be referenced via `call` or `uncall` instructions (Fig. 2).

The optimization techniques presented in this paper deal with RSSA's local control flow, which – like in classical computing [2] – can be represented using a directed multigraph. Labels in RSSA connect entry and exit points, so they can be used to identify edges within the graph. Consequently, we model RSSA's intraprocedural control flow as follows:

Definition 1. *A reversible control flow graph in RSSA is a multigraph* $G = (B, L, s, t, c, a, begin, end)$, *where*

- B *is the finite set of basic blocks in a procedure and vertices of the graph.*
- L *is the set of labels identifying the edges of the graph.*
- $s : L \to B$ *assigns each label to the block of the exit point it is used in.*
- $t : L \to B$ *assigns each label to the block of the entry point it is used in.*
- $c : L \to \{\, T, F, U \,\}$ *assigns each label to how it appears in its exit point.*[1]
- $a : L \to \{\, T, F, U \,\}$ *assigns each label to how it appears in its entry point.*
- $begin \in B$ *is the block containing the* `begin` *instruction.*
- $end \in B$ *is the block that contains the* `end` *instruction.*

Definition 2. *Given a control flow graph* $G = (B, L, s, t, c, a, begin, end)$, *the auxiliary functions* $exit : B \to \wp\,(L)$ *and* $entry : B \to \wp\,(L)$ *determine the set of labels occurring in the entry/exit point of a basic block, with*

$$exit(b) = \{\, l \in L : s(l) = b \,\}$$
$$entry(b) = \{\, l \in L : t(l) = b \,\}$$

Different shapes are used to visualize the nodes of such a graph. In total there are four different shapes, as shown in Fig. 3. A node's shape describes the nature of the represented basic block: A flat top indicates that the block's entry point is unconditional. Similarly, a flat bottom indicates an unconditional exit point. Triangular tops and bottoms indicate conditional entry and exit points. Edges represent labels and have their name written next to them. By convention, a label l connected to the left side of a triangular border indicates that it is used in the **true**-position of the conditional entry/exit ($c(t) = T$ or $a(l) = T$). Labels connected to the right side are used in the **false**-position ($c(t) = F$ or $a(l) = F$). The *begin* node has no incoming edges, while the *end* node has no outgoing edges.

---

[1] T = conditional **T**rue, F = conditional **F**alse and U = **U**nconditional.

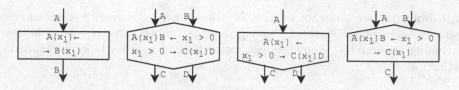

Fig. 3. Shapes for different combinations of entry and exit points in basic blocks.

3 Reversible Control Flow Optimizations

Now that we have laid out the basics of reversible control flow, we will look at specific optimization vectors.

3.1 Removal of Unreachable Code

A common optimization technique for control flow replaces branching instructions whose conditions are constant with unconditional jumps. Doing so in RSSA without further thought will lead to invalid code, as it could leave a label with only one usage, which is illegal. As a solution, we propose an integrated optimization that performs the removal of both static branching and unreachable code, thereby preserving the integrity of the procedure.

Both constant conditions and unreachable code are rarely intentionally created by a programmer. More commonly, they are created by other program transformations such as inlining, constant propagation, or partial evaluation. Another form of unreachable code is debug code that is unused in a production environment. Unreachable code increases a program's size and complexity without contributing to its functionality. This gives reason for an optimizing compiler to remove such code in order to reduce memory consumption and the complexity of control flow. Removing unreachable sections of code can also create additional opportunities for dataflow optimizations like constant propagation or dead code elimination.

As basic blocks are either executed in their entirety or are not executed at all, it suffices to consider reachability as a property of basic blocks instead of individual instructions. Overall, our goal is to remove all basic blocks from a routine that are unreachable. For a multigraph, a sequence of nodes does not uniquely identify an execution path, but a sequence of labels does. Therefore, we perform the reachability analysis on labels. A label is reachable when a jump using that label can occur during runtime. Given a set of reachable labels, we can infer a set of unreachable and therefore removable blocks, as well as a set of entry and exit point transformations required to keep the remaining code valid.

We obtain the set of reachable labels in forwards direction by tracing paths through the control flow graph, starting at the *begin* block and following along the labels of the exit point. This is where we take static branching into account: Constant conditions cause one of the labels in a conditional exit point to not be followed. For our purposes, a condition is considered constant when either both operands are constant or are the same variable. Formally specified, we use a function $fw : B \rightarrow \wp(L)$, giving the set of labels directly reachable (i.e. excluding transitivity) from the exit instruction of a given block b, which is defined as:

$$
fw(b) = \begin{cases} \{\, l \in exit(b) : c(l) = T \,\} & \textbf{if } b\text{'s exit condition evaluates to } true \\ \{\, l \in exit(b) : c(l) = F \,\} & \textbf{if } b\text{'s exit condition evaluates to } false \\ exit(b) & \textbf{otherwise} \end{cases}
$$

The result of fw is determined by the exit point of the given basic block. If the condition in a conditional exit point has a statically known value, only the label on the true or the false side is returned depending on the condition's value. Otherwise, all the exit labels are returned. No labels are returned for the *end* block, as it terminates a routine's control flow and has no successors.

The set R_{fw} of all reachable labels in forward direction is then defined as the transitive closure of reachable labels starting from *begin* and using the *fw* function. It can be computed using the worklist algorithm in Fig. 4.

procedure $ComputeR_{fw}$ ($G = (B, L, s, t, c, a, begin, end)$)
> $R_{fw} \leftarrow \varnothing$
> $q \leftarrow fw\,(begin)$
> **while** $q \neq \varnothing$ **do**
>> $l \leftarrow$ remove any element from q
>> **if** $l \notin R_{fw}$ **then**
>>> $R_{fw} \leftarrow R_{fw} \cup \{\, l \,\}$
>>> $q \leftarrow q \cup fw\,(t\,(l))$
>
> **return** R_{fw}

Fig. 4. Algorithm computing the set of reachable labels.

This algorithm uses a worklist q containing labels that have not yet been processed. When the worklist is depleted, the result set contains all labels reachable from the *begin* block of a routine. As only unprocessed reachable labels cause the worklist to grow and at most all labels in the finite L are processed, the algorithm always terminates.

Only using R_{fw} is not sufficient to conclusively answer which labels are reachable in a control flow graph. There might be labels that are not considered reachable in the forwards direction, but will be reachable during backwards execution. To rectify this, we perform the same analysis in reverse direction by tracing the edges of the graph in backwards direction starting at *end*. In analogy to fw, we define the function bw for directly reachable labels in backwards direction.

$$bw(b) = \begin{cases} \{\, l \in entry(b) : a(l) = T \,\} & \text{if } b\text{'s entry condition evaluates to } true \\ \{\, l \in entry(b) : a(l) = F \,\} & \text{if } b\text{'s entry condition evaluates to } false \\ entry(b) & \textbf{otherwise} \end{cases}$$

The same worklist algorithm as before can be used to compute the transitive closure R_{bw} by replacing $begin$ with end, fw with bw and t with s. Consider the small example in Fig. 5. Both conditions in this control flow graph are constant, so the reachability analysis will result in $R_{fw} = R_{bw} = \{B\}$.

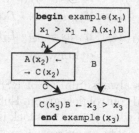

Fig. 5. Control flow graph with $R_{fw} = R_{bw} = \{B\}$.

Working with two distinct sets of reachable labels as the result of analysis raises an obvious question: What happens if the sets are not equal – if some labels are reachable in one execution direction but not the other? The short answer is that differing sets for R_{fw} and R_{bw} indicate a potential reversibility violation lingering in the program. The implications of conflicting reachability for labels are discussed in more detail in Sect. 3.2. For now, we consider a label to be reachable if it is reachable in either direction by using the union set $R = R_{fw} \cup R_{bw}$ as the set of reachable labels.

procedure *RemoveUnreachable* (R, $G = (B, L, s, t, c, a, begin, end)$)
    $p \leftarrow \varnothing$
    foreach $b \in B$ **do**
        if $\exists l \in (exit(b) \cup entry(b)) : l \in R$ **then**
            Update entry and exit point of b to remove unreachable labels.
            $p \leftarrow p \cup \{b\}$
    return p

Fig. 6. Algorithm for the removal of unreachable code.

To remove unreachable code, all of the procedure's basic blocks are processed as shown in Fig. 6. Blocks with at least one reachable entry or exit label are preserved, all other blocks are unreachable and are discarded. *begin* and *end* always have at least one reachable connected label and are therefore always preserved.

The entry and exit points of preserved blocks are updated to remove references to labels that are not in R. That is, a conditional exit point is converted into an unconditional exit point that jumps to the remaining, reachable label. The same is done for conditional entry points, which are converted into unconditional entry points. All other instructions remain unchanged. The changes made to conditional entry and exit points are given by:

$$update\ (ins) = \begin{cases} L_1(as) \leftarrow & \text{if } ins = L_1(as)L_2 \leftarrow c \text{ and } L_2 \notin R \\ L_2(as) \leftarrow & \text{if } ins = L_1(as)L_2 \leftarrow c \text{ and } L_1 \notin R \\ \rightarrow L_2(as) & \text{if } ins = c \rightarrow L_1(as)L_2 \text{ and } L_1 \notin R \\ \rightarrow L_1(as) & \text{if } ins = c \rightarrow L_1(as)L_2 \text{ and } L_2 \notin R \\ ins & \textbf{otherwise} \end{cases}$$

The resulting basic blocks always fulfil all of RSSA's properties and can be used to construct an optimized control flow graph. Entry and exit instructions are only ever completely removed when the entire block is removed. Therefore, there is no basic block without an entry or an exit. Unreachable labels are removed from both the entry and exit points, therefore the requirement that labels must be used exactly twice is not violated. As the remaining parts of the program remain unchanged, no invalid code is generated for valid input.

3.2   A More Aggressive Approach

Previously, we considered a label to be reachable when it is either in R_{fw} or R_{bw}. The union of both acted as the basis for optimization. A more aggressive variant of the optimization uses the intersection set $R_{fw} \cap R_{bw}$ instead. A label is then only considered reachable when it is reachable in both directions. In this case, we assume that a label being unreachable in one direction implies that it also should be unreachable in the other direction. As we will later see, this view of reachability has some pitfalls and requires caution during optimization to not create invalid RSSA code. We also alter the program's behavior when the above assumption does not hold.

To illustrate this further, consider the control flow graph in Fig. 7. Reachability analysis will produce $R_{fw} = \{B\}$, but $R_{bw} = \{A, B, C\}$. During forwards execution, the label A and subsequently the left block can never be reached, as the condition $x_1 > x_1$ always evaluates to false. During backwards execution, this block could be executed if a value greater than zero is passed to x_3. This however always results in a reversibility violation, because the assertion $x_1 > x_1$ can never evaluate to true.

In fact, reaching any block of code that is unreachable in the opposite direction will always lead to a reversibility violation. After all, if there is no valid path connecting the begin instruction to a block of code, there also can never be a valid path from that block of code to the begin instruction during backwards execution. It must either result in a reversibility violation or loop indefinitely,

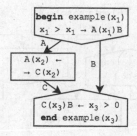

Fig. 7. Control flow graph with $R_{fw} = \{B\}$ and $R_{bw} = \{A, B, C\}$.

which – given bounded memory – also terminates with a reversibility violation at some point [10,17]. The same is true regarding backwards execution and the **end** instruction.

Let us now assume for a moment that only well-behaving programs, which never produce runtime reversibility violations, are considered for optimization. With this assumption, we can also assume that code that we know would trigger a reversibility violation is never executed. This creates room for more potent optimization. On the other hand, assuming that reversibility violations never occur makes RSSA (and any reversible programming language translating to RSSA) less resilient against programming errors, which manifests itself in altered program behavior for programs they do occur in.

In the specific case of removing unreachable code, a label being unreachable in only one direction according to the analysis allows the optimizer to infer that reaching this label would result in a reversibility violation, implying that it is actually unreachable in both directions and therefore removable. This allows the removal of unreachable code in cases where the compiler is otherwise not "smart" enough to determine the constant value of some condition.

As hinted at, there are pitfalls when doing this. Using the intersection of reachable labels (and therefore the union of unreachable labels) leads to situations where the removal of unreachable labels creates invalid RSSA code. This always happens when there is no label reachable in both directions, i.e. $R_{fw} \cap R_{bw} = \varnothing$. In this case, all execution paths through the procedure result in a reversibility violation. We call such a routine disconnected, as no executable path connects *begin* and *end*. An example is shown in Fig. 8, where no label is reachable in both execution directions. This indicates that the entire procedure is unreachable and to be removed, making other parts of the program invalid.

This issue is not limited to visually disconnected control flow graphs. It can also materialize in procedures that appear to be fine at first glance, as seen in Fig. 9. For the left procedure, the condition $x_1 > x_1$ always evaluates to false, leading to $R_{fw} = \{B\}$. $x_3 \geq x_3$ evaluates to true, so that $R_{bw} = \{A, C\}$. Using the new interpretation of reachability leads to $R = \varnothing$. Even though the graph visually seems connected and does not contain loops, all labels are considered unreachable. Furthermore, the problem is also not limited to graphs where no

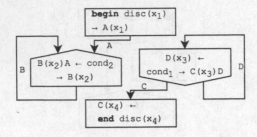

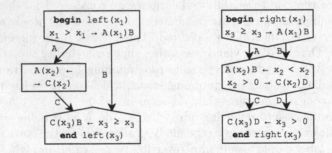

Fig. 8. A disconnected control flow graph.

label is reachable, as shown by the right procedure. Analysis results in $R_{fw} = \{A, C, D\}$, $R_{bw} = \{B, C, D\}$, and subsequently, $R = \{C, D\}$. Both A and B are unreachable, leaving *begin* without any reachable label.

Fig. 9. Control flow graphs with disagreeing reachability.

These examples highlight a problem: There should always be at least one reachable label connected to *begin* and *end* so they are not removed by the optimization, as this would break the procedure. In the right example, the basic block in the center is also problematic: Its exit labels are reachable, but its entry labels are not. The optimization cannot remove the block because it contains reachable labels, but it also cannot update its entry instruction, because it does not contain any reachable label.

We have previously asserted that using an unreachable label during execution always leads to a reversibility violation. We can use this fact to infer additional information about unreachable labels: If exiting a block always leads to a reversibility violation, entering it also leads to one at some point. As reversibility violations are assumed to never occur, the block itself and therefore its entry labels are also unreachable. The same is true for the inverse direction. The algorithm in Fig. 10 implements this idea by removing labels from R whenever such a block is found. This can cause other blocks to become broken, so the process is repeated until a fixed point is reached. The algorithm always terminates because the number of reachable labels strictly decreases and cannot go below

0, in which case no label is reachable and executing the procedure always results in a reversibility violation. Care must be taken regarding *begin* and *end* because they have no reachable entry/exit labels.

$$
\begin{aligned}
&\textbf{procedure } Fix_R \ (\ R, \ G = (B, L, s, t, c, a, begin, end) \ ) \\
&\quad | \ \textbf{repeat until } \textit{no more changes to R occur} \\
&\quad | \quad | \ \textbf{foreach } b \in B \ \textbf{do} \\
&\quad | \quad | \quad | \ \textbf{if } b \neq begin \textbf{ and } entry(b) \cap R = \varnothing \textbf{ then} \\
&\quad | \quad | \quad | \quad \lfloor \ R \leftarrow R \setminus exit(b) \\
&\quad | \quad | \quad | \ \textbf{if } b \neq end \textbf{ and } exit(b) \cap R = \varnothing \textbf{ then} \\
&\quad | \quad | \quad | \quad \lfloor \ R \leftarrow R \setminus entry(b) \\
&\quad | \ \textbf{return } R
\end{aligned}
$$

Fig. 10. Algorithm reducing the set of reachable labels.

After this algorithm is applied, no more blocks with disagreeing entry and exit reachability remain, except *begin* or *end* when all labels connected to them are unreachable. In fact, if all labels attached to either are unreachable, there cannot be a valid execution path through the procedure, resulting in all labels of the procedure being unreachable and the procedure being disconnected.

Definition 3. *A control graph G with a set of reachable labels R fixed by algorithm Fix_R degenerates when removing unreachable code if $R = \varnothing$, making it a disconnected graph.*

There are multiple ways to handle degenerating procedures during optimization. One way to go about this is to fall back to the first variant, where a label is considered reachable when it is reachable in either direction, as this will never lead to blocks with disagreeing reachability. Alternatively, we can continue to assume that reversibility violations do not occur at runtime. Procedures without reachable labels cannot be executed without reversibility violations and therefore can be assumed to never be executed. An optimizer making that assumption can do anything to that procedure without altering the assumed program behavior. It can transform it into a constant function or even remove it completely along with any calls to it. It could even consider all basic blocks in the program that contain a call to it to be unreachable because they trigger reversibility violations.

3.3 Merging Consecutive Blocks

RSSA code can include basic blocks that directly follow each other but are unnecessarily separated by a jump. This situation can arise as a result of unreachable code elimination, but can also exist on its own. To remove the unnecessary jump an optimizing compiler can combine such blocks into one.

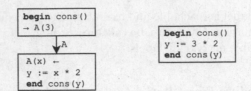

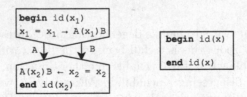

Fig. 11. Optimization of two strictly consecutive basic blocks.

Figure 11 shows an optimizable example along with its simplification. The blocks have been merged and the unnecessary entry and exit points were removed. This reduces code size and empowers optimizations that are local to a single basic block, such as local constant propagation. Two basic blocks can be merged into a single one when they are always executed in sequence without interruptions. We call such blocks *strictly consecutive*. In RSSA strictly consecutive blocks can be identified by checking whether all labels exiting a block b_1 lead to a block b_2. This is possible because every label appears exactly twice and therefore all jumps using that label are trivially known.

Definition 4. *For two distinct basic blocks b_1 and b_2, b_2 is said to be strictly consecutive to b_1 iff $exit(b_1)$ equals $entry(b_2)$ and is not empty.*

This definition also includes strictly consecutive blocks that are connected by more than one label, which happens when the relevant exit and entry instructions are conditional, like in Fig. 12.

Fig. 12. Optimization of strictly consecutive blocks with conditions.

Merging two blocks connected by a conditional potentially alters a program's behavior if the involved assertion can fail at runtime. Continuing our earlier assumption that only well-behaving programs are optimized, we can still merge these blocks and remove the assertion. Otherwise, the optimizer needs to prove that the entry point's assertion never fails, which is not trivially possible. If we cannot prove this and we do not want to assume that only well-behaving programs are optimized, it is still possible to optimize two blocks connected via unconditional entry and exit points. In this case, there is *exactly one* label connecting the strictly consecutive blocks.

In RSSA, the jump from an exit point to an entry point passes a series of atoms from one parameter list to the other. The effects of this must be preserved when merging strictly consecutive blocks to ensure variables are correctly final-ized and initialized. As a simple approach, two strictly consecutive basic blocks can be glued together by generating explicit assignments for every passed atom. Given exit parameters $a_1, \ldots, a_n$ and entry parameters $b_1, \ldots, b_n$, this is done by inserting an assignment $b_i := a_i$ for every $i \in \{1, \ldots, n\}$. On closer inspec-tion, some of these assignments can be omitted by replacing the occurrences of one atom with another atom. This idea leads to the following rules:

1. If a constant c is passed to a variable v, replace all occurrences of v with c.
2. If a variable v is passed to a constant c, replace all occurrences of v with c.
3. If a variable v is passed to another variable u, **either** replace all occurrences of v with u **or** replace all occurrences of u with v.
4. If a constant c is passed to the same constant, no replacements are necessary.
5. If a constant c is passed to a different constant k, this jump will always lead to a reversibility violation. To preserve this behavior, generate an assignment $k := c$ explicitly triggering the reversibility violation at runtime.

Again, merging strictly consecutive blocks enables further optimizations. For example, it is possible to use local common-subexpression-elimination (as described in [5]) to eliminate computations that were done in both of the previ-ously disjoint blocks.

3.4   Elimination of Empty Blocks

The final optimization technique presented in this paper aims to remove basic blocks that serve no function other than redirecting control flow. These blocks only contain an unconditional entry and exit point with no other instructions and their parameter lists consist of the same variables in the same order. We call such basic blocks *empty*. If variables are reordered by a block's parameter list or constants are present, a block performs the function of initializing or finalizing atoms and is more than just a redirection. Empty blocks correspond to a jump immediately followed by another jump in classical computing.

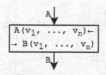

Fig. 13. An empty basic block.

Blocks following the pattern shown in Fig. 13 can be eliminated by simul-taneously modifying the blocks connected to it via A and B. This is done by either replacing the remaining occurrence of label A with B or the remaining

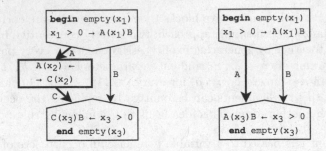

Fig. 14. Elimination of an empty basic block.

occurrence of B with A. In Fig. 14, which shows the control graph of an exemplary procedure before and after performing the optimization, the empty block is highlighted.

If A and B are the same label, the block is connected to itself and replacing them does not change the code. However, in this case, the block is always unreachable and can be removed as previously shown.

Under the assumption that only well-behaved programs are optimized, we can improve this optimization as well. Consider the left basic block pictured in Fig. 15. This block fulfils all the requirements for being a redirecting empty block, except the one that calls for the entry and exit point to be unconditional. However, the conditions used are identical and always evaluate to the same value. Provided that the entry assertion never fails – which we are assuming –, the block fits our expectations for empty blocks and performs two redirections. If entered via A, the block is always exited via C. The same is true for B and D.

Generally speaking, both conditions are not required to be equivalent. Whenever the optimizer can statically infer a bijection relating the value of the entry condition to the value of the exit condition, this optimization can be applied. Instead of being equivalent, the conditions may also be inverses of each other. This is shown on the right-hand side of Fig. 15, where A is redirected to D and B to C.

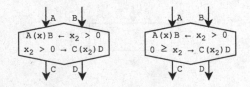

Fig. 15. Examples of redirecting basic blocks with conditions.

4   Conclusion

We have introduced a formalization of RSSA's intraprocedural control flow in form of a directed multigraph, which serves as a foundation for local control flow analysis. On that foundation, we have presented three distinct but related optimization techniques. They fill a gap in the field of optimization for reversible programming languages, as previous work was mostly concerned with optimizing dataflow, for example by eliminating common subexpressions, propagating constants or eliminating dead code [5,6]. Control flow optimizations benefit from those optimizations and also complement them. Constants may be propagated into conditions, which creates static knowledge of formerly dynamic control flow, which in turn allows constant propagation to act more effectively as the number of potential execution paths is reduced. Merging strictly consecutive blocks benefits local optimizations such as common subexpression elimination.

Control flow optimizations are well known and established in classical computing. Transferring them to the reversible world is made challenging by the restrictions placed by RSSA. Novel solutions are required to make sure the program is valid RSSA after every optimization step. The removal of statically evaluable branching required the removal of unreachable code to preserve the program's integrity, which necessitates an integrated solution doing both. While its restrictions make some optimizations more challenging, we still believe RSSA is the right tool for analysis and optimization, as these restrictions also verify that we do not inadvertently break a program during optimization.

An interesting aspect for reversible optimizations is the assumption that only well-behaving programs without reversibility violations are optimized. Optimization variants using that assumption are allowed to change the behavior of programs that do trigger reversibility violations, but at the same time open up more optimization potential for well behaving programs without reversibility violations. This creates a trade-off between the increased optimization potential and safety of a programming language. The presented optimizations allow the choice between both options depending on the safety guarantees by a higher level programming language or even the needs of an individual user. A compromise solution could generate explicit assertions wherever assertions are removed based on the assumption that only well-behaving programs are optimized.

Even without the intention of optimizing a program, reachability analysis can be useful. Warning users about disconnected procedures for example helps spotting software faults before runtime.

4.1   Future Work

Further control flow optimizations established in classical computing have yet to be transferred into the world of reversible computation. The scope of this paper was limited to intraprocedural control flow, leaving analysis and optimization of interprocedural control flow largely unexplored. In close relation to control flow optimizations, loop optimizations such as loop tiling, unrolling, and skewing are promising avenues to explore. While current optimizations for RSSA are general in nature and do not make assumptions regarding the underlying hardware, loop optimizations trying to improve cache locality are very dependent on hardware.

The idea that reversibility violations cause a block of code to be considered unreachable can be explored further. We have hinted at considering calls to disconnected procedures unreachable, which effectively allows the property of being unreachable to spread across procedure boundaries. Similarly, other instructions could be considered unreachable, if an optimizer can prove that they always cause a reversibility violation, such as the assignment $1 := 2$.

References

1. Aho, A.V., Lam, M.S., Sethi, R., Ullman, J.D.: Compilers: Principles, Techniques, & Tools. Pearson Education (2006)
2. Allen, F.E.: Control flow analysis. In: Proceedings of a Symposium on Compiler Optimization, pp. 1–19. Urbana-Champaign, Illinois (1970)
3. Axelsen, H.B., Glück, R., Yokoyama, T.: Reversible machine code and its abstract processor architecture. In: Computer Science – Theory and Applications, pp. 56–69. Ekaterinburg, Russia (2007)
4. Bennett, C.H.: Logical reversibility of computation. IBM J. Res. Dev. **17**(6), 525–532 (1973)
5. Deworetzki, N., Kutrib, M., Meyer, U., Ritzke, P.D.: Optimizing reversible programs. In: Reversible Computation, pp. 224–238. Urbino, Italy (2022)
6. Deworetzki, N., Meyer, U.: Program analysis for reversible languages. In: Proceedings of the 10th ACM SIGPLAN International Workshop on the State Of the Art in Program Analysis, pp. 13–18. Virtual, Canada (2021)
7. Frank, M.P.: The future of computing depends on making it reversible. IEEE Spectrum (2017)
8. Glück, R., Yokoyama, T.: Reversible computing from a programming language perspective. Theoretical Comput. Sci. (2023)
9. Haulund, T.: Design and implementation of a reversible object-oriented programming language. arXiv preprint arXiv:1707.07845 (2017)
10. Kaarsgaard, R., Axelsen, H.B., Glück, R.: Join Inverse categories and reversible recursion. J. Logical Algebraic Methods Program. **87**, 33–50 (2017)
11. Landauer, R.: Irreversibility and heat generation in the computing process. IBM J. Res. Dev. **5**(3), 183–191 (1961)
12. Mogensen, T.Æ.: RSSA: a reversible SSA form. In: Mazzara, M., Voronkov, A. (eds.) PSI 2015. LNCS, vol. 9609, pp. 203–217. Springer, Cham (2016). https://doi.org/10.1007/978-3-319-41579-6_16
13. Storrs Hall, J.: A reversible instruction set architecture and algorithms. In: Proceedings Workshop on Physics and Computation. PhysComp '94, pp. 128–134 (1994)
14. Vieri, C.J.: Pendulum: a reversible computer architecture. Ph.D. thesis, Massachusetts Institute of Technology (1995)
15. Yokoyama, T., Axelsen, H.B., Glück, R.: Principles of a reversible programming language. In: Proceedings of the 5th Conference on Computing Frontiers, pp. 43–54 (2008)
16. Yokoyama, T., Axelsen, H.B., Glück, R.: Towards a reversible functional language. In: International Workshop on Reversible Computation, pp. 14–29 (2011)
17. Yokoyama, T., Axelsen, H.B., Glück, R.: Fundamentals of Reversible Flowchart Languages. Theoret. Comput. Sci. **611**, 87–115 (2016)

Tail Recursion Transformation for Invertible Functions

Joachim Tilsted Kristensen[1]([✉]) [ID], Robin Kaarsgaard[2] [ID],
and Michael Kirkedal Thomsen[1,3] [ID]

[1] University of Oslo, Oslo, Norway
{joachkr,michakt}@ifi.uio.no
[2] University of Southern Denmark, Odense, Denmark
kaarsgaard@imada.sdu.dk
[3] University of Copenhagen, Copenhagen, Denmark

Abstract. Tail recursive functions allow for a wider range of optimisations than general recursive functions. For this reason, much research has gone into the transformation and optimisation of this family of functions, in particular those written in continuation passing style (CPS).

Though the CPS transformation, capable of transforming any recursive function to an equivalent tail recursive one, is deeply problematic in the context of reversible programming (as it relies on troublesome features such as higher-order functions), we argue that relaxing (local) reversibility to (global) invertibility drastically improves the situation. On this basis, we present an algorithm for tail recursion conversion specifically for invertible functions. The key insight is that functions introduced by program transformations that preserve invertibility, need only be invertible in the context in which the functions subject of transformation calls them. We show how a bespoke data type, corresponding to such a context, can be used to transform invertible recursive functions into a pair of tail recursive function acting on this context, in a way where calls are highlighted, and from which a tail recursive inverse can be straightforwardly extracted.

Keywords: tail recursion · CPS transformation · program transformation · program inversion

1 Introduction

When a function calls itself, either directly or indirectly, we say that the function is recursive. Furthermore, when the recursive calls performed by a recursive function all occur as the last operation in its own definition, we say that the function is tail recursive. Unlike generally recursive functions, tail recursive functions can be easily compiled into loops in imperative languages (in particular assembly languages) doing away with the overhead of function calls entirely. This makes tail recursion a desirable programming style.

Recall that a program is *reversible* when it is written such that it only consists of invertible combinations of invertible atomic operations; this is the idea of reversibility as *local* phenomenon. While every reversible program is also *invertible* (in the sense that it has an inverse), the converse is not the case, as an invertible program may consist of a number of non-invertible functions that simply happen to interact in a way as to make the program invertible. As such, invertibility is a *global* phenomenon.

While recursion has been employed in both imperative and functional reversible programming languages [12,24] for many years, tail recursion has been more cumbersome to handle. Here, we argue that relaxing (local) reversibility to (global) invertibility can drastically simplify the handling of tail recursion and even make it possible to use (adaptations of) conventional CPS transformation methods for transforming general recursive to tail recursive functions. To see this, consider the list reversal and list append functions

```
reverse1 [      ] = []               snoc1 ([     ], x) = x : []
reverse1 (x : xs) =                  snoc1 (y : ys, x) =
  let ys      = reverse1 xs   in       let (zs:_x) = snoc1 (ys, x) in
  let (zs:_x) = snoc1 (ys, x) in       (y : zs:_x)
  (zs:_x)
```

The careful reader will have already realised that `reverse1` is its own inverse. Here, we will refrain from clever realisations and focus on purely mechanical ways of providing inverse functions. For instance, the inverses

```
unsnoc1 (y : zs:_x) =                unreverse1 (zs:_x) =
  let (ys, x) = unsnoc1 (zs:_x) in     let (ys, x) = unsnoc1 (zs:_x) in
  (y : ys, x)                          let xs      = unreverse1 ys    in
unsnoc1 (x : [   ]) = ([ ], x)         (x : xs)
                                     unreverse1 [      ] = [ ]
```

are produced by rewriting "`let y = f x in t`" to "`let x = unf y in t`", and then swapping the order of bindings in the remaining program t, starting from the last line and ending with the first, much in the style of Romanenko [19]. To transform these recursive functions into tail recursive functions, the standard technique is to introduce an iterator that passes around an explicit argument for accumulating the deferred part of the computation, e.g.,

```
reverse2 xs = reverse2_iter (xs, [])

reverse2_iter ([     ], accum) = accum
reverse2_iter (x : xs, accum) = reverse2_iter (xs, x : accum)
```

Implementing list reversal in this style makes it tail recursive, but it also loses an important property, namely *branching symmetry*. This is crucial, since branching symmetry was the entire reason why we could mechanically invert the implementations of `snoc1` and `reverse1` so easily: because the leaves of their cases are syntactically orthogonal. For instance, in `reverse1`, when the input is an empty list, the result is also an empty list, and when the input is nonempty, the result is also nonempty.

As a consequence of this loss of symmetry, the iterator function `reverse2_iter` it is not considered *well-formed for inversion* as defined by Glück & Kawabe [6]. Consequently, it cannot be implemented in a reversible functional programming language such as RFun [20,24] or CoreFun [8], as it breaks the symmetric first match policy; the base case returning `accum` will also return the same value from the iterative case. Even worse, `reverse2_iter` cannot be inverted to a deterministic function using known methods [5,16,18]. Of course, this is because `reverse2_iter` is not injective, so the outputs of a particular input is not unique.

It does not take much effort to show that `reverse1` and `reverse2` are semantically equivalent. Thus, since the latter does nothing but call `reverse2_iter` it is surprising that we cannot invert it. A brief analysis of the problem concludes that `reverse2` restricts itself to a subset of the domain of `reverse2_iter`, and since `reverse2` is clearly injective, `reverse2_iter` as restricted to this smaller domain must be injective as well. By further analysis, we realise that the second component of the arguments to `reverse2_iter`, as called by `reverse2`, is static and can be ignored. In this context `reverse2_iter` is in one of three configurations: accepting the restricted input, iterating, or returning an output. By introducing a data type, we can explicitly restrict `reverse2_iter` to this smaller domain:

```
data Configuration a = Input a | Iteration (a, a) | Output a

reverse3 xs = let (Output ys) = iterate (Input xs) in ys

iterate   (Input xs)                = iterate (Iteration (xs, [    ]))
iterate   (Iteration (x : xs, ys)) = iterate (Iteration (xs, x : ys))
iterate   (Iteration ([    ], ys)) = (Output ys)
```

Even further, just like `reverse1` this definition can be mechanically inverted:

```
uniterate (Output ys)              = uniterate (Iteration ([    ], ys))
uniterate (Iteration (xs, x : ys)) = uniterate (Iteration (x : xs, ys))
uniterate (Iteration (xs, [    ])) = (Input xs)

unreverse3 ys = let (Input xs) = uniterate (Output ys) in xs
```

Moreover, these four function definitions are all tail recursive, which was what we wanted.

Structure: In this article we will show an algorithm that can perform this transformation. First, in Sect. 2, we illustrate the program transformation by example, before describing it formally in Sect. 3 and prove its correctness. Afterwards, we discuss a couple of known limitations (Sect. 4) of our approach, and show how the resulting constructs can be compiled to a flow-chart language (Sect. 5). Finally, we discuss related in Sect. 6 and end in Sect. 7 with some concluding remarks.

2   Tail Recursion Transformation, by Example

The transformation we propose assumes a functional programming language with
first order functions, algebraic datatypes, and recursion, as these are the features
commonly found in reversible functional programming languages [8,9,20,24].
Moreover, as the subject of the transformation, we only consider functions that
are *well-formed for inversion* [6] as usual, meaning that the patterns of case-
expressions are orthogonal, either syntactically, or by guard statements as suggested in Mogensen's semi-inversion for guarded-equations [15]. Furthermore,
we require that expressions and patterns are linear (any variable binding is used
exactly once), and (for simplicity) that a variable cannot be redefined in expressions that nest binders (such as let and case).

Such programming languages usually introduce the notion of tail recursion
by introducing an imperative style language feature. For instance, Mogensen's
language for guarded equations [15] features a loop construct that allows it to
call a partial function until it fails (by pattern matching not exhaustive), as
illustrated by the function reverse4, defined by:

```
reverse4(xs) = let ([], acc) = loop revStep (xs, []) in acc
  where revStep(x : xs, acc) = (xs, x : acc);
```

Likewise, the Theseus programming language [9] provides a trace operation
encoded via so-called *iteration labels*, as demonstrated in reverse5 below.

```
iso reverse5 :: [a] <-> [a]
| xs                        = iterate $ inL xs, []
| iterate inL $ (x : xs) ys = iterate $ inL xs, (x : ys)
| iterate inL $ [],      ys = iterate $ inR ys
| iterate      $ inR     ys = ys
  where
    iterate :: ([a] * [a]) + [a]
```

We *do not* introduce a new language feature, but instead relax the requirement
that *all functions* must be well-formed for inversion. In particular, the requirement is relaxed to say that *only the subject of the transformation* must be well-
formed for inversion. For instance, recall that the function snoc1 from Sect. 1 is
well-formed for inversion, and consider Nishida & Vidal's CPS transformation
of first-order functions [17]

```
data Continuation a = Id | F a (Continuation a)

snoc2 p = snoc2_iter (p, Id)
  where
    snoc2_iter (([   ], x), g) = snoc2_call (g, x : [])
    snoc2_iter ((y : ys, x), g) = snoc2_iter ((ys, x), F y g)
    snoc2_call (Id   , zs:_x) = zs:_x
    snoc2_call (F y g, zs:_x) = snoc2_call (g, y : zs:_x)
```

Here, the computation has been split into two parts; one that computes a structure corresponding to the closure of the usual continuation function, and another

that corresponds to evaluating the call to said continuation. Now, just as with `reverse2_iter`, `snoc2_iter` and `snoc2_call` are not injective functions, but can be restricted to such when recognizing that one or more of its arguments are static (`Id` and `[]` respectively). Consequently, we can introduce a datatype that does away with these, and invert `snoc2` as

```
data Configuration' input acc arg output =
    Input'     input
  | Iterate   (input, Continuation acc)
  | Call      (Continuation acc, arg)
  | Output'    output

snoc6 (ys, x) =
  let (Output' (zs:_x)) = snoc6_call (snoc6_iter (Input' (ys, x))) in  (zs:_x)

snoc6_iter (Input' (ys, x))            = snoc6_iter (Iterate ((ys, x), Id))
snoc6_iter (Iterate ((y : ys, x), g))  = snoc6_iter (Iterate ((ys, x), F y g))
snoc6_iter (Iterate (([    ], x), g))  = (Call (g, [x]))

snoc6_call (Call (g, [x]))             = snoc6_call (Iterate ([x], g))
snoc6_call (Iterate ((zs:_x), F y g))  = snoc6_call (Iterate (y : (zs:_x), g))
snoc6_call (Iterate ((zs:_x), Id))     = (Output' ((zs:_x)))

unsnoc6_call (Output' ((zs:_x)))       = unsnoc6_call (Iterate ((zs:_x), Id))
unsnoc6_call (Iterate (y : (zs:_x), g)) = unsnoc6_call (Iterate ((zs:_x), F y g))
unsnoc6_call (Iterate ([x], g))        = (Call (g, [x]))

unsnoc6_iter (Call (g, [x]))           = unsnoc6_iter (Iterate (([ ], x), g))
unsnoc6_iter (Iterate ((ys, x), F y g)) = unsnoc6_iter (Iterate ((y : ys, x), g))
unsnoc6_iter (Iterate ((ys, x), Id))   = (Input' (ys, x))

unsnoc6 (zs:_x) =
  let (Input' (ys, x)) = unsnoc6_iter (unsnoc6_call (Output' (zs:_x))) in (ys, x)
```

Moreover, because the iterator does not use `Output'` and the call simulation does not use `Input'`, we can introduce two separate datatypes, and a couple of gluing functions to improve composition.

```
data Configuration2 input acc arg
  = Input2    input
  | Iterate2 (input, Continuation acc)
  | Output2  (Continuation acc, arg)

data Configuration3 acc arg output
  = Input3    (Continuation acc, arg)
  | Iterate3 (Continuation acc, output)
  | Output3   output

input      a            = (Input2 a)
uninput    (Input2  a)  = a
glue       (Output2 a)  = (Input3 a)
unglue     (Input3  a)  = (Output2 a)
```

```
output     (Output3 a)  = a
unoutput   a            = (Output3 a)
```

Now, because `reverse1` was also well-formed for inversion, we can apply the usual CPS transformation, and obtain a tail-recursive inverse program by the exact same procedure:

```
reverse6    = output . call6 . glue . iterate6 . input

iterate6    (Input2 xs)              = iterate6    (Iterate2 (xs, Id))
iterate6    (Iterate2 (x : xs, g))   = iterate6    (Iterate2 (xs, F x g))
iterate6    (Iterate2 ([], g))       =             (Output2  (g, []))
call6       (Input3  (g, []))        = call6       (Iterate3 (g, []))
call6       (Iterate3 (F x g, ys))   = call6       (Iterate3 (g, zs:_x))
   where zs:_x = snoc6 (ys, x)
call6       (Iterate3 (Id  , ys))    =             (Output3 ys)
uncall6     (Output3 ys)             = uncall6     (Iterate3 (Id  , ys))
uncall6     (Iterate3 (g, zs:_x))    = uncall6     (Iterate3 (F x g, ys))
   where (ys, x) = unsnoc6 (zs:_x)
uncall6     (Iterate3 (g, []))       =             (Input3  (g, []))
uniterate6 (Output2  (g, []))        = uniterate6 (Iterate2 ([], g))
uniterate6 (Iterate2 (xs, F x g))    = uniterate6 (Iterate2 (x : xs, g))
uniterate6 (Iterate2 (xs, Id))       =             (Input2 xs)
```

```
unreverse6 = uninput . uniterate6 . unglue . uncall6 . unoutput
```

It is important to note that even though `reverse6` seems a bit more complicated than `reverse3`, we did not start with a tail recursive function, and the transformation process was entirely mechanical. First we converted into tail recursive form using continuation passing style. Then, we restricted the functions introduced by the transformation, to the domain on which they are called by the function you are inverting. Finally, we inverted all the operations performed by `reverse1`, and this was also entirely mechanical (since `reverse1` was well-formed for inversion), and produced the inverse program by swapping the input and output arguments (keeping the recursive call in front of the `Iterate` data structure).

3   Tail Recursion Transformation, Formally

In the interest of simplicity we will show how the transformation works on a small, idealised subset of the Haskell programming language as shown in Fig. 1, restricted to first order function application and conditionals. A term is a pattern, a function applied to a pattern, or a case-expression, though in program examples, we might use a `where`-clause or a `let`-statement when the syntactic disambiguation is obvious. Functions applied to terms, patterns that consist of terms, and let-statements are disambiguated as shown in Fig. 2.

$$p ::= c(p_i) \qquad\qquad\qquad\qquad\qquad \text{(Constructor).}$$
$$\mid x \qquad\qquad\qquad\qquad\qquad\qquad\quad \text{(Variable).}$$
$$t ::= p \mid f\, p \mid \textbf{case } t \textbf{ of } p_i \rightarrow t_i \qquad\qquad \text{(Terms.)}$$
$$\Delta ::= f\, p = t\ [\textbf{where } p_i = t_i].\ \Delta \mid \textbf{data } d\ =\ c_j(d_i)\ .\ \Delta \mid \epsilon \qquad \text{(Programs).}$$

Fig. 1. The syntax for a first order functional programming language.

$$[\![f\, t]\!] ::= \textbf{case } [\![t]\!] \textbf{ of } p \rightarrow f\, p$$
$$[\![c(t_i)]\!] ::= \textbf{case } [\![t_i]\!] \textbf{ of } p_i \rightarrow c(p_i)$$
$$[\![\textbf{let } p\ =\ t_1 \textbf{ in } t_2]\!] ::= \textbf{case } [\![t_1]\!] \textbf{ of } p \rightarrow [\![t_2]\!]$$
$$[\![f\, p_i = t_i]\!] ::= f\, x =\ \textbf{case } x \textbf{ of } p_i \rightarrow [\![t_i]\!]$$
$$[\![f\, p = t \textbf{ where } p_i = t_i]\!] ::= f\, p = \textbf{case } [\![t_i]\!] \textbf{ of } p_i \rightarrow [\![t]\!]$$

Fig. 2. Disambiguation of syntactic sugar.

First, we give the definition of the requirements for the transformation to work.

Definition 1. *A term t is closed under a pattern p precisely if all of the variables that occur in p appear in t exactly once.*

Definition 2. *A function f, as defined by the equation $f\, p = t$, is well-formed for inversion if t is closed under p. Moreover,*

- *If t is an application then $t \equiv g\, p_0$, where g is well-formed for inversion as well.*
- *If t is a case-expression then $t \equiv \textbf{case } t_0 \textbf{ of } p_i \rightarrow t_i$, where then t_0 is well-formed for inversion, each t_i is closed under the corresponding pattern p_i, and for all indices j and k, if $j < k$ then p_j is syntactically distinguishable from p_k and the last occurring patterns in all branches of t_j are pairwise syntactically distinguishable from the last occurring patterns in t_k.*

When a function is *well-formed for inversion* in this way, we know how to invert it using existing methods, even though such methods may require some expensive search. However, functions that do not contain a `case`-expression are all trivially and efficiently invertible, and we can focus on the hard part, namely conditionals.

Functions that are well-formed for inversion will be implemented with function clauses of the following two forms

$$f\ p_k = t_k$$
$$f\ p_i = g_i(t_{i0},\ t_{i1})$$

Each term t_k is well-formed for inversion and do not contain recursive calls to f, k is less than i, and g_i is well-formed for inversion. Furthermore, t_{i0} may contain recursive calls to f but t_{i1} is free of such calls. Moreover, the result of calling g_i with these arguments yield patterns that are distinguishable from the results of calling g_j on (t_{j0}, t_{j1}) whenever $i < j$.

The first order CPS transformation proposed by Nishida & Vidal [17] essentially defers the call to g_i by storing the result of evaluating t_{i1} in a data structure that mimics the closure of the continuation from the usual CPS transformation (here called CC in the interest of saving space in examples). The resulting transformation as applied to f becomes

```
data CC = Id | Gᵢ(d_{tᵢ₁}, CC)
f₀ x                    = f₁(Id, x)
fⱼ (g, pₖ)              = fₙ(g, tₖ)
fⱼ (g, pᵢ)              = fᵢ(Gᵢ(tᵢ₁, g), tᵢ₀)
fₙ (Id, y)              = y
fₙ (Gᵢ(pᵢ₁, g), pᵢ₀)    = fₙ(g, gᵢ(pᵢ₀, pᵢ₁))
```

where $d_{t_{i1}}$ is the data type name of the term t_{i1} for each constructor G_i of the data type CC. The transformation introduces a helper function f_j with $1 \leq j < n$ (and $1 \leq i < n$) for each equation in the definition of f, and the argument of these helper functions are all products where the first component is a CC. The semantics are clearly preserved since each f_j simply builds up a stack of closures G_i, while f_n calls the corresponding function g_i from the definition of f in the expected order.

However, the individual f_j may not be well-formed for inversion, and f_n is certainly not well-formed as the variable pattern in the first case is a catch-all that later cases cannot be syntactically orthogonal to. Consequently, we cannot use existing methods to invert these functions. Instead, we realize that their origins are well-formed for inversion, so we should have been able to invert them in a way that is "well formed enough". The idea is to represent each intermediate function with a datatype, and use the fact that each g_i is well-formed for inversion. We define the following data type

```
data Configuration1 = Input(dₓ) | Iterateⱼ(CC, d_{tᵢ₀}) | Outputₖ(CC, d_{tₖ})
data Configuration2 = Inputₖ(CC, d_{tₖ}) | Eval(CC, d_{tₖ}) | Output(d_y)
```

and use it to define following invertible program

```
1   f₀'                                    = f₂' ∘ h ∘ f₁'
2   h (Outputₖ(g, x))                      = Inputₖ(g, x)
3   f₁' (Input(pₗ))                        = f₁'(Iterateₗ(Id, pₗ))
4   f₁' (Iterateᵢ(g, pᵢ))                  = f₁'(Iterateᵢ(Gᵢ(tᵢ₁, g), tᵢ₀)
5   f₁' (Iterateₖ(g, pₖ))                  = Outputₖ(g, tₖ)
6   f₂' (Inputₖ(g, pₖ))                    = f₂' (Eval(g, pₖ))
7   f₂' (Eval(Iterateᵢ₀(Gᵢ(pᵢ₁, g)), pᵢ₀)) = f₂'(g, yᵢ)
8         where yᵢ = gᵢ(pᵢ₀, pᵢ₁)
9   f₂' (Eval(Id, y))                      = Output(y)
```

Now, just as with the CPS transformation, f_0' is semantically equivalent to f because f_1' collects calls G_j and f_2' evaluates them. As such, the only difference is that the input is wrapped in Input and Output. However, this time we can derive an inverse program as

```
10   f₀'⁻¹                   = f₁'⁻¹ ∘ h⁻¹ ∘ f₂'⁻¹
11   h⁻¹(Inputₖ(g, x))       = Outputₖ(g, x)
12   f₂'⁻¹(Output(y))        = f₂'⁻¹(Eval(Id, y))
```

13 $f_2'^{-1}(\text{g, } y_i)$ $= f_2'^{-1}(\text{Eval}(\text{Iterate}_{i0}(\text{G}_i(p_{i1}, \text{ g})), p_{i0}))$

14        $\text{where } (p_{i0}, p_{i1}) = g_i^{-1}(y_i)$

15 $f_2'^{-1}(\text{Eval}(\text{g, } p_k))$ $= \text{Input}_k(\text{g, } p_k)$

16 $f_1'^{-1}(\text{Output}_k(\text{g, } p_k))$ $= f_1'^{-1}(\text{Iterate}_k(\text{g, } p_k))$

17 $f_1'^{-1}(\text{Iterate}_i(\text{G}_i(p_{i1}, \text{ g}), p_{i0}))\} = f_1'^{-1}(\text{Iterate}_j(\text{g, } p_i))$

18 $f_1'^{-1}(\text{Iterate}_l(\text{Id, } p_l))$ $= \text{Input}(p_l)$

Now $f_0'^{-1}$ is tail recursive by construction. So, it remains to show that it is also the inverse to the function f that we started with. We do so by proving three lemmas that we combine in a theorem which concludes the section.

Lemma 1. *The function h^{-1} is inverse to h.*

Proof. We inspect program lines 2 and 11 above – Trivially, h is invertible, and its inverse is exactly h^{-1}.

Lemma 2. *The function $f_1'^{-1}$ is inverse to f_1'.*

Proof. By cases on the lines 16–18.

- (16) We inspect lines 1–9, and see that there is only one way of constructing $\text{Output}_k(g, p_k)$; It is the output of f_1' in line 5. So, it suffices to invert f_1' on $\text{Iterate}_k(g, p_k)$ and we are done.
- (17) Since the first component of the argument is not Id, there is only line 4 to consider. So, p_{i0} and p_{i1} must be the result of evaluating the terms t_{i0} and t_{i1}. Since f was well-formed for inversion, these terms must be closed under p_i (Definition 2), which we may thus reconstruct by copying.
- (18) Since the first component of the argument is Id, there is only line 3 to consider. In this equation, the argument of f_1' was $\text{Input}(p_l)$ which is exactly the result of $f_1'^{-1}$ in this case.

Lemma 3. *The function $f_2'^{-1}$ is inverse to the function f_2'*

Proof. By cases on the lines 12–15.

- (12) Analogous to the case for line 16.
- (13–14) Since g_i was well-formed for inversion, the output y_i is syntactically orthogonal to outputs of g_j when $i \neq j$. The patterns it takes as arguments (p_{i0}, p_{i1}) are syntactically orthogonal to all other such patterns, so the choice of constructors Iterate_{i0} and G_i has to be unique as well.
- (15) Analogous to the case for line 18.

Theorem 1. *The function $f_0'^{-1}$ is inverse to f.*

Proof. $f_0'^{-1}$ is the inverse to f_0' (by definition of function composition) because h^{-1}, $f_1'^{-1}$, and $f_2'^{-1}$ are the inverses to h, f_1', and f_2' by lemmas 1, 2 and 3 respectively. Now, since f_0' was semantically equivalent to f_0, $f_0'^{-1}$ must be inverse to f_0. Since f_0 was the CPS transformation of f, it must also preserve its semantics, and so $f_1'^{-1}$ is the inverse of f, which is what we set out to show.

4   Known Limitations

In Definition 1 we required linearity, which is slightly stronger than it needs to be. The reason why we chose this restriction is because it commonly occurs in reversible programming [20,24], and makes it easy to reject programs that are trivially non-invertible. However, the linearity restriction could be relaxed to *relevance* (i.e., that variables must occur *at least once* rather than *exactly once*) as in [8]. Moreover, we might even want to relax this restriction even further to say that all values that were available to a particular function of interest must be used at least once on every execution path. We do not believe that it can relaxed further than that, as an invertible program cannot lose information when it is not redundant.

Additionally, one may want to relax the constraints of local invertibility to operations for which an inverse is symbolically derivable. For instance, consider extending the syntax for patterns with integer literals, and terms with addition and subtraction. Hence, the following formulation of the Fibonacci-pair function is possible.

```
fib (a, b) = (a + b, a)
dec n      = n - 1

fib_pair 0 = (1, 1)
fib_pair n = fib (fib_pair (dec n))
```

While this program is invertible, it requires a bit of inference to derive the inverse. For instance, that one of the arguments of `fib` is preserved in its output, which is needed to infer `unfib`. Likewise for `dec` and `undec`, the compiler must infer that subtracting a constant can be automatically inverted.

Additionally, while the algebraic data-representation of natural number constants is syntactically distinguishable, with integer constants and variables the compiler has to insert guards, as in

```
fib_pair =  output . call7 . glue . iterate7 . input

iterate7    (Input2 n)                    = iterate7    (Iterate2 (n, Id))
iterate7    (Iterate2 (n, f)) | n /= 0    = iterate7    (Iterate2 (n', F () f))
  where n' = dec n
iterate7    (Iterate2 (0, f))             =             (Output2 (f, (1,1)))
call7       (Input3  (f, (1, 1)))         = call7       (Iterate3 (f, (1, 1)))
call7       (Iterate3 (F () f, pair))     = call7       (Iterate3 (f, y))
  where y = fib pair
call7       (Iterate3 (Id , x))           =             (Output3 x)
uncall7     (Output3 x)                   = uncall7     (Iterate3 (Id, x))
uncall7     (Iterate3 (f, y)) | y /= (1, 1) = uncall7   (Iterate3 (F () f, pair))
  where pair = unfib y
uncall7     (Iterate3 (f, (1, 1)))        =             (Input3 (f, (1, 1)))
uniterate7  (Output2 (f, (1, 1)))         = uniterate7  (Iterate2 (0, f))
uniterate7  (Iterate2 (n', F () f))       = uniterate7  (Iterate2 (n, f))
  where n = undec n'
uniterate7  (Iterate2 (n, Id ))           =             (Input2 n)
```

```
unfib_pair = uninput . uniterate7 . unglue . uncall7 . unoutput

unfib (ab, a) = (a, ab - a)
undec       n = n + 1
```

However, the necessary guards are essentially predicates stating that future clauses do not match (so, they can all be formulated using the $\neq$-operator). Moreover, the additional meta theory needed for this kind of support is fairly simple. In this case, that adding a constant can be inverted by subtracting it, and that one of the arguments of addition must be an available expression in the term returned by the call.

5   Translation to Flowchart Languages

One reason for putting recursive functions on a tail recursive form is for efficiency, as tail recursive programs can be easily compiled to iterative loop-constructs, eliminating the overhead of function calls. We sketch here how the transformed programs can be translated to a reversible loop-construct from flowchart languages [23] (see also [3, 4]), which can be implemented in Janus [12, 25] and later be compiled [2] to reversible abstract machines such as PISA [22] or BobISA [21].

We remind the reader that the reversible loop has the following structure:

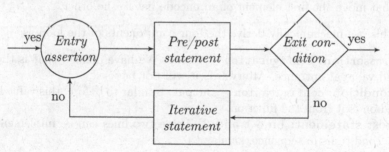

The entry assertion must only be true on entry to the loop, while the exit condition will only be true in the final iterations. For completeness there are two statements in the loop: the upper (called *pre/post statement*) we can use to transform between the input/output state and the iterative state, while the lower (called *iterative statement*) is the most widely used as this has similar semantics to the normal while-loop.

We will show the translation based on the `reverse3` example from before.

```
data Configuration a = Input a | Iteration (a, a) | Output a

reverse3 xs = let (Output ys) = interpret (Input xs) in ys

interpret   (Input xs)              = interpret (Iteration (xs, [   ]))
interpret   (Iteration (x : xs, ys)) = interpret (Iteration (xs, x : ys))
interpret   (Iteration ([   ], ys))  = (Output ys)
```

The first step is to apply our transformation to yield a tail recursive function; here, this has already been done. Next, we must translate the functional abstract data types to imperative values. The `Configuration` type will be translated into an enumeration type, with the values `Input`, `Iteration`, and `Output` encoded at integers (e.g. 1, 2, and 3). We would also need to encoded the function data (here the two lists), which could be done with an arrays and a given length. We will, however, not dwell on the data encoding, as our focus is the translation of code that our translation generates.

We can now construct the `reverse3` procedure that will contain the loop. This will be given the encoded list and return the reversed encoded list. Here a full compiler (again outside our scope) should also be aware that e.g. Janus restricts to call-by-reference, making it needed to compile the function to inline data handling. Though, this is not a restriction in reversible assembly languages. In the beginning of `reverse3` we will create a local variable `configuration` that is initialised to `Input`. After the loop, this variable will be delocalised with the value `Output`. At the entry to the loop, the available variables will, thus, be `configuration` and the function data (i.e. the encoding of the two lists).

The reversible loop will implement the `interpret` function. We assume that there exists a translation of the data handling, meaning that we have the two procedures

`empty` that checks if the encoded list is empty, and
`move` that that move the first element of an encode list to the other.

With this, we mechanically derive the four components of the loop as

Entry assertion: `configuration = Input`. We have defined that is the only valid value at entrance. Afterwards it will not be used.

Exit condition: `configuration = Output`. Similar to before, this value is only used on exit from the function.

Pre/post statement: Line 1 and 3. These two lines can be implemented as two conditions in sequence, similar to

```
if    (configuration = Input)
then configuration++ // Update from enum Input to Iteration.
fi    (configuration = Iteration and empty(ys))
if    (configuration = Iteration and empty(xs))
then configuration++ // Update from enum Iteration to Output.
fi    (configuration = Output)
```

Here, the first condition transforms the `Input` value to an `Iteration` value with the assertion that the resulting list is empty, while the second condition transforms a `Iteration` value with an empty list to an `Output` value with an assertion that we now have an output value.

Iterative statement: Line 2. This performs the iterative computation, generating code similar to

```
if    (configuration = Iteration and (not empty(xs)))
then move(xs,ys) // Execute the iterative statement.
fi    (configuration = Iteration and (not empty(ys)))
```

For completeness we check and assert that `configuration = Iteration`, though this is clear from the translation. We also assure correct data handling, by checking that the relevant lists are non-empty (matching the pattern matching of the function) and implement the relevant data handling (the move function).

The generated program could be more efficient, but it clearly demonstrates how the datatype `Configuration` translates to a reversible loop. The hard work is in the encoding of the data. This approach also applies to functions that have more one function clause with `Input` and `Output` cases, and more iterative clauses.

6   Discussion and Related Work

While it is possible to invert all injective functions [1,14], inverse programs constructed this way are often not very efficient. In spite of this, specific inversion methods tend to have well-defined subsets of programs for which they can produce efficient inverses. Precisely classifying the problems which can be efficiently inverted is hard, so the problem is usually approached from a program-specific perspective. One approach is to restrict programs to be formulated in a way that is particularly conducive to inversion. Another approach is grammar-based-inversion, which works by classifying how hard it is to invert a function, based on the properties of a grammar derived from the function body that decides whether or not a given value is in its range [7,13].

An alternative perspective on finding efficient inverse programs is to acknowledge the huge body of knowledge that has been produced in order to optimized programs running in the forward direction for time complexity, and see if we can bring those optimizations into the realm of reversible computing. In doing so we have not found a need to invent new classes of programs to invert. Instead, we enable existing techniques for optimizing CPS transformed programs to be leveraged on programs which do not naturally allow for CPS transformation.

The technique we use for transforming programs into tail recursive form is essentially Nishida & Vidal's method for continuation passing style for first order programs [17]. In doing so, we introduce an extra function that evaluates a data type that represents a continuation. In related work on grammar/syntax based inversion techniques [6,18], *well-formed with respect to inversion* means that the function is linear in its arguments (and so does not throw anything away), and that cases are syntactically orthogonal. Programs that are well-formed in this sense allow inversion by applying known inversion methods to the iteration function, which then becomes a non-deterministic inverse program (since it need not be injective). However, existing methods for non-determinism elimination can be applied to solve this problem since the original program was *well-formed*.

7   Conclusion

In this work we have shown that invertible programs admit a tail recursion transformation, provided that they are syntactically well-formed. This was achieved using a version of the first order CPS transformation tailored to invertible programs. Alternatives that do not have tail recursion optimisation must instead rely on search, which can be prohibitively expensive. Instead of searching, we can enforce determinism by pattern matching. That is, transformations where the non-injective part is introduced by the compiler, we can use a "*new datatype trick*". Finally, we have shown correctness of our transformation and how the transformed programs can be efficiently compiled to the reversible loops found in reversible flowchart languages, which in turn may serve as a basis for efficient implementations in reversible abstract machines.

7.1 Future Work

Currently, the transformation is implemented for at subset of Haskell. Future work will be to integrate it into an invertible functional programming language such as Jeopardy [10,11]. This work avoids the need for a symbolic and relational intermediate representation. Perhaps future iterations on such an approach will enable a relaxation of the existing methods' very strict requirements (such as linearity), and thus a less restrictive notion of well-formedness, but also a less syntactic notion of the complexity of function invertibility.

A major improvement to the complexity of function invertibility would also be to eschew classifying *programs* that are hard to invert in favor of classifying *problems*. One approach could be to see if the grammar-based approach from [13] can be relaxed to grammars that recognize the *output* of the function, rather than grammars *generated by the syntactic structure of the output* of a program.

An example of such a relaxation would allow existential variables. That is, to split the mechanism of introducing a variable symbol from the mechanism that associates it with a value (its binder). This is customary in logic programming languages such as `Prolog`, where programs express logical relationships that are solved for all possible solutions based on backtracking that redefines variable bindings. In a functional language, such a mechanism could try to postpone the need to use a free variable until as late as possible, allowing partially invertible functions that accept and return partial data structures (containing logical variables) that may be combined to complete ones (free of logical variables) when composed in certain ways. We are currently exploring this concept further in related work on the Jeopardy programming language [11].

References

1. Abramov, S., Robert, G.: The universal resolving algorithm and its correctness: inverse computation in a functional language. Sci. Comput. Program. **43**(23), 193–229 (2002). https://doi.org/10.1016/S0167-6423(02)00023-0. Mathematics of Program Construction (MPC 2000)
2. Axelsen, H.B.: Clean translation of an imperative reversible programming language. In: Knoop, J. (ed.) CC 2011. LNCS, vol. 6601, pp. 144–163. Springer, Heidelberg (2011). https://doi.org/10.1007/978-3-642-19861-8_9

3. Glück, R., Kaarsgaard, R.: A categorical foundation for structured reversible flowchart languages: soundness and adequacy. Logical Methods Comput. Sci. **14**(3) (2018). https://doi.org/10.1016/j.entcs.2018.03.021

4. Glück, R., Kaarsgaard, R., Yokoyama, T.: From reversible programming languages to reversible metalanguages. Theoret. Comput. Sci. **920**, 46–63 (2022). https://doi.org/10.1016/j.tcs.2022.02.024

5. Glück, R., Kawabe, M.: A program inverter for a functional language with equality and constructors. In: Ohori, A. (ed.) APLAS 2003. LNCS, vol. 2895, pp. 246–264. Springer, Heidelberg (2003). https://doi.org/10.1007/978-3-540-40018-9_17

6. Glück, R., Kawabe, M.: Derivation of deterministic inverse programs based on LR parsing. In: Kameyama, Y., Stuckey, P.J. (eds.) FLOPS 2004. LNCS, vol. 2998, pp. 291–306. Springer, Heidelberg (2004). https://doi.org/10.1007/978-3-540-24754-8_21

7. Glück, R., Kawabe, M.: A method for automatic program inversion based on LR(0) parsing. Fund. Inform. **66**(4), 367–395 (2005)

8. Jacobsen, P.A.H., Kaarsgaard, R., Thomsen, M.K.: CoreFun: a typed functional reversible core language. In: Kari, J., Ulidowski, I. (eds.) RC 2018. LNCS, vol. 11106, pp. 304–321. Springer, Cham (2018). https://doi.org/10.1007/978-3-319-99498-7_21

9. James, R.P., Sabry, A.: Theseus: a high level language for reversible computing (2014). Work in progress paper at RC 2014. https://www.cs.indiana.edu/sabry/papers/theseus.pdf

10. Kristensen, J.T., Kaarsgaard, R., Thomsen, M.K.: Branching execution symmetry in Jeopardy by available implicit arguments analysis. In: Rutle, A. (ed.) Proceedings of 34th Norwegian ICT Conference for Research and Education, NIKT 2022. No. 1 (2022)

11. Kristensen, J.T., Kaarsgaard, R., Thomsen, M.K.: Jeopardy: an invertible functional programming language (2022). https://doi.org/10.48550/ARXIV.2209.02422. Work-in-progress paper presented at 34th Symposium on Implementation and Application of Functional Languages

12. Lutz, C., Derby, H.: Janus: a time-reversible language. A letter to R. Landauer (1986). http://tetsuo.jp/ref/janus.pdf

13. Matsuda, K., Mu, S.-C., Hu, Z., Takeichi, M.: A grammar-based approach to invertible programs. In: Gordon, A.D. (ed.) ESOP 2010. LNCS, vol. 6012, pp. 448–467. Springer, Heidelberg (2010). https://doi.org/10.1007/978-3-642-11957-6_24

14. McCarthy, J.: The inversion of functions defined by Turing machines. In: Shannon, C.E., McCarthy, J. (eds.) Automata Studies. Annals of Mathematics Studies, Princeton University Press, Princeton (1956)

15. Mogensen, T.Æ.: Semi-inversion of guarded equations. In: Glück, R., Lowry, M. (eds.) GPCE 2005. LNCS, vol. 3676, pp. 189–204. Springer, Heidelberg (2005). https://doi.org/10.1007/11561347_14

16. Mogensen, T.Æ.: Semi-inversion of functional parameters. In: Proceedings of the 2008 ACM SIGPLAN Symposium on Partial Evaluation and Semantics-Based Program Manipulation, PEPM 2008, pp. 21–29. ACM (2008). https://doi.org/10.1145/1328408.1328413

17. Nishida, N., Vidal, G.: Conversion to tail recursion in term rewriting. J. Logic Algebraic Program. **83**(1), 53–63 (2014). https://doi.org/10.1016/j.jlap.2013.07.001

18. Nishida, N., Vidal, G.: Program inversion for tail recursive functions. In: 22nd International Conference on Rewriting Techniques and Applications, RTA 2011, vol. 10, pp. 283–298 (2011)

19. Romanenko, A.: The generation of inverse functions in REFAL. In: Proceedings of the International Workshop on Partial Evaluation and Mixed Computation, vol. 427. North-Holland, Amsterdam (1988). https://cir.nii.ac.jp/crid/1571135649260521472

20. Thomsen, M.K., Axelsen, H.B.: Interpretation and programming of the reversible functional language. In: Proceedings of the 27th Symposium on the Implementation and Application of Functional Programming Languages, IFL 2015, pp. 8:1–8:13. ACM (2016). https://doi.org/10.1145/2897336.2897345

21. Thomsen, M.K., Axelsen, H.B., Glück, R.: A reversible processor architecture and its reversible logic design. In: De Vos, A., Wille, R. (eds.) RC 2011. LNCS, vol. 7165, pp. 30–42. Springer, Heidelberg (2012). https://doi.org/10.1007/978-3-642-29517-1_3

22. Vieri, C.J.: Reversible computer engineering and architecture. Ph.D. thesis, MIT, EECS (1999)

23. Yokoyama, T., Axelsen, H.B., Glück, R.: Reversible flowchart languages and the structured reversible program theorem. In: Aceto, L., Damgård, I., Goldberg, L.A., Halldórsson, M.M., Ingólfsdóttir, A., Walukiewicz, I. (eds.) ICALP 2008. LNCS, vol. 5126, pp. 258–270. Springer, Heidelberg (2008). https://doi.org/10.1007/978-3-540-70583-3_22

24. Yokoyama, T., Axelsen, H.B., Glück, R.: Towards a reversible functional language. In: De Vos, A., Wille, R. (eds.) RC 2011. LNCS, vol. 7165, pp. 14–29. Springer, Heidelberg (2012). https://doi.org/10.1007/978-3-642-29517-1_2

25. Yokoyama, T., Glück, R.: A reversible programming language and its invertible self-interpreter. In: Partial Evaluation and Program Manipulation, PEPM 2007, pp. 144–153. ACM (2007). https://doi.org/10.1145/1244381.1244404

Saving Memory Space in Deep Neural Networks by Recomputing: A Survey

Irek Ulidowski[1,2]([✉]) [iD]

[1] School of Computing and Mathematical Sciences, University of Leicester,
Leicester, UK
iu3@le.ac.uk
[2] Department of Applied Informatics, AGH University of Science and Technology,
Kraków, Poland

Abstract. Training a multilayered neural network involves execution of the network on the training data, followed by calculating the error between the predicted and actual output, and then performing back-propagation to update the network's weights in order to minimise the overall error. This process is repeated many times, with the network updating its weights until it produces the desired output with a satisfactory level of accuracy. It requires storage in memory of activation and gradient data for each layer during each training run of the network. This paper surveys the main approaches to recomputing the needed activation and gradient data instead of storing it in memory. We discuss how these approaches relate to reversible computation techniques.

Keywords: Deep Neural Networks · recomputing activations

1 Introduction

Many products and services have been developed in recent years as a result of incredible advances in neural networks and generative models. Recognition and classification of images and ChatGPT are excellent examples of application of *Convolutional Neural Networks* (CNNs) [25] and *Generative Pre-trained Transformer* models [30,37] respectively. One of the characteristics of these networks and models is the large number of transformation modules in their architectures, referred to as their *depth*. Their capability and usefulness can be attributed to being able to train on vast amounts of data employing powerful computing facilities. There is, however, a cost to this success, and in this paper we focus generally on resources used during training of deep neural networks. There are some well known approaches to saving energy while training networks, and we briefly summarise them at the end of the next section. We shall concentrate in this paper on reducing memory space used and, to a smaller extent, by using more

I. Ulidowski has been partially supported by JSPS Fellowship grant S21050.

M. Kutrib and U. Meyer (Eds.): RC 2023, LNCS 13960, pp. 89–105, 2023.
https://doi.org/10.1007/978-3-031-38100-3_7

energy-efficient algorithms. This paper also explores if and how these measures are related to, and can be improved with, reversible computation techniques.

Neural networks are trained in order to fine tune their parameters (weights) so that they become more accurate. A single training run of a network involves a forward pass, where outputs of each layer are computed from inputs and stored in memory, and a backwards pass when backpropagation is performed. Outputs of all layers are fed into backpropagation, which produces adjustment to the weights that make the network slightly more accurate. Typically, there are thousands of such training runs before an acceptable level of precision is reached. The training is performed on dedicated hardware, such as GPUs or TPUs, which has limited cache capacity, meaning that the saved outputs need to be stored in local memory instead. One alternative to using local memory, which slows down computation, is to recompute outputs during the backwards pass. This will require more computation but can be mitigated, to some extent, by hardware working at full capacity having most of the date in cache.

Since a layer's input is the output of the previous layer, we can recompute inputs from the outputs of the last layer, then using those inputs as outputs of the penultimate layer we can recompute the inputs of that layer, and so on until we have recomputed the original inputs to the network, namely the inputs of the first layer. This process can be seen as uncomputing the effects of layers' transformations. In some cases this is done by developing an algorithm for the inverse of such transformation [7,16,22]. At other times, indirect methods are used and special algorithms are developed [20,27]. Optimised implementations of such algorithms use a lot of temporary data, thus space, which needs to be garbage collected. It would be worthwhile to consider how the usage of temporary data can be reduced, or even removed, by employing reversibility [4,7,11,18,39].

The amount of energy needed to train a neural network depends on its depth, the number of images to be trained on, dimension of their pixel representation, the number of weights (parameters) that are used to represent the relationship between pixel values, and the number of times the network needs to be run before all its parameters are trained up to an acceptable accuracy. Average neural networks have around 50 layer modules, and around 25 million weights to train [31] . Such networks require 64 thousands or more runs to fully train, so the values of approximately 1.6 billion weights need to be calculated, stored, retrieved and eventually deleted, all of which contributes to the overall energy cost of training [31]. The scale of practically useful generative models is several magnitudes larger, and consequently the energy cost is huge. To give an indication of potential costs, training the GPT-3 model (the backbone of ChatGPT) with 175 billion of parameters consumed several thousand petaflop/s-days [5], which some experts estimate costed at least 10.9 million USD [26].

Paper organisation: An introduction to deep neural networks and their training, as well as to two types of networks, is given in the next two sections. Then the subsequent sections present three different approaches to recomputing outputs: matrix inversion, inverting convolutions and by using shortcuts.

2   Training Deep Neural Networks

Neural networks are collections of neurons that are connected in an acyclic graph. Neurons are normally grouped into layers, and a network is a chain of such layers. Neurons within a layer are not connected but neurons of two adjacent layers are normally connected. Several adjacent layers make up a module consisting of an input layer, several hidden layers and an output layer; see below:

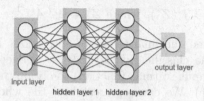

Fig. 1. Module of four fully connected layers. (Color figure online)

A module may represent a linear transformation of input data to output data, but a neural network gets its power by using modules which combine both linear and non-linear transformations. A typical deep neural network for image recognition consists of three parts, where each part is a chain of layers or modules of layers. The first part prepares image data for processing, for example by normalising pixel values of the image, or possibly also applying whitening. Then we have a (large) number of layers or modules of layers connected in a chain, where the main processing of the image data takes place. This is where feature learning occurs. Finally, we have several layers where the processed data is flattened and classified using a fully-connected layer. In a fully-connected layer, every input neuron is connected to every output neuron.

The main part of neural network is a chain of layers, with each layer feeding transformed data to the next layer, in other words the outputs of a layer become inputs of the next layer. Data is transformed by a set of weights, one for each pair of connected neurons, which is typically a linear transformation. Or, by a function which is applied element-wise to the input data to produce the output data, and which can be non-linear. We shall now use the notation as in [23,40]. If we represent image data as tensors X and Z, then transformation defined by the weights W and bias b can be written as $Z = WX + b$. For example, consider CIFAR-10 dataset [24]. There are 50,000 training images and 10,000 test images arranged into 10 classes (including car, truck, and ship). Each image is 32×32 pixels in RGB (Red Green and Blue), so each image is represented by $32 \times 32 \times 3 = 3072$ pixel values, which can be arranged as a 3072×1 vector. The weights are then a 3072×3072 matrix and b is a 3072×1 vector. Alternatively, we can apply a function f, typically non-linear, to the input data to obtain the outputs: $Z = f(X)$. Such functions are called *activation* functions, for example the *Rectified Linear Unit* [28] (ReLU), sigmoid and tanh. The values of such functions are called *activations*. In order to achieve the full potential of multilayer architectures, layers representing linear transformations are followed by applying non-linear functions:

$$A = f(Z), \text{ where } Z = WX + b, \tag{1}$$

where A is a tensor of activations. Original input image data X is pre-processed to give A^0. Then, A^0 is fed to a chain of n layers producing n tensors of activations A^i, for $1 \leq i \leq n$, as follows:

$$A^i = f^i(Z^i), \text{ where } Z^i = W^i A^{i-1} + b^i \tag{2}$$

Once we have calculated the final tensor of activations A^n we can apply the transformation g of the classification layer (fully connected layer followed by application of, for example, softmax function) to obtain the final outcome values O, namely $O = g(A^n)$. We can represent how the whole network calculates O given A^0 (the pre-processed training input data) as a combination of tensor product, addition and function composition:

$$O = g(f^n(W^n(f^{n-1}(W^{n-1}(\cdots(f^1(A^0) + b^1))\cdots + b^{n-1})) + b^n)) \tag{3}$$

We can then evaluate how the obtained values compare with the actual target values Y (that we expected to achieve). This is done by defining an *objective* function J which measures the difference between the obtained outputs and the target values, in other words the overall error:

$$J = l(O, Y) + s,$$

where l is a common *loss* function such as, for example, mean squared error, and s is a *regularisation* term (which is a function of the network's weight tensors).

2.1   Backpropagation

The goal of training a neural network is to minimise the value of the objective function, so that the values predicted by the network are as close as possible to the actual values. A neural network is trained using a process called *backpropagation* [32]. The training data is fed into the network and the output O is compared to the desired output Y. The backpropagation algorithm updates the values of all the weights in the network so that the updated network produces outputs that are closer the target values, thereby minimising the overall error. This process is repeated multiple times (at least thousands of times), with the network updating its weights each time until it reaches a satisfactory level of accuracy. A common method for optimisation is Stochastic Gradient Descent (SGD) [23,40].

Initial weights and parameters in a neural network are usually set randomly. This is done to ensure that the network is not biased towards any specific solution. The common approach is to initialise the weights with small random values chosen from a Gaussian or normal distribution with a mean of 0 and a small standard deviation, such as 0.1. Then the pre-processed data A^0 is input and the network calculates all the activation tensors A^i and the predicted outcome O for this run of the network. The tensors A^i and O need to be stored in memory to assist in backpropagation.

We also need compute the gradient of the objective function with respect to any individual weight W_{jk}^i. We shall denote the gradients of J with respect individual weights in W^i as $\partial J/\partial W^i$. These individual gradients can be computed by the chain rule using (many) "intermediate" partial derivatives. Eqs. (2) and (3) help us to work this out:

$$\partial J/\partial W^i = \partial J/\partial O \cdot \partial O/\partial A^n \cdot \partial A^n/\partial Z^n \cdot \partial Z^n/\partial A^{n-1} \cdots \partial A^i/\partial Z^i \cdot \partial Z^i/\partial W^i$$

To keep things simple we have omitted the bias terms b and the regularisation term s. Here $\cdot$ is the tensor product, and when tensors are 2D matrices then $\cdot$ is matrix multiplication (or layer convolution transformation). These intermediate derivatives have the following meaning:

- $\partial J/\partial O$: this depends on a particular loss function and a regularisation term;
- $\partial O/\partial A^n$: this is related to the derivative of g;
- $\partial A^j/\partial Z^j$: this is related to the derivatives of f^j for $j > i$;
- $\partial Z^j/\partial A^{j-1}$: these are just tensors W^i for $j > i$;
- $\partial Z^i/\partial W^i$: this is just the tensor A^{i-1}.

The gradient of J with respect to W^n, written $\overline{W^n}$, is $\partial J/\partial O \cdot \partial O/\partial A^n \cdot \partial A^n/\partial Z^n \cdot A^{n-1}$, which can be rewritten as

$$\overline{W^n} = \overline{A^n} \cdot \partial A^n/\partial Z^n \cdot A^{n-1},$$

where $\overline{A^n}$ $(= \partial J/\partial O \cdot \partial O/\partial A^n)$ is the gradient of J with respect to A^n. So the gradient of the activations of the last layer and the activations of the penultimate layer are needed to compute the weight gradient of the last layer. We can also calculate $\overline{A^{n-1}}$ as follows:

$$\overline{A^{n-1}} = \overline{A^n} \cdot \partial A^n/\partial Z^n \cdot \partial Z^n/\partial A^{n-1}$$

Typically, the values of $\overline{A^n}$, $\overline{A^{n-1}}$ and A^{n-1} are stored in memory, but A^{n-1} could also be re-computed.

We can next calculate the weight gradient of the penultimate layer

$$\overline{W^{n-1}} = \overline{A^{n-1}} \cdot \partial A^{n-1}/\partial Z^{n-1} \cdot A^{n-2}$$

and continue thus backwards all the way to $\overline{W^1}$, using previously computed and stored in memory values of activations and gradients of activations. Finally, all the weights are updated for the next round of training: $W^i_{next} = W^i - \overline{W^i}$.

Performing these derivatives by "hand" separately for each weight is error-prone and inefficient. *Automatic differentiation* technology [1] helps backpropagation to efficiently compute the gradients by avoiding duplicate calculations and not computing unnecessary intermediate values. This is done by computing the gradients of each layer from back to front as we have illustrated above, where we have calculated gradients of the last two layers. More specifically, we use the stored activations, weights and the previously calculated gradients (from the subsequent layers since we are computing from back to front) to compute the gradients of the current layer.

2.2   Energy-Saving Measures

Having described a typical structure and the training process of a neural network, we can identify several reasons why training has a very high energy cost, and for each of the reasons there are measures to reduce the cost. It is clear that specialised hardware, such as GPUs or TPUs optimised for deep learning, will be more energy efficient for performing millions and millions calculation than the ordinary hardware. Another measure we can take is to reduce the number of networks' weights, which we will see when we move from MLPs to CNNs in the next section. Additional techniques such as pruning, quantisation, and low-rank factorisation [15] can also help. We can also employ inference optimisation, which relies on reducing the computational cost of making predictions with a trained model through techniques such as dynamic quantisation or model distillation. In this paper, however, we only explore the approaches to saving energy by saving memory space during training and via more energy-efficient algorithms.

3   Multilayer Perceptron and Convolutional Neural Networks

The presented above neural network architecture resembles most closely that of *Multilayer Perceptron* (MLP) [23,40]. Given that layers are fully connected, an MLP with even a small number of layers will have a huge number of weights, activations and gradients to save in memory during training. Numerical data in this and the next paragraph are taken from Section 7 of [31]. Consider an MLP with four fully connected layers: an input (with 3072 neurons for CIFAR-10 images) and an output layer (with 10 neurons for 10 classes of images), plus two hidden layers (each with 128 neurons). This requires 410,880 weights to be saved in just one training run, and typically we need around 10 runs for MPL to reach an acceptable success rate (around 55%) in classifying CIFAR-10 images. So, this is 4.1 million weights. Since we have 50,000 images we also need to store 13.3 million intermediate pixel values (50,000 times (128+128+10)) for a single run on all images, or 133 million values for 10 runs. In total, we need 137 million values to be stored without even considering the gradient values.

Despite conceptual advantages of MLPs they are not sufficiently effective. Convolutional Neural Networks [25] (CNNs) are more potent neural networks. The main improvement compared with MLPs stems from realisation that only groups of closely located pixels represent a basic shape like an eye or mouth, and they do not depend on pixels far away. Also, to recognise a particular shape in an image, only a small same number of parameters (representing closely located pixels) is needed. Consequently, CNNs use convolution transformations where input image tensors are *convolved* with series of small *filters* (which are typically $1 \times 1, 3 \times 3, 5 \times 5$ matrices) instead of being transformed by large weight tensors: see Fig. 3. This means that a typical layer of a CNN uses many fewer weights (typically 1, 9 or 25) than a typical layer of an MLP. However, CNNs are much deeper, having many more layers than MLPs. A basic CNN with three convolution layers, such as in Fig. 2, containing 54 convolutions uses 5954 parameters (weights) and achieves success rate of 67%. If we increase the number of weights tenfold, we obtain respectful 82% precision [31]. So, the rate increases from 55% for an MLP with 410,880 weights to 82% for a CNN with 59,540 weights.

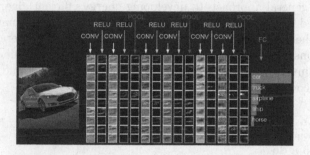

Fig. 2. Simple CNN classifying an image. It has three convolution layers and a fully connected layer. The outcome is the set of probabilities that the input image belongs to one of 10 classes of images [36].

CNNs can classify images with a very high accuracy by employing more modules each with many convolutional layers. For example ResNet50 [17], a version of *Residual Neural Network*, has 50 layers arranged into 6 modules and over 25 million trainable weights which allows it to reach 87.3% accuracy [29]. There are other CNN that achieve around 97% (top 5) accuracy, namely NFNets, but they use prohibitory large number of trainable parameters [29] (5 to 15 times more than ResNet50). We also need to remember that deep neural networks require many runs during training. For example, versions of the original ResNet, including ResNet50, were trained over 64,000 runs [17]. In summary, it is easy to estimate that the state-of-the-art CNNs calculate, store and delete many hundreds of billions of values of activations, weights and gradients during their training process. The main focus of developers is to maximise accuracy of networks, and the cost at which this is achieved is rarely considered, let alone estimated or measured. There are only very few studies that address the modelling and measuring of computation cost of AI applications [14].

4   Recalculation via Function and Matrix Inverse

Transformation of inputs into activations in several adjacent layers of MLP is given in Eq. (1). Let's assume for simplicity that input, intermediate, and activation tensors X, Z and A, respectively, are $n \times 1$ vectors, W is an $n \times n$ weight matrix and b is an $n \times 1$ bias vector. If the activation function has an inverse f^{-1} and W has an inverse W^{-1}, then we can recalculate X from A:

$$X = W^{-1}(Z - b), \text{ where } Z = f^{-1}(A). \tag{4}$$

Many popular activation functions, such as sigmoid and tanh, are invertible but not the mentioned above ReLU (Rectified Linear Unit [28]), defined by $ReLU(x) = max(x, 0)$. However, *paratremised* ReLU given by $pReLU(x) = max(x, 0) + \alpha min(x, 0)$, for some small α, has the inverse: $pReLU^{-1}(x) = max(x, 0) + \alpha^{-1} min(x, 0)$.

Efficient reversible algorithms for inverting a matrix are given in [8, 12]. They benefits from general approach to developing energy efficient algorithms in [7]. They are based on *Gaussian Elimination* (GE), where a given matrix is transformed into the Identity matrix by performing simple row operations. If the same operations are simultaneously applied to a copy of the Identity matrix, we obtain an inverse of the given matrix. A slightly improved and corrected in places pseudocode based on that in [8] is given below[1].

Input: I: $n \times n$ Identity matrix, W has non-zero determinant, $row = red = 0$
1: % loop forwards over all rows
2: **for** $i = 0$ **to** n **do**
3:     % loop over all prior rows
4:     **for** $j = 1$ **to** $i - 1$ **do**
5:         % calculate row multiplier row needed to reduce $W[i, j]$ to zero
6:         $row+ = W[i, j]/W[j, j]$
7:         **for** $k = 1$ **to** n **do**
8:             % write over values in row i in W and I reducing $W[i, j]$ to zero
9:             $W[i, k]- = row W[j, k]$ $I[i, k]- = row I[j, k]$
10:         **end for**
11:         $row+ = I[i, j]/I[j, j]$ % reduce row to 0
12:     **end for**
13:     % normalise rows i by multiplying by reducing scalar red ($=W[i, i]$)
14:     $red+ = W[i, i]$
15:     **for** $k = 1$ **to** n **do**
16:         $W[i, k] = W[i, k]/red$ $I[i, k] = I[i, k]/red$
17:     **end for**
18:     $red+ = 1/I[i, k]$ % reduce red to 0
19: **end for**
20: % W is upper echelon with determinant 1, I is a lower echelon
21: % loop backwards over all rows
22: **for** $i = n$ **to** 1 **do**
23:     % loop over all prior rows
24:     **for** $j = i + 1$ **to** n **do**
25:         % calculate row multiplier row needed to reduce $W[i, j]$ to zero
26:         $row+ = W[i, j]/W[j, j]$ % note that $W[j, j] = 1$
27:         **for** $k = 1$ **to** n **do**
28:             % write over values in row i in W and I reducing $W[i, j]$ to zero
29:             $W[i, k]- = row W[j, k]$ $I[i, k]- = row I[j, k]$

---

[1] Detailed explanation how the algorithm works is given in [8].

30:      **end for**
31:         $row+ = I[i,j]/I[j,j]$ % reduce row to 0
32:      **end for**
33: **end for**
34: **return** I
Output: W: $n \times n$ Identity matrix, I is W^{-1}, $row = red = 0$

GE works correctly in precise arithmetic. However, when executed as a program there may be problems with numerical instability. When the leading coefficient of one of the rows ($W[i,i]$ on line 14) is very close to zero, then to row-reduce the matrix we need to divide by that number (line 16), thus amplifying error. Numerical stability can be improved by using partial pivoting, which is not implemented here.

An alternative approach is to perform QR decomposition of W using *Modified Gram-Schmidt* (MGS) process [13,21], which is numerically stable. It allows us to compute matrices Q and R such that $W = QR$, where Q is orthogonal and R is upper triangular. We can employ the approach inspired by reversible computation that we have used in GE to redevelop MGS algorithm.

Substituting in Eq. (1), we obtain $QRX = Z - b$. Since $Q^T Q = I$, we get $RX = Q^T(Z - b)$, where $Z = f^{-1}(A)$. Since R is upper triangular, we can easily compute X by backwards substitution.

Both of these approaches to inverting matrices have asymptotic time of $O(n^3)$ and space $O(n^2)$. This approach may be worth considering for small images like those of CIFAR-10, where a weight matrix in a fully-connected layer is 3072×3072. However, there are datasets, such as *ImageNet* [33], with images with 256×256 pixels or larger, which would require inverting 65536×65536 matrices. This may not be cost efficient.

5   Recalculation via Inverting Convolution

The main transformation between layers of a CNN is *convolution*. In the two dimensional (2D) setting, input values are $n \times n$ matrices (representing pixel values of an image) and w are small $p \times p$ matrices called *filters*, where p is typically 1, 3, 5 or 7. The main idea is that a filter passes over a matrix and a sum product is calculated between the corresponding elements of the filter (sometime called kernel) and the overlap. This value is used to update the pixel value of the activation matrix in the cell that corresponds to the central cell of the overlap. In order to be able to pass the filter over every cell of a matrix, we need to add extra cells (with values 0) around the edges of the matrix, called *padding*. *Stride* is the number of cells (in the input matrix) by which the filter moves during convolution. Typically filters are 3×3 and we use padding of 1 and stride 1: The result of $w \star_l X$, where $\star_l$ is a *convolution layer* transformation[2], is a $n + p - 1 \times n + p - 1$ matrix C. See Fig. 3. We can take advantage of the

---

[2] This operation, which is depicted in Fig. 3 and given in (5), is a *cross-correlation* operation, although is commonly called convolution or convolution layer transformation. The real *convolution* operation is denoted by $*$ and is defined in (8) below.

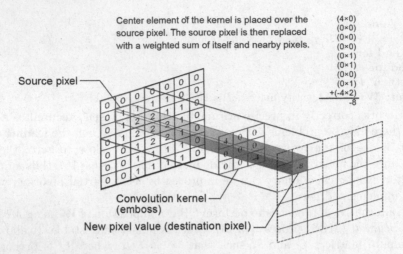

Fig. 3. Convolution layer transformation of 5×5 input with padding 1 and stride 1 image by 3×3 filter [38].

space saving matrix multiplication approach [8,12] to do the corresponding when computing convolutions. A typical element $C[k,l]$ is calculated as follows, where $m = (p-1)/2$ and $0 \le k, l \le n + 1$ due to padding of 1.

$$C[k,l] = \sum_{i=-m}^{m} \sum_{j=-m}^{m} w[i,j] X[k+i, l+j] \qquad (5)$$

We can implement this to save space by computing and uncomputing individual products as follows, assuming that $C[k,l]$ is set to 0:

```
for i = −m to m do
    for j = −m to m do
        temp += w[i,j]X[k+i, l+j]
        C[k,l] += temp
        temp −= w[i,j]X[k+i, l+j] % uncompute temp
    end for
end for
```

Can we recompute X given w and C? We are not aware of any direct method, where some operation is performed on w and C to give X. However, this can be done indirectly [20]. If X is represented as a $n^2 \times 1$ vector, denoted by $\vec{X}$, then there exists a $n^2 \times n^2$ matrix W such that the vectorised version of $w \star_l X$ is the same as matrix multiplication of W and $\vec{X}$:

$$\vec{C} = \overrightarrow{w \star_l X} = W\vec{X} \qquad (6)$$

An illustration of this is given in Fig. 4, where both input and filter have size 3×3, and we use one pixel padding and stride 1. This means that once we compute the inverse of W using one of the approaches from the previous section, then we can recompute inputs from the results of a convolution layer transformation: $\vec{X} = W^{-1} \vec{C}$.

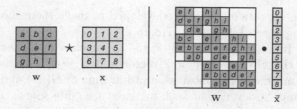

Fig. 4. Vectorised $w \star_l X$ equals to matrix multiplication $W\vec{X}$ [20].

Inspecting W in Fig. 4 we notice that if f, g h and i are 0, then the resulting W is lower triangular. Then we can calculate $\vec{X}$ from $\vec{C}$ and W by forward substitution. If the values of a, b, c and d are 0, then W is an upper triangular matrix, and we can use backwards substitution instead. Such filters are called *autoregressive*. It is shown in [20] that some filters can be "produced" from smaller square autoregressive filters (where values c and g are also 0). Such filters give rise to so-called *emerging* convolutions. Consider a (say 3×3) filter w and two square autoregressive filters k_1 and k_2 of the same (2×2) size such that $w = k_2 * k_1$. We have the following property [20]:

$$(k_2 * k_1) \star X = k_2 \star (k_1 \star X) = C \tag{7}$$

where $\star$ is cross-correlation [40] (also called here "convolution layer transformation", and "convolution" in most of the AI literature) and $*$ is the real convolution operation defined as follows. Given w and X as before, $w * X = Conv$, where a typical $[k, l]$ element of $Conv$ is

$$Conv[k, l] = \sum_{i=-m}^{m} \sum_{j=-m}^{m} w[i, j] X[k - i, l - j]. \tag{8}$$

Equation (7) gives another method for recalculating X. Assume wlog that the vectorised version of k_2 is a lower triangular K_2 and the vectorised version of k_1 is an upper triangular K_1. Using forward substitution with K_2 and $\vec{C}$ we obtain $\vec{Y}$ such that $k_1 \star X = Y$. Then using backwards substitution with K_1 and $\vec{Y}$ we obtain $\vec{X}$, which gives us X.

The above presented method may not work well in the training process (for example become unstable) when 1×1 convolutions are used. Therefore, it is proposed in [20] to use QR decomposition instead as we have argued in Sect. 4.

In [27] the authors build upon the outcomes in [20] and propose a new method for invertible convolution, which relies on a novel approach to padding which is used with emerging convolutions, namely two pixel padding only on the top and on the left for 3×3 convolutions with stride 1. It results in matrices associated with such padded convolutions being lower triangular, which can be "inverted" by forward substitution.

The approaches presented in this section rely on inverting matrices and solving sets of linear equations by either forward or backward substitution. Algorithms for these operations can be redeveloped to make them more energy efficient by utilising reversibility as in [7,8,18,39].

Given $n \times n$ input image and a filter, the approaches of this section represent the input and the filter as a $n^2 \times 1$ vector and $n^2 \times n^2$ matrix respectively. Inverting such matrix has at most asymptotic time of $O(n^6)$ and space $O(n^4)$. It is worth noting, however, that such matrices are quite sparse. Also, if we use auto-regressive convolutions, the resulting matrices will be triangular, so overall easier to invert or solve. Overall, this approach works for CIFAR-10 images [20] but it remains to be seen if larger ImageNet images can be processed this way.

6   Recalculation from Shortcut Connections

An ingenious idea to ease recalculation of layer inputs from outputs and transformation parameters is based on using connection shortcuts between neighbouring layers [9,10,35]. The input data is split into two blocks $\boldsymbol{X}_1$ and $\boldsymbol{X}_2$, and they are transformed to the corresponding blocks $\boldsymbol{Y}_1$ and $\boldsymbol{Y}_2$ by

$$
\begin{aligned}
\boldsymbol{Y}_1 &= \boldsymbol{X}_1 \\
\boldsymbol{Y}_2 &= \boldsymbol{X}_2 + m(\boldsymbol{X}_1),
\end{aligned}
\tag{9}
$$

where function m represents an arbitrary transformation (convolution layer followed by an activation function). The input blocks can be easily recomputed:

$$
\begin{aligned}
\boldsymbol{X}_1 &= \boldsymbol{Y}_1 \\
\boldsymbol{X}_2 &= \boldsymbol{Y}_2 - m(\boldsymbol{Y}_1)
\end{aligned}
\tag{10}
$$

ResNets [6,17] are CNNs that use shortcuts. A typical ResNet module is made up from several convolutional layers interleaved with ReLU and possibly batch normalisation, all surrounded by a shortcut, with ReLU applied outside, as can be seen in Fig. 5. If we apply the splitting of image into blocks approach to ResNet we obtain *Reversible* ResNet [16], or RevNet for short. The corresponding equations are

$$
\begin{aligned}
\boldsymbol{Y}_1 &= \boldsymbol{X}_1 + \mathcal{F}(\boldsymbol{X}_2) \\
\boldsymbol{Y}_2 &= \boldsymbol{X}_2 + \mathcal{G}(\boldsymbol{Y}_1),
\end{aligned}
\tag{11}
$$

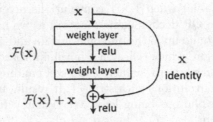

Fig. 5. A typical ResNet layer architecture [17]. Batch normalisation not shown.

where $\mathcal{F}, \mathcal{G}$ are *residual* functions (representing arbitrary layer transformations). The input values can be recomputed as follows, first $\boldsymbol{X_2}$ and then $\boldsymbol{X_1}$:

$$\boldsymbol{X_2} = \boldsymbol{Y_2} - \mathcal{G}(\boldsymbol{Y_1})$$
$$\boldsymbol{X_1} = \boldsymbol{Y_1} - \mathcal{F}(\boldsymbol{X_2}) \tag{12}$$

Since such shortcut modules leave part of the input unchanged, they typically have several layers where different subsets of the original input $\boldsymbol{X}$ are passed unchanged. It is suggested in [9,16] to use three or four such layers in a shortcut module to make sure that all blocks of input are transformed. In [41] the authors propose three different types of shortcut connection transformers, which are reversible and thus can be used to recompute activations.

In order to compute gradients of weights and activations of a typical ResNet layer using the recomputed activations as in (12), we rewrite (11) as follows:

$$\boldsymbol{Z_1} = \boldsymbol{X_1} + \mathcal{F}(\boldsymbol{X_2})$$
$$\boldsymbol{Y_2} = \boldsymbol{X_2} + \mathcal{G}(\boldsymbol{Z_1}) \tag{13}$$
$$\boldsymbol{Y_1} = \boldsymbol{Z_1}$$

The computation graph of this layer is given if Fig. 6 . When backpropagation works on this layer, it is given the activations $\boldsymbol{Y_1}$ and $\boldsymbol{Y_2}$, and their gradients $\overline{\boldsymbol{Y_1}}$, $\overline{\boldsymbol{Y_2}}$. We can recompute $\boldsymbol{Z_1}$, $\boldsymbol{X_2}$, and $\boldsymbol{X_1}$ using (13). Next, $\overline{\boldsymbol{Z_1}}$, $\overline{\boldsymbol{X_2}}$ and $\overline{\boldsymbol{X_1}}$ can be calculated [16] using the computation graph in Fig. 6 as follows:

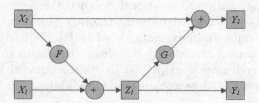

Fig. 6. A computation graph for forward propagation

$$\overline{\boldsymbol{Z_1}} = \overline{\boldsymbol{Y_1}} \cdot \partial\boldsymbol{Y_1}/\partial\boldsymbol{Z_1} + \overline{\boldsymbol{Y_2}} \cdot \partial\boldsymbol{Y_2}/\partial\boldsymbol{Z_1} = \overline{\boldsymbol{Y_1}} + \overline{\boldsymbol{Y_2}} \cdot \partial\mathcal{G}/\partial\boldsymbol{Z_1}$$
$$\overline{\boldsymbol{X_2}} = \overline{\boldsymbol{Z_1}} \cdot \partial\boldsymbol{Z_1}/\partial\boldsymbol{X_2} + \overline{\boldsymbol{Y_2}} \cdot \partial\boldsymbol{Y_2}/\partial\boldsymbol{X_2} = \overline{\boldsymbol{Z_1}} \cdot \partial\mathcal{F}/\partial\boldsymbol{X_2} + \overline{\boldsymbol{Y_2}} \tag{14}$$
$$\overline{\boldsymbol{X_1}} = \overline{\boldsymbol{Z_1}} \cdot \partial\boldsymbol{Z_1}/\partial\boldsymbol{X_1} = \overline{\boldsymbol{Z_1}}$$

Finally, we can compute weight gradients of the transformations $\mathcal{F}$ ad $\mathcal{G}$, namely $\overline{\boldsymbol{W}}_{\mathcal{F}}$ and $\overline{\boldsymbol{W}}_{\mathcal{G}}$, using the same approach [16]:

$$\overline{\boldsymbol{W}}_{\mathcal{F}} = \overline{\boldsymbol{Z_1}} \cdot \partial\boldsymbol{Z_1}/\partial\boldsymbol{W}_{\mathcal{F}} = \overline{\boldsymbol{Z_1}} \cdot \partial\mathcal{F}/\partial\boldsymbol{W}_{\mathcal{F}}$$
$$\overline{\boldsymbol{W}}_{\mathcal{G}} = \overline{\boldsymbol{Y_2}} \cdot \partial\boldsymbol{Y_2}/\partial\boldsymbol{W}_{\mathcal{G}} = \overline{\boldsymbol{Y_2}} \cdot \partial\mathcal{G}/\partial\boldsymbol{W}_{\mathcal{G}} \tag{15}$$

Since RevNet has the same architecture as ResNet, including downsampling layers, where the dimension of data is reduced, meaning information is lost, not all activations can be recomputed from the layers' outputs using the above described method. Activation for those non-reversible layers must be stored in memory, but it is stated in [16] that there are only a handful of such layers.

RevNet has been applied to image classification benchmarks CIFAR-10 and ImageNet [16]. It produces roughly the same classification error rates as ResNet, so saving large amounts of memory does not come at the expense of lost accuracy. The authors have also confirmed that although there was a small build up of numerical error while recomputing activations, both networks performed equally well in terms of training efficiency and final performance. However, the additional computation overhead of recalculating activations and, as a result, adjusting backpropagation was around 50% as compared with ResNet [16].

The shortcoming with non-reversible layers has been addressed by proposing a fully invertible form of RevNets, called *i-RevNet* [22]. Downsampling transformations, for example *max-pooling* or convolutions with strides larger than 1, are replaced with linear and invertible modules that can reduce the spatial resolution (referred to as a spatial downsampling) while maintaining the layer's size by increasing the number of channels. i-RevNets achieve the same performance results, in terms of accuracy of classification, as RevNets and ResNets with the corresponding number of layers. Also, [22] provides the first empirical evidence that learning invertible representations that do not discard any information about their input on large-scale supervised problems is possible.

There is also initial work on invertible ResNets [2], called *i-ResNets*. Instead of partitioning image data into additional channels this approach only requires adding a simple normalisation step during training. However, i-ResNets as well as i-RevNets may suffer from exploding inverses [3]. Similarly as with exploding gradients, theoretical invertibility not always translates to stable numerical invertibility. Although inverse maps may exists sometime they lead to serious reconstruction errors [3]. More work is needed to address this issue.

7   Conclusion

We have provided a short survey on three different approaches to saving memory space in deep neural networks by recomputing activations, namely by matrix inversion, inverting convolutions and by using shortcuts in Residual networks. They work correctly in precise arithmetic but inversion of matrices or convolutions may encounter calculation error build-up when performed electronically. However, more numerically stable algorithms for inversion can be used. Overall, we conclude that the shortcut method and neural networks with shortcuts, such as ResNets and RevNets, are most effective in recomputing activations.

As far as we are aware no effort has been made so far to adjust the algorithms or the code for the three methods to compute "more reversibly". Although [8] provides a reversible algorithm for matrix inversion, no experiment data is provided on how its implementation affects energy used as compared with a standard irreversible version. Optimised implementations of the algorithms for convolution inversion and for Residual networks use a lot of temporary data, thus space, which needs to be garbage collected. It would be worthwhile to consider how the usage of temporary data can be reduced, or even removed, by employing reversibility techniques [4,7,11,18,19,39]. It would also be interesting to reformulate some of the discussed algorithms (matrix inversion) so that they can be rendered in a reversible language (such as Janus) [7,34,39].

References

1. Baydin, A.G., Pearlmutter, B.A., Radul, A.A., Siskind, J.M.: Automatic differentiation in machine learning: a survey. J. Mach. Learn. Res. **18**(153), 1–43 (2017)
2. Behrmann, J., Duvenaud, D., Jacobsen, J.: Invertible residual networks. CoRR abs/1811.00995 (2018)
3. Behrmann, J., Vicol, P., Wang, K., Grosse, R.B., Jacobsen, J.: Understanding and mitigating exploding inverses in invertible neural networks. In: AISTATS 2021. PMLR, vol. 130, pp. 1792–1800 (2021)
4. Bennett, C.H.: Logical reversibility of computation. IBM J. Res. Dev. **17**(6), 525–532 (1973). https://doi.org/10.1147/rd.176.0525
5. Brown, T.B., et al.: Language models are few-shot learners. In: NeurIPS 2020, Proceedings (2020)
6. Chang, B., Meng, L., Haber, E., Ruthotto, L., Begert, D., Holtham, E.: Reversible architectures for arbitrarily deep residual neural networks. In: AAAI-18. IAAI-18, EAAI-18, Proceedings, pp. 2811–2818. AAAI Press, Washington (2018)
7. Demaine, E.D., Lynch, J., Mirano, G.J., Tyagi, N.: Energy-efficient algorithms. In: ITCS 2016, Proceedings, pp. 321–332. ACM, New York (2016)
8. Demaine, E.D., Lynch, J., Sun, J.: An efficient reversible algorithm for linear regression. In: ICRC 2021, Proceedings, pp. 103–108, IEEE, Washington (2021)
9. Dinh, L., Krueger, D., Bengio, Y.: NICE: non-linear independent components estimation. In: Bengio, Y., LeCun, Y. (eds.) ICLR 2015, Workshop Track Proceedings (2015)
10. Dinh, L., Sohl-Dickstein, J., Bengio, S.: Density estimation using real NVP. In: ICLR 2017, Proceedings. OpenReview.net (2017)
11. Frank, M.P.: Reversibility for efficient computing, Ph. D. thesis, MIT (1999)
12. Frank, M.P.: Introduction to reversible computing: motivation, progress, and challenges. In: Bagherzadeh, N., Valero, M., Ramírez, A. (eds.) Computing Frontiers 2005, Proceedings, pp. 385–390. ACM (2005)
13. Gander, W.: Algorithms for the QR decomposition (2003)
14. García-Martín, E., Rodrigues, C.F., Riley, G.D., Grahn, H.: Estimation of energy consumption in machine learning. J. Parallel Distributed Comput. **134**, 75–88 (2019). https://doi.org/10.1016/j.jpdc.2019.07.007
15. Goel, A., Tung, C., Lu, Y., Thiruvathukal, G.K.: A survey of methods for low-power deep learning and computer vision. In: WF-IoT 2020, Proceedings, pp. 1–6. IEEE, New Orleans (2020). https://doi.org/10.1109/WF-IoT48130.2020.9221198
16. Gomez, A.N., Ren, M., Urtasun, R., Grosse, R.B.: The reversible residual network: backpropagation without storing activations. In: NIPS 2017, Proceedings, pp. 2214–2224 (2017)
17. He, K., Zhang, X., Ren, S., Sun, J.: Deep residual learning for image recognition. In: CVPR 2016, Proceedings, pp. 770–778. IEEE Computer Society (2016)

18. Hoey, J., Ulidowski, I.: Reversing an imperative concurrent programming language. Sci. Comput. Program. **223**, 102873 (2022). https://doi.org/10.1016/j.scico.2022.102873
19. Hoey, J., Ulidowski, I., Yuen, S.: Reversing parallel programs with blocks and procedures. In: EXPRESS/SOS 2018, Proceedings, EPTCS, vol. 276, pp. 69–86 (2018). https://doi.org/10.4204/EPTCS.276.7
20. Hoogeboom, E., van den Berg, R., Welling, M.: Emerging convolutions for generative normalizing flows. In: Chaudhuri, K., Salakhutdinov, R. (eds.) ICML 2019, Proceedings. PMLR, vol. 97, pp. 2771–2780 (2019)
21. Imakura, A., Yamamoto, Y.: Efficient implementations of the modified Gram-Schmidt orthogonalization with a non-standard inner product. CoRR (2017)
22. Jacobsen, J., Smeulders, A.W.M., Oyallon, E.: i-RevNet: deep invertible networks. CoRR abs/1802.07088 (2018). http://arxiv.org/abs/1802.07088
23. Kaelbling, L.: Introduction to Machine Learning. Course Notes, MIT Open Learning Library (2020)
24. Krizhevsky, A., Nair, V., Hinton, G.: The CIFAR-10 dataset. https://www.cs.toronto.edu/~kriz/cifar.html (2009)
25. LeCun, Y., Bottou, L., Bengio, Y., Haffner, P.: Gradient-based learning applied to document recognition. Proc. IEEE **86**(11), 2278–2324 (1998)
26. Morgan, T.P.: Counting the cost of training large language models. https://www.nextplatform.com/2022/12/01/counting-the-cost-of-training-large-language-models/ (2022)
27. Nagar, S., Dufraisse, M., Varma, G.: CInC flow: Characterizable invertible 3×3 convolution. CoRR abs/2107.01358 (2021)
28. Nair, V., Hinton, G.E.: Rectified linear units improve restricted Boltzmann machines. In: ICML-10, Proceedings, pp. 807–814. Omnipress (2010)
29. Image classification on ImageNet. Papers with Code. https://paperswithcode.com/sota/image-classification-on-imagenet (2022)
30. Radford, A., Narasimhan, K., Salimans, T., Sutskever, I.: Improving language understanding by generative pre-training (1998)
31. Rambhatla, S.S., Jones, M., Chellappa, R.: To boost or not to boost: on the limits of boosted neural networks. CoRR abs/2107.13600 (2021)
32. Rumelhart, D., Hinton, G., Williams, R.: Learning representations by back-propagating errors. Nature **323**, 533–536 (1986)
33. Russakovsky, O., et al.: ImageNet large scale visual recognition challenge. Int. J. Comput. Vision **115**(3), 211–252 (2015). https://doi.org/10.1007/s11263-015-0816-y
34. Schordan, M., Oppelstrup, T., Thomsen, M.K., Glück, R.: Reversible languages and incremental state saving in optimistic parallel discrete event simulation. In: Ulidowski, I., Lanese, I., Schultz, U.P., Ferreira, C. (eds.) RC 2020. LNCS, vol. 12070, pp. 187–207. Springer, Cham (2020). https://doi.org/10.1007/978-3-030-47361-7_9
35. Srivastava, R.K., Greff, K., Schmidhuber, J.: Highway networks (2015). https://arxiv.org/abs/1505.00387
36. Convolutional neural networks for visual recognition. CS231n Course Notes. https://cs231n.github.io/. Stanford University (2023)
37. Vaswani, A., et al.: Attention is all you need. In: NIPS2017, Proceedings, pp. 5998–6008 (2017)
38. Wu, Z., et al.: Application of image retrieval based on convolutional neural networks and hu invariant moment algorithm in computer telecommunications. Comput. Commun. **150**, 729–738 (2020)

39. Yokoyama, T., Glück, R.: A reversible programming language and its invertible self-interpreter. In: PESPM 2007, pp. 144–153. ACM (2007). https://doi.org/10.1145/1244381.1244404
40. Zhang, A., Lipton, Z.C., Li, M., Smola, A.J.: Dive into deep learning. CoRR abs/2106.11342 (2021)
41. Zhao, Y., Zhou, S., Zhang, Z.: Multi-split reversible transformers can enhance neural machine translation. In: EACL 2021, Proceedings, pp. 244–254. Association for Computational Linguistics (2021). https://doi.org/10.18653/v1/2021.eacl-main.19

Towards a Dereversibilizer: Fewer Asserts, Statically

Jonas Wolpers Reholt[1]([⊠]), Robert Glück[1] [ID], and Matthis Kruse[2] [ID]

[1] DIKU, Department of Computer Science, University of Copenhagen, Copenhagen, Denmark
jonas.reholt@di.ku.dk, glueck@acm.org
[2] CISPA Helmholtz Center for Information Security, Saarbrücken, Germany
matthis.kruse@cispa.de

Abstract. Reversible programming is an unconventional paradigm that offers new ways to construct software. When programs have inherent inverse counterparts, such as compression/decompression, the invertibility of reversible implementations enables a "write once, verify once" approach. The nature of today's computers is, however, irreversible.

This work-in-progress contribution explores the dereversibilization of *reversible* source programs into *irreversible* target programs. As a first step into this space, we explore the use of state-of-the-art Satisfiability-Modulo-Theories (SMT) solvers to statically remove redundant assertions. We divide the problem space into two parts: High-level dereversibilization of Janus-like source programs and classical compilation to machine code.

In this contribution, we focus on the semantics-preserving removal of assertions from reversible control-flow statements. Our prototype reduces the size of the assembly code and marks the first step towards automatic dereversibilization and new opportunities of using reversible programs.

Keywords: Reversible Languages · Program Transformation · Satisfiability-Modulo-Theories (SMT) Solver · Static Analysis · Compilation

1 Introduction

Reversible languages allow to write programs that can be run in both directions, forward and backward. When programs have inherent inverse counterparts, such as compression/decompression, this enables writing and verifying a single reversible program instead of two separate programs. This *"write once, verify once"* approach offers new ways to develop correct-by-construction software components.

However, the nature of today's computers is irreversible. Thus, in order to execute a program written in a reversible language, one must *dereversibilize* [11] it by compiling it into a one-way program in conventional machine code. To guarantee correct behavior, a dereversibilization introduces runtime assertions, which impose overhead on the translated code. As can be seen in Listing 1.1, the optimizing compiler g++ (version 11.2) translates an assert into seven lines of Intel x86-64 assembly code containing a conditional branch, which destroys linearity. This can pose considerable overhead in performance-critical code. Typically, assertions are required at the join points of the control flow [23]. However, those assertions are not always necessary for correct runs on conventional hardware.

Compilers available for mainstream (irreversible) languages, such as C++, will usually not try to remove any assertion [13]. The closest related works we know of are 1) Dafny, a compiled language that actively uses assertions to verify the correctness of programs [14], and 2) Astrée, a static analyzer that uses abstract interpretation to guarantee the absence of run-time errors [6].

Listing 1.1. Statement assert(a == 0) translated to x86-64 assembler by g++

```
...                                    1
cmp     DWORD PTR [rbp-4], 0           2
je      .L3                            3
mov     ecx, OFFSET FLAT:.LC0          4
mov     edx, 5                         5
mov     esi, OFFSET FLAT:.LC1          6
mov     edi, OFFSET FLAT:.LC2          7
call    __assert_fail                  8
.L3:                                   9
...                                    10
```

However, both of these projects do not follow the path of using Satisfiability-Modulo-Theories (SMT) solvers to carry out optimizations on the target programs.

This work-in-progress contribution focuses on creating an *optimizer for removing redundant run-time assertions* introduced by dereversibilization. Hence, there is no focus on classical program optimizations because industry-tested compilers, such as the gcc compiler collection, can be used for this purpose. This paper should be seen as a step towards a full-featured dereversibilizing compiler geared to improve code quality, minimizing the overhead, while retaining the benefits of reversible languages. On our benchmarks, our prototype implementation[1] typically reduces the size of the generated assembly code by 18%.

2 Preliminaries

2.1 Querying SMT Solvers

We briefly review SMT solvers and describe how we use them to identify assertions that can never fail during the execution of a program. An assertion that is true for all program executions can be removed safely.

Solving with SMT: SMT solvers can check satisfiability of first-order formulas. Formulas may use symbols from different kinds of theories. SMT solvers implement decision procedures for them and are able to check formulas containing symbols from multiple theories [19]. Thus, SMT solvers can be used to check program properties. However, because SMT solvers work on immutable states, the analyzed program must first be transformed into Static-Single-Assignment (SSA) form to build a program execution model from it.

---

[1] Sources and benchmarks at https://github.com/jonasreholt/Japa-Dereversibilizer.

An SMT solver S applied to a formula f has three possible results: 1) *satisfiable* if f has a satisfying state; 2) *unsatisfiable* if f does not have a satisfying state; 3) *undecided* if, e.g., a timeout occurs.

Using SMT for Assertion Removal: SMT solvers are geared towards deciding property *satisfaction*, but safe assertion removal necessitates proving *validity*. A program property ϕ, which we want to prove valid, is negated before it is given to the SMT solver: If $\neg\phi$ is *not* satisfiable, then there is no state in which $\neg\phi$ is true, and therefore ϕ must be valid. Property ϕ is a formula that can be given by reversible conditionals, reversible loops, and explicit assert statements.

Programs can contain assertions that are fallacies. A fallacy in the program execution model leads the SMT solver to classify subsequent assertions as unsatisfiable. As a result, they are removed. Listing 1.2 shows a simple example where the fallacy in lines 1-2 leads to the `assert` in line 3 always being removed.

This has two practical consequences: 1) The optimizer emits programs with all subsequent assertions removed, and 2) finds at most one fallacy at each run. Our pragmatic choice is to emit a warning for fallacies and continue optimizing as if the fallacy was not present. Figure 1 shows how this is done. When reaching a program assertion ϕ', its satisfiability is checked in the current execution model Φ. This is used to discover fallacies. If ϕ' is satisfiable, the optimizer checks the validity of ϕ' to decide whether it is safe to remove it from the emitted program, and continues with the extended program execution model $\phi' \wedge \Phi$. Otherwise, the optimizer emits a warning and continues without ϕ'.

Choosing a Solver: We want our findings to be independent of any particular system. Thus, we selected a solver adhering to the international SMT-LIB standard [21], such that our queries can be directly mapped to any SMT solver conforming to this standard. In this work, we use the open-source solver Z3 [1,17].

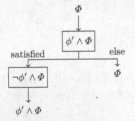

Listing 1.2. Due to an unsatisfiable `delocal` (line 2) the assertion in line 3 is optimized away.

```
local int i = 2      1
delocal int i = 3    2
assert(x > 42)       3
```

Fig. 1. Scheme for proving validity of assertion ϕ' in execution model Φ.

2.2 Typed Language Extension with For-Loops and Asserts

We extend Janus [22] with `for`-loops, local variables, and assertions. The main difference between `for`-loops and `from`-loops is the addition of an explicit loop variable. An explicit loop variable makes it easier to reason about loop termination for unrolling. The initialization of the loop variable then becomes the initial loop condition, which is required to be false after the first iteration. Additionally, an `invariant` attribute can be added to `for`-loops, allowing the programmer to add more information than what our system is capable of inferring. The user-provided loop invariant is checked at *initialization* of the loop, at the start of each iteration (*maintenance*), and at *termination*.

The semantics of local variables requires an explicit deallocation to ensure reversibility of the language. That is, `local int x = 0` allocates and initializes an integer variable x, and `delocal int x = 0` deallocates it and checks that it has the expected value. Because of this, an `assert` statement has to be introduced to model `delocal`'s semantics correctly. Both statements are inverse to each other: When running in reverse, `delocal` becomes `local`, and vice versa.

Our extension, called `Japa`, is statically typed, the details of which we have to omit for the sake of brevity. Typing provides information needed to choose the right theories (e.g., arithmetic, arrays) when interacting with the SMT solver.

3 Dereversibilization Using SMT Solvers

3.1 SMT Query Information and Query Points

There are several language constructs that require emitting assertions when performing dereversibilization. Consulting the language specification of Janus [22] and Sect. 2.2, we see that run-time assertions stem from four sources: 1) Deallocation of local variables, 2) conditional statements, 3) loops, and 4) assert statements. We query the SMT solver for each of these points in the program.

The more information SMT solvers have, the more likely it is that they can decide satisfiability of a given formula. Because of this, we encode the entire procedure when performing an SMT query.

3.2 Logic Formula Generation

State Updates: The `SMT-LIB` standard implemented by many SMT solvers does not consider mutability. A common trick in the compiler literature is to use SSA form. Because the abstract syntax tree (AST) represents a reversible program, we can transform it into a reversible SSA [16]. However, as no `SMT-LIB` logic is reversible, we instead dereversibilize the AST to generate `SMT-LIB` queries. To do so, we mimic a single-pass SSA algorithm [4].

As an example, fresh variables are introduced into the query to model state updates, and we can simply assert the changes to these fresh variables. Listing 1.3 and Listing 1.4 illustrate this, where id' is the fresh variable, and $op=$ is a *reversible update* [11], such as `+=` and `-=`.

Listing 1.3. Update of a variable.

```
1  id op= e
```

Listing 1.4. SSA-esque `SMT-LIB` query of a variable update.

```
(declare-const id' type)          1
(assert (= id' (op id e)))        2
```

Conditional Statements: Whenever an assertion occurs after a conditional, the if-then-else verification condition `ite` can be used to choose the appropriate value depending on the path taken at runtime. This conditionally sets the value of some *id* either to its original value or the latest value associated with a descendant of *id*. This is illustrated in Listing 1.5 and Listing 1.6.

Listing 1.5. Local separated from deallocation by conditional flow.

```
1   local type id = e₁
2   if (if-e)
3   {
4       stmts
5   } fi (fi-e)
6   delocal type id = e₂
```

Listing 1.6. Handling conditional branch flow with SMT-LIB.

```
(define-fun id () type e₁)              1
                                        2
... ; if-body conversion + fi-e.       3
                                        4
(declare-const new-id type)             5
(assert (= new-id (ite (if-e)           6
     id if-body-last-id)))
(assert not (= new-id e₂))              7
```

If the assertion is associated with the `fi`-condition of a conditional, it can be handled by asserting the entrance-condition *if-e*, handling the body, and finally validating the exit-condition *fi-e*. See Listing 1.7 and Listing 1.8.

Listing 1.7. Simple conditional flow.

```
1   if (if-e)
2   {
3       stmts
4   } fi (fi-e)
```

Listing 1.8. Transformation of conditional flow into Z3 for query.

```
(declare-const if-e-id Bool)            1
(assert (= if-e-id if-e)                2
                                        3
... ; if-body conversion.               4
                                        5
(assert (not (= last-body-id fi-e)      6
   ))
```

Loop Constructs: In general, loops may not terminate. Because of this, SMT-LIB does not provide reasoning about loops. Therefore, we handle loops either by means of unrolling or by analyzing them in a generalized scope to emulate an arbitrary iteration.

If a `for`-loop is unrollable, it can be transformed into a series of nested conditionals as seen in Listing 1.9 and Listing 1.10.

Listing 1.9. Simple loop construct.

```
1   stmts₁
2   for type id = e₁ {
3       stmts₂
4   } id op= e₂; until (type id = e₃)
5   stmts₃
```

Listing 1.10. Unrolling of `for`-loop.

```
stmts₁                                  1
local type id = e₁                      2
if (!(id == e₃)) {                      3
    stmts₂                              4
    id op= e₂                           5
    if (!(id == e₃)) {                  6
        ...                             7
    } fi (id == e₃)                     8
} fi (id == e₃)                         9
delocal type id = e₃                    10
stmts₃                                  11
```

The optimizer uses four cases to gather information for the SMT solver during `from`-loop analysis: 1) Loop has invariant and is unrollable, 2) loop is not unrollable but has invariant, 3) loop has no invariant but can be unrolled, and 4) loop has no invariant and cannot be unrolled.

Loops are deemed unrollable if all updates of loop variables are statically expressible, if they are unmodified in the loop body the loop is not based on overflow/underflow, and if the iteration count does not exceed an arbitrary given bound. If a loop is not deemed unrollable, the loop statement must be analyzed in a more general scope, as explained below.

Loops that are Not Unrollable: To model an arbitrary iteration, all modified variables are generalized. Then the solver tries to determine an upper and lower bound for the loop variable in order to avoid failing state caused by over- or underflow. Finally, the generalized loop body is analyzed to deem the loop-assertion's validity.

Loops with Invariants: Because loop invariants are user-generated, the analysis phase must prove an invariant's validity before information can be used past an unrollable loop. *Initialization* is proven before a loop begins. *Maintenance* is proven by simulating an arbitrary iteration and then validating the invariant. *Termination* is proven by assuring loop variable increase/decrease in an arbitrary iteration.

4 Experimental Results

The results of the benchmark can be seen in Fig. 2 and Fig. 3.[2] Our compiler is written in Haskell and can be found in the repository together with the benchmark programs. Figure 3 shows the factor difference in average compile time with and without the SMT-optimization module, measured as $\frac{opt}{noOpt}$. So lower is better. The absolute compile time difference was in the range [0.095 s;6 s]. We tested the reversible version of Djikstra's perm-to-code program [23] with (marked $\mathcal{I}$) and without an explicit loop invariant.

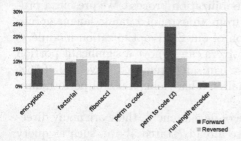

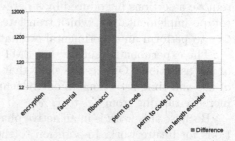

Fig. 2. Number of removed assembly lines in percent. Higher percentage is better. (Color figure online)

Fig. 3. Factor difference in compilation time with and without the SMT-optimization module.

---

[2] Run on a 2.3 GHz Intel i5-8300H CPU. Compiled using gcc's C++ compiler g++ (version 11.2) with no optimizations to isolate the impact of our assertion remover.

Overall Results: As benchmark programs, we adapted to Japa common reversible programs taken from the literature [10,11,20,23].

The optimization improves the wall-clock runtime by 11% for the Fibonacci program and by an average of 2% for the rest. Considering that assertion removal is the only optimization used, this runtime improvement is useful on its own.

The results show that the code size is significantly reduced (measured as total number of assembly lines generated by the g++ compiler). The code size reduction is 18% on average, which is due to an average removal of 56% of the assertions. The results also show that the program (blue bar) and its inverse (yellow bar) are about equally well improved. The outlier in Fig. 2 is perm-to-code ($\mathcal{I}$). Here, the added invariant only helps optimizing the forward-version because it guards against variable overflow. An invariant guarding against underflow would equally benefit the inverted program.

Run-length-encoder: Our optimizer performs worst for the run-length encoder. We argue that the reason is the loop structure of the implementation. Here, the end condition is a boolean expression depending on values computed in the body, rather than a predetermined counter. The current analysis strategy will therefore require manually inserted information, such as a loop invariant, in order to optimize the program safely.

Compile Time: We did not optimize the runtime of our prototype implementation. Unsurprisingly, most time is spent in the SMT solver. Hence, a next step will be query optimization [3,12], helping the solver select theories by using input parameters [18] and looking into exploiting parallelism [3, Sect. 7.4] from many queries being independent of each other.

5   Conclusion and Future Work

This work-in-progress contribution investigates the use of an SMT solver to remove assertions introduced by a dereversibilization process. We present a prototype implementation, which translates from an extended Janus language into C++ to perform an experimental evaluation of our SMT-optimization module.

The experiments indicate that SMT solvers can remove a significant portion of the assertions. Our results show that we can safely remove an average of 56% of the run-time assertions in our benchmarks. This yields a useful performance increase ranging from 2% to 11%.

Because this work is in an active phase of development, there are many directions for future work. In addition to those already stated above, such as query optimization, the benchmark programs show that a frequent problem is that the solver theory has to consider the edge case that a loop variable could overflow or underflow. This could be mitigated by 1) changing the language semantics to illegalize arithmetic overflow or underflow; 2) loop bound detection, e.g., as introduced in [15]; 3) automatic loop invariant generation [5], as introducing invariants showed promising results. Furthermore, for handling unbounded loops, we may use constrained Horn clauses [2,7].

Finally, this paper's contribution can be combined with the work of others to create a full-featured compilation chain. A first step could be to make use of RSSA [16] and subsequent optimizations on that level [8,9], as this could directly benefit the results of our optimizer pass. Another task is to show the correctness of the logic formula generation.

Acknowledgments. The authors thank Maurizio Proietti and the anonymous reviewers for their useful feedback.

References

1. Abal, I., Castro, D.: Z3: bindings for the Z3 theorem prover. http://hackage.haskell.org/package/z3. Accessed 30 Apr 2022
2. Bjørner, N., Gurfinkel, A., McMillan, K., Rybalchenko, A.: Horn clause solvers for program verification. In: Beklemishev, L.D., Blass, A., Dershowitz, N., Finkbeiner, B., Schulte, W. (eds.) Fields of Logic and Computation II. LNCS, vol. 9300, pp. 24–51. Springer, Cham (2015). https://doi.org/10.1007/978-3-319-23534-9_2
3. Bjørner, N., de Moura, L., Nachmanson, L., Wintersteiger, C.M.: Programming Z3. In: Bowen, J.P., Liu, Z., Zhang, Z. (eds.) SETSS 2018. LNCS, vol. 11430, pp. 148–201. Springer, Cham (2019). https://doi.org/10.1007/978-3-030-17601-3_4
4. Braun, M., Buchwald, S., Hack, S., Leißa, R., Mallon, C., Zwinkau, A.: Simple and efficient construction of static single assignment form. In: Jhala, R., De Bosschere, K. (eds.) CC 2013. LNCS, vol. 7791, pp. 102–122. Springer, Heidelberg (2013). https://doi.org/10.1007/978-3-642-37051-9_6
5. Cimatti, A., et al.: Infinite-state invariant checking with IC3 and predicate abstraction. Form Method Syst. Des. **49**(3), 190–218 (2016)
6. CNRS: The Astrée static analyzer. https://www.astree.ens.fr/. Accessed 27 May 2022
7. De Angelis, E., et al.: Analysis and transformation of constrained Horn clauses for program verification. Theory Practice Logic Progr. **22**(6), 974–1042 (2022)
8. Deworetzki, N., Meyer, U.: Program analysis for reversible languages. In: Workshop on the State of the Art in Program Analysis, Proceedings, pp. 13–18. ACM (2021)
9. Deworetzki, N., et al.: Optimizing reversible programs. In: Mezzina, C.A., Podlaski, K. (eds.) Reversible Computation. RC 2022. Lecture Notes in Computer Science, vol. 13354, pp. 224–238. Springer, Cham (2022). https://doi.org/10.1007/978-3-031-09005-9_16
10. Glück, R., Kawabe, M.: A method for automatic program inversion based on LR(0) parsing. Fund. Inform. **66**(4), 367–395 (2005)
11. Glück, R., Yokoyama, T.: Reversible computing from a programming language perspective. Theoret. Comput. Sci. **953**, 113429 (2023)
12. Gupta, S., Saxena, A., Mahajan, A., Bansal, S.: Effective use of SMT solvers for program equivalence checking through invariant-sketching and query-decomposition. In: Beyersdorff, O., Wintersteiger, C.M. (eds.) SAT 2018. LNCS, vol. 10929, pp. 365–382. Springer, Cham (2018). https://doi.org/10.1007/978-3-319-94144-8_22
13. IEEE: The open group base specifications: assert.h. https://pubs.opengroup.org/onlinepubs/9699919799/basedefs/assert.h.html. Accessed 02 Feb 2023

14. Leino, K.R.M.: Dafny: an automatic program verifier for functional correctness. In: Clarke, E.M., Voronkov, A. (eds.) LPAR 2010. LNCS (LNAI), vol. 6355, pp. 348–370. Springer, Heidelberg (2010). https://doi.org/10.1007/978-3-642-17511-4_20

15. de Michiel, M., et al.: Static loop bound analysis of C programs based on flow analysis and abstract interpretation. In: IEEE Conference on Embedded and Real-Time Computing Systems and Applications, Proceedings. pp. 161–166. IEEE (2008)

16. Mogensen, T.Æ.: RSSA: a reversible SSA form. In: Mazzara, M., Voronkov, A. (eds.) PSI 2015. LNCS, vol. 9609, pp. 203–217. Springer, Cham (2016). https://doi.org/10.1007/978-3-319-41579-6_16

17. de Moura, L., Bjørner, N.: Z3: an efficient SMT solver. In: Ramakrishnan, C.R., Rehof, J. (eds.) TACAS 2008. LNCS, vol. 4963, pp. 337–340. Springer, Heidelberg (2008). https://doi.org/10.1007/978-3-540-78800-3_24

18. de Moura, L.: Z3 performance with non-linear arithmetic. http://stackoverflow.com/questions/12511503. Accessed 09 Jun 2022

19. Nelson, G., Oppen, D.C.: Simplification by cooperating decision procedures. ACM TOPLAS 1(2), 245–257 (1979)

20. Táborský, D., Larsen, K.F., Thomsen, M.K.: Encryption and reversible computations. In: Kari, J., Ulidowski, I. (eds.) RC 2018. LNCS, vol. 11106, pp. 331–338. Springer, Cham (2018). https://doi.org/10.1007/978-3-319-99498-7_23

21. The SMT-LIB Initiative: SMT-LIB: The satisfiability modulo theories library. http://smtlib.cs.uiowa.edu/index.shtml. Accessed 28 Jun 2022

22. Yokoyama, T., Glück, R.: A reversible programming language and its invertible self-interpreter. In: PEPM, Proceedings, pp. 144–153. ACM Press (2007)

23. Yokoyama, T., et al.: Fundamentals of reversible flowchart languages. Theoret. Comput. Sci. **611**, 87–115 (2016)

Quantum Computing

Quantum String Matching Unfolded and Extended

Domenico Cantone[1] (ID), Simone Faro[1]([✉]) (ID), and Arianna Pavone[2] (ID)

[1] Department of Mathematics and Computer Science, University of Catania,
Catania, Italy
{domenico.cantone,simone.faro}@unict.it
[2] Department of Mathematics and Computer Science, University of Palermo,
Palermo, Italy
ariannamaria.pavone@unipa.it

Abstract. The string matching problem is one of the fundamental problems in computer science with applications in a variety of fields. Basically, it consists in finding all occurrences of a given pattern within a larger text. Despite its straightforward formulation, it has given rise to a huge number of solutions based on very different approaches and varied computational paradigms. But it is only very recently that the first solution based on quantum computation has been proposed by Niroula and Nam, allowing the problem to be solved in $\mathcal{O}(\sqrt{n}(\log^2(n) + \log(m)))$ time, with a quadratic speed-up compared to classical computation. To date, these two research fields have remained almost entirely separate, mainly because the technical aspects typical of the quantum computation field remain almost obscure to those involved in text processing. This paper aims to reconcile the two fields by unfolding the technical aspects of the Niroula-Nam quantum solution and providing a detailed general procedure working in $\mathcal{O}(\sqrt{n}\log^2(n))$ time that can be used as a framework for solving other string matching problems, including nonstandard ones. In this direction, the paper also proposes an extension of the algorithm to the approximate string matching problem with swaps, reporting the configuration of the occurrence together with its position, and achieving a quasi-linear $\mathcal{O}(\sqrt{n}\log^2(n))$ time complexity when $m = \mathcal{O}(\log(n))$.

1 Introduction

Quantum computing represents a cutting-edge domain within computer science, harnessing the principles of quantum mechanics to engineer more formidable computing systems capable of operating noticeably different from classical computers. Unlike the latter, which process information using binary bits (i.e., either 0 or 1), quantum computing leverages *quantum bits* (or *qubits*) capable of existing in multiple states simultaneously. Two or more qubits can also be placed in a condition of *quantum entanglement*, a physical phenomenon that allows two

This work is partially funded by the National Centre for HPC, Big Data and Quantum Computing, Project CN00000013, affiliated to Spoke 10.

or more qubits to perform certain operations simultaneously, resulting in faster and more efficient operations than classical bits. These features confer quantum computers a significant advantage over classical ones, enabling them to perform certain types of calculations with remarkable speed, particularly in areas such as code-breaking and optimization.

Quantum computing has produced substantial advancements in the realm of algorithms. Among the most notable ones, we mention Shor's algorithm [18] for factoring large numbers and Grover's algorithm [10] for unstructured search, offering exponential and quadratic speed-up over classical algorithms, respectively. As a result, they serve as compelling demonstrations of the potential of quantum computing and have generated significant interest in further research and development in the field. But it is only with the recent demonstration of quantum supremacy that a wave of interest in quantum computing has been unleashed, and solutions based on these new technologies have invaded various fields of computer science.

Text processing, and *string matching* in particular, is among the areas that have recently attracted attention in quantum computation. Formally, given a pattern x of length m and a text y of length n, the string matching problem consists in finding all occurrences of x in y, figuring out not only their number but also their positions within the text. In a classical model of computation the problem has an $\Omega(n)$ time complexity. The first linear solution was proposed by Knuth, Morris and Pratt [13] as early as 1977. A number of solutions based on their algorithm were subsequently developed, enabling the problem to be solved in sub-linear time for practical applications, thus reaching the theoretical limit $\mathcal{O}(n/m \log_\sigma m)$ in the average case proved by Yao [20].

Some early solutions to the problem through the use of quantum computing appeared in 2003 [16] and more recently in 2017 [14]. However, the first solution to offer $\mathcal{O}(\sqrt{n}(\log^2(n) + \log(m)))$ complexity has been presented by Niroula and Nam in 2021 [15]. However, the presentation given by Niroula and Nam is cut out for experts in the quantum field, as it is particularly succinct and glosses over many implementation details useful for a full understanding of the solution.

The goal that this paper sets is twofold. Firstly, it aims to be a bridge between two very distant fields of research that have had little contamination so far, explaining in detail the implementation and the theoretical aspects related to the solution proposed in [15] and showing how it can be generalized to solving nonstandard string matching problems. Secondly, it provides an extension of the Niroula-Nam algorithm to the approximate string matching problem in the presence of non-overlapping swaps of adjacent characters, which achieves a $\mathcal{O}(\sqrt{n2^m} \log^2(n))$ time complexity. Unlike the other solutions to the problem our algorithm also computes the swap configuration of the occurrence as well as its location. In the case of short patterns, i.e. if $m = \mathcal{O}(\log(n))$, our algorithm achieves a $\mathcal{O}(n \log^2(n))$ time complexity. For patterns that are very short to be considered of constant length, the complexity is still $\mathcal{O}(\sqrt{n} \log^2(n))$.

The paper is organized as follows. In Sect. 2, we provide some preliminaries useful for understanding the whole paper, and we introduce the essential notation. In Sect. 3, we present a minimal set of quantum operators that will be used in Sect. 4 for the specification of the Niroula-Nam quantum algorithm. Then, in Sect. 5, we present an extension of the Niroula-Nam algorithm to the approximate string matching problem with swaps. Finally, in Sect. 6, we present our conclusions and discuss potential directions for future research.

2 Preliminaries

Given a string x of length $n \geqslant 0$, we represent it as a finite array $x[0 .. n-1]$. We denote by $x[i]$ the $(i+1)$-st character of x, for $0 \leqslant i < n$, and by $x[i .. j]$ the substring of x contained between the $(i+1)$-st and the $(j+1)$-st characters of x, for $0 \leqslant i \leqslant j < n$. For ease of notation, the $(i+1)$-th character of the string x will also be denoted by the symbol x_i, so that $x = x_0, x_1, \ldots, x_{n-1}$.

The fundamental unit in quantum computation is the *qubit*. A qubit is a coherent superposition of the two orthonormal basis states, which are denoted by $|0\rangle$ and $|1\rangle$, using the conventional *bra-ket* notation. The mathematical formulation for a qubit $|\psi\rangle$ is then a linear combination of the two basis states, i.e., $|\psi\rangle = \alpha|0\rangle + \beta|1\rangle$, where the values α and β, called *amplitudes*, are complex numbers such that $|\alpha|^2 + |\beta|^2 = 1$, representing the probability of finding the qubit in the state $|0\rangle$ or $|1\rangle$, respectively, when measured. A quantum measurement is the only operation through which information is gained about the state of a qubit, however causing the qubit to collapse to one of the two basis states. The measurement of the state of a qubit is irreversible, meaning that it irreversibly alters the magnitudes of α and β. If b is a binary value, equal to 0 or 1, we use the symbol $|b\rangle$ to indicate the qubit in the corresponding basis state, $|0\rangle$ or $|1\rangle$, respectively. Multiple qubits taken together are referred to as *quantum registers*. A quantum register $|\psi\rangle = |q_0, q_1, .., q_{n-1}\rangle$ of n qubits is the tensor product of the constituent qubits, i.e., $|\psi\rangle = \bigotimes_{i=0}^{n-1} |q_i\rangle$. If k is an integer value that can be represented by a binary string of length n, we use the symbol $|k\rangle$ to denote the register of n qubits such that $|k\rangle = \bigotimes_{i=0}^{n-1} |k_i\rangle$, where $|k_i\rangle$ takes the value of the i-th least significant binary digit of k. For example, the quantum register $|9\rangle$ with 4 qubits is given by $|9\rangle = |1\rangle \otimes |0\rangle \otimes |0\rangle \otimes |1\rangle$. The mathematical formulation of a quantum register is then $|\psi\rangle = \sum_{k=0}^{2^n-1} \alpha_k |k\rangle$, where the values α_k represent the probability of finding the register in the state $|k\rangle$ when measured, with $\sum_{k=0}^{2^n-1} |\alpha_k|^2 = 1$.

The model of computation we adopt in this paper is that of *reversible circuits*. Circuits are networks composed of wires that carry qubit values to *gates* that perform elementary operations on qubits. The qubits move through the circuit in a linear fashion, where the input values are written onto the wires entering the circuit from the left side, while the output values are read-off the wires leaving the circuit on the right side. At every time step, each wire can enter at most one gate. In the definition of a circuit, it is often necessary to include *ancillæ* qubits, which are needed to achieve some specific tasks in computation that otherwise could not be achieved.

For the circuit model of computation, a natural measure of complexity is the *number of gates* used in the circuit. If we assume the circuit as being divided into a sequence of discrete time-steps, where the application of a single gate requires a single time-step, another measure of complexity is the *depth* of the circuit, which is the total number of required time-steps. We observe that this is not necessarily the same as the total number of gates in the circuit, since gates that act on disjoint qubits can often be applied in parallel.

3 Quantum Building Blocks

Operators in quantum computing are mathematical entities used to represent functional processes that result in the change of the state of a quantum register. Although there are no problems in realizing any quantum operator capable of working in constant time on a quantum register of fixed size, operators of variable size can only be implemented through the composition of elementary gates. In this section we briefly list some of the basic components for building a quantum circuit, with special focus on those that are useful for the purpose of this paper.

3.1 Basic Quantum Gates

Firstly, the *Pauli*-X (or X or NOT) gate is the quantum equivalent of the NOT gate for classical computers with respect to the standard basis $|0\rangle$ and $|1\rangle$. It operates on a single qubit, mapping $|0\rangle$ to $|1\rangle$ and $|1\rangle$ to $|0\rangle$. The *Hadamard* (or H) gate is a well known single-qubit operation that maps the basis states $|0\rangle$ and $|1\rangle$ to $\frac{1}{\sqrt{2}}(|0\rangle+|1\rangle)$ and to $\frac{1}{\sqrt{2}}(|0\rangle-|1\rangle)$, respectively, thus creating a superposition of the two basis states with equal amplitudes. The *Pauli*-Z (or Z or *phase-flip gate*) is the third single-qubit operator of our interest. It leaves the basis state $|0\rangle$ unchanged while mapping $|1\rangle$ to $-|1\rangle$, by applying a negative phase to it. Based on the equivalence $Z = HXH$, the Z operator can be obtained from the previous two operators. The *controlled* NOT *gate* (or CNOT) is a quantum logic gate operating on a register of two qubits $|q_0, q_1\rangle$. If the control qubit $|q_0\rangle$ is set to 1, it inverts the target qubit $|q_1\rangle$, otherwise all qubits stay the same. Formally, it maps $|q_0, q_1\rangle$ to $|q_0, q_0 \oplus q_1\rangle$. The *Toffoli gate* (also CCNOT gate) is a universal reversible logic gate that works on 3 qubits: if the first two qubits are both set to 1, it inverts the third qubit, otherwise all bits stay the same. Formally, it maps a 3 qubits register $|q_0, q_1, q_2\rangle$ to $|q_0, q_1, q_0 q_1 \oplus q_2\rangle$. Generalizations of the CNOT gate are the *n*-ary *fanout* operator and the *multiple*-CNOT. The former uses a single control qubit and $n - 1$ target qubits, while the latter uses $n - 1$ control qubits and a single target qubit. We will discuss these two operators in detail in Sect. 3.2. The *Swap gate* is a two-qubit operator: expressed in basis states, it swaps the state of the two qubits $|q_0, q_1\rangle$ involved in the operation, mapping them to $|q_1, q_0\rangle$. Finally the *Fredkin gate* (or *controlled-Swap gate*) is a universal gate which consists in a Swap gate controlled by a single qubit. Both Swap and Fredkin gates can be obtained from the application of 3 CNOT gates and 3 Toffoli gates, respectively. The gates just described are depicted in Fig. 1.

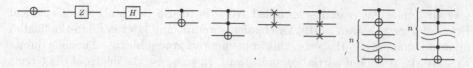

Fig. 1. The representation of the following basic gates (from left to right): Pauli-X, Pauli-Z, Hadamard, CNOT, Toffoli, Swap, Fredkin, Fanout and MCNOT.

3.2   The Fanout and the Multiple-CNOT Operators

Given a quantum register $|\psi\rangle = |q_0, q_1, \ldots, q_{n-1}\rangle$ of n qubits, a *fanout* operator simultaneously copies the control qubit $|q_0\rangle$ onto the $n - 1$ target qubits $|q_i\rangle$, for $i = 1, .., n - 1$. Formally the fanout operator applies the following mapping $|q_0, q_1, q_2, .., q_{n-1}\rangle$ to $|q_0, q_0 \oplus q_1, q_0 \oplus q_2, \ldots, q_0 \oplus q_{n-1}\rangle$.

Although a constant time fanout can be obtained by the product of n controlled-not gates, the no-cloning theorem makes it difficult to directly fanout qubits in constant depth [12]. However, assuming that the target qubits are all initialized to $|0\rangle$, it is easy to see that, by a divide-and-conquer strategy, we can compute fanout in depth $\Theta(\log(n))$ using controlled-not gates and 0 ancillæ qubits [8].

More specifically, the operator can be divided into $\lceil \log(n) \rceil$ time-steps. The i-th step, for $i = 0, \ldots, \lceil \log(n) \rceil - 1$, copies in parallel, through controlled-CNOT, the states $|q_j\rangle$ into the states $|q_{2^i + j}\rangle$, for $j = 0, \ldots, 2^i - 1$. Thus, the i-th time-step consists in 2^i parallel CNOT gates, with the exception of the last time-step, which may contain less. See Fig. 2 for an example on an 8 qubit register.

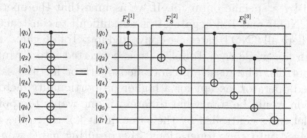

Fig. 2. The fanout operator F_8 for a register of 8 qubits.

A *multiple*-CNOT (or M-CNOT) operator flips the unique target qubit $|q_{n-1}\rangle$ if all the $n - 1$ control qubits $|q_i\rangle$ (for $i = 0, .., n - 2$) are set to $|1\rangle$. Formally, the M-CNOT maps $|q_0, q_1, q_2, .., q_{n-1}\rangle$ to $|q_0, q_1, \ldots, q_{n-2}, (q_0 \cdot q_1 \cdots q_{n-2}) \oplus q_{n-1}\rangle$.

Although Toffoli showed in 1980 that the construction of multicontrolled gates is impossible in the context of classical reversible computation without the use of auxiliary bits [19], this construction is instead possible in the context of quantum computation, but it requires an exponential number of gates, which is impractical for a number of control qubits greater than 5. The most direct way to implement a multi-controlled NOT is to use the concepts of classical Boolean logic as shown in [19] for classical circuits, and later in [3] in the field of quantum computing. However, this implementation requires $n-2$ ancillæ qubits to store the results of partial computations. In this case the depth of the circuit is linear with respect to the number of control qubits, since parallelism cannot be used, since the operations are executed in sequential order. In more recent papers [2,11], it was shown that a construction rearranging the circuit gates to achieve logarithmic depth by exploiting parallelism is possible, using $n-2$ and $n/2$ ancillæ qubits, respectively. For the sake of completeness, we also mention a recent result [17] that enables the implementation of multi-controlled NOT gates in constant time in architectures with trapped ions and neutral atoms.

3.3 Quantum Oracles

Given a function $f\colon \{0,1\}^n \to \{0,1\}$, any quantum operator that maps a register containing the value of a given input $x \in \{0,1\}^n$ into a register whose value depends on $f(x)$ is called a *quantum oracle*. In this paper we refer to a specific class of quantum oracles called *phase oracles*. A phase oracle U_f for a function $f\colon \{0,1\}^n \to \{0,1\}$ takes as input a quantum register $x \in \{0,1\}^n$ and leaves its value unchanged, applying to it a negative global phase only in the case in which $f(x) = 1$, that is, only if x is a solution for the function. More formally, $U_f|x\rangle = (-1)^{f(x)}|x\rangle$.

3.4 Controlled Operators

In many circumstances, it is necessary to apply in a quantum circuit an operator controlled by a specific qubit $|c\rangle$. If we assume that the operator consists exclusively of CNOTs and Toffoli gates, it is not difficult to construct a controlled version of it, where all CNOT gates are converted into Toffoli gates, adding a new control qubit in $|c\rangle$, while each Toffoli gate is converted into a Multiple-CNOT gate with 3 controls. The resulting controlled operator has the same depth as the uncontrolled operator, except for a higher proportionality factor.

The situation would be somewhat different if one wants to apply a number, say t, of parallel gates controlled by the same qubit $|c\rangle$. Since the control qubit would be involved into the t operations, the resulting gates would no longer be executable in parallel. Assume that $|c\rangle$ is the control qubit and G is an operator which consists in the parallel execution of the set of mutually disjoint gates $\{G_0, G_1, .., G_{t-1}\}$, each operating on a register of n qubits in time $T(n)$. Let $|q_0, q_1, .., q_{n-1}\rangle$ be the quantum register to which one wants to apply the t gates in parallel. The state of $|c\rangle$ is transferred into t ancillæ qubits $|a_i\rangle$, all initialized to $|0\rangle$, for $0 \leqslant i < t$, , through a fan-out operator. In this way, t copies of the state $|c\rangle$ are obtained. The ancilla qubit $|a_i\rangle$ is then used as a control qubit for applying the gate G_i. Finally, the ancillæ qubits are cleaned up by the application of a new fan-out operator, controlled again by $|c\rangle$. Such technique applies the t gates in parallel in $T(n)$ time, but requires $\mathcal{O}(\log(n))$ time for the fanout operator. The following figure schematizes (on the right) how the technique is implemented and proposes (on the left) a succinct graphic representation of the whole compound operator.

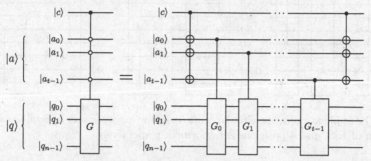

3.5   The Circular Shift Operator

A *circular shift operator* (or rotation operator) R_s applies a leftforward shift of s positions to a register of n qubits so that the startung position is moved of s position to the right, modulo n. In other words, the elements whose position exceeds the size n of the register are moved, in a circular fashion, to the first positions of the register. Formally, the operator R_s applies the following permutation

$$|q_0, q_1, \ldots, q_{n-1}\rangle \longrightarrow |q_s, q_{s+1}, \ldots, q_{n-1}, q_0, q_2, \ldots, q_{s-1}\rangle$$

A circular shift operation can always be decomposed into a product of Swap operations. We need at most n Swaps to transform a sequence into a specific permutation. For example, rotating a register by one position consists of moving q_{i+1} to position q_i and, finally, q_0 to position q_{n-1}. However, in a quantum circuit, multiple Swap operators can be applied in parallel when they involve mutually disjoint pairs of qubits. With a register with n qubits, we can apply at most $n/2$ Swap operations in parallel, moving $n/2$ qubits to their final positions in a single time step. The best case is when it is necessary to rotate the register exactly by $n/2$ positions. In that case, it is enough to apply $n/2$ parallel Swaps, exchanging q_i with $q_{n/2+i}$, for $i = 0, \ldots, n/2-1$. This operation takes $\mathcal{O}(1)$ time.

For lack of space, we do not formalize the construction of circuits allowing for circular rotations. However, we observe that, in the worst case, with $n/2$ swap operations we manage to correctly place at most $n/2$ elements, leaving the remaining $n/2$ elements to be placed. Likewise, at each subsequent step the number of qubits to be correctly placed decreases by half. This allows to perform a complete rotation in $\mathcal{O}(\log(n))$ steps (see Fig. 3).

Let us now assume that we want to apply a circular shift operator that can apply a rotation of a number of positions dependent on an input value k. In this context, we suppose to operate on a circuit containing two quantum registers: the first register $|k\rangle$, of size $\lceil \log(n) \rceil$, contains the input value related to the rotation, while the second register $|q\rangle$, of size n, represents the register that is to be rotated. We have then $|k\rangle = \bigotimes_{i=0}^{\log(n)-1} |k_i\rangle$, where $|k_i\rangle$ is initialized with the

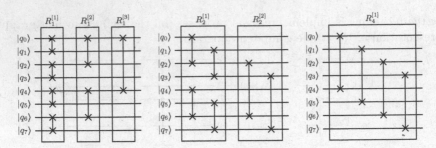

Fig. 3. The application of the circular shift operator for a register of 8 qubits in which a rotation of 1, 2, and 4 positions is performed, respectively.

value of the i-th least significant bit of the binary representation of the k-value. It will then be enough, for any value of i, such that $0 \leqslant i < \log(n)$, to apply to register $|q\rangle$ the rotation operator R_{2^i} controlled by the qubit $|k_i\rangle$. Note that the rotation operator R_{2^i} can be composed of, at most, $\log(n)$ parallel gates, so it will be necessary to apply the technique described in Sect. 3.4, which involves the use of $\log(n)$ ancillæ qubits.

Accordingly, the circular shift operator dependent on the value of an input quantum register k can be schematized as in Fig. 4. The resulting operator uses $n + \log(n) - 1$ input qubits, plus $\log(n) - 1$ ancillæ qubits, and its depth is equal to $\mathcal{O}(\log^2(n))$.

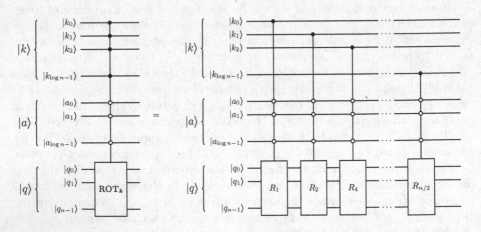

Fig. 4. A circular shift operator on a n-qubit register $|q\rangle$ controlled by a $\log(n)$-qubit register $|k\rangle$. The circuit makes use of a register $|a\rangle$ of $\log(n)$ ancillæ qubits.

3.6   A Brief Detour to Grover's Search Algorithm

Grover's is a well-known quantum search algorithm for searching a desired item within an unstructured dataset of n items with $\mathcal{O}(\sqrt{n})$ operations [10], which is quadratically lower than classical methods. The algorithm is inherently bounded-error, but we know there is no quantum algorithm with less than n queries that solves the problem with certainty for an arbitrary dataset [4].

Specifically, given a function $f \colon \{0,1\}^{\log(n)} \to \{0,1\}$ with a unique solution $w \in \{0,1\}^{\log(n)}$ such that $f(w) = 1$, the algorithm uses a rotation of the quantum register representing the superimposition of all inputs $x \in \{0,1\}^{\log(n)}$ to bring the desired solution w to a higher probability of being obtained.

Going into more detail, the algorithm starts with the vector obtained from the superimposition of all possible inputs $x \in \{0,1\}^{\log(n)}$. Note that the objective vector, in which the unique solution w has amplitude 1 and all other items have amplitudes 0, is nearly orthogonal to the starting vector. Thus the goal of the algorithm is to apply to the initial vector a rotation as close as possible to $\pi/2$ so as to bring it close to the objective vector. A single iterative step of the algorithm consists in two rotations. The first rotation consists in applying the Phase Oracle U_f of the function f, with the effect of flipping the amplitude of the unique input w, leaving the amplitudes of all other inputs unchanged. The second rotation consists in applying the Grover's Diffusion operator (or Diffuser), which represents a reflection with respect to the vector $|+\rangle^{\oplus n}$ and can be mathematically expressed through the algebraic operator $2|0\rangle\langle 0| - I_{\log(n)}$. The overall rotation performed during a single Grover iteration is approximately of $2/\sqrt{n}$ radiants, where n is the condominium size of the function f. Thus, it is enough to perform $\pi/4\sqrt{n}$ iterations. The following figure schematizes the circuit related to Grover's algorithm in which the typical structure of the Diffusion operator (Diffuser) used by the algorithm is also provided in detail.

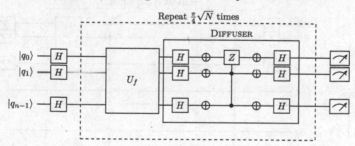

Regarding the complexity of Grover's algorithm, we must take into account that each iteration consists in the application of the phase oracle and the Diffuser. Since the latter requires a multicontrolled Z gate on n qubits, its depth is logarithmic in n (see Sect. 3.2). Thus, Grover's algorithm has complexity $\mathcal{O}(\sqrt{n}(T(n) + \log(n)))$[1], where $T(n)$ is the time complexity of the phase oracle.

In the case that the function f has r solutions, with $r > 1$, $\mathcal{O}(\sqrt{n})$ iterations are still enough for finding a solution, but it can be shown that roughly $\frac{\pi}{4}\sqrt{\frac{n}{r}}$ iterations are required [6], and that this bound is optimal [5]. However, in

---

[1] If we assume to be able to implement the multi-controlled NOT gate in constant time [17], a Grover's search on a dataset of n items achieves $\mathcal{O}(\sqrt{n}T(n))$ time.

general, the value r is not known a priori and can only be obtained through a complex procedure based on the Quantum Phase Estimation. Finally, if we have r solutions and we would like to find all of them, $\Theta(\sqrt{nr})$ iterations are sufficient and necessary [1].

4   A General Quantum String Matching Algorithm

We are now ready to describe the quantum algorithm for solving the string matching problem introduced in [15]. To this end, let y be a binary text of size n and let x be a binary pattern of size m. The algorithm is presented in Fig. 5.

The quantum algorithm uses a 4 registers state $|\psi\rangle = |k\rangle \otimes |a\rangle \otimes |y\rangle \otimes |x\rangle$. The $|y\rangle$ register, of size n, is initialized to contain the characters of the text. The $|x\rangle$ register, of size m, on the other hand, is initialized to contain the characters of the pattern. The algorithm also uses a register of size $\log(n)$ that can contain a text shift value and a register $|a\rangle$ of $\log(n)$ ancillæ qubits. The two registers $|k\rangle$ and $|a\rangle$ are both initialized to $|0\rangle^{\otimes n}$.

During the initialization, the algorithm applies the Hadamard operator to all qubits in the $|k\rangle$ register, so that it represents the superimposition of all possible shift values between 0 and $n - 1$. Then, in the preprocessing phase, the circular rotation operator controlled by the $|k\rangle$ register is applied to the $|y\rangle$ register, as described in Sect. 3.5. At the end of the preprocessing phase, the $|y\rangle$ register represents the superimposition of all possible circular rotations of the text.

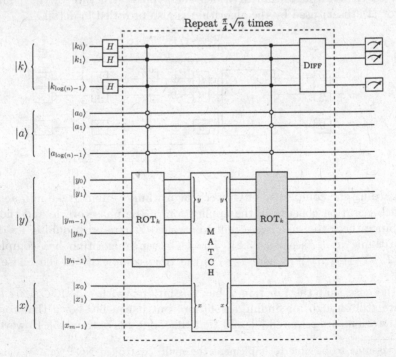

Fig. 5. The circuit of the general quantum string matching algorithm. The gray gate indicate the inverse of the ROT operator.

The algorithm proceeds with a search phase based on Grover's algorithm in order to identify a possible alignment i, with $0 \leqslant i < n - m$, such that $x = y[i .. i + m - 1]$. The search phase of the algorithm makes use of a phase oracle (denoted by MATCH in Fig. 5) for identifying a match between two binary strings. More formally, the phase oracle implements the function $f : \{0,1\}^m \times \{0,1\}^m \to \{0,1\}$, defined, for any $x, y \in \{0,1\}^m$, as

$$f(x,y) = \begin{cases} 1 & \text{if } x \text{ matches against } y \\ 0 & \text{otherwise.} \end{cases}$$

In this context, whether two strings, x and y of length m, make a match depends on the type of matching problem we want to solve. In the case of standard string matching, an exact match between strings is considered, that is, x matches against y if and only if $x[i] = y[i]$, for $0 \leqslant i < m$. However, several definitions of nonstandard string matching exist. A straightforward generalization admits the presence of at most δ errors in the comparison between x and y. Further generalizations assume the presence of some editing operations (such as insertions, deletions, substitutions, or swaps) to transform x in y.

The phase oracle takes as input two registers of size m, containing the elements of the binary strings to be compared. In the context of the algorithm in Fig. 5, the register $|x\rangle$, which contains the pattern, is compared with the first m qubits of the register $|y\rangle$. The latter contains the superimposition of all substrings of the text of length m. This allows the algorithm to compare the pattern in parallel with all the substrings in the text and to extrapolate, through Grover's search algorithm, the index of a position in the text (if any) where an occurrence of the pattern begins.

Regarding the time complexity of the algorithm, the Grover search needs to repeat the entire process $\pi/4\sqrt{n}$ times. Since the Diffuser is applied to a register of size $\log(n)$, its complexity is $\mathcal{O}(\log(\log(n)))$, so that, if the phase oracle requires $M(n)$ time then the total complexity of the algorithm is equal to $\mathcal{O}(\sqrt{n}(\log^2(n) + M(n) + \log(\log(n))))$. Observe also that, if we assume to be able to implement a multi-controlled NOT gate in constant time, then the algorithm achieves $\mathcal{O}(\sqrt{n}M(n))$ time.

In the next subsection we show how to construct a reversible phase oracle for the exact string matching problem working in $\mathcal{O}(\log(m))$ time, so that the resulting algorithm achieves a $\mathcal{O}(\sqrt{n}(\log^2(n) + \log(m))) = \mathcal{O}(\sqrt{n}\log^2(n))$ time complexity.

4.1 A Phase Oracle for the Exact String Matching Problem

The phase oracle for checking an exact match between two strings, x and y, both strings of length m, is shown in Fig. 6. The oracle is obtained by comparing characters in corresponding positions, through the use of m CNOT gates. Specifically the i-th CNOT gate, for $0 \leqslant i < m$, operates using $|y_i\rangle$ as control qubit and $|x_i\rangle$ as target qubit. Note that if the two qubits are concordant in their value, then $|x_i\rangle$ takes the value $|0\rangle$, otherwise it takes the value $|1\rangle$. Hence, it is enough to flip the value of all the qubits in the $|x\rangle$ register, through the use of m X gates, and to use a flip-phase gate (a Z gate) multi-controlled on all the values of $|x\rangle$ in order to add a negative phase in case $|x\rangle = |1\rangle^{\otimes n}$. The oracle concludes the computation through an uncompute process by applying the same set of gates in reverse order.

Note that the n CNOT gates can be executed in parallel as well as the set of n X gates. Finally, the application of the multicontrolled flip-phase gate takes $\mathcal{O}(\log(m))$ time. Thus, the total complexity of the operator is $\mathcal{O}(\log(m))$.

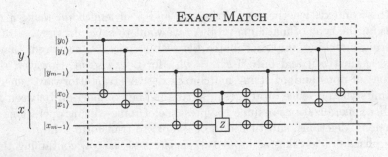

Fig. 6. A circuit for detecting an exact match between two strings of length m.

5   Extension to Swap String Matching

The *string matching problem with swaps* (swap matching problem, for short) [7,9] is a well-studied variant of the classic string matching problem. In this context the pattern is said to *swap-match the text at a given location j* if adjacent pattern characters can be swapped, if necessary, so as to make it identical to the substring of the text starting at location j. All swaps are constrained to be disjoint, i.e., each character can be involved in at most one swap. Moreover, we make the agreement that identical adjacent characters are not allowed to be swapped.

For instance the pattern $x =$ "abaab" swap-matches the text $y =$ "baababa" at three different locations. Specifically, at position 0 the substring "$\underline{ba}ab\underline{a}$" needs two swaps to match the pattern, while at positions 1 and 2 the substrings "$a\underline{ab}ab$" and "$aba\underline{ba}$" need a single swap to match the pattern, respectively.

Definition 1 (Swap permutation). *A* swap permutation *for a string x of length m is a permutation $\pi : \{0, \ldots, m-1\} \to \{0, \ldots, m-1\}$ such that:*

1. if $\pi(i) = j$, then $\pi(j) = i$ (characters at positions i and j are swapped);
2. for all i, $\pi(i) \in \{i-1, i, i+1\}$ (only adjacent characters can be swapped);
3. if $\pi(i) \neq i$, then $x[\pi(i)] \neq x[i]$ (identical characters can not be swapped).

For a given string x and a swap permutation π for x, we write $\pi(x)$ to denote the *swapped version* of x, namely $\pi(x) = x[\pi(0)] \cdot x[\pi(1)] \cdots x[\pi(m-1)]$.

Definition 2 (Swap match). *Given a text y of length n and a pattern x of length m, x is said to* swap-match *(or to have a* swapped occurrence*) at location $j \geqslant m-1$ of y if there exists a swap permutation π of x such that $\pi(x)$ matches y at location j. In such a case we write $x \propto y[j .. j + m - 1]$.*

If a pattern x of length m has a swap-match starting at location j of a text y, then the number k of swaps needed to transform x into its swapped version $\pi(x) = y[j .. j + m - 1]$ is equal to half the number of mismatches of x at location j. Thus the value of k lies between 0 and $\lfloor m/2 \rfloor$.

Lemma 1 ([7]). *Let x and y be strings of length m and suppose that there exists a swap permutation π such that $\pi(x) = y$. Then π is unique.*

Corollary 1. *Given a text y of length n and a pattern x of length m, if $x \propto y_j$, for a given position $j \in \{0, \ldots, n - m\}$, there exists a unique swapped occurrence of x in y starting at position j.* □

Definition 3 (Swap outline). *Let x be a string of length m and let π be a swap permutation for x. A* swap outline *for the string $\pi(x)$ is a binary sequence $s = \langle s_0, s_1, \ldots, s_{n-2} \rangle$ of size $n - 1$, where $s_i = 1$ if and only if character $x[i]$ is swapped with character $x[i + 1]$, i.e., $\pi(i) = i + 1$ and $\pi(i + 1) = i$.*

Thus, by Corollary 1, if we have $x \propto y[j .. j + m - 1]$ for a given position $j \in \{0, \ldots, n - m\}$, there exists a unique swap outline s such that

$$x[i] = \begin{cases} y[j + i + s_i] & \text{if } i = 0 \\ y[j + i + s_i - s_{i-1}] & \text{if } 0 < i < n - 1 \\ y[j + i - s_{i-1}] & \text{if } i = n - 1. \end{cases}$$

From Definition 1 it follows that, for any position $i > 0$ in a swap outline s, we have $s_i = 1$ only if $s_{i-1} = 0$. In other words, any swap outline has no occurrences of consecutive bits set to 1. For instance the two strings "*abaab*" and "*baaba*" swap matches and their swap outline is $\langle 1001 \rangle$, while the two strings "*abaab*" and "*aabab*" swap matches and their swap outline is $\langle 0100 \rangle$.

Definition 4 (Improper swap outline set). *Let x be a string of length m and let s be proper swap outline for x. We say that a binary sequence s' is an* improper swap outline *associated with s if s' has length $m - 1$ and*

1. *$s_i' = 1$ whenever $s_i = 1$;*
2. *if $s_i' = 1$ and $s_i = 0$ then it must be $s_{i-1}' = 1$ and $s_{i+1} = 0$.*

Observe that it is possible to obtain, from an improper outline s', the corresponding proper swap outline s in linear time. This can be done by clearing all the bits in s' that are set to 1 and are preceded by another bit set to 1. For example, the corresponding proper swap outline of the sequence $\langle 110010111 \rangle$ is given by the sequence $\langle 100010100 \rangle$. Observe also that, given a string x of length m and a (proper or improper) swap outline s of length $m - 1$, it is possible to reconstruct in linear time the swapped version of x, which we call x_s. This can be done by scanning the bits in the sequence s and swapping the two adjacent characters $x[i]$ and $x[i-1]$ if and only if $s_i = 1$ and $s_{i-1} = 0$ (or $i = 0$).

The quantum operator depicted in Fig. 7 is a direct translation of this logical construction. The circuit takes as input two registers of size m: the first register s is initialized with information about the swap outline to be applied to the second register x. While the register s remains unchanged at the end of the computation, the register x is modified in x_s. The depth of this circuit is $\Theta(m)$ when it is executed on a quantum register x of size m. However, the circuit is highly parallelizable, since the controlled swap operators can be divided into two operationally disjointed groups. Specifically, in a first time-step, it is possible to execute in parallel the controlled swap operations acting on the pairs of qubits (x_{2i}, x_{2i+1}) by preceding and following X operators on the qubits x_{2i}. In a second time-step, it will be possible to perform in parallel controlled swap operations acting on the pairs of qubits (x_{2i-1}, x_{2i}), by preceding and following X operators on the qubits x_{2i-1}. Thus the Swap circuit can be executed in time $\Theta(1)$. Figure 8 shows the structure of the parallelized Swap operator acting on a register with 8 qubits.

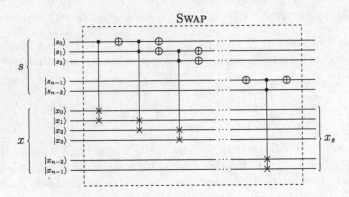

Fig. 7. A Swap operator for the computation of a swapped version of a string x.

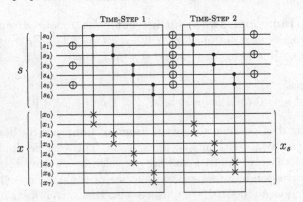

Fig. 8. A parallelized Swap operator acting on a register with 8 qubits.

To obtain the string x again from its swapped version x_s, the inverted circuit can be applied. Observe, however, that even with two applications of the same SWAP circuit the same result is obtained since we have that $x = \pi(\pi(x))$ for any swap permutation π of a string x. Finally, it is possible to use the SWAP circuit depicted in Fig. 9 to obtain a quantum operator that, given two strings x and y (both of length m), is able to search for an outline s, such that $y = x_s$. The operator works on three quantum registers. The first register $|s\rangle$, of size $n - 1$, is initialized to $|0\rangle^{n-1}$. The second and third registers, $|x\rangle$ and $|y\rangle$, are initialized with the characters of the strings x and y, respectively. In order to evaluate all the possible swap outlines of x the first register is transformed to $|+\rangle^{n-1}$ by applying n Hadamard operators. The SWAP operator, followed by an EXACT-MATCH operator, is used to apply the permutation s to the string x and compare x_s against the string y. The EXACT-MATCH operator is squeezed between two SWAP operators in order to implement the uncomputation process.

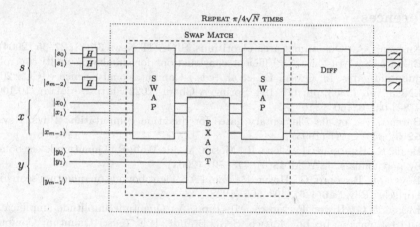

Fig. 9. A circuit to search for an outline s such that $y = x_s$.

It is straightforward to observe that the proposed circuit depicted in Fig. 9 is able to detect a swap outline in time $\mathcal{O}(\sqrt{n}\log(m))$. The circuit returns as output a binary sequence s' that can represent a proper or improper outline. If s' is an improper outline, it is possible to obtain the corresponding proper outline in linear time with respect to the length of the string x. Finally the SWAP MATCH operator in Fig. 9 can be used within the circuit in Fig. 5 for solving the swap string matching matching problem in time $\mathcal{O}(\sqrt{n2^m}\log^2(n))$ computing the swap configuration of the occurrence as well as its location. In the case of short patterns, i.e. if $m = \mathcal{O}(\log(n))$, our algorithm achieves a $\mathcal{O}(n\log^2(n))$ time complexity, while for very short patterns, i.e. patterns of constant length, the complexity is still $\mathcal{O}(\sqrt{n}\log^2(n))$.

6   Conclusions

In this paper we addressed the problem of string matching through the use of the quantum paradigm. We analyzed in detail the solution of Niroula and Nam [15] that solves the problem in $\mathcal{O}(\sqrt{n}(\log^2(n) + \log(m)))$ time and extended it to the approximate string matching problem by admitting the presence of possible swaps between adjacent characters of the pattern obtaining a solution whose complexity is $\mathcal{O}(\sqrt{n 2^m}(\log^2(n) + \log(m))$. For fairly short patterns for which the relationship $m = \mathcal{O}(\log(n))$ holds, the time complexity reduces to $\mathcal{O}(n \log^2(n))$. In the case of short patterns, whose value can be assumed to be a constant, then the algorithm achieves a time complexity equal to $O(\sqrt{n} \log^2(n))$. Our future research will be directed toward defining quantum circuits that allow the definition of other nonstandard matching problems based on the Hamming distance, the editing distance, or other editing operations involving larger substrings.

References

1. Ambainis, A.: Quantum search algorithms. SIGACT News **35**(2), 22–35 (2004)
2. Balauca, S., Arusoaie, A.: Efficient constructions for simulating multi controlled quantum gates. In: Groen, D., et al. (eds.) Computational Science - ICCS 2022. LNCS, vol. 13353, pp. 179–194. Springer, Cham (2022). https://doi.org/10.1007/978-3-031-08760-8_16
3. Barenco, A., et al.: Elementary gates for quantum computation. Phys. Rev. A **52**(5), 3457–3467 (1995)
4. Beals, R., Buhrman, H., Cleve, R., Mosca, M., de Wolf, R.: Quantum lower bounds by polynomials. J. ACM **48**(4), 778–797 (2001)
5. Boyer, M., Brassard, G., Høyer, P., Tapp, A.: Tight bounds on quantum searching. Fortschr. Phys. **46**(4–5), 493–505 (1998)
6. Brassard, G., Høyer, P., Mosca, M., Tapp, A.: Quantum amplitude amplification and estimation. In: Lo Monaco, S.G., Brandt, H.E. (eds.) Quantum Computation and Information. Contemporary Mathematics, vol. 305, pp. 53–74. American Mathematical Society (2002)
7. Cantone, D., Faro, S.: Pattern matching with swaps for short patterns in linear time. In: Nielsen, M., Kučera, A., Miltersen, P.B., Palamidessi, C., Tůma, P., Valencia, F. (eds.) SOFSEM 2009. LNCS, vol. 5404, pp. 255–266. Springer, Heidelberg (2009). https://doi.org/10.1007/978-3-540-95891-8_25
8. Fang, M., Fenner, S., Green, F., Homer, S., Zhang, Y.: Quantum lower bounds for fanout. Quantum Info. Comput. **6**(1), 46–57 (2006)
9. Faro, S., Pavone, A.: An efficient skip-search approach to swap matching. Comput. J. **61**(9), 1351–1360 (2018)
10. Lov K. Grover. A fast quantum mechanical algorithm for database search. In: Proceedings of the Twenty-Eighth Annual ACM Symposium on Theory of Computing, STOC 1996, New York, NY, USA, pp. 212–219. ACM (1996)
11. He, Y., Luo, M., Zhang, E., Wang, H.-K., Wang, X.-F.: Decompositions of n-qubit Toffoli gates with linear circuit complexity. Int. J. Theor. Phys. **56**, 07 (2017)
12. Høyer, P., Spalek, R.: Quantum fan-out is powerful. Theory C. **1**, 81–103 (2005)
13. Knuth, D.E., Morris, J.H., Jr., Pratt, V.R.: Fast pattern matching in strings. SIAM J. Comput. **6**(2), 323–350 (1977)

14. Montanaro, A.: Quantum pattern matching fast on average. Algorithmica **77**(1), 16–39 (2017)
15. Niroula, P., Nam, Y.: A quantum algorithm for string matching. NPJ Quant. Inf. **7**, 37 (2021)
16. Ramesh, H., Vinay, V.: String matching in $\tilde{o}(\sqrt{n} + \sqrt{m})$ quantum time. J. Discr. Algorithms **1**(1), 103–110 (2003)
17. Rasmussen, S.E., Groenland, K., Gerritsma, R., Schoutens, K., Zinner, N.T.: Single-step implementation of high-fidelity n-bit Toffoli gates. Phys. Rev. A **101**, 022308 (2020)
18. Shor, P.W.: Polynomial-time algorithms for prime factorization and discrete logarithms on a quantum computer. SIAM J. Comp. **26**(5), 1484–1509 (1997)
19. Toffoli, T.: Reversible computing. In: de Bakker, J., van Leeuwen, J. (eds.) ICALP 1980. LNCS, vol. 85, pp. 632–644. Springer, Heidelberg (1980). https://doi.org/10.1007/3-540-10003-2_104
20. Yao, A.C.: The complexity of pattern matching for a random string. Technical report, Stanford, CA, USA (1977)

Optimizing Quantum Space Using Spooky Pebble Games

Arend-Jan Quist[✉][iD] and Alfons Laarman[iD]

Leiden Institute of Advanced Computer Science, Leiden University,
Leiden, The Netherlands
{a.quist,a.w.laarman}@liacs.leidenuniv.nl

Abstract. Pebble games are usually used to study space/time trade-offs. Recently, spooky pebble games were introduced to study classical space/quantum space/time trade-offs for simulation of classical circuits on quantum computers. In this paper, the spooky pebble game framework is applied for the first time to general circuits. Using this framework we prove an upper bound for quantum space in the spooky pebble game. Moreover, we present a solver for the spooky pebble game based on a SAT solver. This spooky pebble game solver is empirically evaluated by calculating optimal classical space/quantum space/time trade-offs. Within limited runtime, the solver could find a strategy reducing quantum space when classical space is taken into account, showing that the spooky pebble model is useful to reduce quantum space.

Keywords: Pebble game · Spooky pebble game · Quantum computing · Satisfiability

1 Introduction

For a long time, scientists have been thinking how specific problems could be calculated within certain computational constraints. For example, the size of the memory and the runtime of the calculation are usually constrained. It could be useful to know whether for example some specific computational problems can be calculated on a machine with certain limited memory. To study the memory usage and runtime for a calculation, pebble games were introduced. Pebble games model the use of space and time in the run of a given circuit. The trade-off between space and time can also be easily studied by a pebble game by studying the maximum number of pebbles and time used.

A pebble game for a given circuit is played on a graph. This graph is the natural underlying graph of the circuit. Every gate in the circuit is a node in the graph. The direct input/output connection between gates is represented by a directed edge from source gate to target gate. Note that such a graph is a directed acyclic graph, as there could not be any cycle in a circuit.

The pebble game is played as follows. Every node can be pebbled and unpebbled. Placing a pebble on a node means that the result/output of the corresponding gate is calculated and stored in memory. Unpebbling a node means that the

M. Kutrib and U. Meyer (Eds.): RC 2023, LNCS 13960, pp. 134–149, 2023.
https://doi.org/10.1007/978-3-031-38100-3_10

calculated value is removed from memory. Thus a node can only be pebbled if its inputs are pebbled already, as the gate depends on its inputs which should be in current memory. The goal of the pebble game is to pebble the final outputs of the circuit, which means that the output values of the circuit are stored in memory.

The memory usage and runtime of a circuit can now be easily studied. The memory is modelled by pebbles, where every pebble represents one memory unit. Thus the space used by a circuit is the maximal number of pebbles used at any time. The runtime is the number of pebblings and unpebblings to play the pebble game.

There exist variations of the pebble game, see for example [5,15] for a (non complete) overview. In this paper, we will consider three types of pebble games: irreversible pebble games, reversible pebble games and the spooky pebble game. For the *irreversible pebble game* all inputs of a node must be pebbled to pebble that node, but there are no constraints for unpebbling a node. This is a model for classical computing. For the *reversible pebble game* all inputs of a node must be pebbled to either pebble or unpebble that node. This is a model for reversible computing in general and, more specific, for quantum computing on a circuit with irreversible gates [13]. This is useful for quantumly simulating a classical circuit. This pebble game was introduced by Bennett [2].

The *spooky pebble game* is an extension of the reversible pebble game for quantum computing which was introduced recently by Gidney [8] and more extensive worked out by Kornerup et al [12]. This game weakens the constraint for unpebbling a node in reversible pebbling at the cost of doing a quantum measurement. In the spooky pebble game, this is represented by a spook, which replaces a pebble and classically stores the measurement outcome. The (classical) value of the measurement outcome is used later by the quantum computer to restore the state. Thus for the spooky pebble game we can study the trade-off between classical memory, quantum memory and time. As quantumly accessible classical space (represented by spooks) is assumed to be much cheaper that quantum space (represented by pebbles) (see e.g. [1,16,17]), studying such a trade-off could be very useful for memory reduction in quantum computing.

The spooky pebble game, similar to reversible pebbling, models quantum computing for an irreversible (classical) circuit. Therefore, it is a useful model for a quantum oracle calculation of a classical function, i.e. quantum calculations of the type

$$\sum_{x \in \{0,\ldots,N-1\}} \alpha_x |x\rangle |j_x\rangle \rightarrow \sum_{x \in \{0,\ldots,N-1\}} \alpha_x |x\rangle |j_x \oplus f(x)\rangle$$

for some classical function $f : \{0, \ldots, N-1\} \rightarrow \{0, \ldots, M-1\}$. In many famous quantum algorithms like Shor's [19] and Grover's [10] such oracle calculations are essential. Thus, studying the spooky pebble game can be useful for quantum memory management for near term quantum computing on machines with constrained space and time.

The remainder of this paper is organized as follows. In Sect. 2, we will explain the theory about the spooky pebble game. Note that we are the first that study the spooky pebble game on general DAGs instead of line graphs as in [12]. In Sect. 3, we will prove a theorem about the maximum memory cost for a quantum oracle computation with respect to the equivalent classical computation when there is also classical memory available. Section 4 describes a solver of the spooky pebble game developed by us. This solver encodes the game as a satisfiability problem and tries to solve it. To our knowledge this is the first solver for the spooky pebble game. In Sect. 5 the details of our open source solver implementation are presented. This section also describes experiments to create optimal quantum space, classical space and time trade-offs with the solver.

2   Background: Spooky Pebble Game

In this section, we will first explain measurement based uncomputation for quantum computing, which is the basis for the spooky pebble game. Then we will formally introduce (spooky) pebble games. Most of this section was introduced by [8,12].

2.1   Measurement-Based Uncomputation

In quantum computing, the only operations one can apply are reversible operations and measurements. Thus, to apply irreversible (classical) operations without using additional space, a measurement is needed. The disadvantage of such measurements is that superpositions of inputs, which usually form the strength of quantum computing, collapse unintendedly. Measurement-based uncomputation is a technique to do an irreversible uncomputing operation using a measurement such that, under certain conditions, the uncollapsed state can be restored using the outcome of the measurement. This technique can be applied for quantum oracles where the quantum input remains in memory during the entire computation and no interference gates are applied in between the measurement-based uncomputation and the restoring of the state. These conditions are satisfied when we quantumly simulate a classical oracle computation, which we will focus on in this paper.

Figure 1 depicts the idea of measurement-based uncomputation in a circuit. Assume that an irreversible function f is computed on some quantum superposition input $\sum_x \alpha_x |x\rangle$. This is done by the reversible operation U_f which writes the outcome in a new register, resulting in the state $\sum_x \alpha_x |x\rangle |f(x)\rangle$. Now, (a part of) the input is changed by another complicated computation, while keeping the function output in memory. If we want to remove the function output from the memory, we cannot simply uncompute the function output by applying U_f again as the input has gone. Instead the function output is measured after applying a Hadamard gate to it. On measurement outcome b, a phase $(-1)^{bf(x)}$ is added to the state. After computing the semi-classical CNOT dependent on the measurement outcome, the memory of the function output is free and can be freely used as an $|0\rangle$ ancilla by other computations. If we want to correct for the phase $(-1)^{bf(x)}$, we need the state with the function outputs in memory again. To get this, we need the input $\sum_x \alpha_x |x\rangle$ again and compute the function f. Now we can apply a Z-gate on the function output register, dependent on the measurement outcome b. Now, the function output can be uncomputed by applying U_f again, and we are back in the state with input $\sum_x \alpha_x |x\rangle$.

Note that this trick of temporary uncomputing the function output of an irreversible function f when the inputs are not available is not possible in usual reversible computing. Hence, measurement-based uncomputation can be seen as quantum semi-reversible computation.

For a more formal and extensive description of measurement-based uncomputation, we refer to [12].

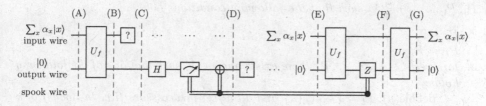

Fig. 1. This circuit describes measurement-based uncomputation. The three wires depict the input and output of the function f and the spook wire to classically store the measurement outcome. The labels (A), (B), etc. correspond to the corresponding spooky pebbling configurations as shown in Fig. 2.

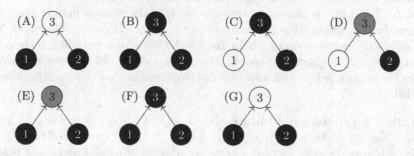

Fig. 2. Spooky pebbling configurations for the labels in the circuit of Fig. 1. In Definition 2, the spooky pebble game is introduced. The function inputs in vertices (1) and (2) are used to compute a function f and store the output in vertex (3). In other words: $f((1), (2)) = (3)$. A white vertex is unpebbled, a black one is pebbled and a grey vertex is spooked. Note that in this example not the entire input is changed: vertex (2) is pebbled (i.e. hold in memory) all over the computation and only vertex (1) is unpebbled (i.e. removed from memory).

2.2 Pebble Games

In this section, we will formally define three types of pebble games: irreversible, reversible and spooky.

We will first define the irreversible and reversible pebble game. The irreversible pebble game is a natural model for classically computing a circuit. The reversible pebble game is a natural model for reversible computation on irreversible circuits, e.g. quantumly computing a classical circuit.

Definition 1 ((Ir)reversible pebbling). *Let $G = (V, E)$ be a directed acyclic graph (DAG). The set of roots R is defined as $R = \{v \in V \mid \text{out-degree}(v) = 0\}$. A (ir)reversible pebbling strategy on G is a sequence of sets of pebbled vertices $P_0, P_1, \ldots, P_T \subseteq V$ such that the following conditions hold:*

1. *$P_0 = \emptyset$;*
2. *$P_T = R$;*
3. *for every $t \in \{1, 2, \ldots, T\}$ there exists one $v \in V$ such that one of the following holds:*
   - *pebble(v): $P_t = P_{t-1} \cup \{v\}$ and all direct predecessors (i.e. in-nodes) of v are in P_{t-1};*
   - *unpebble(v):*
     For irreversible pebbling: $P_t = P_{t-1} \setminus \{v\}$;
     For reversible pebbling: $P_t = P_{t-1} \setminus \{v\}$ and all direct predecessors (i.e. in-nodes) of v are in P_{t-1}.

Now, we will define the spooky pebble game, a natural model for quantumly computing a classical circuit using measurement-based uncomputation. The definition for this game is mainly adapted from [12]. The spooky pebble game can be viewed as an extended generalization of the (ir)reversible pebble game. The main difference between spooky pebbling and (ir)reversible pebbling is the addition of spooks. To regulate the spooks, the actions *spook* and *unspook* are added, and for the actions *pebble* and *unpebble* the requirement that no spook is changed is added.

Definition 2 (Spooky pebbling). *Let $G = (V, E)$ be a directed acyclic graph (DAG). The set of roots R is defined as $R = \{v \in V \mid \text{out-degree}(v) = 0\}$. A spooky pebbling strategy on G is a sequence of pairs of pebbles and spook pebbles $(P_0, S_0), (P_1, S_1), \ldots, (P_T, S_T) \subseteq V \times V$ such that the following conditions hold:*

1. *$P_0 = \emptyset$ and $S_0 = \emptyset$;*
2. *$P_T = R$ and $S_T = \emptyset$;*
3. *for every $t \in \{1, 2, \ldots, T\}$ there exists one $v \in V$ such that one of the following holds:*
   - *pebble(v): $P_t = P_{t-1} \cup \{v\}$ and $S_t = S_{t-1}$ and all direct predecessors (i.e. in-nodes) of v are in P_{t-1};*
   - *unpebble(v): $P_t = P_{t-1} \setminus \{v\}$ and $S_t = S_{t-1}$ and all direct predecessors (i.e. in-nodes) of v are in P_{t-1};*
   - *spook(v): $P_t = P_{t-1} \setminus \{v\}$ and $S_t = S_{t-1} \cup \{v\}$;*

– unspook(v): $P_t = P_{t-1} \cup \{v\}$ and $S_t = S_{t-1} \setminus \{v\}$ and all direct predecessors (i.e. in-nodes) of v are in P_{t-1}. [1]

For a pebbling strategy on a DAG G, the following three quantities are useful. The *pebbling time* is the integer T. The *pebbling cost* is $\max_{t \in [T]} |P_t|$ and (for the spooky pebbling game) the *spook cost* is $\max_{t \in [T]} |S_t|$.

In Fig. 3 we see some examples of moves for the different types of pebble games. For the configuration on the top, the move *unpebble(5)* can be applied for all irreversible, reversible and spooky pebbling. The move *unpebble(4)* can only be applied in the irreversible pebble game, as its input vertex 1 is not pebbled. The move *spook(4)* can only be applied in the spooky pebble game, as the (ir)reversible pebble game don't have spooks.

In Figs. 1 and 2, the relation between the spooky pebble game and measurement-based uncomputation is depicted. Quantum space is represented by pebbles and spooks represent classical space. Like in the reversible pebble game, pebbling and unpebbling are just applying classical (irreversible) gates on a quantum computer, storing the gate-outputs in additional space. Placing a spook can be interpreted as applying measurement-based uncomputation and storing the measurement outcome in memory. Unspooking can be interpreted as restoring the uncomputated state by recomputing the function.

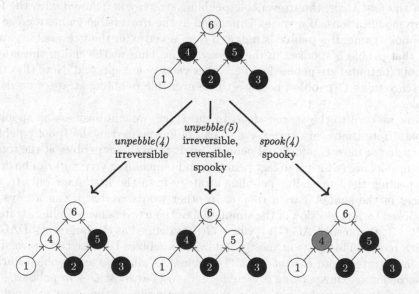

Fig. 3. Three examples of steps for different types of pebble games. A white node represents an empty vertex, a black vertex is a pebbled vertex and a grey vertex is a spooked vertex.

---

[1] Note that a pebble is placed on v when v is unspooked.

3   Theorem: Spooky Pebble Cost Equals Irreversible Pebble Cost

In this section, we present some results to relate pebble cost and price of different types of pebble games presented above. We will show first that if a DAG with m roots (outputs) can be irreversible pebbled with C pebbles, then it can be spooky pebbled with at most $C+m$ pebbles. Intuitively, this result holds because the irreversible pebble game can be simulated by the spooky pebble game with additional pebbles at all roots. Gidney [8] already proved a similar result for line graphs where an optimal irreversible pebble strategy with $C = 2$ pebbles is obvious, but we generalize this to arbitrary DAGs and arbitrary irreversible pebbling strategies. The statement can be formalized as follows.

Theorem 1. *Let $G = (V, E)$ be a DAG with m roots. Assume there exists a irreversible pebbling strategy to pebble G with irreversible pebble cost C. Then there exists a spooky pebbling strategy to pebble G with spooky pebble cost at most $C + m$.*

Proof. Let $P_0, P_1, \ldots, P_T$ be a irreversible pebbling strategy with irreversible pebble cost C. Now we can simulate this strategy by a spooky pebble game. This simulation consists of two stages.

In the *first stage*, the irreversible pebbling strategy is followed with the following modifications. If a vertex is pebbled in the irreversible game, then so in the spooky game. If a pebble is removed from a vertex in the irreversible game, then that pebble is spooked in the spooky game. Thus at the end of this stage, all roots (outputs) are pebbled and all other vertices are spooked. Note that this first stage takes C pebbles, because the irreversible pebbling strategy needs C pebbles.

Now we turn to the *second stage*. In this stage, we will unspook all spooked pebbles. Note that every vertex $v \in V$ can be unspooked in the spooky pebble game using at most C additional pebbles, apart from the m pebbles at the roots. This unspooking (which is in fact pebbling and unpebbling vertex v) can be done by repeating the irreversible pebbling strategy from the first stage only to the vertices in the subDAG with root v. In other words, vertex v can always be unspooked by a projection of the simulation of the irreversible pebbling strategy $P_0, P_1, \ldots, P_T$ on subDAG $\hat{G}(v)$, where $\hat{G}(v)$ is defined as the largest subDAG of G with root v. This costs at most C additional pebbles because the irreversible pebbling strategy can cost at most C pebbles. As all roots are pebbled during the second stage, unspooking a vertex $v \in V$ costs at most $C + m$ pebbles.

We can unspook the vertices in the reverse order as the order we pebbled them (for the first time t) in the irreversible pebbling strategy. This is to ensure that unspooking a vertex v can never be done when there is still a spook on a successor w of v. Unspooking such w could then give a spook on v. So if all vertices are unspooked in this reverse of placement order, all spooks will be removed at the end of the second stage. Thus we end up with the DAG in the final state without spooks and with pebbles on all roots.   □

Now we will analyse the spooky pebble time and the spook cost of the strategy described in the above theorem.

First we analyse the spook cost. We observe that at most $|V| - m$ spooks are needed in the first stage, because every non-root vertex is spooked. Note that this bound is an upper bound: in most cases there is a strategy such that less spooks are needed. One could spare spooks by unpebbling a vertex v if possible instead of always spooking it in the first stage. This in general reduces the number of spooks.

For the spooky pebble time we can do the following observations. If the irreversible pebble time is T, then the first stage takes also time T. In the second stage, for every vertex $v \in V \backslash R$ a projection of the first stage strategy to $\hat{G}(v)$ is applied to unspook vertex v. Thus the time to unspook any vertex $v \in V \backslash R$ can be at most T. So the spooky pebble time of the strategy of Theorem 1 is at most $T(|V| - m + 1)$, as every of the $|V| - m$ non-root vertices $v \in V \backslash R$ needs to be unspooked.

4   Spooky Pebble Game Solver

In this section, we present our solver algorithm for the spooky pebble game. This solver tries to find a solution to the pebble game with a constrained number of pebbles and spooks. For the irreversible [9] and reversible [6] pebble game, optimizing the number of pebbles is shown to be PSPACE-complete. For the spooky pebble game no such result exist, but presumably it is a difficult problem too. Thus, the spooky pebble game is encoded as a satisfiablilty problem, similar to the method of [14] for the reversible pebble game.

To encode the spooky pebble game into a satisfiability problem, we use the boolean variables $p_{v,i}$ and $s_{v,i}$ with v the vertex and i the time. The variable $p_{v,i}$ indicates whether vertex v is pebbled at time i, and similar for spooking with variable $s_{v,i}$. We use the shorthand $x_i = \bigcup_{v \in V} p_{v,i} \cup \bigcup_{v \in V} s_{v,i}$ to describe all variables at time i.

We use the clauses as stated below to describe the game. If there is an assignment of variables that satisfies all clauses, i.e. evaluates to true, this assignment describes a solution of the game. The clauses below are for the game with T timesteps.

Initial clauses: For V the set of vertices in DAG G we have initial clauses:

$$I(x_0) = \bigwedge_{v \in V} \neg p_{v,0} \land \neg s_{v,0} \tag{1}$$

Final clauses: For R the set of outputs (roots) in DAG G we have final clauses:

$$F(x_T) = \bigwedge_{v \in R} p_{v,T} \land \bigwedge_{v \notin R} \neg p_{v,T} \land \bigwedge_{v \in V} \neg s_{v,T} \tag{2}$$

Move clauses: There are the following move clauses for edgeset E of DAG G, for every time $i = 0, \ldots, T - 1$:

To add a pebble all predecessors must be pebbled and a spook on this vertex should be removed[2]:

$$M_1(x_i, x_{i+1}) = \bigwedge_{(v,w) \in E} [(\neg p_{v,i} \wedge p_{v,i+1}) \implies (p_{w,i} \wedge p_{w,i+1})] \wedge$$

$$\bigwedge_{v \in V} [(\neg p_{v,i} \wedge p_{v,i+1}) \implies \neg s_{v,i+1}] \quad (3)$$

To remove a pebble all predecessors must be pebbled or the pebble must be changed into a spook:

$$M_2(x_i, x_{i+1}) = \bigwedge_{(v,w) \in E} [(p_{v,i} \wedge \neg p_{v,i+1}) \implies ((p_{w,i} \wedge p_{w,i+1}) \vee s_{v,i+1})] \quad (4)$$

To add a spook the vertex must be unpebbled:

$$M_3(x_i, x_{i+1}) = \bigwedge_{v \in V} [(\neg s_{v,i} \wedge s_{v,i+1}) \implies (p_{v,i} \wedge \neg p_{v,i+1})] \quad (5)$$

To remove a spook all predecessors must be pebbled and the spook must be changed into a pebble:

$$M_4(x_i, x_{i+1}) = \bigwedge_{(v,w) \in E} [(s_{v,i} \wedge \neg s_{v,i+1}) \implies ((p_{w,i} \wedge p_{w,i+1}) \wedge p_{v,i+1})] \quad (6)$$

Cardinality clauses: For P the maximal number of pebbles and S the maximal number of spooks we have for every $i = 0, 1, \ldots, T$ the clauses:

$$C(x_i) = \left(\sum_{v \in V} p_{v,i} \leq P \right) \wedge \left(\sum_{v \in V} s_{v,i} \leq S \right) \quad (7)$$

Using these clauses, we actually encode our problem as in Bounded Model Checking format (BMC) [3, Chapter 18]. Using this formula the problem can be easily defined for arbitrary times T. The following BMC formula is used:

$$I(x_0) \wedge C(x_0) \wedge M(x_0, x_1) \wedge C(x_1) \wedge \cdots \wedge M(x_{T-1}, x_T) \wedge C(x_T) \wedge F(x_T). \quad (8)$$

Here, M is the conjunction $M = M_1 \wedge M_2 \wedge M_3 \wedge M_4$ of the move clauses from Eq. (3)–(6). With this BMC formula, the time T can be gradually unrolled until a solution is found. This formula can be given to a SAT solver to find a solution for the spooky pebble game problem.

In Algorithm 1 we state our heuristic for the spooky pebble game solver. The solver starts with time $T = 0$. If the formula is proven to be *unsatisfiable* (i.e. the solver shows that there is no solution for the given SAT formula), T is incremented by 1. If the SAT solver cannot find a solution in runtime T_{wait}

---

[2] Hereby we prevent a vertex to be pebbled and spooked at the same time.

Algorithm 1. Heuristic for spooky pebble game solver (runtime timeout T_{max})

$T := 0$
formula = setup_SAT_formula(T)
while result $\neq$ sat **do**
   result := run_SAT_solver(formula) $\triangleright$ returns timeout after T_{wait} seconds
   if result = timeout **then**
      $T := T + T_{skip}$
   if result = unsat **then**
      $T := T + 1$
   formula = unroll_SAT_formula(T) $\triangleright$ update formula upto time T

Algorithm 2. Sequential time optimizer heuristic
(T is parallel time of the game solution)

for $t_0 = T, T-1, \ldots, 1$ **do**
   for v in V **do**
      if v is unpebbled at time t_0 **then**
         for $t = t_0, t_0 - 1, \ldots, 0$ **do**
            if v was used to (un)pebble or unspook a succesor at time t **then**
               break
            if v was unspooked at time t **then**
               break
            if v is pebbled at time t **then**
               remove the pebble from v between time t and t_0
               break

but the formula cannot be proven to be unsatisfiable, we have a *timeout* and T is incremented with T_{skip}[3]. If the SAT solver finds a *satisfiable* solution, the program is stopped as a strategy for the spooky pebble game is found. This entire heuristic has a timeout of T_{max}.

Using push and pop statements for the final clauses, incremental SAT solving can be used, which updates the SAT formula for every new time T. This incremental extension of the formula speeds up the SAT solver in next runs.

Note that our implementation of clauses uses parallel time. In other words, multiple pebbles and spooks can be added or removed at the same timestep. For example, in the pebble configuration at the top of Fig. 3, the steps *unpebble(2)*, *unpebble(3)* and *pebble(6)* can be applied in one parallel timestep. In general, the parallel pebbling time for a game is much smaller than the sequential pebbling time as multiple sequential steps can be applied in one parallel step. This highly reduces the number of BMC enrollings to find a solution. As every BMC enrolling duplicates the move and cardinality clauses as well as the variables all the time, the size of the SAT formula can be highly reduced too. This reduction of clauses and variables in the SAT formula speeds up the SAT solver.

---

[3] We define T_{skip} (which is possibly greater than 1) because every call to the SAT solver takes some 'useless' time to optimize the SAT formula. Thus the heuristic usually can find a spooky pebble game solutions faster when $T_{skip} > 1$.

We built a tool that converts a parallel solution to a sequential solution such that only one pebble or spook is added or removed at the same time. This tool also detects useless pebbling and unpebblings. More precisely, if a pebble is placed but not used to pebble any successor, this pebbling and corresponding unpebbling is detected and removed. The precise procedure is stated in Algorithm 2. With this algorithm, the sequential time and the number of used pebbles of the parallel solution provided by the solver can be reduced. These sequential times are usually reported for pebbling strategies, see e.g. [14].

5   Implementation and Experiment

We implement our spooky game solver algorithm from Sect. 4 in Python. Our code is open source can be found in [18]. The open source Z3 solver for satisfiability is used as SAT solver [7].

To test the performance of our implementation, we use an Intel Core i7-6700 CPU @ 3.40GHz × 8 processor. The benchmark circuits we use are the well known ISCAS85 benchmarks [4]. Using the open source tool mockturtle, the circuits are transformed to XOR-majority graphs (DAGs), which can be easily transformed to circuits with common quantum gates [20]. Table 1 shows the information on the DAGs of the ISCAS85 benchmarks.

Table 1. Properties of the DAGs of the ISCAS85 benchmarks used to benchmark the spooky pebble game solver.

name	vertices	roots	edges
c432	172	7	260
c499	177	32	246
c880	276	26	374
c1355	177	32	246
c1908	193	25	257
c2670	401	46	533
c3540	830	22	1395
c5315	1089	96	1503
c6288	979	32	1639
c7552	988	62	1584

For all these benchmarks we run a performance test. The goal is to find a front of spooky pebble game solutions with optimal parameters (sequential) time, number of pebbles and number of spooks. The procedure is described in detail in Algorithm 3. For various numbers of spooks a solution is searched with a decreasing number of pebbles. For each constraint, the solver is run 5 times with different seeds. If at least one solution is found, the number of pebbles is decreased by 5. If no solution is found, the number of pebbles is not decreased anymore and the iteration with next number spooks is started.

As runtime parameters for the solver (Algorithm 1), we use $T_{wait} = 15$ s and $T_{max} = 2$ min. The solver gives quite little results for these runtimes on large benchmarks[4].

Thus, we used a longer runtime for the large benchmarks. For the four largest benchmarks, $T_{wait} = 60$ s and $T_{max} = 8$ min is used. For all benchmarks, T_{skip} is set to 5.

---

[4] Large benchmarks need many clauses and variables to encode one BMC iteration, and usually also take a larger pebbling time (more BMC iterations). Hence, their SAT formula is much larger, which makes it a harder job for the SAT solver to find a solution.

Algorithm 3. Optimal solutions search for benchmarks

Function spooky_pebble_game_solver(pebbles, spooks) is described in Algorithm 1

---

for spooks = vertices, vertices/5, vertices/10, vertices/20, 0 **do**
    spooky_pebble_game_solver(∞, spooks)   ▷ run solver 5 times
    pb := minimal #pebbles in found solutions
    for pebbles = pb, pb-5, pb-10, ... **do**
        spooky_pebble_game_solver(pebbles, spooks)   ▷ run solver 5 times
        if no solution is found by solver **then**
            break

In Figs. 4 and 5 the results of the runs of the spooky pebble game solver are depicted. Figure 4 shows the solutions found by the solver for each benchmark. The color of the datapoint indicates the number of spooks used by the solution. Figure 5 depicts the runtime of the solver with respect to the constraints on the number of pebbles and spooks (P resp. S in Eq. (7)). Note that the number of spooks is plotted on power scale to clarify the different colors of the datapoints. The runs with infinite pebbles (base case runs in Algorithm 3) are omitted from the plots as no constraints are needed[5]. Also the runs with a timeout (that did not find a solution) are omitted from the plots.

From the data as shown in Figs. 4 and 5 we see that for the large benchmarks with more than 800 vertices the datapoints are less coherent, despite the longer timeout times T_{wait} and T_{max} for these benchmarks. Especially for c3540, c5315 and c7552 still not so many datapoints are found, their sequential time plots don't show the same general behaviour as the others, and their runtimes are less uniform. This might be due to the large size of the benchmarks and the specific structure of their DAGs which causes instabilities in the performance of the underlying SAT engine.

From the data in Fig. 4 we observe the following. First observation is that for almost all benchmarks the solver could find a solution with less pebbles when spooks are allowed. In the case with 0 spooks, no solution can be found below a certain value of pebbles, while there are solutions with less pebbles that use spooks. In fact, within the runtime constraints of the solver, we can find a quantum/classical memory management strategy that reduces the quantum space needed to quantumly simulate a classical circuit. Thus, the spooky pebble framework is useful to reduce quantum space for a calculation.

Another direct observation is that in general the sequential time for a solution increases when the number of pebbles decreases. This is exactly what we would expect, because this is the usual space-time trade-off for calculations.

On the other hand, we observe that for solutions with relatively many pebbles the sequential time increases when the number of spooks increases. We would not expect this from first instance, as with more classical space we expect the time

---

[5] One could also argue that the pebble constraint equals the number of vertices. But the number of vertices is much larger than all other pebble constraints and would be far beyond the plot range.

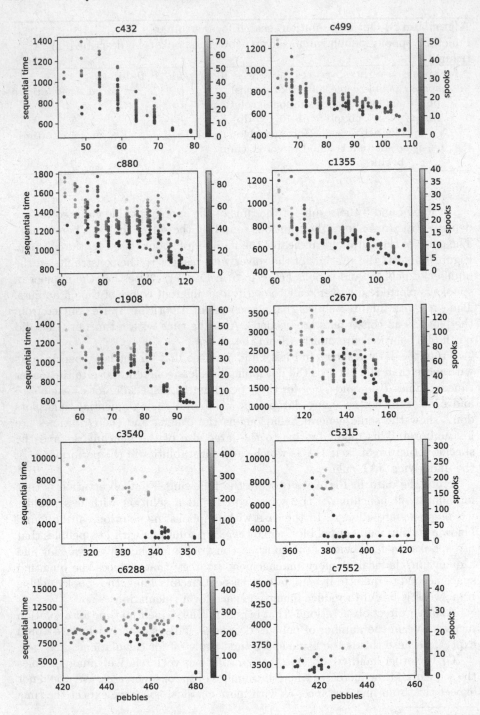

Fig. 4. Solutions of the spooky pebble game with sequential time, number of pebbles and number of spooks found by the heuristic of Algorithm 3.

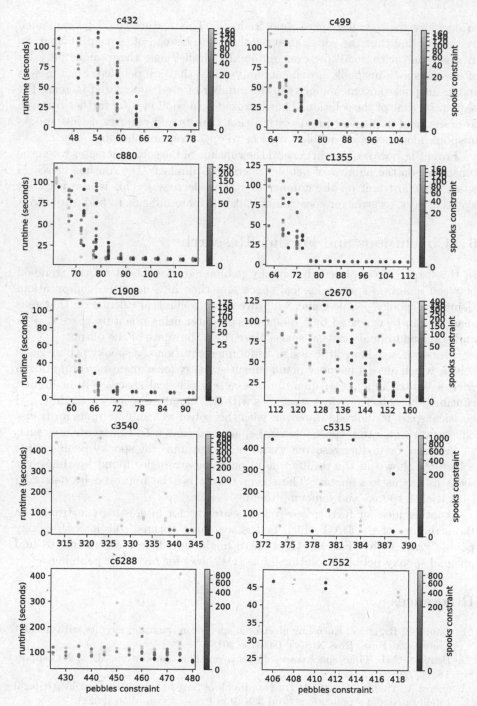

Fig. 5. Runtime of the heuristic spooky pebble game solver in Algorithm 3 for given constraints on number of pebbles and spooks. The runs with timeout (120 s resp. 480 s) are not shown in the figures.

to decrease by a similar space-time trade-off. This feature could be explained by considering that the solver uses parallel time instead of sequential time. So in a solution with small (or even minimal) parallel time there might be a lot of useless spook-unspook movements on vertices that are pebbled. Such useless spook-unspook movements increase the number of used spooks and increase the sequential time of the solution. Thus it would be a good idea for further research to design and implement an algorithm that detects and removes useless spook-unspook movements on pebbled vertices to optimize the solutions.

From Fig. 5 we see that in general the runtime of the solver increases when the constraint on the number of pebbles decreases. Similarly, the runtime increases when the constraint on the number of spooks decreases. This is also what we would expect, as stronger constraints makes it more difficult to find a solution.

6   Conclusions and Further Research

In this paper, we explored the spooky pebble game, a model for the trade-off between quantum space, classical space and time in a quantum computation. Using the spooky pebble game, we proved that a classical calculation that uses space C can be executed by a quantum computer using quantum space $C + m$ and some additional classical space. Here, m is the space of the output.

Moreover, we showed the design and implementation of a spooky pebble game solver, which gives a memory management strategy for a quantum computation with a limited amount of quantum space and classical space. Within limited runtime, this solver provides strategies with less quantum space when additional classical space is allowed. Moreover, with this solver we can find fronts for trade-offs between quantum space, classical space and time used to execute a circuit.

An idea for further research would be to optimize the spooky pebble game solver. As shown in the results, many pebbling strategies found by the solver seem to use useless spooks. The solver results can be improved by detecting such useless spooks and removing them.

Another idea for further research is searching for interesting constraints on the structure of the DAG which makes searching optimal solutions of spooky pebble game easier. For e.g. trees there might be efficient algorithms to find optimal spooky pebbling solutions, like [11] shows for reversible pebbling.

References

1. Babbush, R., et al.: Encoding electronic spectra in quantum circuits with linear t complexity. Phys. Rev. X **8**(4), 041015 (2018)
2. Bennett, C.H.: Time/space trade-offs for reversible computation. SIAM J. Comput. **18**(4), 766–776 (1989)
3. Biere, A., Heule, M., van, M.H.: Handbook of Satisfiability. Frontiers in Artificial Intelligence and Applications, 2nd 336. IOS Press, Amsterdam (2021)
4. Brglez, F., Fujiwara, H.: A neutral netlist of 10 combinational benchmark circuits. In: Proceedings of IEEE International Symposium Circuits and Systems, June 1985, pp. 695–698 (1985)

5. Chan, S.M.: Just a pebble game. In: 2013 IEEE Conference on Computational Complexity, pp. 133–143. IEEE (2013)
6. Chan, S.M., Lauria, M., Nordstrom, J., Vinyals, M.: Hardness of approximation in pspace and separation results for pebble games. In: 2015 IEEE 56th Annual Symposium on Foundations of Computer Science, pp. 466–485. IEEE (2015)
7. de Moura, L., Bjørner, N.: Z3: an efficient SMT solver. In: Ramakrishnan, C.R., Rehof, J. (eds.) TACAS 2008. LNCS, vol. 4963, pp. 337–340. Springer, Heidelberg (2008). https://doi.org/10.1007/978-3-540-78800-3_24
8. Gidney, C.: Spooky pebble games and irreversible uncomputation (2019). https://algassert.com/post/1905
9. Gilbert, J.R., Lengauer, T., Tarjan, R.E.: The pebbling problem is complete in polynomial space. In: Proceedings of the Eleventh Annual ACM Symposium on Theory of Computing, pp. 237–248 (1979)
10. Grover, L.K.: A fast quantum mechanical algorithm for database search. In: Proceedings of the Twenty-Eighth Annual ACM Symposium on Theory of Computing, pp. 212–219 (1996)
11. Komarath, B., Sarma, J., Sawlani, S.: Reversible pebble game on trees. In: Xu, D., Du, D., Du, D. (eds.) COCOON 2015. LNCS, vol. 9198, pp. 83–94. Springer, Cham (2015). https://doi.org/10.1007/978-3-319-21398-9_7
12. Kornerup, N., Sadun, J., Soloveichik, D.: The spooky pebble game. arXiv preprint arXiv:2110.08973 (2021)
13. Li, M., Tromp, J., Vitányi, P.: Reversible simulation of irreversible computation. Physica D **120**(1–2), 168–176 (1998)
14. Meuli, G., Soeken, M., Roetteler, M., Bjorner, N., De Micheli, G.: Reversible pebbling game for quantum memory management. In: 2019 Design, Automation & Test in Europe Conference & Exhibition (DATE), pp. 288–291. IEEE (2019)
15. Nordström, J.: New wine into old wineskins: a survey of some pebbling classics with supplemental results (2015). https://www.csc.kth.se/~jakobn/research/PebblingSurveyTMP.pdf
16. Park, D.K., Petruccione, F., Rhee, J.K.K.: Circuit-based quantum random access memory for classical data. Sci. Rep. **9**(1), 3949 (2019)
17. Peikert, C.: He gives C-sieves on the CSIDH. In: Canteaut, A., Ishai, Y. (eds.) EUROCRYPT 2020. LNCS, vol. 12106, pp. 463–492. Springer, Cham (2020). https://doi.org/10.1007/978-3-030-45724-2_16
18. Quist, A.J.: Spooky pebble game. GitHub repository (2023). https://github.com/Quist-A/spooky-pebble-game
19. Shor, P.W.: Algorithms for quantum computation: discrete logarithms and factoring. In: Proceedings 35th Annual Symposium on Foundations of Computer Science, pp. 124–134. IEEE (1994)
20. Soeken, M., Roetteler, M., Wiebe, N., De Micheli, G.: Design automation and design space exploration for quantum computers. In: Design, Automation & Test in Europe Conference & Exhibition (DATE), 2017, pp. 470–475. IEEE (2017)

Uncomputation in the Qrisp High-Level Quantum Programming Framework

Raphael Seidel[1]([✉])[iD], Nikolay Tcholtchev[1][iD], Sebastian Bock[1][iD], and Manfred Hauswirth[1,2][iD]

[1] Fraunhofer Institute for Open Communications Systems, Kaiserin-Augusta-Allee 31, 10589 Berlin, Germany
{Raphael.Seidel,Nikolay.Tcholtchev,Sebastian.Bock, Manfred.Hauswirth}@fokus.fraunhofer.de
[2] TU Berlin, Straße des 17. Juni 135, 10623 Berlin, Germany
Manfred.Hauswirth@tu-berlin.de

Abstract. Uncomputation is an essential part of reversible computing and plays a vital role in quantum computing. Using this technique, memory resources can be safely deallocated without performing a non-reversible deletion process. For the case of quantum computing, several algorithms depend on this as they require disentangled states in the course of their execution. Thus, uncomputation is not only about resource management, but is also required from an algorithmic point of view. However, synthesizing uncomputation circuits is tedious and can be automated. In this paper, we describe the interface for automated generation of uncomputation circuits in our Qrisp framework. Our algorithm for synthesizing uncomputation circuits in Qrisp is based on an improved version of "Unqomp", a solution presented by Paradis et al. Our paper also presents some improvements to the original algorithm, in order to make it suitable for the needs of a high-level programming framework. Qrisp itself is a fully compilable, high-level programming language/framework for gate-based quantum computers, which abstracts from many of the underlying hardware details. Qrisp's goal is to support a high-level programming paradigm as known from classical software development.

Keywords: Quantum computation · Uncomputation · High-level programming · Qrisp

1 Introduction

While the hardware side of quantum computing has seen steady improvements, significant progress in quantum software development methods is still lacking. This is due to the fact that coding algorithms for the main available physical backends is still done using quantum circuit objects, which are indeed expressive but provide little structure. In order to better support more complex algorithms,

M. Kutrib and U. Meyer (Eds.): RC 2023, LNCS 13960, pp. 150–165, 2023.
https://doi.org/10.1007/978-3-031-38100-3_11

which might include a multitude of concepts, a more abstract programming workflow is necessary.

This problem has been identified by the community and two solutions have been proposed: Q# [11] and Silq [2]. Unfortunately, these proposals currently provide no straightforward way of compiling their algorithms into quantum circuits. In previous work on Qrisp [9], we demonstrated several constructs and abstractions, which permit a high-level programming workflow, while still maintaining full platform-independent compilability. The fundamental paradigm behind Qrisp's design has always been the automation of as many of the repetitive steps of low-level programming as possible without losing expressiveness. As uncomputation is a central and re-occurring topic in many quantum algorithms, it is natural to investigate the automation of this procedure and how Qrisp can support it. In the following, we present an interface for automatic uncomputation within Qrisp as well as some adjustments to the underlying algorithm "Unqomp" [7].

The rest of this paper is organized as follows: Sect. 2 overviews our Qrisp framework for high-level programming of quantum computers. Then Sect. 3 motivates the role of uncomputation for quantum software development. Sections 4 and 5 discuss the possible methods for implementing uncomputation and present the corresponding Qrisp interface. After that, in Sect. 6 the improvements to established uncomputation methods, which make those more comfortable to use in the scope of Qrisp, are discussed. The final section summarizes and concludes our paper.

2   Brief Overview of Qrisp

The state of the art in programming a quantum computer is currently similar to programming in assembler on a classical computer. Even worse, while assembly programming offers at least some basic instructions, e.g. commands, registers, loops, etc., which are more abstract than accessing the actual hardware gates through binary codes, in quantum computing gates and qubits is the current standard way of programming. Frameworks such as Qiskit [12] or Cirq [4] enable the user to create sub-circuits that can be reused in larger, more complex circuits. However, the handling of the circuits is still quite complicated and tedious.

The Qrisp framework [1] consists of a set of Python modules and language extensions that attempt to overcome the above challenge by abstracting the qubit and gate structure of the underlying circuits as far as possible. This is achieved by conceptually replacing gates and qubits with functions and variables. In this way, it is possible to create much more complex circuits than would be possible with the current low-level approach. It goes without saying that the transition to variables and functions does not mean the end of programming with gates and qubits. The elementary quantum functions must of course still be implemented in the background with the help of gates and qubits.

3   The Need for Uncomputation in Quantum Computing

Uncomputation is an important aspect of quantum information processing (and reversible computing in general), because it facilitates the efficient use of quantum resources. In classical computing, resource efficiency can be achieved by deleting information from main memory and reusing the deleted bits for other purposes.[1] Deleting or resetting a qubit, however, is not a reversible process and is usually performed by measuring the qubit in question and performing a bit flip based on the outcome. This measurement collapses the superposition of other entangled qubits, which are supposed to be unaffected. In many cases this collapse interferes with the quantum algorithm, such that the resulting state can no longer be used.

In some situations, uncomputation is not only relevant as a way to manage quantum resources but is actually required, in order for a quantum algorithm to produce a correct result. One such example is Grover's algorithm [3], which utilizes an oracle function and a diffusing process, in order to search for suitable solutions in a given space based on the logic of the above mentioned oracle function. Assume that we have two quantum variables, of which one is in a state of uniform superposition:

$$|\psi_0\rangle = \sum_{i=0}^{2^n-1} |i\rangle \, |0\rangle . \tag{1}$$

In Grover's algorithm, an oracle now calculates a boolean value $f(i)$, which is required to perform a phase tag on the correct solution, for which the algorithm is searching:

$$|\psi_1\rangle = \sum_{i=0}^{2^n-1} |i\rangle \, |f(i)\rangle . \tag{2}$$

After performing the phase tag, the state is:

$$|\psi_2\rangle = Z_{|f(i)\rangle} |\psi_1\rangle = \sum_{i=0}^{2^n-1} (-1)^{f(i)} |i\rangle \, |f(i)\rangle . \tag{3}$$

---

[1] A good correspondence in classical computing to uncomputation in quantum computing is the concept of garbage collection as, e.g., in Java. While classical garbage collection usually simply performs a non-reversible deletion of the collected data, uncomputation in contrast means performing the necessary (reversible) steps to bring the data back into some initial state.

In order for Grover's diffuser to actually amplify the amplitude of the tagged state, we need the state to be disentangled, i.e.,

$$|\psi_3\rangle = \sum_{i=0}^{2^n-1} (-1)^{f(i)} |i\rangle |0\rangle \tag{4}$$

Therefore we need to uncompute the variable containing $f(i)$. This shows clearly why uncomputation is required even within the implementation and execution of one of the most popular quantum algorithms, in order to enable the efficient search of solutions for a particular problem based on an oracle function.

4   The Challenge of Implementing Uncomputation

In many cases, uncomputing a set of qubits can be achieved by applying the inverse of the steps required for the computation. While this seems like a simple approach, it can be ambiguous, e.g., because it might not be clear which gates actually contributed to the computation. For instance, consider the Z gate in Eq. 3. In any case, it is a tedious amount of extra programming work, which should be automated.

To remedy this problem, an algorithm called "Unqomp" for automatic uncomputation has been devised [7]. An important advantage of Unqomp is, that it does not follow the philosophy of simply reverting the computation, but rather enables the algorithm to skip "un-uncomputation" or recomputation. Recomputation is a phenomenon that happens if one naively reverts the computation process. If that computation process contained an uncomputation itself, the reversed process contains a recomputation. Unqomp enables skipping that recomputation, by inserting the reverted operations at the correct point within the circuit instead of appending them at the end. While skipping recomputation is generally a truly useful feature, it also has a drawback: Due to the insertion of the reverted operations within the circuit, the qubits holding the values that would potentially be recomputed cannot be deallocated until the uncomputation is completed. If we recompute them, these qubits can be used for other purposes between their un- and recomputation.

In Qrisp the developer can choose[2] whether they want to perform recomputation: Using the `gate_wrap` decorator, functions of quantum variables can be packed into self-contained gate objects, which are not dissolved by the Unqomp implementation. Any uncomputed quantum variables inside these objects will be recomputed if required. The advantages and drawbacks of uncomputation with and without recomputation are summarized in Fig. 1.

---

[2] An algorithm for automatic determination wether a variable should be recomputed has been presented in [6]. This method is however not yet implemented within Qrisp.

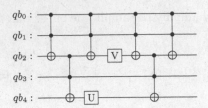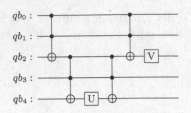

(a) Conceptual visualisation of an uncomputation, which simply reverts the computation. A value is computed into qubit 4 using some temporary result in qubit 2. Subsequently some process U is applied and afterwards, the computation is reversed. Note that qubit 2 is available for some other process V while U is running. Within Qrisp, automatic qubit allocation permits that the recomputation of qubit 2 can even happen on a differing qubit, enabling automated and flexible resource management.

(b) Conceptual visualisation of an uncomputation as done in Unqomp. Note, that only 4 instead of 6 Toffoli gates are needed, because qubit 2 does not need to be recomputed. However, this comes at the cost that qubit 2 is not uncomputed until qubit 4 is uncomputed. Therefore the process V needs to wait until after the uncomputation is done. If the duration of the (re)computation is small compared to the duration of U and V, this implementation requires twice the time compared to the approach in 1a.

Fig. 1. Conceptual visualisation of different uncomputation strategies.

5   Utilizing the Unqomp Method in Qrisp

Unqomp has been implemented in Qrisp and we provide two ways to call this function as described in the following subsections.

5.1   Decorator Based Uncomputation in Qrisp

The first option is the `auto_uncompute` decorator, which automatically uncomputes all local quantum variables, i.e., `QuantumVariable` class instances, of a function. To demonstrate this functionality, we create a function which returns a `QuantumBool` instance in Qrisp containing the AND value of the three associated inputs. To do so, this function creates a local QuantumBool, which stores the temporary result of the AND value of the first two inputs.

```
from qrisp import QuantumBool, mcx

def triple_AND(a, b, c):

    local = QuantumBool()
    result =  QuantumBool()

    mcx([a, b], local_quantum_bool)
    mcx([local_quantum_bool, c], result)
```

```
    return result

a = QuantumBool()
b = QuantumBool()
c = QuantumBool()

result = triple_AND(a, b, c)
```

Executing this piece of code and visualizing the `.qs` attribute (the QuantumSession[3]) of any of the participating SPSVERBc3s produces the following circuit:

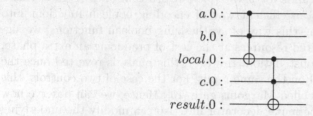

We see that the qubit containing the local `QuantumBool` does not end up in the $|0\rangle$ state, if a and b are in the $|1\rangle$ state. Therefore this qubit is still entangled and cannot be reused for other purposes.

We will now rewrite this function with the `auto_uncompute` decorator:

```
from qrisp import QuantumBool, mcx, auto_uncompute

@auto_uncompute
def triple_AND(a, b, c):

    local = QuantumBool()
    result =  QuantumBool()

    mcx([a, b], local_quantum_bool)
    mcx([local_quantum_bool, c], result)

    return result

a = QuantumBool()
b = QuantumBool()
c = QuantumBool()

result = triple_AND(a, b, c)
```

---

[3] In Qrisp, a `QuantumSession` contains all the high-level objects and steer the interaction with the hardware or simulation backend.

This snippet produces the following `QuantumCircuit`:

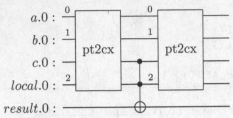

As an effect of the `auto_uncompute` decorator, we see that the multi-controlled X-gate acting on the local QuantumBool has been replaced by a gate called *pt2cx*, which stands for *phase tolerant two controlled X* gate. Phase tolerant logic synthesis is an efficient way of encoding boolean functions into quantum circuits [8]. Using this way of synthesizing boolean functions, we significantly reduce the required resources at the cost of producing an extra phase, depending on the input constellation. However, this phase is reverted once the inverted gate is performed on the same input. For the case of two controls, this is implemented as the so-called Margolus gate [10]. Hence, we can observe how the usage of the `auto_uncompute` decorator in Qrisp can modify the underlying quantum circuits in a way, such that resources, i.e., qubits, that are not needed can be freed and disentangled when required.

5.2   Uncomputation over Qrisp QuantumVariables

The second way of invoking uncomputation is the `.uncompute` method of the `QuantumVariable` class in Qrisp. A `QuantumVariable` in Qrisp is an abstraction that allows the user to manage several qubits simultaneously and to implement data types such as `QuantumFloat`, `QuantumChar` or `QuantumString`.

We demonstrate the use of the `uncompute` method of the `QuantumVariable` class based on the example from above:

```
def triple_AND(a, b, c):

    local = QuantumBool()
    result =  QuantumBool()

    mcx([a, b], local_quantum_bool)
    mcx([local_quantum_bool, c], result)

    local_quantum_bool.uncompute()

    return result

a = QuantumBool()
b = QuantumBool()
c = QuantumBool()

result = triple_AND(a, b, c)
```

This produces the following quantum circuit:

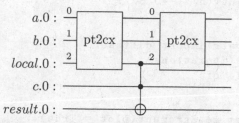

The `uncompute` method and the `auto_uncompute` decorator automatically call the `delete` method after successful uncomputation, which frees the used qubit. If we allocate a new `QuantumBool`, the compiled quantum circuit will reuse that qubit:

```
from qrisp import cx
d = QuantumBool()
cx(result, d)
```

And the quantum circuit is updated to:

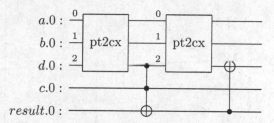

We can see how the qubit holding the local `QuantumBool` has been reused to now accomodate the `QuantumBool` d.

5.3   Case Study: Solving Quadratic Equations Using Grover's Algorithm

We want to close this section with an example given in our previous article [9], where we highlighted how Qrisp can be used to solve a quadratic equation using Grover's algorithm. To achieve this in Qrisp, we employed manual uncomputation using the `invert` environment. Using the `auto_uncompute` decorator we reformulate the code from [9] as follows:

```
from qrisp import QuantumFloat, h, z, auto_uncompute

@auto_uncompute
def sqrt_oracle(qf):
    z(qf*qf == 0.25)

qf = QuantumFloat(3, -1, signed = True)
```

```
n = qf.size
iterations = int((n/2)**0.5) + 1
h(qf)

from qrisp.grover import diffuser
for i in range(iterations):
    sqrt_oracle(qf)
    diffuser(qf)

result = qf.get_measurement(plot = True)
```

The function `sqrt_oracle` applies a Z gate onto the `QuantumBool` generated by evaluating the comparison. Note that this `QuantumBool` and the result of the multiplication `qf*qf` (a `QuantumFloat`) are uncomputed automatically.

The histogram of the simulated outcome probabilities is shown in Fig. 2, demonstrating the correctness of the quadratic equation solving procedure, while in parallel uncomputing qubits using the Qrisp infrastructure for the efficient execution of the Grover's algorithm.

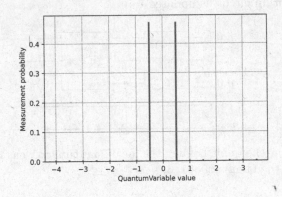

Fig. 2. Histogram of the simulation results of the quadratic solver.

6 Uncomputation Beyond Unqomp

Even though the Unqomp algorithm provides a very convenient way of solving automatic uncomputation, it comes with a few restrictions. We will not detail them too deeply here as they are well documented in the original publication [7], however, the most important one can be overcome using the Qrisp implementation of the algorithm which is described in the following section.

6.1 Uncomputing Synthesized Gates

The main restriction Unqomp imposes is that only a certain class of gates can be uncomputed, which the authors of Unqomp call *qfree*: A quantum gate is *qfree* if it neither introduces nor destroys states of superposition. In more mathematical terms, this implies that the unitary matrix of a *qfree* gate can only have a single non-zero entry per column.

This is a serious restriction, since many quantum functions make use of non-*qfree* gates such as the Hadamard, even though their net-effect is *qfree*. An example of such a situation is Fourier arithmetic (of which Qrisp's arithmetic module makes heavy use). Even though the multiplication function

$$U_{mul} \left| a \right\rangle \left| b \right\rangle \left| 0 \right\rangle = \left| a \right\rangle \left| b \right\rangle \left| a \cdot b \right\rangle \tag{5}$$

itself is qfree, it makes use of Hadamard gates, which are not qfree. In order to overcome this major restriction, the Qrisp implementation of Unqomp does not decompose gates but instead check the combined gate for *qfree*-ness.

This feature, in combination with the previously mentioned `gate_wrap` decorator, can be used to create quantum functions that can be successfully uncomputed even though their inner workings contain non-*qfree* gates.

We demonstrate this with an implementation of the Margolus gate taken from [5]

```
from qrisp import cx, ry
from numpy import pi

def margolus(control, target):
    ry(pi/4, target[0])
    cx(control[1], target[0])
    ry(-pi/4, target[0])
    cx(control[0], target[0])
    ry(pi/4, target[0])
    cx(control[1], target[0])
    ry(-pi/4, target[0])
```

While the Margolus gate itself is *qfree*, the constituents (to be specific, the RY gates) are not. Therefore the following code results in an error:

```
from qrisp import QuantumVariable

control = QuantumVariable(2)
target = QuantumVariable(1)

margolus(control, target)

target.uncompute()
```

We can circumvent this error by applying the `gate_wrap` decorator to margolus.

```
from qrisp import gate_wrap
control = QuantumVariable(2)
target = QuantumVariable(1)

margolus_wrapped = gate_wrap(margolus)
margolus_wrapped(control, target)

target.uncompute()
```

Qrisp now automatically checks the combined gate for *qfree*-ness instead of the constituents. Since *qfree*-ness corresponds to the unitary having only a single non-zero entry per column, this property can be checked in linear time if the unitary is known.

6.2   Permeability

Permeability is a concept, which is introduced in the Qrisp implementation of Unqomp and generalizes the notion of a controlled operation. The permeability status of a gate on a certain input qubit q decides how this gate is treated, when q is uncomputed. We choose this definition, because it permits a broader scope of uncomputable circuits than Unqomp [7] and can be decided in linear time, if the unitary matrix is available. A gate is called permeable on qubit i, if it commutes with the Z operator on this qubit.

$$\text{U is permeable on qubit i} \Leftrightarrow UZ_i = Z_iU \tag{6}$$

This implies that any controlled gate is permeable on its control qubit because

$$Z_0cU = \begin{pmatrix} 1 & 0 \\ 0 & -1 \end{pmatrix} \begin{pmatrix} 1 & 0 \\ 0 & U \end{pmatrix}$$

$$= \begin{pmatrix} 1 & 0 \\ 0 & -U \end{pmatrix}$$

$$= cUZ_0$$

However, not every permeable unitary is equal to a controlled gate, for example, Z_0CX_{01}.

Why is this property relevant for the Unqomp algorithm? The defining feature of the DAG (directed acyclic graph) representation of Unqomp, is the fact that multiple "control edges" can be connected to the same node. This is due to the commutative property of control knobs:

The DAG representation of Uncomp no longer contains any information about the order in which controlled gates are applied. It therefore supports a flexible insertion of the inverse "uncomputation" gates, since it is not necessary to specify, the concrete position in a sequence of controlled gates. In other words, Unqomp's DAG representation abstracts away equivalence classes of gate sequence permutations based on non-trivial commutation relations.

At this point we need the following theorem, which is proved in the appendix:

Theorem 1. *Let $U \in U(2^n)$ and $V \in U(2^m)$ be n and m qubit operators, respectively. If U is permeable on its last p qubits and V is permeable on its first p qubits, the two operators commute, if they intersect only on these qubits:*

$$(U \otimes \mathbb{1}^{\otimes m-p})(\mathbb{1}^{\otimes n-p} \otimes V) = (\mathbb{1}^{\otimes n-p} \otimes V)(U \otimes \mathbb{1}^{\otimes m-p}) \tag{7}$$

According to Theorem 1, it is not only control knobs that possess the above non-trivial commutation relation but the same is also true for two general gates, U, V if they are both permeable on q_1:

We therefore modify the Unqomp algorithm in such a way that, every time it determines whether a gate is controlled on a certain qubit, we instead return the permeability status on that qubit. This simple modification has proved to provide a uniform way of treating uncomputation of synthesized gates. In addition, it also expanded the class of circuits that can be uncomputed. For example, an important class of synthesized gates, that is permeable but not controlled, is quantum logic synthesis.

As mentioned before, permeability can be determined efficiently. This is due to the fact, that according to Theorem 2 (in the appendix), the matrix representation is block diagonal. For instance, if $p = 2$:

$$U = \begin{pmatrix} \tilde{U}_0 & 0 & 0 & 0 \\ 0 & \tilde{U}_1 & 0 & 0 \\ 0 & 0 & \tilde{U}_2 & 0 \\ 0 & 0 & 0 & \tilde{U}_3 \end{pmatrix} \tag{8}$$

Therefore, permeability can be decided by iteratively checking the off-diagonal blocks for non-zero entries.

7 Summary and Conclusions

In this paper, we gave a short introduction to why uncomputation is necessary in general and how to perform it. We introduced two ways of implementing and using the state-of-the-art algorithm Unqomp [7] (the `auto_uncompute` decorator and the `uncompute` method of the `QuantumVariable` class) in the Qrisp high-level programming framework. Moreover, we gave a short example of how to deploy these techniques, in order to have an even more elegant formulation of solving quadratic equations using Grover's algorithm [3] than in our previous article about Qrisp [9]. Finally, we elaborated on our extension of the Unqomp algorithm, which supports the uncomputation of more general quantum circuits an efficient way of deciding the necessary properties (permeability, qfree-ness) required for it to work.

Acknowledgement. This work was funded by the Federal Ministry for Economic Affairs and Climate Action (German: Bundesministerium für Wirtschaft und Klimaschutz) under the funding number Qompiler project. The authors are responsible for the content of this publication.

Appendix: Proof of Theorem 1

This appendix contains the proofs for theorem 1 from Sect. 6. In order to derive the arguments for theorem 1, we first need the following theorem.

Theorem 2. *Let $U \in U(2^n)$ be an n-qubit operator. If U is permeable on the first p qubits, there are operators $\tilde{U}_0, \tilde{U}_1 .. \tilde{U}_{2^p-1}$ such that:*

$$U = \sum_{i=0}^{2^p-1} |i\rangle \langle i| \otimes \tilde{U}_i. \tag{9}$$

Proof. We will treat the case $p = 1$ first and generalize via induction afterwards. We start by inserting identity operators $\mathbb{1} = \sum_{i=0} |i\rangle \langle i|$:

$$U = \mathbb{1} U \mathbb{1} \tag{10}$$

$$= \sum_{i,j=0}^{1} |i\rangle \langle i| U |j\rangle \langle j| \tag{11}$$

$$= \sum_{i,j=0}^{1} |i\rangle \langle j| \otimes \hat{U}_{ij}. \tag{12}$$

where $\hat{U}_{ij} = \langle i| U |j\rangle$. Due to the permeability condition, we have

$$0 = Z_0 U - U Z_0 \tag{13}$$

$$= \left(\sum_{k=0}^{1} (-1)^k |k\rangle \langle k| \otimes \mathbb{1}^{\otimes n-1} \right) \left(\sum_{i,j=0}^{1} |i\rangle \langle j| \otimes \hat{U}_{ij} \right) \tag{14}$$

$$- \left(\sum_{i,j=0}^{1} |i\rangle \langle j| \otimes \hat{U}_{ij} \right) \left(\sum_{k=0}^{1} (-1)^k |k\rangle \langle k| \otimes \mathbb{1}^{\otimes n-1} \right) \tag{15}$$

$$= \sum_{i,j,k=0}^{1} (-1)^k \left(|k\rangle \langle k|i\rangle \langle j| \otimes \hat{U}_{ij} - |i\rangle \langle j|k\rangle \langle k| \otimes \hat{U}_{ij} \right) \tag{16}$$

$$= \sum_{i,j,k=0}^{1} (-1)^k \left(|k\rangle \langle k|i\rangle \langle j| - |i\rangle \langle j|k\rangle \langle k| \right) \otimes \hat{U}_{ij} \tag{17}$$

$$= \sum_{i,j=0}^{1} \left((-1)^i |i\rangle \langle j| - (-1)^j |i\rangle \langle j| \right) \otimes \hat{U}_{ij}. \tag{18}$$

From this form, we see that the index constellations, where $i = j$ cancel out. We end up with

$$0 = 2(|0\rangle \langle 1| \otimes \hat{U}_{01} - |1\rangle \langle 0| \otimes \hat{U}_{10}). \tag{19}$$

Since both summands act on disjoint subspaces, we conclude

$$\hat{U}_{01} = 0 = \hat{U}_{10}. \tag{20}$$

Finally, we set

$$\tilde{U}_0 = \hat{U}_{00} \tag{21}$$

$$\tilde{U}_1 = \hat{U}_{11} \tag{22}$$

yielding the claim for p = 1. To complete the proof we give the induction step, that is we will proof the claim for $p = p_0 + 1$ under the assumption that it is true for $p = p_0$: Since U is permeable on qubit $p_0 + 1$, we have

$$0 = Z_{p_0+1} U - U Z_{p_0+1} \tag{23}$$

As the claim is true for $p = p_0$, we insert

$$U = \sum_{i=0}^{2^{p_0}-1} |i\rangle \langle i| \otimes \tilde{U}_i \tag{24}$$

yielding

$$0 = \sum_{i=0}^{2^{p_0}-1} |i\rangle \langle i| \otimes (Z_{p_0+1} \tilde{U}_i - Z_{p_0+1} \tilde{U}_i) \tag{25}$$

Since each of the summand operators act on disjoint subspaces, we conclude

$$0 = Z_{p_0+1} \tilde{U}_i - Z_{p_0+1} \tilde{U}_i \tag{26}$$

Implying

$$\tilde{U}_i = \sum_{j=0}^{1} |j\rangle \langle j| \otimes (\tilde{U}_i)_j. \tag{27}$$

We insert this form into Eq. 24 to retrieve the claim for $p = p_0 + 1$:

$$U = \sum_{i=0}^{2^{p_0+1}-1} |i\rangle \langle i| \otimes \tilde{U}_i \tag{28}$$

$\square$

Having proved the above theorem, the next step is to employ it in argumentation for the validity of Theorem 1.

Proof. According to Theorem 2 we can write

$$(U \otimes 1^{\otimes m-p}) = \sum_{i=0}^{2^p-1} \tilde{U}_i \otimes |i\rangle \langle i| \otimes 1^{\otimes m-p} \tag{29}$$

$$(1^{\otimes n-p} \otimes V) = \sum_{j=0}^{2^p-1} 1^{\otimes n-p} \otimes |j\rangle \langle j| \otimes \tilde{V}_j \tag{30}$$

Multiplying these operators gives

$$(U \otimes 1^{\otimes m-p})(1^{\otimes n-p} \otimes V) \tag{31}$$

$$= \left(\sum_{i=0}^{2^p-1} \tilde{U}_i \otimes |i\rangle \langle i| \otimes 1^{\otimes m-p} \right) \left(\sum_{j=0}^{2^p-1} 1^{\otimes n-p} \otimes |j\rangle \langle j| \otimes \tilde{V}_j \right) \tag{32}$$

$$= \sum_{i,j=0}^{2^p-1} \tilde{U}_i \otimes |i\rangle \langle i|j\rangle \langle j| \otimes \tilde{V}_j \tag{33}$$

$$= \sum_{i=0}^{2^p-1} \tilde{U}_i \otimes |i\rangle \langle i| \otimes \tilde{V}_i \tag{34}$$

Multiplication in reverse order yields the same result:

$$(1^{\otimes n-p} \otimes V)(U \otimes 1^{\otimes m-p}) \tag{35}$$

$$= \left(\sum_{j=0}^{2^p-1} 1^{\otimes n-p} \otimes |j\rangle \langle j| \otimes \tilde{V}_j \right) \left(\sum_{i=0}^{2^p-1} \tilde{U}_i \otimes |i\rangle \langle i| \otimes 1^{\otimes m-p} \right) \tag{36}$$

$$= \sum_{i,j=0}^{2^p-1} \tilde{U}_i \otimes |j\rangle \langle j|i\rangle \langle i| \otimes \tilde{V}_j \tag{37}$$

$$= \sum_{i=0}^{2^p-1} \tilde{U}_i \otimes |i\rangle \langle i| \otimes \tilde{V}_i \tag{38}$$

$\square$

References

1. Qrisp online. http://www.qrisp.eu/. Accessed 19 Feb 2023
2. Bichsel, B., Baader, M., Gehr, T., Vechev, M.: SILQ: a high-level quantum language with safe uncomputation and intuitive semantics. In: Proceedings of the 41st ACM SIGPLAN Conference on Programming Language Design and Implementation, PLDI 2020, New York, NY, USA, pp. 286–300. Association for Computing Machinery (2020)
3. Grover, L.K.: A fast quantum mechanical algorithm for database search (1996)
4. Heim, B., et al.: Quantum programming languages. Nat. Rev. Phys. **2**(12), 709–722 (2020)
5. Maslov, D.: Advantages of using relative-phase Toffoli gates with an application to multiple control Toffoli optimization. Physical Re. A **93**(2) (2016)
6. Meuli, G., Soeken, M., Roetteler, M., Bjorner, N., Micheli, G.D.: Reversible pebbling game for quantum memory management (2019)
7. Paradis, A., Bichsel, B., Steffen, S., Vechev, M.: Unqomp: synthesizing uncomputation in quantum circuits. In: Proceedings of the 42nd ACM SIGPLAN International Conference on Programming Language Design and Implementation, PLDI 2021, New York, NY, USA, pp. 222–236. Association for Computing Machinery (2021)
8. Seidel, R., Becker, C.K.-U., Bock, S., Tcholtchev, N., Gheorghe-Pop, I.-D., Hauswirth, M.: Automatic generation of Grover quantum oracles for arbitrary data structures. Quant. Sci. Technol. **8**(2), 025003 (2023)
9. Seidel, R., Bock, S., Tcholtchev, N., Hauswirth, M.: Qrisp: a framework for compliable high-level programming of gate-based quantum computers. In: PlanQC - Programming Languages for Quantum Computing, September 2022
10. Song, G., Klappenecker, A.: The simplified Toffoli gate implementation by Margolus is optimal (2003)
11. Svore, K., et al.: Q#. In: Proceedings of the Real World Domain Specific Languages Workshop 2018 on - RWDSL2018. ACM Press (2018)
12. Wille, R., Van Meter, R., Naveh, Y.: Ibm's qiskit tool chain: working with and developing for real quantum computers. In: 2019 Design, Automation & Test in Europe Conference & Exhibition (DATE), pp. 1234–1240 (2019)

Quantum Circuits

Improved Synthesis of Toffoli-Hadamard Circuits

Matthew Amy[1] (ID), Andrew N. Glaudell[2] (ID), Sarah Meng Li[3]([✉]) (ID),
and Neil J. Ross[4] (ID)

[1] School of Computing Science, Simon Fraser University, Burnaby, Canada
matt_amy@sfu.ca
[2] Photonic Inc., Vancouver, Canada
[3] Institute for Quantum Computing, University of Waterloo, Waterloo, Canada
sarah.li@uwaterloo.ca
[4] Department of Mathematics and Statistics, Dalhousie University, Halifax, Canada
neil.jr.ross@dal.ca

Abstract. The matrices that can be exactly represented by a circuit over the Toffoli-Hadamard gate set are the orthogonal matrices of the form $M/\sqrt{2}^k$, where M is an integer matrix and k is a nonnegative integer. The exact synthesis problem for this gate set is the problem of constructing a circuit for a given such matrix. Existing methods produce circuits consisting of $O(2^n \log(n)k)$ gates, where n is the dimension of the matrix. In this paper, we provide two improved synthesis methods. First, we show that a technique introduced by Kliuchnikov in 2013 for Clifford+T circuits can be straightforwardly adapted to Toffoli-Hadamard circuits, reducing the complexity of the synthesized circuit from $O(2^n \log(n)k)$ to $O(n^2 \log(n)k)$. Then, we present an alternative synthesis method of similarly improved cost, but whose application is restricted to circuits on no more than three qubits. Our results also apply to orthogonal matrices over the dyadic fractions, which correspond to circuits using the 2-qubit gate $H \otimes H$, rather than the usual single-qubit Hadamard gate H.

Keywords: Quantum circuits · Exact synthesis · Toffoli-Hadamard

1 Introduction

Recent experimental progress has made it possible to carry out large computational tasks on quantum computers faster than on state-of-the-art classical supercomputers [3,26]. However, qubits are incredibly sensitive to decoherence, which leads to the degradation of quantum information. Moreover, physical gates implemented on real quantum devices have poor gate fidelity, so that every additional gate in a circuit introduces a small error to the computation. To harness the full power of quantum computing, it is therefore crucial to design resource-efficient compilation techniques.

Over the past decade, researchers have taken advantage of a correspondence between quantum circuits and matrices of elements from algebraic number rings [2,7,10,14,15]. This number-theoretic perspective can reveal important properties of gate sets and has resulted in several improved synthesis protocols.

An important instance of this correspondence occurs in the study of the Toffoli-Hadamard gate set $\{X, CX, CCX, H\}$ [2,9]. Circuits over this gate set correspond exactly to orthogonal matrices of the form $M/\sqrt{2}^k$, where M is an integer matrix and k is a nonnegative integer. A closely related instance of this correspondence arises with the gate set $\{X, CX, CCX, H \otimes H\}$, where the 2-qubit gate $H \otimes H$ replaces the usual single-qubit Hadamard gate H. Circuits over this second gate set correspond exactly to orthogonal matrices over the ring of dyadic fractions $\mathbb{Z}[1/2]$ [2]. The Toffoli-Hadamard gate set is arguably the simplest universal gate set for quantum computation [1,22]; the corresponding circuits have been studied in the context of diagrammatic calculi [23], path-sums [24], and quantum logic [5], and play a critical role in quantum error correction [4,6,20], fault-tolerant quantum computing [11,19,25], and the quantum Fourier transform [17].

In this paper, we leverage the number-theoretic structure of the aforementioned circuits to design improved synthesis algorithms. Our approach is to focus on the matrix groups associated with the gate sets $\{X, CX, CCX, H\}$ and $\{X, CX, CCX, H \otimes H\}$. For each group, we use a convenient set of generators and study the factorization of group elements into products of these generators. Because each generator can be expressed as a short circuit, a good solution to this factorization problem yields a good synthesis algorithm.

Exact synthesis algorithms for Toffoli-Hadamard circuits were introduced in [9] and independently in [2]. We refer to the algorithm of [2], which we take as our baseline, as the *local synthesis algorithm* because it factors the input matrix column by column. This algorithm produces circuits of $O(2^n \log(n)k)$ gates, where n is the dimension of the input matrix.

We propose two improved synthesis methods. The first, which we call the *Householder synthesis algorithm*, is an adaptation to the Toffoli-Hadamard gate set of the technique introduced by Kliuchnikov in [13] for the Clifford+T gate set. This algorithm proceeds by embedding the input matrix in a larger one, and then expressing this larger matrix as a product of Householder reflections. The Householder synthesis algorithm produces circuits of $O(n^2 \log(n)k)$ gates. We then introduce a *global synthesis algorithm*, inspired by the work of Russell in [21] and of Niemann, Wille, and Drechsler in [18]. In contrast to the local synthesis algorithm, which proceeds one column at a time, the global algorithm considers the input matrix in its entirety. In its current form, this last algorithm is restricted to matrices of dimensions 2, 4, and 8. As a result of this restriction, the dimension of the input matrix can be dropped in the asymptotic analysis, and the circuits produced by the global algorithm consist of $O(k)$ gates.

The rest of this paper is organized as follows. In Sect. 2, we introduce the exact synthesis problem, as well as the matrices, groups, and rings that will be used throughout the paper. In Sect. 3, we review the local synthesis algorithm of [2]. The Householder synthesis algorithm and the global synthesis algorithm are discussed in Sects. 4 and 5, respectively. We conclude in Sect. 6.

2   The Exact Synthesis Problem

In this section, we introduce the *exact synthesis problem*. We start by defining the matrices, groups, and rings that will be used in the rest of the paper.

Definition 1. *The ring of dyadic fractions is defined as* $\mathbb{Z}[1/2] = \{u/2^k; \ u \in \mathbb{Z}, k \in \mathbb{N}\}$.

Definition 2. $\mathcal{O}_n(\mathbb{Z}[1/2])$ *is the group of n-dimensional orthogonal dyadic matrices. It consists of the $n \times n$ orthogonal matrices of the form $M/2^k$, where M is an integer matrix and k is a nonnegative integer. For brevity, we denote this group by* $\mathcal{O}_n$.

Definition 3. $\mathcal{L}_n$ *is the group of n-dimensional orthogonal scaled dyadic matrices. It consists of the $n \times n$ orthogonal matrices of the form $M/\sqrt{2}^k$, where M is an integer matrix and k is a nonnegative integer.*

$\mathcal{O}_n$ is infinite if and only if $n \geq 5$. Moreover, $\mathcal{O}_n$ is a subgroup of $\mathcal{L}_n$. When n is odd, we in fact have $\mathcal{O}_n = \mathcal{L}_n$ [2, Lemma 5.9]. When n is even, $\mathcal{O}_n$ is a subgroup of $\mathcal{L}_n$ of index 2. As a result, it is also the case that $\mathcal{L}_n$ is infinite if and only if $n \geq 5$.

Definition 4. *Let $t \in \mathbb{Z}[1/2]$. A natural number k is a denominator exponent of t if $2^k t \in \mathbb{Z}$. The least such k is called the least denominator exponent of t, and is denoted by* $\mathrm{lde}(t)$.

Definition 5. *Let $t = u/\sqrt{2}^k$, where $u \in \mathbb{Z}$ and $k \in \mathbb{N}$. A natural number k is a scaled denominator exponent of t if $\sqrt{2}^k t \in \mathbb{Z}$. The least such k is called the least scaled denominator exponent of t, and is denoted by* $\mathrm{lde}_{\sqrt{2}}(t)$.

We extend Definitions 4 and 5 to matrices with appropriate entries as follows. A natural number k is a *(scaled) denominator exponent* of a matrix M if it is a (scaled) denominator exponent of all of the entries of M. Similarly, the least such k is called the *least (scaled) denominator exponent* of M. We denote the least denominator exponent of M and the least scaled denominator of M by $\mathrm{lde}(M)$ and $\mathrm{lde}_{\sqrt{2}}(M)$, respectively.

We now leverage some well-known quantum gates to define generators for $\mathcal{O}_n$ and $\mathcal{L}_n$.

Definition 6. *The matrices* (-1), X, CX, CCX, H, *and K are defined as follows:*

$$(-1) = [-1], \qquad X = \begin{bmatrix} 0 & 1 \\ 1 & 0 \end{bmatrix}, \qquad H = \frac{1}{\sqrt{2}} \begin{bmatrix} 1 & 1 \\ 1 & -1 \end{bmatrix},$$

$CX = \mathrm{diag}(I_2, X)$, $CCX = \mathrm{diag}(I_6, X)$, *and $K = H \otimes H$.*

The matrix (-1) is a scalar. The matrices X, CX, and CCX are known as the *NOT*, *CNOT*, and *Toffoli* gates, respectively, while the matrix H is the *Hadamard* gate. In Definition 6, CX and CCX are defined as block matrices, while K is defined as the twofold tensor product of H with itself. Below we explicitly write out matrices for CX, CCX, and K:

$$CX = \begin{bmatrix} 1 & 0 & 0 & 0 \\ 0 & 1 & 0 & 0 \\ 0 & 0 & 0 & 1 \\ 0 & 0 & 1 & 0 \end{bmatrix}, \quad CCX = \begin{bmatrix} 1 & 0 & 0 & 0 & 0 & 0 & 0 & 0 \\ 0 & 1 & 0 & 0 & 0 & 0 & 0 & 0 \\ 0 & 0 & 1 & 0 & 0 & 0 & 0 & 0 \\ 0 & 0 & 0 & 1 & 0 & 0 & 0 & 0 \\ 0 & 0 & 0 & 0 & 1 & 0 & 0 & 0 \\ 0 & 0 & 0 & 0 & 0 & 1 & 0 & 0 \\ 0 & 0 & 0 & 0 & 0 & 0 & 0 & 1 \\ 0 & 0 & 0 & 0 & 0 & 0 & 1 & 0 \end{bmatrix}, \quad K = \frac{1}{2} \begin{bmatrix} 1 & 1 & 1 & 1 \\ 1 & -1 & 1 & -1 \\ 1 & 1 & -1 & -1 \\ 1 & -1 & -1 & 1 \end{bmatrix}.$$

Definition 7. *Let M be an $m \times m$ matrix, $m \leq n$, and $0 \leq a_0 < \ldots < a_{m-1} < n$. The m-level matrix of type M is the $n \times n$ matrix $M_{[a_0,\ldots,a_{m-1}]}$ defined by*

$$M_{[a_0,\ldots,a_{m-1}]_{i,j}} = \begin{cases} M_{i',j'} & \text{if } i = a_{i'} \text{ and } j = a_{j'} \\ I_{i,j} & \text{otherwise.} \end{cases}$$

The dimension n of the matrix $M_{[a_0,\ldots,a_{m-1}]}$ is left implicit most of the time, as it can often be inferred from the context. As an example, the 2-level matrix $H_{[0,2]}$ of dimension 4 is

$$H_{[0,2]} = \frac{1}{\sqrt{2}} \begin{bmatrix} 1 & 0 & 1 & 0 \\ 0 & \sqrt{2} & 0 & 0 \\ 1 & 0 & -1 & 0 \\ 0 & 0 & 0 & \sqrt{2} \end{bmatrix}.$$

Definition 8. *The set $\mathcal{G}_n$ of n-dimensional generators of $\mathcal{O}_n$ is the subset of $\mathcal{O}_n$ defined as*

$$\mathcal{G}_n = \{(-1)_{[a]}, X_{[a,b]}, K_{[a,b,c,d]} \; ; \; 0 \leq a < b < c < d < n\}.$$

Definition 9. *The set $\mathcal{F}_n$ of n-dimensional generators of $\mathcal{L}_n$ is the subset of $\mathcal{L}_n$ defined as $\mathcal{F}_n = \mathcal{G}_n$ when n is odd and as*

$$\mathcal{F}_n = \{(-1)_{[a]}, X_{[a,b]}, K_{[a,b,c,d]}, I_{n/2} \otimes H \; ; \; 0 \leq a < b < c < d < n\}$$

when n is even.

In Definition 9, the condition on the parity of n ensures that $I_{n/2} \otimes H$ is only included when it is meaningful to do so. In what follows, for brevity, we ignore the subscript in $I_{n/2} \otimes H$ and simply write $I \otimes H$. It is known that $\mathcal{G}_n$ and $\mathcal{F}_n$ are indeed generating sets for $\mathcal{O}_n$ and $\mathcal{L}_n$, respectively [2].

Circuits over a set $\mathbb{G}$ of quantum gates are constructed from the elements of $\mathbb{G}$ through composition and tensor product. Circuits can use ancillary qubits, but these must be initialized and terminated in the computational basis state $|0\rangle$. For example, in the diagram below the circuit C uses a single ancilla.

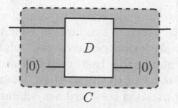

Ancillas provide additional computational space and, as we will see below, can be useful in reducing the gate count of circuits.

If C is a circuit over some gate set, we write $[\![C]\!]$ for the matrix represented by C and we say that C *represents* $[\![C]\!]$. If $\mathbb{G}$ is a gate set, we write $\mathcal{U}(\mathbb{G})$ for the collection of matrices representable by a circuit over $\mathbb{G}$. That is, $\mathcal{U}(\mathbb{G}) = \{[\![C]\!] \; ; \; C \text{ is a circuit over } \mathbb{G}\}$.

Definition 10. *The* exact synthesis problem *for a gate set $\mathbb{G}$ is the following: given $U \in \mathcal{U}(\mathbb{G})$, find a circuit C over $\mathbb{G}$ such that $[\![C]\!] = U$. A constructive solution to the exact synthesis problem for $\mathbb{G}$ is known as an* exact synthesis algorithm *for $\mathbb{G}$.*

The *Toffoli-Hadamard* gate set consists of the gates CCX and H. Because the Toffoli gate is universal for classical reversible computation with ancillary bits in the 0 or 1 state [8], one can express both X and CX over this gate set. As a result, and by a slight abuse of terminology, we refer to the gate set $\{X, CX, CCX, H\}$ as the Toffoli-Hadamard gate set.

It was shown in [9] and later, independently, in [2], that the operators exactly representable by an m-qubit Toffoli-Hadamard circuit are precisely the elements of $\mathcal{L}_{2^m}$. The proof of this fact takes the form of an exact synthesis algorithm. The algorithm of [2], following prior work of [10], proceeds in two steps. First, one shows that, when n is a power of 2, every operator in $\mathcal{F}_n$ can be exactly represented by a circuit over $\{X, CX, CCX, H\}$. Then, one shows that every element of $\mathcal{L}_n$ can be factored as a product of matrices from $\mathcal{F}_n$. Together, these two steps solve the exact synthesis problem for the Toffoli-Hadamard gate set. By considering the gate set $\{X, CX, CCX, K\}$, rather than the gate set $\{X, CX, CCX, H\}$, one obtains circuits that correspond precisely to the elements of $\mathcal{O}_n$ [2]. The exact synthesis problem for this gate set is solved similarly, with the exact synthesis algorithm using $\mathcal{G}_n$ rather than $\mathcal{F}_n$.

Each element of $\mathcal{F}_n$ (resp. $\mathcal{G}_n$) can be represented by a circuit containing $O(\log(n))$ gates (so a constant number of gates when n is fixed). It is therefore the complexity of the factorization of elements of $\mathcal{L}_n$ (resp. $\mathcal{O}_n$) into elements of $\mathcal{F}_n$ (resp. $\mathcal{G}_n$) that determines the complexity of the overall synthesis algorithm. For this reason, in the rest of the paper, we focus on finding improved solutions to this factorization problem.

3   The Local Synthesis Algorithm

In this section, we revisit the solution to the exact synthesis problem for $\{X, CX, CCX, H\}$ (and $\{X, CX, CCX, K\}$) proposed in [2]. The algorithm, which we call the *local synthesis algorithm*, is an analogue of the *Giles-Selinger algorithm* introduced in [10] for the synthesis of Clifford+T circuits. In a nutshell, the local synthesis algorithm proceeds one column at a time, reducing each column of the input matrix to a basis vector. This process is repeated until the input matrix is itself reduced to the identity. The algorithm is local in the sense that the matrix factorization is carried out column by column and that, at each step, the algorithm only uses information about the column currently being reduced. We now briefly recall the main points of [2, Section 5.1] in order to better understand the functionality of the local synthesis algorithm. We encourage the reader to consult [2] for further details.

Lemma 1. *Let v_0, v_1, v_2, v_3 be odd integers. Then there exists $\tau_0, \tau_1, \tau_2, \tau_3 \in \mathbb{Z}_2$ such that*

$$K_{[0,1,2,3]}(-1)^{\tau_0}_{[0]}(-1)^{\tau_1}_{[1]}(-1)^{\tau_2}_{[2]}(-1)^{\tau_3}_{[3]}\begin{bmatrix} v_0 \\ v_1 \\ v_2 \\ v_3 \end{bmatrix} = \begin{bmatrix} v'_0 \\ v'_1 \\ v'_2 \\ v'_3 \end{bmatrix},$$

where v'_0, v'_1, v'_2, v'_3 are even integers.

Lemma 2. *Let $|u\rangle \in \mathbb{Z}[1/2]^n$ be a unit vector with $\mathrm{lde}(|u\rangle) = k$. Let $|v\rangle = 2^k |u\rangle$. If $k > 0$, the number of odd entries in $|v\rangle$ is a multiple of 4.*

Proof. Since $\langle u|u\rangle = 1$, $\langle v|v\rangle = 4^k$. Thus $\sum v_j^2 = 4^k$. Since the only squares modulo 4 are 0 and 1, and $v_j^2 \equiv 1 \pmod 4$ if and only if v_j is odd, the number of v_j in $|v\rangle$ such that $v_j^2 \equiv 1 \pmod 4$ is a multiple of 4. □

Lemmas 1 and 2 imply the *Column Lemma*, the crux of the local synthesis algorithm.

Lemma 3 (Column Lemma). *Let $|u\rangle \in \mathbb{Z}[1/2]^n$ be a unit vector and $|j\rangle$ be a standard basis vector. There exists a sequence of generators $G_0, \ldots, G_q \in \mathcal{G}_n$ such that $(G_q \cdots G_1)|u\rangle = |j\rangle$.*

Proof. Let $k = \mathrm{lde}(|u\rangle)$ and proceed by induction on k. When $k = 0$, $|u\rangle = \pm |j'\rangle$ for some $0 \le j' < n$. Indeed, since $|u\rangle$ is a unit vector, we have $\sum u_i^2 = 1$. Since $u_i \in \mathbb{Z}$, there must be exactly one i such that $u_i = \pm 1$ while all the other entries of $|u\rangle$ are 0. If $|j'\rangle = |j\rangle$ there is nothing to do. Otherwise, map $|u\rangle$ to $|j\rangle$ by applying an optional one-level (-1) generator followed by an optional two-level X generator. When $k > 0$, by Lemma 2, the number of odd entries in $|v\rangle = 2^k |u\rangle$ is a multiple of 4. We can then group these odd entries into quadruples and apply Lemma 1 to each quadruple to reduce the least denominator exponent of the vector. By induction, we can continuously reduce k until it becomes 0, which is the base case. □

Proposition 1. *Let U be an $n \times n$ matrix. Then $U \in \mathcal{O}_n$ if, and only if, U can be written as a product of elements of $\mathcal{G}_n$.*

Proof. The right-to-left direction follows from the fact that $\mathcal{G}_n \subseteq \mathcal{O}_n$. For the converse, use Lemma 3 to reduce the leftmost unfixed column U_j to $|j\rangle$, $0 \leq j < n$. After that, repeat the column reduction on the next leftmost unfixed column until U is reduced to the identity. □

The local synthesis algorithm establishes the left-to-right implication of Proposition 1. It expresses an element of $\mathcal{O}_n$ as a product of generators from $\mathcal{G}_n$ and thereby solves the exact synthesis problem for $\{X, CX, CCX, K\}$. A small extension of the algorithm shows that $\mathcal{F}_n$ generates $\mathcal{L}_n$, solving the exact synthesis problem for $\{X, CX, CCX, H\}$.

Corollary 1. *Let U be an $n \times n$ matrix. Then $U \in \mathcal{L}_n$ if, and only if, U can be written as a product of elements of $\mathcal{F}_n$.*

Proof. As before, the right-to-left direction follows from the fact that $\mathcal{F}_n \subseteq \mathcal{L}_n$. Conversely, let $U \in \mathcal{L}_n$ and write U as $U = M/\sqrt{2}^q$, where M is an integer matrix and $q = \mathrm{lde}_{\sqrt{2}}(U)$. If q is even, then $U \in \mathcal{O}_n$. By Proposition 1, U can be written as a product of elements of $\mathcal{G}_n \subset \mathcal{F}_n$. If q is odd, then by [2, Lemma 5.9] n must be even. It follows that $(I \otimes H)U \in \mathcal{O}_n$. We can conclude by applying Proposition 1 to $(I \otimes H)U$. □

In the rest of this section, we analyze the gate complexity of the local synthesis algorithm. In the worst case, it takes exponentially many generators in $\mathcal{G}_n$ to decompose a unitary in $\mathcal{O}_n$. Since $\mathcal{L}_n$ is simply a scaled version of $\mathcal{O}_n$, the same gate complexity holds for the local synthesis of $\mathcal{L}_n$ over $\mathcal{F}_n$.

Lemma 4. *Let $|u\rangle \in \mathbb{Z}[1/2]^n$ with $\mathrm{lde}(|u\rangle) = k$. Let $|j\rangle$ be a standard basis vector. The number of generators in $\mathcal{G}_n$ required by Lemma 3 to reduce $|u\rangle$ to $|j\rangle$ is $O(nk)$.*

Proof. Let $|v\rangle = 2^k |u\rangle$, then $|v\rangle \in \mathbb{Z}^n$. We proceed by case distinction. When $k = 0$, there is precisely one non-zero entry in $|v\rangle$, which is either 1 or -1. We need at most a two-level X gate and a one-level (-1) gate to send $|v\rangle$ to $|j\rangle$. Hence the gate complexity over $\mathcal{G}_n$ is $O(1)$. When $k > 0$, there are odd entries in $|v\rangle$ and the number of such entries must be doubly-even (i.e., a multiple of 4). To reduce k by 1 as in Lemma 3, we need to make all of the odd entries even. By Lemma 1, for each quadruple of odd entries, we need at most four one-level (-1) gates and precisely one four-level K gate. In the worst case, there are $\lfloor n/4 \rfloor$ quadruples of odd entries in $|v\rangle$. To reduce k to 0, we thus need at most $(4+1)\lfloor n/4 \rfloor k \in O(nk)$ elements of $\mathcal{G}_n$. Therefore, the total number of generators in $\mathcal{G}_n$ required by Lemma 3 to reduce $|u\rangle$ to $|j\rangle$ is $\max(O(nk), O(1)) = O(nk)$. □

Proposition 2. *Let $U \in \mathcal{O}_n$ with $\mathrm{lde}(U) = k$. Then, using the local synthesis algorithm, U can be represented by a product of $O(2^n k)$ elements of $\mathcal{G}_n$.*

Proof. The local synthesis algorithm starts from the leftmost column of U that is not yet reduced. In the worst case, this column is U_0 and $\mathrm{lde}(U_0) = k$. By Lemma 4, we need $O(nk)$ generators in $\mathcal{G}_n$ to reduce U_0 to $|0\rangle$. While reducing

U_0, the local synthesis algorithm may increase the least denominator exponent of the other columns of U. Each row operation potentially increases the least denominator exponent by 1. Therefore, the least denominator exponent of any other column in U may increase to $2k$ during the reduction of U_0. Now let f_{U_i} be the cost of reducing U_i to $|i\rangle$. As the algorithm proceeds from the left to the right of U, f_{U_i} increases as shown below.

$$f_{U_0} \in O(nk), \quad f_{U_1} \in O((n-1)2k), \quad f_{U_2} \in O((n-2)2^2k), \quad \ldots, \quad f_{U_{n-1}} \in O(2^{n-1}k).$$

In total, the number of generators from $\mathcal{G}_n$ that are required to synthesize U is

$$S_n = \sum_{i=0}^{n-1} f_{U_i} = \sum_{i=0}^{n-1} (n-i)2^i k. \tag{1}$$

Multiplying both sides of Eq. (1) by 2 yields

$$2S_n = \left(2n + (n-1)2^2 + (n-2)2^3 + (n-3)2^4 + \ldots + 2^n\right)k. \tag{2}$$

Subtracting Eq. (1) from Eq. (2) yields

$$S_n = \left(-n + 2 + 2^2 + \ldots + 2^{n-1} + 2^n\right)k = \left(-n + 2^{n+1} - 2\right)k \in O(2^n k).$$

Hence, the complexity of the local synthesis algorithm of $\mathcal{O}_n$ over $\mathcal{G}_n$ is $O(2^n k)$.
□

Corollary 2. *Let $U \in \mathcal{L}_n$ with $\mathrm{lde}_{\sqrt{2}}(U) = k$. Then, using the local synthesis algorithm, U can be represented by a product of $O(2^n k)$ elements of $\mathcal{F}_n$.*

Proof. When k is even, $U \in \mathcal{O}_n$ and, by Proposition 2, U can be represented by $O(2^n k)$ generators in $\mathcal{G}_n \subset \mathcal{F}_n$. When k is odd then, by [2, Lemma 5.9], n must be even so that $(I \otimes H)U \in \mathcal{O}_n$. Applying Proposition 2 to $(I \otimes H)U$ yields a sequence of $O(2^n k)$ generators over $\mathcal{G}_n$ for $(I \otimes H)U$. Hence, the complexity of synthesizing U over $\mathcal{F}_n$ is $O(2^n k)$.
□

In the context of quantum computation, the dimension of the matrix to be synthesized is exponential in the number of qubits. That is, $n = 2^m$, where m is the number of qubits. Moreover, the cost of synthesizing an m-qubit circuit for any element of $\mathcal{F}_{2^m}$ is linear in m. Therefore, the gate complexity of an m-qubit Toffoli-Hadamard circuit synthesized using the local synthesis algorithms is $O(2^{2^m} mk)$.

4   The Householder Synthesis Algorithm

In this section, we explore how using additional dimensions can be helpful in quantum circuit synthesis. These results are a direct adaptation to the Toffoli-Hadamard gate set of the methods introduced in [13] for the Clifford+T gate set. Compared to the local synthesis algorithm, the algorithm presented in this section, which we call the *Householder synthesis algorithm*, reduces the gate complexity of the produced circuits from $O(2^n \log(n)k)$ to $O(n^2 \log nk)$, where n is the dimension of the input matrix.

Definition 11. *Let $|\psi\rangle$ be an n-dimensional unit vector. The reflection operator $R_{|\psi\rangle}$ around $|\psi\rangle$ is defined as*

$$R_{|\psi\rangle} = I - 2|\psi\rangle\langle\psi|.$$

Note that if R is a reflection operator about some unit vector, then R is unitary. Indeed, $R = R^\dagger$ and $R^2 = I$. As a result, if $|\psi\rangle$ is a unit vector of the form $|v\rangle/\sqrt{2}^k$ for some integer vector $|v\rangle$, then $R_{|\psi\rangle} \in \mathcal{L}_n$.

We start by showing that if $U \in \mathcal{L}_n$, then there is an operator U' constructed from U that can be conveniently factored as a product of reflections. In what follows, we will use two single-qubit states:

$$|+\rangle = \frac{|0\rangle + |1\rangle}{\sqrt{2}} \quad \text{and} \quad |-\rangle = \frac{|0\rangle - |1\rangle}{\sqrt{2}}.$$

Proposition 3. *Let $U \in \mathcal{L}_n$ and define*

$$U' = |+\rangle\langle-| \otimes U + |-\rangle\langle+| \otimes U^\dagger.$$

Then $U' \in \mathcal{L}_{2n}$ and U' can be factored into n reflections in $\mathcal{L}_{2n}$. That is, $U' = R_{|\phi_0\rangle} \cdots R_{|\phi_{n-1}\rangle}$, where $R_{|\phi_0\rangle}, \ldots, R_{|\phi_{n-1}\rangle} \in \mathcal{L}_{2n}$.

Proof. Let U and U' be as stated. It can be verified by direct computation that U' is unitary. Moreover, since $U \in \mathcal{L}_n$ and $|+\rangle\langle-|$ and $|-\rangle\langle+|$ are integral matrices scaled by $1/2$, it follows that $U' \in \mathcal{L}_{2n}$. It remains to show that U' is a product of reflection operators. Define

$$|\omega_j^\pm\rangle = \frac{|-\rangle|j\rangle \pm |+\rangle|u_j\rangle}{\sqrt{2}},$$

where $|u_j\rangle$ is the j-th column vector in U and $|j\rangle$ denotes the j-th computational basis vector. Since $\langle\omega_j^+|\omega_j^+\rangle = \langle\omega_j^-|\omega_j^-\rangle = 1$, both $|\omega_j^+\rangle$ and $|\omega_j^-\rangle$ are unit vectors. Moreover, it is easy to show that any two distinct $|\omega_j^\pm\rangle$ are orthogonal, so that $\{|\omega_j^\pm\rangle \mid j = 0, \ldots, n-1\}$ forms an orthonormal basis. Now let $P_j^+ = |\omega_j^+\rangle\langle\omega_j^+|$ and $P_j^- = |\omega_j^-\rangle\langle\omega_j^-|$. It follows from the completeness equation that

$$I = \sum_{j=0}^{n-1}\left(|\omega_j^+\rangle\langle\omega_j^+| + |\omega_j^-\rangle\langle\omega_j^-|\right) = \sum_{j=0}^{n-1}(P_j^+ + P_j^-). \tag{3}$$

Furthermore, $|\omega_j^+\rangle$ and $|\omega_j^-\rangle$ are the $+1$ and -1 eigenstates of U', respectively. Now note that U' is Hermitian and thus normal. Hence, by the spectral theorem, we have

$$U' = \sum_{j=0}^{n-1}\left(|\omega_j^+\rangle\langle\omega_j^+| - |\omega_j^-\rangle\langle\omega_j^-|\right) = \sum_{j=0}^{n-1}(P_j^+ - P_j^-). \tag{4}$$

From Eqs. (3) and (4), $I - U' = 2\sum_{j=0}^{n-1} P_j^-$, which implies that

$$U' = I - 2\sum_{j=0}^{n-1} P_j^- = I - 2\sum_{j=0}^{n-1}|\omega_j^-\rangle\langle\omega_j^-| = \prod_{j=0}^{n-1}\left(I - 2|\omega_j^-\rangle\langle\omega_j^-|\right) = \prod_{j=0}^{n-1} R_{|\omega_j^-\rangle}. \tag{5}$$

Since $|\omega_j^-\rangle$ is a unit vector of the form $|v_j\rangle/\sqrt{2^k}$ where $|v_j\rangle$ is an integer vector, $R_{|\omega_j^-\rangle} \in \mathcal{L}_{2n}$. This completes the proof. $\qquad\square$

By noting that $|+\rangle\langle-|$ and $|-\rangle\langle+|$ are matrices with dyadic entries, one can reason as in the proof of Proposition 3 to show that an analogous result holds for $U \in \mathcal{O}_n$, rather than $U \in \mathcal{L}_n$.

Proposition 4. *Let $U \in \mathcal{O}_n$ and define*

$$U' = |+\rangle\langle-| \otimes U + |-\rangle\langle+| \otimes U^\dagger.$$

Then $U' \in \mathcal{O}_{2n}$ and U' can be factored into n reflections in $\mathcal{O}_{2n}$. That is, $U' = R_{|\phi_0\rangle} \cdots R_{|\phi_{n-1}\rangle}$, where $R_{|\phi_0\rangle}, \ldots, R_{|\phi_{n-1}\rangle} \in \mathcal{O}_{2n}$.

Proposition 5. *Let $|\psi\rangle = |v\rangle/\sqrt{2^k}$ be an n-dimensional unit vector, where $|v\rangle$ is an integer vector. Assume that $\mathrm{lde}_{\sqrt{2}}(|\psi\rangle) = k$. Then the reflection operator $R_{|\psi\rangle}$ can be exactly represented by $O(nk)$ generators over $\mathcal{F}_n$.*

Proof. Let $|\psi\rangle$ be as stated. When k is even, then, by Lemma 3, there exists a word G over $\mathcal{G}_n$ such that

$$G|\psi\rangle = |0\rangle. \tag{6}$$

Since the elements of $\mathcal{G}_n$ are self-inverse, the word $G^\dagger$ obtained by reversing G is a word over $\mathcal{G}_n$ such that $G^\dagger|0\rangle = |\psi\rangle$. Moreover, we have $G^\dagger R_{|0\rangle} G = R_{|\psi\rangle}$, since

$$G^\dagger R_{|0\rangle} G = G^\dagger (I - 2|0\rangle\langle0|) G = I - 2(G^\dagger|0\rangle)(G^\dagger|0\rangle)^\dagger = R_{G^\dagger|0\rangle} = R_{|\psi\rangle}. \tag{7}$$

Hence the number of elements of $\mathcal{G}_n$ that are needed to represent $R_{|\psi\rangle}$ is equal to the number of generators needed to represent G, $G^\dagger$, and $R_{|0\rangle}$. Note that

$$R_{|0\rangle} = I - 2|0\rangle\langle0| = (-1)_{[0]} \in \mathcal{G}_n.$$

Moreover, the number of generators needed to represent $G^\dagger$ is equal to the number of generators needed to represent G. By Lemma 4, $O(nk)$ generators are needed for this. Hence, $R_{|\psi\rangle}$ can be exactly represented by $O(nk)$ generators over $\mathcal{G}_n \subset \mathcal{F}_n$. When k is odd, we can reason as in Corollary 1 to show that $R_{|\psi\rangle}$ can be represented as a product of $O(nk)$ generators from $\mathcal{F}_n$. $\qquad\square$

Proposition 6. *Let $U \in \mathcal{L}_n$ and $U' \in \mathcal{L}_{2n}$ be as in Proposition 3 and assume that $\mathrm{lde}_{\sqrt{2}}(U) = k$. Then U' can be represented by $O(n^2k)$ generators from $\mathcal{F}_n$.*

Proof. By Proposition 3, U' can be expressed as a product n reflections. By Proposition 5, each one of these reflections can be exactly represented by $O(nk)$ generators from $\mathcal{F}_n$. Therefore, to express U', we need $n \cdot O(nk) = O(n^2k)$ generators from $\mathcal{F}_n$. $\qquad\square$

Corollary 3. *Let $U \in \mathcal{O}_n$ and $U' \in \mathcal{O}_{2n}$ be as in Proposition 4 and assume that $\mathrm{lde}(U) = k$. Then U' can be represented by $O(n^2k)$ generators from $\mathcal{G}_n$.*

To conclude this section, we use Proposition 3 to define the Householder synthesis algorithm, which produces circuits of size $O(4^m mk)$. Suppose that $n = 2^m$, where m is the number of qubits on which a given operator $U \in \mathcal{L}_{2^m}$ acts. Suppose moreover that $\text{lde}_{\sqrt{2}}(U) = k$. The operator U' of Proposition 6 can be represented as a product of $O(n^2 k) = O(4^m k)$ elements of $\mathcal{F}_{2^m+1}$. Since any element of $\mathcal{F}_{2^m+1}$ can be represented by a Toffoli-Hadamard circuit of gate count $O(m)$, we get a circuit D of size $O(4^m mk)$ for U'. Now consider the circuit $C = (H \otimes I)D(HX \otimes I)$. For any state $|\phi\rangle$, we have

$$C\,|0\rangle\,|\phi\rangle = (H \otimes I)D(HX \otimes I)\,|0\rangle\,|\phi\rangle = (H \otimes I)D\,|-\rangle\,|\phi\rangle = (H \otimes I)\,|+\rangle\,U\,|\phi\rangle = |0\rangle\,U\,|\phi\rangle\,.$$

Hence, C is a Toffoli-Hadamard circuit for U (which uses an additional ancillary qubit).

The Householder exact synthesis algorithm can be straightforwardly defined in the case of circuits over the gate set $\{X, CX, CCX, K\}$, with the small caveat that two additional ancillary qubits are required, since one cannot prepare a single qubit in the state $|-\rangle$ over $\{X, CX, CCX, K\}$.

5   The Global Synthesis Algorithm

The local synthesis algorithm factorizes a matrix by reducing one column at a time. As we saw in Sect. 3, this approach can lead to large circuits, since reducing the least (scaled) denominator exponent of one column may increase that of the subsequent columns. We now take a global view of the matrix, focusing on matrices of dimension 2, 4, and 8 (i.e., matrices on 1, 2, and 3 qubits). Through a careful study of the structure of these matrices, we define a synthesis algorithm that reduces the least (scaled) denominator exponent of the entire matrix at every iteration. We refer to this alternative synthesis algorithm as the *global synthesis algorithm*.

5.1   Binary Patterns

We associate a binary matrix (i.e., a matrix over $\mathbb{Z}_2$) to every element of $\mathcal{L}_n$. These binary matrices, which we call *binary patterns*, will be useful in designing a global synthesis algorithm.

Definition 12. *Let $U \in \mathcal{L}_n$ and write U as $U = M/\sqrt{2}^k$ with $\text{lde}_{\sqrt{2}}(U) = k$. The* binary pattern *of U is the binary matrix $\overline{U}$ defined by $\overline{U}_{i,j} = M_{i,j} \pmod 2$.*

The matrix $\overline{U}$ is the binary matrix obtained by taking the residue modulo 2 of every entry of the integral part of U (when U is written using its least scaled denominator exponent). The next two lemmas establish important properties of binary patterns.

Lemma 5. *Let $U \in \mathcal{L}_n$ with $\text{lde}_{\sqrt{2}}(U) = k$. If $k > 1$, then the number of 1's in any column of $\overline{U}$ is doubly-even.*

Proof. Consider an arbitrary column $|u\rangle = |v\rangle / \sqrt{2^k}$ of U. Let $|\overline{u}\rangle$ be the corresponding column in $\overline{U}$. Since $\langle u|u\rangle = 1$, we have $\sum v_i^2 = 2^k$. Thus, when $k > 1$, we have $\sum v_i^2 \equiv 0 \pmod 4$. Since $v_i^2 \equiv 1 \pmod 4$ if and only if $v_i \equiv 1 \pmod 2$, and since the only squares modulo 4 are 0 and 1, the number of odd v_i must be a multiple of 4. Hence, the number of 1's in any column of $\overline{U}$ is doubly-even. $\square$

Lemma 6. *Let $U \in \mathcal{L}_n$ with* $\mathrm{lde}_{\sqrt{2}}(U) = k$. *If $k > 0$, then any two distinct columns of $\overline{U}$ have evenly many 1's in common.*

Proof. Consider two distinct columns $|u\rangle$ and $|w\rangle$ of U. Let $|\overline{u}\rangle$ and $|\overline{w}\rangle$ be the corresponding columns in $\overline{U}$. Since U is orthogonal, we have

$$\langle u|w\rangle = \sum_{i=0}^{n-1} u_i w_i = 0. \qquad (8)$$

Taking Eq. (8) modulo 2 implies that $|\{i \; ; \; \overline{u}_i = \overline{w}_i = 1\}| \equiv 0 \pmod 2$, as desired. $\square$

Lemmas 5 and 6 also hold for the rows of $\overline{U}$. The proofs are similar, so they are omitted here. These lemmas show that the binary matrices that are the binary pattern of an element of $\mathcal{L}_n$ form a strict subset of $\mathbb{Z}_2^{n \times n}$. The proposition below gives a characterization of this subset for $n = 8$. The proof of the proposition is a long case distinction which can be found in Appendix A.

Proposition 7. *Let $U \in \mathcal{L}_8$ with $\mathrm{lde}_{\sqrt{2}}(U) \geq 2$. Then up to row permutation, column permutation, and taking the transpose, $\overline{U}$ is one of the 14 binary patterns in Fig. 1.*

Definition 13. *Let n be even and let $B \in \mathbb{Z}_2^{n \times n}$. We say that B is* row-paired *if the rows of B can be partitioned into identical pairs. Similarly, we say that B is* column-paired *if the columns of B can be partitioned into identical pairs.*

Note that, for $U \in \mathcal{L}_n$, if $\overline{U}$ is row-paired, then $\overline{U^\mathsf{T}}$ is column-paired. Indeed, if $\overline{U}$ is row-paired, then $\overline{U}^\mathsf{T}$ is column-paired so that $\overline{U^\mathsf{T}} = \overline{U}^\mathsf{T}$ is column-paired.

Row-paired binary patterns will play an important role in the global synthesis algorithm. Intuitively, if $\overline{U}$ is row-paired, then one can permute the rows of U to place identical rows next to one another, at which point a single Hadamard gate can be used to globally reduce the least scaled denominator exponent of U. This intuition is detailed in Lemma 7, where S_n denotes the symmetric group on n letters.

Lemma 7. *Let n be even and let $U \in \mathcal{L}_n$. If $\overline{U}$ is row-paired, then there exists $P \in S_n$ such that*

$$\mathrm{lde}_{\sqrt{2}}((I \otimes H)PU) < \mathrm{lde}_{\sqrt{2}}(U).$$

$$A = \begin{bmatrix} 1&1&1&1&1&1&1&1 \\ 1&1&1&1&1&1&1&1 \\ 1&1&1&1&1&1&1&1 \\ 1&1&1&1&1&1&1&1 \\ 1&1&1&1&1&1&1&1 \\ 1&1&1&1&1&1&1&1 \\ 1&1&1&1&1&1&1&1 \\ 1&1&1&1&1&1&1&1 \end{bmatrix}, \quad B = \begin{bmatrix} 1&1&1&1&1&1&1&1 \\ 1&1&1&1&1&1&1&1 \\ 1&1&1&1&1&1&1&1 \\ 1&1&1&1&1&1&1&1 \\ 1&1&1&1&0&0&0&0 \\ 1&1&1&1&0&0&0&0 \\ 1&1&1&1&0&0&0&0 \\ 1&1&1&1&0&0&0&0 \end{bmatrix},$$

$$C = \begin{bmatrix} 1&1&1&1&1&1&1&1 \\ 1&1&1&1&1&1&1&1 \\ 1&1&1&1&0&0&0&0 \\ 1&1&1&1&0&0&0&0 \\ 1&1&0&0&1&1&0&0 \\ 1&1&0&0&1&1&0&0 \\ 1&1&0&0&0&0&1&1 \\ 1&1&0&0&0&0&1&1 \end{bmatrix}, \quad D = \begin{bmatrix} 1&1&1&1&0&0&0&0 \\ 1&1&1&1&0&0&0&0 \\ 1&1&1&1&0&0&0&0 \\ 1&1&1&1&0&0&0&0 \\ 1&1&0&0&1&1&0&0 \\ 1&1&0&0&1&1&0&0 \\ 1&1&0&0&1&1&0&0 \\ 1&1&0&0&1&1&0&0 \end{bmatrix},$$

$$E = \begin{bmatrix} 1&1&1&1&1&1&1&1 \\ 1&1&1&1&1&1&1&1 \\ 1&1&1&1&0&0&0&0 \\ 1&1&1&1&0&0&0&0 \\ 0&0&0&0&1&1&1&1 \\ 0&0&0&0&1&1&1&1 \\ 0&0&0&0&0&0&0&0 \\ 0&0&0&0&0&0&0&0 \end{bmatrix}, \quad F = \begin{bmatrix} 1&1&1&1&0&0&0&0 \\ 1&1&1&1&0&0&0&0 \\ 1&1&0&0&1&1&0&0 \\ 1&1&0&0&1&1&0&0 \\ 1&0&1&0&1&0&1&0 \\ 1&0&1&0&1&0&1&0 \\ 1&0&0&1&0&1&1&0 \\ 1&0&0&1&0&1&1&0 \end{bmatrix},$$

$$G = \begin{bmatrix} 1&1&1&1&0&0&0&0 \\ 1&1&1&1&0&0&0&0 \\ 1&1&0&0&1&1&0&0 \\ 1&1&0&0&1&1&0&0 \\ 0&0&1&1&1&1&0&0 \\ 0&0&1&1&1&1&0&0 \\ 0&0&0&0&0&0&0&0 \\ 0&0&0&0&0&0&0&0 \end{bmatrix}, \quad H = \begin{bmatrix} 1&1&1&1&0&0&0&0 \\ 1&1&1&1&0&0&0&0 \\ 1&1&0&0&1&1&0&0 \\ 1&1&0&0&1&1&0&0 \\ 0&0&1&1&0&0&1&1 \\ 0&0&1&1&0&0&1&1 \\ 0&0&0&0&1&1&1&1 \\ 0&0&0&0&1&1&1&1 \end{bmatrix},$$

$$I = \begin{bmatrix} 1&1&1&1&0&0&0&0 \\ 1&1&1&1&0&0&0&0 \\ 1&1&1&1&0&0&0&0 \\ 1&1&1&1&0&0&0&0 \\ 0&0&0&0&1&1&1&1 \\ 0&0&0&0&1&1&1&1 \\ 0&0&0&0&1&1&1&1 \\ 0&0&0&0&1&1&1&1 \end{bmatrix}, \quad J = \begin{bmatrix} 1&1&1&1&0&0&0&0 \\ 1&1&1&1&0&0&0&0 \\ 1&1&1&1&0&0&0&0 \\ 1&1&1&1&0&0&0&0 \\ 0&0&0&0&0&0&0&0 \\ 0&0&0&0&0&0&0&0 \\ 0&0&0&0&0&0&0&0 \\ 0&0&0&0&0&0&0&0 \end{bmatrix},$$

$$K = \begin{bmatrix} 1&1&1&1&1&1&1&1 \\ 1&1&1&1&1&1&1&1 \\ 1&1&1&1&1&1&1&1 \\ 1&1&1&1&1&1&1&1 \\ 0&0&0&0&0&0&0&0 \\ 0&0&0&0&0&0&0&0 \\ 0&0&0&0&0&0&0&0 \\ 0&0&0&0&0&0&0&0 \end{bmatrix}, \quad L = \begin{bmatrix} 1&1&1&1&1&1&1&1 \\ 1&1&1&1&0&0&0&0 \\ 1&1&0&0&1&1&0&0 \\ 1&1&0&0&0&0&1&1 \\ 1&0&1&0&1&0&1&0 \\ 1&0&1&0&0&1&0&1 \\ 1&0&0&1&1&0&0&1 \\ 1&0&0&1&0&1&1&0 \end{bmatrix},$$

$$M = \begin{bmatrix} 1&1&1&1&0&0&0&0 \\ 1&1&0&0&1&1&0&0 \\ 1&0&1&0&1&0&1&0 \\ 1&0&0&1&0&1&1&0 \\ 0&1&1&0&1&0&0&1 \\ 0&1&0&1&0&1&0&1 \\ 0&0&1&1&0&0&1&1 \\ 0&0&0&0&1&1&1&1 \end{bmatrix}, \quad N = \begin{bmatrix} 1&1&1&1&0&0&0&0 \\ 1&1&0&0&1&1&0&0 \\ 1&0&1&0&1&0&1&0 \\ 1&0&0&1&0&1&1&0 \\ 0&1&1&0&0&1&1&0 \\ 0&1&0&1&1&0&1&0 \\ 0&0&1&1&1&1&0&0 \\ 0&0&0&0&0&0&0&0 \end{bmatrix}.$$

Fig. 1. Binary patterns for the elements of $\mathcal{L}_8$.

Proof. Let $U = M/\sqrt{2}^k$ and let $r_0, \ldots, r_{n-1}$ be the rows of M. Because $\overline{U}$ is row-paired, there exists some $P \in S_n$ such that

$$PU = \frac{1}{\sqrt{2}^k} \begin{bmatrix} r_0 \\ \vdots \\ r_{n-1} \end{bmatrix},$$

with $r_0 \equiv r_1$, $r_2 \equiv r_3$, $\ldots$, and $r_{n-2} \equiv r_{n-1}$ modulo 2. Since $I \otimes H$ is the block diagonal matrix $I \otimes H = \mathrm{diag}(H, H, \ldots, H)$, left-multiplying PU by $I \otimes H$ yields

$$(I \otimes H)\, PU = \begin{bmatrix} r_0 \\ \vdots \\ r_{n-1} \end{bmatrix} = \frac{1}{\sqrt{2}^{k+1}} \begin{bmatrix} r_0 + r_1 \\ r_0 - r_1 \\ \vdots \\ r_{n-2} + r_{n-1} \\ r_{n-2} - r_{n-1} \end{bmatrix} = \frac{2}{\sqrt{2}^{k+1}} \begin{bmatrix} r'_0 \\ \vdots \\ r'_{n-1} \end{bmatrix} = \frac{1}{\sqrt{2}^{k-1}} \begin{bmatrix} r'_0 \\ \vdots \\ r'_{n-1} \end{bmatrix},$$

for some integer row vectors $r'_0, \ldots, r'_{n-1}$. Thus, $\mathrm{lde}_{\sqrt{2}}((I \otimes H)PU) < \mathrm{lde}_{\sqrt{2}}(U)$ as desired. $\square$

Lemma 8. *Let n be even and let $U \in \mathcal{L}_n$. If $\overline{U}$ is column-paired, then there exists $P \in S_n$ such that*

$$\mathrm{lde}_{\sqrt{2}}(UP(I \otimes H)) < \mathrm{lde}_{\sqrt{2}}(U).$$

Proof. Since $\overline{U}$ is column-paired, $\overline{U}^\mathsf{T}$ is row-paired. By Lemma 7, there exists $Q \in S_n$ such that $\mathrm{lde}_{\sqrt{2}}((I \otimes H)QU^\mathsf{T}) < \mathrm{lde}_{\sqrt{2}}(U^\mathsf{T})$. Hence, letting $P = Q^\mathsf{T}$, and using the fact that the least scaled denominator exponent of an element of $\mathcal{L}_n$ is the same as that of its transpose, we get

$$\mathrm{lde}_{\sqrt{2}}(UP(I \otimes H)) = \mathrm{lde}_{\sqrt{2}}((UP(I \otimes H))^\mathsf{T}) = \mathrm{lde}_{\sqrt{2}}((I \otimes H)QU^\mathsf{T}) < \mathrm{lde}_{\sqrt{2}}(U^\mathsf{T}) = \mathrm{lde}_{\sqrt{2}}(U).$$
$\square$

Lemma 9. *Let $U \in \mathcal{L}_8$ with $\mathrm{lde}_{\sqrt{2}}(U) = k$. If $\overline{U}$ is neither row-paired nor column-paired, then, up to row permutation, column permutation, and taking the transpose, $\overline{(I \otimes H)U(I \otimes H)}$ is row-paired and $\mathrm{lde}_{\sqrt{2}}((I \otimes H)U(I \otimes H)) \leq \mathrm{lde}_{\sqrt{2}}(U)$.*

Proof. Let U be as stated. By Proposition 7, up to row permutation, column permutation, and taking the transpose, $\overline{U}$ is one of the binary patterns in Fig. 1. Since $\overline{U}$ is neither row-paired nor column-paired, $\overline{U}$ is L, M, or N. Write $\overline{U}$ as the 4×4 block matrix

$$\overline{U} = \begin{bmatrix} P_{0,0} & P_{0,1} & P_{0,2} & P_{0,3} \\ P_{1,0} & P_{1,1} & P_{1,2} & P_{1,3} \\ P_{2,0} & P_{2,1} & P_{2,2} & P_{2,3} \\ P_{3,0} & P_{3,1} & P_{3,2} & P_{3,3} \end{bmatrix},$$

where $P_{i,j}$ is a 2×2 binary matrix. By inspection of Fig. 1, since $\overline{U}$ is one of L, M, or N, we see that each $P_{i,j}$ is one of the binary matrices below:

$$\begin{bmatrix} 1 & 1 \\ 1 & 1 \end{bmatrix}, \quad \begin{bmatrix} 0 & 0 \\ 0 & 0 \end{bmatrix}, \quad \begin{bmatrix} 1 & 1 \\ 0 & 0 \end{bmatrix}, \quad \begin{bmatrix} 0 & 0 \\ 1 & 1 \end{bmatrix}, \quad \begin{bmatrix} 1 & 0 \\ 1 & 0 \end{bmatrix}, \quad \begin{bmatrix} 0 & 1 \\ 0 & 1 \end{bmatrix}, \quad \begin{bmatrix} 1 & 0 \\ 0 & 1 \end{bmatrix}, \quad \text{and} \quad \begin{bmatrix} 0 & 1 \\ 1 & 0 \end{bmatrix}.$$

In particular, each $P_{i,j}$ has evenly many nonzero entries. Now write U as the 4×4 block matrix

$$U = \frac{1}{\sqrt{2}^k} \begin{bmatrix} Q_{0,0} & Q_{0,1} & Q_{0,2} & Q_{0,3} \\ Q_{1,0} & Q_{1,1} & Q_{1,2} & Q_{1,3} \\ Q_{2,0} & Q_{2,1} & Q_{2,2} & Q_{2,3} \\ Q_{3,0} & Q_{3,1} & Q_{3,2} & Q_{3,3} \end{bmatrix},$$

where $Q_{i,j}$ is a 2×2 integer matrix such that $Q_{i,j} = P_{i,j}$ modulo 2. As $I \otimes H = \mathrm{diag}(H, H, H, H)$, we have

$$(I \otimes H)U(I \otimes H) = \frac{1}{\sqrt{2}^k} \begin{bmatrix} Q'_{0,0} & Q'_{0,1} & Q'_{0,2} & Q'_{0,3} \\ Q'_{1,0} & Q'_{1,1} & Q'_{1,2} & Q'_{1,3} \\ Q'_{2,0} & Q'_{2,1} & Q'_{2,2} & Q'_{2,3} \\ Q'_{3,0} & Q'_{3,1} & Q'_{3,2} & Q'_{3,3} \end{bmatrix},$$

where $Q'_{i,j} = HQ_{i,j}H$. Since $Q_{i,j}$ is an integer matrix with evenly many odd entries and, since for any integers w, x, y, and z, we have

$$H \begin{bmatrix} w & x \\ y & z \end{bmatrix} H = \frac{1}{2} \begin{bmatrix} w+x+y+z & w-x+y-z \\ w+x-y-z & w-x-y+z \end{bmatrix},$$

it follows that $Q'_{i,j} = HQ_{i,j}H$ is itself an integer matrix. Thus, $\mathrm{lde}_{\sqrt{2}}((I \otimes H) U (I \otimes H)) \leq \mathrm{lde}_{\sqrt{2}}(U)$. A long but straightforward calculation shows that $\overline{(I \otimes H)U(I \otimes H)}$ is in fact row-paired.   □

5.2   The 1- And 2-Qubit Cases

We now discuss the exact synthesis problem for $\mathcal{L}_2$ and $\mathcal{L}_4$. The problem is simple in these cases because the groups are finite. Despite their simplicity, these instances of the problem shed some light on our method for defining a global synthesis algorithm for $\mathcal{L}_8$.

Proposition 8. *If $U \in \mathcal{L}_2$, then* $\mathrm{lde}_{\sqrt{2}}(U) \leq 1$.

Proof. Let $k = \mathrm{lde}_{\sqrt{2}}(U)$ and suppose that $k \geq 2$. Let $|u\rangle$ be the first column of U with $\mathrm{lde}(|u\rangle) = k$ and let $|v\rangle = 2^k |u\rangle$. As $\langle u|u \rangle = 1$, we have $v_0^2 + v_1^2 = 2^k \equiv 0$ (mod 4), since $k \geq 2$. Therefore, $v_0 \equiv v_1 \equiv 0$ (mod 2). This is a contradiction since at least one of v_0 and v_1 must be odd for k to be minimal.   □

Lemma 10. *Let $a \in \mathbb{Z}$. Then $a^2 \equiv 1$ (mod 8) if and only if $a \equiv 1$ (mod 2).*

Proof. If $a \equiv 0$ (mod 2), then a^2 is even, so $a^2 \not\equiv 1$ (mod 8). If $a \equiv 1$ (mod 2), then $a = 2q + 1$ for some $q \in \mathbb{Z}$, so that $a^2 = 4q^2 + 4q + 1$. If $q = 2p$ for some $p \in \mathbb{Z}$, then $a^2 = 1 + 8(2p^2 + p) \equiv 1$ (mod 8). Otherwise, $q = 2p + 1$ for some $p \in \mathbb{Z}$ and $a^2 = 1 + 8(2p^2 + 3p + 1) \equiv 1$ (mod 8).   □

Proposition 9. *If $U \in \mathcal{L}_4$ then* $\mathrm{lde}_{\sqrt{2}}(U) \leq 2$.

Proof. Let $k = \mathrm{lde}_{\sqrt{2}}(U)$ and suppose that $k \geq 3$. Let $|u\rangle$ be the first column of U with $\mathrm{lde}_{\sqrt{2}}(|u\rangle) = k$ and let $|v\rangle = \sqrt{2}^k |u\rangle$. By reasoning as in Lemma 2, we see that the number of odd entries in $|v\rangle$ must be doubly-even. Hence, $v_0 \equiv v_1 \equiv v_2 \equiv v_3 \equiv 1$ (mod 2). By Lemma 10, $v_0^2 \equiv v_1^2 \equiv v_2^2 \equiv v_3^2 \equiv 1$ (mod 8). As $\langle u|u \rangle = 1$, we have $v_0^2 + v_1^2 + v_2^2 + v_3^2 = 4^k \equiv 0$ (mod 8). This is a contradiction since we in fact have $v_0^2 + v_1^2 + v_2^2 + v_3^2 \equiv 4$ (mod 8).   □

It follows from Proposition 9 that $\mathcal{L}_4$ is finite. Indeed, by Proposition 9, the least scaled denominator exponent of an element of $\mathcal{L}_4$ can be no more than 2. As a consequence, the number of possible columns for a matrix in $\mathcal{L}_4$ is upper bounded by the number of integer solutions to the equation $v_0^2 + v_1^2 + v_2^2 + v_3^2 = 2^k$, which is finite since $k \leq 2$. Proposition 8 similarly implies that $\mathcal{L}_2$ is finite.

In principle, one can therefore define an exact synthesis algorithm for $\mathcal{L}_4$ by explicitly constructing a circuit for every element of the group using, e.g., the local algorithm of Sect. 3. We now briefly outline a different approach to solving this problem.

Lemma 11. *Let $U \in \mathcal{L}_4$. If $\mathrm{lde}_{\sqrt{2}}(U) \geq 1$, then, up to row permutation and column permutation $\overline{U}$ is one of the binary patterns below.*

$$B_0 = \begin{bmatrix} 1 & 1 & 0 & 0 \\ 1 & 1 & 0 & 0 \\ 0 & 0 & 0 & 0 \\ 0 & 0 & 0 & 0 \end{bmatrix}, \qquad B_1 = \begin{bmatrix} 1 & 1 & 0 & 0 \\ 1 & 1 & 0 & 0 \\ 0 & 0 & 1 & 1 \\ 0 & 0 & 1 & 1 \end{bmatrix}, \qquad B_2 = \begin{bmatrix} 1 & 1 & 1 & 1 \\ 1 & 1 & 1 & 1 \\ 1 & 1 & 1 & 1 \\ 1 & 1 & 1 & 1 \end{bmatrix}.$$

Proof. By Proposition 9, we only need to consider the cases $\mathrm{lde}_{\sqrt{2}}(U) = 1$ and $\mathrm{lde}_{\sqrt{2}}(U) = 2$. When $\mathrm{lde}_{\sqrt{2}}(U) = 2$, by Lemma 5, $\overline{U} = B_2$. When $\mathrm{lde}_{\sqrt{2}}(U) = 1$, then the rows and columns of $\sqrt{2}U$ are integer vectors of norm no more than 2 and must therefore contain 0 or 2 odd entries. It then follows from Lemma 6 that the only two possible binary patterns for U are B_0 and B_1, up to row permutation and column permutation. □

Proposition 10. *Let $U \in \mathcal{L}_4$. Then U can be represented by $O(1)$ generators in $\mathcal{F}_4$.*

Proof. Let $\mathrm{lde}_{\sqrt{2}}(U) = k$. By Proposition 9, $k \leq 2$. When $k = 0$, U is a signed permutation matrix and can therefore be written as a product of no more than 3 two-level X gates and 4 one-level (-1) gates. When $k > 0$, then, by Lemma 11, $\overline{U}$ is one of B_0, B_1, or B_2. Since all of these binary patterns are row-paired, we can apply Lemma 7 to reduce the least scaled denominator exponent of U. □

The exact synthesis algorithm given in the proof of Proposition 10 is the global synthesis algorithm for $\mathcal{L}_4$. The algorithm relies on Lemma 11, which characterizes the possible binary patterns for elements of $\mathcal{L}_4$.

5.3   The 3-Qubit Case

We now turn to the case of $\mathcal{L}_8$ (and $\mathcal{O}_8$). This case is more complex than the one discussed in the previous section, because $\mathcal{L}_8$ is an infinite group. Luckily, the characterization given in Proposition 7 allows us to proceed as in Proposition 10.

Proposition 11. *Let $U \in \mathcal{L}_8$ with $\mathrm{lde}_{\sqrt{2}}(U) = k$. Then U can be represented by $O(k)$ generators in $\mathcal{F}_8$ using the global synthesis algorithm.*

Proof. By induction on k. There are only finitely many elements in $\mathcal{L}_8$ with $k \leq 1$, so each one of them can be represented by a product of $O(1)$ elements of $\mathcal{F}_8$. When $k \geq 2$, by Proposition 7, $\overline{U}$ must be one of the 14 binary patterns in Fig. 1. When $\overline{U}$ is row-paired, by Lemma 7, there exists some $P \in S_8$ such that

$$\mathrm{lde}_{\sqrt{2}}((I \otimes H) \, PU) \leq k - 1.$$

If $\overline{U}$ is not row-paired, then, by inspection of Fig. 1, $\overline{U}$ is neither row-paired nor column-paired and so, by Lemma 9, $U' = (I \otimes H) \, U \, (I \otimes H)$ is row-paired and $\mathrm{lde}_{\sqrt{2}}(U') \leq \mathrm{lde}_{\sqrt{2}}(U)$. Thus, by Lemma 7, there exists $P \in S_8$ such that

$$\mathrm{lde}_{\sqrt{2}}((I \otimes H) \, PU') \leq k - 1.$$

Continuing in this way, and writing each element of S_8 as a constant number of elements of $\mathcal{F}_8$, we obtain a sequence of $O(k)$ elements of $\mathcal{F}_8$ whose product represents U. □

We end this section by showing that the global synthesis algorithm for $\mathcal{L}_8$ given in Proposition 11 can be used to define a global synthesis algorithm $\mathcal{O}_8$ of similar asymptotic cost. The idea is to consider an element U of $\mathcal{O}_8$ as an element of $\mathcal{L}_8$ (which is possible since $\mathcal{O}_8 \subseteq \mathcal{L}_8$) and to apply the algorithm of Proposition 11 to U. This yields a decomposition of U that contains evenly many $I \otimes H$ gates, but these can be removed through rewriting as in [16].

Lemma 12. *For any word W over $\{(-1)_{[a]}, X_{[a,b]} ; 0 \le a < b < n\}$, there exists a word W' over $\mathcal{G}_n$ such that $(I \otimes H)W = W'(I \otimes H)$. Moreover, if W has length ℓ, then W' has length $c\ell$ for some positive integer c that depends on n.*

Proof. Consider the relations below, where a is assumed to be even in Eqs. (10) and (12) and a is assumed to be odd in Eqs. (11) and (13).

$$(I \otimes H)(I \otimes H) = \epsilon \tag{9}$$

$$(I \otimes H)(-1)_{[a]} = (-1)_{[a]}X_{[a,a+1]}(-1)_{[a]}(I \otimes H) \tag{10}$$

$$(I \otimes H)(-1)_{[a]} = X_{[a-1,a]}(I \otimes H) \tag{11}$$

$$(I \otimes H)X_{[a,a+1]} = (-1)_{[a+1]}(I \otimes H) \tag{12}$$

$$(I \otimes H)X_{[a,a+1]} = K_{[a-1,a,a+1,a+2]}X_{[a,a+1]}(I \otimes H) \tag{13}$$

The relations show that commuting $I \otimes H$ with $(-1)_{[a]}$ or $X_{[a,a+1]}$ adds only a constant number of gates. To commute $I \otimes H$ with $X_{[a,b]}$, one can first express $X_{[a,b]}$ in terms of $X_{[a,a+1]}$, and then apply the relations above. The result then follows by induction on the length of W. □

Proposition 12. *Let $U \in \mathcal{O}_8$ with $\mathrm{lde}(U) = k$. Then U can be represented by $O(k)$ generators in $\mathcal{G}_8$ using the global synthesis algorithm.*

Proof. By Proposition 11, one can find a word W of length $O(k)$ over $\mathcal{F}_8$ that represents U and contains evenly many occurrences of $I \otimes H$. By construction, each pair of $I \otimes H$ gates is separated by a word over $\{(-1)_{[a]}, X_{[a,b]} ; 0 \le a < b < n\}$ and can thus be eliminated by an application of Lemma 12. This yields a new word W' over $\mathcal{G}_8$ of length $O(k)$. □

6   Conclusion

In this paper, we studied the synthesis of Toffoli-Hadamard circuits. We focused on circuits over the gate sets $\{X, CX, CCX, H\}$ and $\{X, CX, CCX, K\}$. Because circuits over these gate sets correspond to matrices in the groups $\mathcal{L}_n$ and $\mathcal{O}_n$, respectively, each circuit synthesis problem reduces to a factorization problem in the corresponding matrix group. The existing local synthesis algorithm was introduced in [2]. We proposed two alternative algorithms.

Our first algorithm, the Householder synthesis algorithm, is an adaptation of prior work by Kliuchnikov [13] and applies to matrices of arbitrary size. The Householder algorithm first factors the given matrix as a product of reflection operators, and then synthesizes each reflection in this factorization. The Householder algorithm uses an additional qubit, but reduces the overall complexity of the synthesized circuit from $O(2^n \log(n)k)$ to $O(n^2 \log(n)k)$.

Our second algorithm, the global synthesis algorithm, is inspired by prior work of Russell, Niemann and others [18, 21]. The global algorithm relies on a small dictionary of binary patterns which ensures that every step of the algorithm strictly decreases the least denominator exponent of the matrix to be synthesized. Because this second algorithm only applies to matrices of dimension 2, 4, and 8, it is difficult to compare its complexity with that of the other methods. However, the global nature of the algorithm makes it plausible that it would outperform the method of [2] in practice, and we leave this as an avenue for future research.

Looking forward, many questions remain. Firstly, it would be interesting to compare the algorithms in practice. Further afield, we would like to find a standalone global synthesis for $\mathcal{O}_8$, rather than relying on the corresponding result for $\mathcal{L}_8$ and the commutation of generators. This may require a careful study of residue patterns modulo 4, rather than modulo 2, as we did here. Finally, we hope to extend the global synthesis method to larger, or even arbitrary, dimensions.

Acknowledgement. Part of this research was carried out during SML's undergraduate honours work at Dalhousie University. The authors would like to thank Jiaxin Huang and John van de Wetering for enlightening discussions. The circuit diagrams in this paper were typeset using Quantikz [12].

A   Proof of Proposition 7

Proposition 7. *Let $U \in \mathcal{L}_8$ with $\mathrm{lde}_{\sqrt{2}}(U) \geq 2$. Then up to row permutation, column permutation, and taking the transpose, $\overline{U}$ is one of the 14 binary patterns in* Fig. 1.

Proof. Let u_i denote the i-th column of U, and $u_i^\dagger$ denote the the i-th row of U, $0 \leq i < 8$. Let $\|v\|$ denote the hamming weight of v, where v is a string of binary bits. Proceed by case distinctions.

Case 1. There are identical rows or columns in U. Up to transposition, suppose U has two rows that are identical. By Proposition 13, $U \in \mathcal{B}_0$ up to permutation.

Case 2. There are no identical rows or columns in U. By Proposition 14, $U \in \mathcal{B}_1$ up to permutation. □

A.1   Binary Patterns that are Either Row-Paired or Column-Paired

Definition 14. *We define the set $\mathcal{B}_0$ of binary matrices as $\mathcal{B}_0 = \{A, B, C, D, E,$ $F, G, H, I, J, K\}$, where*

$$
A = \begin{bmatrix}
1 & 1 & 1 & 1 & 1 & 1 & 1 & 1 \\
1 & 1 & 1 & 1 & 1 & 1 & 1 & 1 \\
1 & 1 & 1 & 1 & 1 & 1 & 1 & 1 \\
1 & 1 & 1 & 1 & 1 & 1 & 1 & 1 \\
1 & 1 & 1 & 1 & 1 & 1 & 1 & 1 \\
1 & 1 & 1 & 1 & 1 & 1 & 1 & 1 \\
1 & 1 & 1 & 1 & 1 & 1 & 1 & 1 \\
1 & 1 & 1 & 1 & 1 & 1 & 1 & 1
\end{bmatrix}, \quad
B = \begin{bmatrix}
1 & 1 & 1 & 1 & 1 & 1 & 1 & 1 \\
1 & 1 & 1 & 1 & 1 & 1 & 1 & 1 \\
1 & 1 & 1 & 1 & 1 & 1 & 1 & 1 \\
1 & 1 & 1 & 1 & 1 & 1 & 1 & 1 \\
1 & 1 & 1 & 1 & 0 & 0 & 0 & 0 \\
1 & 1 & 1 & 1 & 0 & 0 & 0 & 0 \\
1 & 1 & 1 & 1 & 0 & 0 & 0 & 0 \\
1 & 1 & 1 & 1 & 0 & 0 & 0 & 0
\end{bmatrix}, \quad
C = \begin{bmatrix}
1 & 1 & 1 & 1 & 1 & 1 & 1 & 1 \\
1 & 1 & 1 & 1 & 1 & 1 & 1 & 1 \\
1 & 1 & 1 & 1 & 0 & 0 & 0 & 0 \\
1 & 1 & 1 & 1 & 0 & 0 & 0 & 0 \\
1 & 1 & 0 & 0 & 1 & 1 & 0 & 0 \\
1 & 1 & 0 & 0 & 1 & 1 & 0 & 0 \\
1 & 1 & 0 & 0 & 0 & 0 & 1 & 1 \\
1 & 1 & 0 & 0 & 0 & 0 & 1 & 1
\end{bmatrix},
$$

$$
D = \begin{bmatrix}
1 & 1 & 1 & 1 & 0 & 0 & 0 & 0 \\
1 & 1 & 1 & 1 & 0 & 0 & 0 & 0 \\
1 & 1 & 1 & 1 & 0 & 0 & 0 & 0 \\
1 & 1 & 1 & 1 & 0 & 0 & 0 & 0 \\
1 & 1 & 0 & 0 & 1 & 1 & 0 & 0 \\
1 & 1 & 0 & 0 & 1 & 1 & 0 & 0 \\
1 & 1 & 0 & 0 & 1 & 1 & 0 & 0 \\
1 & 1 & 0 & 0 & 1 & 1 & 0 & 0
\end{bmatrix}, \quad
E = \begin{bmatrix}
1 & 1 & 1 & 1 & 1 & 1 & 1 & 1 \\
1 & 1 & 1 & 1 & 1 & 1 & 1 & 1 \\
1 & 1 & 1 & 1 & 0 & 0 & 0 & 0 \\
1 & 1 & 1 & 1 & 0 & 0 & 0 & 0 \\
0 & 0 & 0 & 0 & 1 & 1 & 1 & 1 \\
0 & 0 & 0 & 0 & 1 & 1 & 1 & 1 \\
0 & 0 & 0 & 0 & 0 & 0 & 0 & 0 \\
0 & 0 & 0 & 0 & 0 & 0 & 0 & 0
\end{bmatrix}, \quad
F = \begin{bmatrix}
1 & 1 & 1 & 1 & 0 & 0 & 0 & 0 \\
1 & 1 & 1 & 1 & 0 & 0 & 0 & 0 \\
1 & 1 & 0 & 0 & 1 & 1 & 0 & 0 \\
1 & 1 & 0 & 0 & 1 & 1 & 0 & 0 \\
1 & 0 & 1 & 0 & 1 & 0 & 1 & 0 \\
1 & 0 & 1 & 0 & 1 & 0 & 1 & 0 \\
1 & 0 & 0 & 1 & 0 & 1 & 1 & 0 \\
1 & 0 & 0 & 1 & 0 & 1 & 1 & 0
\end{bmatrix},
$$

$$
G = \begin{bmatrix}
1 & 1 & 1 & 1 & 0 & 0 & 0 & 0 \\
1 & 1 & 1 & 1 & 0 & 0 & 0 & 0 \\
1 & 1 & 0 & 0 & 1 & 1 & 0 & 0 \\
1 & 1 & 0 & 0 & 1 & 1 & 0 & 0 \\
0 & 0 & 1 & 1 & 1 & 1 & 0 & 0 \\
0 & 0 & 1 & 1 & 1 & 1 & 0 & 0 \\
0 & 0 & 0 & 0 & 0 & 0 & 0 & 0 \\
0 & 0 & 0 & 0 & 0 & 0 & 0 & 0
\end{bmatrix}, \quad
H = \begin{bmatrix}
1 & 1 & 1 & 1 & 0 & 0 & 0 & 0 \\
1 & 1 & 1 & 1 & 0 & 0 & 0 & 0 \\
1 & 1 & 0 & 0 & 1 & 1 & 0 & 0 \\
1 & 1 & 0 & 0 & 1 & 1 & 0 & 0 \\
0 & 0 & 1 & 1 & 0 & 0 & 1 & 1 \\
0 & 0 & 1 & 1 & 0 & 0 & 1 & 1 \\
0 & 0 & 0 & 0 & 1 & 1 & 1 & 1 \\
0 & 0 & 0 & 0 & 1 & 1 & 1 & 1
\end{bmatrix}, \quad
I = \begin{bmatrix}
1 & 1 & 1 & 1 & 0 & 0 & 0 & 0 \\
1 & 1 & 1 & 1 & 0 & 0 & 0 & 0 \\
1 & 1 & 1 & 1 & 0 & 0 & 0 & 0 \\
1 & 1 & 1 & 1 & 0 & 0 & 0 & 0 \\
0 & 0 & 0 & 0 & 1 & 1 & 1 & 1 \\
0 & 0 & 0 & 0 & 1 & 1 & 1 & 1 \\
0 & 0 & 0 & 0 & 1 & 1 & 1 & 1 \\
0 & 0 & 0 & 0 & 1 & 1 & 1 & 1
\end{bmatrix},
$$

$$
J = \begin{bmatrix}
1 & 1 & 1 & 1 & 0 & 0 & 0 & 0 \\
1 & 1 & 1 & 1 & 0 & 0 & 0 & 0 \\
1 & 1 & 1 & 1 & 0 & 0 & 0 & 0 \\
1 & 1 & 1 & 1 & 0 & 0 & 0 & 0 \\
0 & 0 & 0 & 0 & 0 & 0 & 0 & 0 \\
0 & 0 & 0 & 0 & 0 & 0 & 0 & 0 \\
0 & 0 & 0 & 0 & 0 & 0 & 0 & 0 \\
0 & 0 & 0 & 0 & 0 & 0 & 0 & 0
\end{bmatrix}, \quad
K = \begin{bmatrix}
1 & 1 & 1 & 1 & 1 & 1 & 1 & 1 \\
1 & 1 & 1 & 1 & 1 & 1 & 1 & 1 \\
1 & 1 & 1 & 1 & 1 & 1 & 1 & 1 \\
1 & 1 & 1 & 1 & 1 & 1 & 1 & 1 \\
0 & 0 & 0 & 0 & 0 & 0 & 0 & 0 \\
0 & 0 & 0 & 0 & 0 & 0 & 0 & 0 \\
0 & 0 & 0 & 0 & 0 & 0 & 0 & 0 \\
0 & 0 & 0 & 0 & 0 & 0 & 0 & 0
\end{bmatrix}.
$$

Proposition 13. *Let $U \in \mathbb{Z}_2^{8 \times 8}$. Suppose U satisfies Lemmas 6 and 5. If U has two rows that are identical, then $U \in \mathcal{B}_0$ up to permutation and transposition.*

Proof. Let u_i denote the i-th column of U, and $u_i^\dagger$ denote the i-th row of U, $0 \le i < 8$. Let $\|v\|$ denote the hamming weight of v, where v is a string of binary bits. Up to permutation, suppose $\|u_0^\dagger\| = \|u_1^\dagger\|$. By Lemma 5, $\|u_0^\dagger\| = 8$ or $\|u_0^\dagger\| = 4$. Proceed by case distinctions, we summarized the derivation of binary patterns in Fig. 2 and Fig. 3.

Case 1. $\|u_0^\dagger\| = \|u_1^\dagger\| = 8$.
Subcase 1.1. $\|u_0\| = 8$.
Subcase 1.1.1. $\|u_1\| = 8$.
Subcase 1.1.1.1. $\|u_2\| = 8$.
Subcase 1.1.1.1.1. $\|u_3\| = 8$.

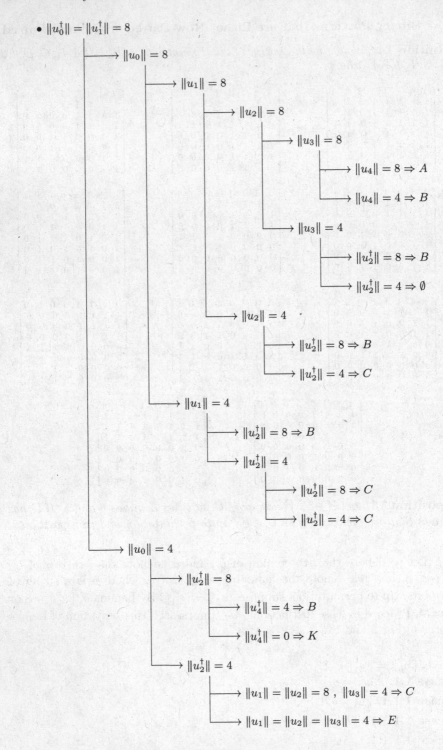

Fig. 2. Case distinction for $\|u_0^\dagger\| = \|u_1^\dagger\| = 8$.

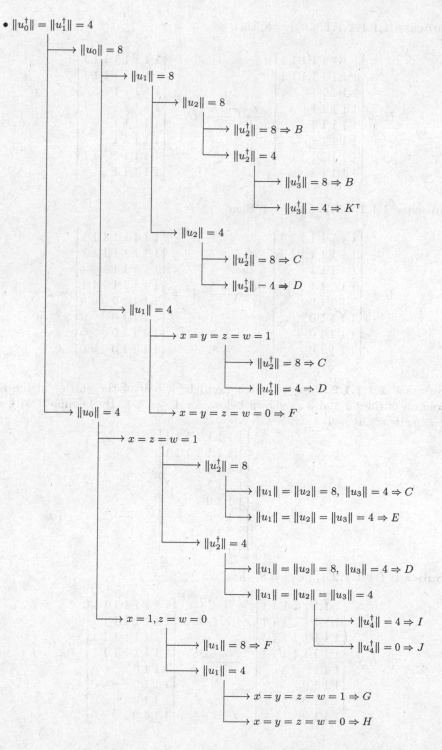

Fig. 3. Case distinction for $\|u_0^\dagger\| = \|u_1^\dagger\| = 4$.

Subcase 1.1.1.1.1.1. $\|u_4\| = 8$, then

$$U = \begin{bmatrix} 1\,1\,1\,1\,1\,1\,1\,1 \\ 1\,1\,1\,1\,1\,1\,1\,1 \\ 1\,1\,1\,1\,1 \\ 1\,1\,1\,1\,1 \\ 1\,1\,1\,1\,1 \\ 1\,1\,1\,1\,1 \\ 1\,1\,1\,1\,1 \\ 1\,1\,1\,1\,1 \end{bmatrix} \xrightarrow{\text{Lemma } 5} U = \begin{bmatrix} 1\,1\,1\,1\,1\,1\,1\,1 \\ 1\,1\,1\,1\,1\,1\,1\,1 \\ 1\,1\,1\,1\,1\,1\,1\,1 \\ 1\,1\,1\,1\,1\,1\,1\,1 \\ 1\,1\,1\,1\,1\,1\,1\,1 \\ 1\,1\,1\,1\,1\,1\,1\,1 \\ 1\,1\,1\,1\,1\,1\,1\,1 \\ 1\,1\,1\,1\,1\,1\,1\,1 \end{bmatrix} = A.$$

Subcase 1.1.1.1.1.2. $\|u_4\| = 4$, then

$$U = \begin{bmatrix} 1\,1\,1\,1\,1\,1\,1\,1 \\ 1\,1\,1\,1\,1\,1\,1\,1 \\ 1\,1\,1\,1\,1 \\ 1\,1\,1\,1\,1 \\ 1\,1\,1\,1\,0 \\ 1\,1\,1\,1\,0 \\ 1\,1\,1\,1\,0 \\ 1\,1\,1\,1\,0 \end{bmatrix} \xrightarrow{\text{Lemma } 5} U = \begin{bmatrix} 1\,1\,1\,1\,1\,1\,1\,1 \\ 1\,1\,1\,1\,1\,1\,1\,1 \\ 1\,1\,1\,1\,1\,1\,1\,1 \\ 1\,1\,1\,1\,1\,1\,1\,1 \\ 1\,1\,1\,1\,0\,0\,0\,0 \\ 1\,1\,1\,1\,0\,0\,0\,0 \\ 1\,1\,1\,1\,0\,0\,0\,0 \\ 1\,1\,1\,1\,0\,0\,0\,0 \end{bmatrix} = B.$$

Subcase 1.1.1.1.2. $\|u_3\| = 4$. Let (x, y) be a pair of the entries in the i-th column of rows 2 and 3 as shown below, for $4 \le i < 8$. By Lemma 6 with u_3, $x = y$. Hence $u_2^\dagger = u_3^\dagger$.

$$U = \begin{bmatrix} 1\,1\,1\,1\,1\,1\,1\,1 \\ 1\,1\,1\,1\,1\,1\,1\,1 \\ 1\,1\,1\,1\,x \\ 1\,1\,1\,1\,y \\ 1\,1\,1\,0 \\ 1\,1\,1\,0 \\ 1\,1\,1\,0 \\ 1\,1\,1\,0 \end{bmatrix}.$$

Subcase 1.1.1.1.2.1. $\|u_2^\dagger\| = 8$, then

$$U = \begin{bmatrix} 1\,1\,1\,1\,1\,1\,1\,1 \\ 1\,1\,1\,1\,1\,1\,1\,1 \\ 1\,1\,1\,1\,1\,1\,1\,1 \\ 1\,1\,1\,1\,1\,1\,1\,1 \\ 1\,1\,1\,0 \\ 1\,1\,1\,0 \\ 1\,1\,1\,0 \\ 1\,1\,1\,0 \end{bmatrix} \xrightarrow{\text{Lemma } 5} \begin{bmatrix} 1\,1\,1\,1\,1\,1\,1\,1 \\ 1\,1\,1\,1\,1\,1\,1\,1 \\ 1\,1\,1\,1\,1\,1\,1\,1 \\ 1\,1\,1\,1\,1\,1\,1\,1 \\ 1\,1\,1\,0\,1\,0\,0\,0 \\ 1\,1\,1\,0\,1\,0\,0\,0 \\ 1\,1\,1\,0\,1\,0\,0\,0 \\ 1\,1\,1\,0\,1\,0\,0\,0 \end{bmatrix} = B.$$

Subcase 1.1.1.1.2.2. $\|u_2^\dagger\| = 4$, then

$$U = \begin{bmatrix} 1\,1\,1\,1\,1\,1\,1\,1 \\ 1\,1\,1\,1\,1\,1\,1\,1 \\ 1\,1\,1\,1\,0\,0\,0\,0 \\ 1\,1\,1\,1\,0\,0\,0\,0 \\ 1\,1\,1\,0 \\ 1\,1\,1\,0 \\ 1\,1\,1\,0 \\ 1\,1\,1\,0 \end{bmatrix}.$$

Note that rows 3 and 4 violate Lemma 6, so this case is not possible.

Subcase 1.1.1.2. $\|u_2\| = 4$. Let (x, y) be a pair of the entries in the i-th column of rows 2 and 3 as shown below, for $3 \leq i < 8$. By Lemma 6 with u_2, $x = y$. Hence $u_2^\dagger = u_3^\dagger$.

$$U = \begin{bmatrix} 1\,1\,1\,1\,1\,1\,1\,1 \\ 1\,1\,1\,1\,1\,1\,1\,1 \\ 1\,1\,1\,x \\ 1\,1\,1\,y \\ 1\,1\,0 \\ 1\,1\,0 \\ 1\,1\,0 \\ 1\,1\,0 \end{bmatrix}.$$

Subcase 1.1.1.2.1.

$$U = \begin{bmatrix} 1\,1\,1\,1\,1\,1\,1\,1 \\ 1\,1\,1\,1\,1\,1\,1\,1 \\ 1\,1\,1\,1\,1\,1\,1\,1 \\ 1\,1\,1\,1\,1\,1\,1\,1 \\ 1\,1\,0 \\ 1\,1\,0 \\ 1\,1\,0 \\ 1\,1\,0 \end{bmatrix} \xrightarrow{Lemma\ 5} \begin{bmatrix} 1\,1\,1\,1\,1\,1\,1\,1 \\ 1\,1\,1\,1\,1\,1\,1\,1 \\ 1\,1\,1\,1\,1\,1\,1\,1 \\ 1\,1\,1\,1\,1\,1\,1\,1 \\ 1\,1\,0\,1\,1\,0\,0\,0 \\ 1\,1\,0 \\ 1\,1\,0 \\ 1\,1\,0 \end{bmatrix} \xrightarrow{Lemma\ 5} \begin{bmatrix} 1\,1\,1\,1\,1\,1\,1\,1 \\ 1\,1\,1\,1\,1\,1\,1\,1 \\ 1\,1\,1\,1\,1\,1\,1\,1 \\ 1\,1\,1\,1\,1\,1\,1\,1 \\ 1\,1\,0\,1\,1\,0\,0\,0 \\ 1\,1\,0\,1\,1 \\ 1\,1\,0\,1\,1 \\ 1\,1\,0\,1\,1 \end{bmatrix}.$$

By Lemma 5 for rows 5, 6, and 7, we have

$$U = \begin{bmatrix} 1\,1\,1\,1\,1\,1\,1\,1 \\ 1\,1\,1\,1\,1\,1\,1\,1 \\ 1\,1\,1\,1\,1\,1\,1\,1 \\ 1\,1\,1\,1\,1\,1\,1\,1 \\ 1\,1\,0\,1\,1\,0\,0\,0 \\ 1\,1\,0\,1\,1\,0\,0\,0 \\ 1\,1\,0\,1\,1\,0\,0\,0 \\ 1\,1\,0\,1\,1\,0\,0\,0 \end{bmatrix} = B.$$

Subcase 1.1.1.2.2. $\|u_2^\dagger\| = 4$, then up to column permutation,

$$
U = \begin{bmatrix} 1\,1\,1\,1\,1\,1\,1\,1 \\ 1\,1\,1\,1\,1\,1\,1\,1 \\ 1\,1\,1\,1\,0\,0\,0\,0 \\ 1\,1\,1\,1\,0\,0\,0\,0 \\ 1\,1\,0 \\ 1\,1\,0 \\ 1\,1\,0 \\ 1\,1\,0 \end{bmatrix} \xrightarrow{\ Lemma\ 6\ }
\begin{bmatrix} 1\,1\,1\,1\,1\,1\,1\,1 \\ 1\,1\,1\,1\,1\,1\,1\,1 \\ 1\,1\,1\,1\,0\,0\,0\,0 \\ 1\,1\,1\,1\,0\,0\,0\,0 \\ 1\,1\,0\,0 \\ 1\,1\,0\,0 \\ 1\,1\,0\,0 \\ 1\,1\,0\,0 \end{bmatrix} \xrightarrow{\ Lemma\ 5\ }
\begin{bmatrix} 1\,1\,1\,1\,1\,1\,1\,1 \\ 1\,1\,1\,1\,1\,1\,1\,1 \\ 1\,1\,1\,1\,0\,0\,0\,0 \\ 1\,1\,1\,1\,0\,0\,0\,0 \\ 1\,1\,0\,0\,1\,1\,0\,0 \\ 1\,1\,0\,0\,x\,y \\ 1\,1\,0\,0 \\ 1\,1\,0\,0 \end{bmatrix}
$$

$$
\xrightarrow{\ Lemma\ 6\ }
\begin{bmatrix} 1\,1\,1\,1\,1\,1\,1\,1 \\ 1\,1\,1\,1\,1\,1\,1\,1 \\ 1\,1\,1\,1\,0\,0\,0\,0 \\ 1\,1\,1\,1\,0\,0\,0\,0 \\ 1\,1\,0\,0\,1\,1\,0\,0 \\ 1\,1\,0\,0\,1\,1 \\ 1\,1\,0\,0\,0\,0 \\ 1\,1\,0\,0\,0\,0 \end{bmatrix}
\xrightarrow{\ Lemma\ 5\ }
\begin{bmatrix} 1\,1\,1\,1\,1\,1\,1\,1 \\ 1\,1\,1\,1\,1\,1\,1\,1 \\ 1\,1\,1\,1\,0\,0\,0\,0 \\ 1\,1\,1\,1\,0\,0\,0\,0 \\ 1\,1\,0\,0\,1\,1\,0\,0 \\ 1\,1\,0\,0\,1\,1\,0\,0 \\ 1\,1\,0\,0\,0\,0\,1\,1 \\ 1\,1\,0\,0\,0\,0\,1\,1 \end{bmatrix} = C.
$$

Subcase 1.1.2. $\|u_1\| = 4$. Let (x, y) be a pair of the entries in the i-th column of rows 2 and 3 as shown below, for $2 \le i < 8$. By Lemma 6 with u_1, $x = y$. Hence $u_2^\dagger = u_3^\dagger$.

$$
U = \begin{bmatrix} 1\,1\,1\,1\,1\,1\,1\,1 \\ 1\,1\,1\,1\,1\,1\,1\,1 \\ 1\,1\,x \\ 1\,1\,y \\ 1\,0 \\ 1\,0 \\ 1\,0 \\ 1\,0 \end{bmatrix}.
$$

Subcase 1.1.2.1. $\|u_2^\dagger\| = 8$, then

$$
U = \begin{bmatrix} 1\,1\,1\,1\,1\,1\,1\,1 \\ 1\,1\,1\,1\,1\,1\,1\,1 \\ 1\,1\,1\,1\,1\,1\,1\,1 \\ 1\,1\,1\,1\,1\,1\,1\,1 \\ 1\,0 \\ 1\,0 \\ 1\,0 \\ 1\,0 \end{bmatrix} \xrightarrow{\ Lemma\ 5\ }
\begin{bmatrix} 1\,1\,1\,1\,1\,1\,1\,1 \\ 1\,1\,1\,1\,1\,1\,1\,1 \\ 1\,1\,1\,1\,1\,1\,1\,1 \\ 1\,1\,1\,1\,1\,1\,1\,1 \\ 1\,0\,1\,1\,1\,0\,0\,0 \\ 1\,0 \\ 1\,0 \\ 1\,0 \end{bmatrix} \xrightarrow{\ Lemma\ 5\ }
$$

$$
\begin{bmatrix}
1\,1\,1\,1\,1\,1\,1\,1 \\
1\,1\,1\,1\,1\,1\,1\,1 \\
1\,1\,1\,1\,1\,1\,1\,1 \\
1\,1\,1\,1\,1\,1\,1\,1 \\
1\,0\,1\,1\,1\,0\,0\,0 \\
1\,0\,1\,1\,1 \\
1\,0\,1\,1\,1 \\
1\,0\,1\,1\,1
\end{bmatrix}
\xrightarrow{Lemma\ 5}
\begin{bmatrix}
1\,1\,1\,1\,1\,1\,1\,1 \\
1\,1\,1\,1\,1\,1\,1\,1 \\
1\,1\,1\,1\,1\,1\,1\,1 \\
1\,1\,1\,1\,1\,1\,1\,1 \\
1\,0\,1\,1\,1\,0\,0\,0 \\
1\,0\,1\,1\,1\,0\,0\,0 \\
1\,0\,1\,1\,1\,0\,0\,0 \\
1\,0\,1\,1\,1\,0\,0\,0
\end{bmatrix}
= B.
$$

Subcase 1.1.2.2. $\|u_2^\dagger\| = 4$. By Lemma 6 with row 3, for u_2 and u_3, precisely one of them has hamming weight 8, and the other has hamming weight 4. Up to column permutation, let $\|u_2\| = 8$ and $\|u_3\| = 4$.

$$
U =
\begin{bmatrix}
1\,1\,1\,1\,1\,1\,1\,1 \\
1\,1\,1\,1\,1\,1\,1\,1 \\
1\,1\,1\,1\,0\,0\,0\,0 \\
1\,1\,1\,1\,0\,0\,0\,0 \\
1\,0\,1\,0 \\
1\,0\,1\,0 \\
1\,0\,1\,0 \\
1\,0\,1\,0
\end{bmatrix}
\xrightarrow{Lemma\ 5}
\begin{bmatrix}
1\,1\,1\,1\,1\,1\,1\,1 \\
1\,1\,1\,1\,1\,1\,1\,1 \\
1\,1\,1\,1\,0\,0\,0\,0 \\
1\,1\,1\,1\,0\,0\,0\,0 \\
1\,0\,1\,0\,1\,1\,0\,0 \\
1\,0\,1\,0\,1 \\
1\,0\,1\,0\,0 \\
1\,0\,1\,0\,0
\end{bmatrix}
\xrightarrow{Lemma\ 6}
\begin{bmatrix}
1\,1\,1\,1\,1\,1\,1\,1 \\
1\,1\,1\,1\,1\,1\,1\,1 \\
1\,1\,1\,1\,0\,0\,0\,0 \\
1\,1\,1\,1\,0\,0\,0\,0 \\
1\,0\,1\,0\,1\,1\,0\,0 \\
1\,0\,1\,0\,1\,1 \\
1\,0\,1\,0\,0 \\
1\,0\,1\,0\,0
\end{bmatrix}
$$

$$
\xrightarrow{Lemma\ 5}
\begin{bmatrix}
1\,1\,1\,1\,1\,1\,1\,1 \\
1\,1\,1\,1\,1\,1\,1\,1 \\
1\,1\,1\,1\,0\,0\,0\,0 \\
1\,1\,1\,1\,0\,0\,0\,0 \\
1\,0\,1\,0\,1\,1\,0\,0 \\
1\,0\,1\,0\,1\,1\,0\,0 \\
1\,0\,1\,0\,0\,0 \\
1\,0\,1\,0\,0\,0
\end{bmatrix}
\xrightarrow{Lemma\ 5}
\begin{bmatrix}
1\,1\,1\,1\,1\,1\,1\,1 \\
1\,1\,1\,1\,1\,1\,1\,1 \\
1\,1\,1\,1\,0\,0\,0\,0 \\
1\,1\,1\,1\,0\,0\,0\,0 \\
1\,0\,1\,0\,1\,1\,0\,0 \\
1\,0\,1\,0\,1\,1\,0\,0 \\
1\,0\,1\,0\,0\,0\,1\,1 \\
1\,0\,1\,0\,0\,0\,1\,1
\end{bmatrix}
= C.
$$

Subcase 1.2. $\|u_0\| = 4$. Let (x, y) be a pair of the entries in the i-th column of rows 2 and 3 as shown below, for $1 \le i < 8$. By Lemma 6 with u_0, $x = y$. Hence $u_2^\dagger = u_3^\dagger$.

$$
U =
\begin{bmatrix}
1\,1\,1\,1\,1\,1\,1\,1 \\
1\,1\,1\,1\,1\,1\,1\,1 \\
1\ x \\
1\ y \\
0 \\
0 \\
0 \\
0
\end{bmatrix}
.
$$

Subcase 1.2.1. $\|u_2^\dagger\| = 8$. By Lemma 5, $\|u_4^\dagger\| = 4$ or $\|u_4^\dagger\| = 0$. Then we have

$$U = \begin{bmatrix} 1\,1\,1\,1\,1\,1\,1\,1 \\ 1\,1\,1\,1\,1\,1\,1\,1 \\ 1\,1\,1\,1\,1\,1\,1\,1 \\ 1\,1\,1\,1\,1\,1\,1\,1 \\ 0 \\ 0 \\ 0 \\ 0 \end{bmatrix}.$$

Subcase 1.2.1.1. $\|u_4^\dagger\| = 4$, then

$$U = \begin{bmatrix} 1\,1\,1\,1\,1\,1\,1\,1 \\ 1\,1\,1\,1\,1\,1\,1\,1 \\ 1\,1\,1\,1\,1\,1\,1\,1 \\ 1\,1\,1\,1\,1\,1\,1\,1 \\ 0\,1\,1\,1\,1\,0\,0\,0 \\ 0 \\ 0 \\ 0 \end{bmatrix} \xrightarrow{\text{Lemma 5}} \begin{bmatrix} 1\,1\,1\,1\,1\,1\,1\,1 \\ 1\,1\,1\,1\,1\,1\,1\,1 \\ 1\,1\,1\,1\,1\,1\,1\,1 \\ 1\,1\,1\,1\,1\,1\,1\,1 \\ 0\,1\,1\,1\,1\,0\,0\,0 \\ 0\,1\,1\,1\,1\,0\,0\,0 \\ 0\,1\,1\,1\,1\,0\,0\,0 \\ 0\,1\,1\,1\,1\,0\,0\,0 \end{bmatrix} = B.$$

Subcase 1.2.1.2. $\|u_4^\dagger\| = 0$, then

$$U = \begin{bmatrix} 1\,1\,1\,1\,1\,1\,1\,1 \\ 1\,1\,1\,1\,1\,1\,1\,1 \\ 1\,1\,1\,1\,1\,1\,1\,1 \\ 1\,1\,1\,1\,1\,1\,1\,1 \\ 0\,0\,0\,0\,0\,0\,0\,0 \\ 0 \\ 0 \\ 0 \end{bmatrix} \xrightarrow{\text{Lemma 5}} \begin{bmatrix} 1\,1\,1\,1\,1\,1\,1\,1 \\ 1\,1\,1\,1\,1\,1\,1\,1 \\ 1\,1\,1\,1\,1\,1\,1\,1 \\ 1\,1\,1\,1\,1\,1\,1\,1 \\ 0\,0\,0\,0\,0\,0\,0\,0 \\ 0\,0\,0\,0\,0\,0\,0\,0 \\ 0\,0\,0\,0\,0\,0\,0\,0 \\ 0\,0\,0\,0\,0\,0\,0\,0 \end{bmatrix} = K.$$

Subcase 1.2.2. $\|u_2^\dagger\| = 4$, then the binary matrix is shown below. By Lemma 6, there can be two cases: precisely two of $\{u_1, u_2, u_3\}$ have hamming weight 8, or all of $\{u_1, u_2, u_3\}$ have hamming weight 4.

$$U = \begin{bmatrix} 1\,1\,1\,1\,1\,1\,1\,1 \\ 1\,1\,1\,1\,1\,1\,1\,1 \\ 1\,1\,1\,1\,0\,0\,0\,0 \\ 1\,1\,1\,1\,0\,0\,0\,0 \\ 0 \\ 0 \\ 0 \\ 0 \end{bmatrix}.$$

Subcase 1.2.2.1. Up to column permutation, let $\|u_1\| = \|u_2\| = 8$ and $\|u_3\| = 4$.

$$U = \begin{bmatrix} 1\,1\,1\,1\,1\,1\,1\,1 \\ 1\,1\,1\,1\,1\,1\,1\,1 \\ 1\,1\,1\,1\,0\,0\,0\,0 \\ 1\,1\,1\,1\,0\,0\,0\,0 \\ 0\,1\,1\,0 \\ 0\,1\,1\,0 \\ 0\,1\,1\,0 \\ 0\,1\,1\,0 \end{bmatrix} \xrightarrow{Lemma\ 5} \begin{bmatrix} 1\,1\,1\,1\,1\,1\,1\,1 \\ 1\,1\,1\,1\,1\,1\,1\,1 \\ 1\,1\,1\,1\,0\,0\,0\,0 \\ 1\,1\,1\,1\,0\,0\,0\,0 \\ 0\,1\,1\,0\,1\,1\,0\,0 \\ 0\,1\,1\,0\,1 \\ 0\,1\,1\,0\,0 \\ 0\,1\,1\,0\,0 \end{bmatrix} \xrightarrow{Lemma\ 6} \begin{bmatrix} 1\,1\,1\,1\,1\,1\,1\,1 \\ 1\,1\,1\,1\,1\,1\,1\,1 \\ 1\,1\,1\,1\,0\,0\,0\,0 \\ 1\,1\,1\,1\,0\,0\,0\,0 \\ 0\,1\,1\,0\,1\,1\,0\,0 \\ 0\,1\,1\,0\,1\,1 \\ 0\,1\,1\,0\,0 \\ 0\,1\,1\,0\,0 \end{bmatrix}$$

$$\xrightarrow{Lemma\ 5} \begin{bmatrix} 1\,1\,1\,1\,1\,1\,1\,1 \\ 1\,1\,1\,1\,1\,1\,1\,1 \\ 1\,1\,1\,1\,0\,0\,0\,0 \\ 1\,1\,1\,1\,0\,0\,0\,0 \\ 0\,1\,1\,0\,1\,1\,0\,0 \\ 0\,1\,1\,0\,1\,1\,0\,0 \\ 0\,1\,1\,0\,0\,0 \\ 0\,1\,1\,0\,0\,0 \end{bmatrix} \xrightarrow{Lemma\ 5} \begin{bmatrix} 1\,1\,1\,1\,1\,1\,1\,1 \\ 1\,1\,1\,1\,1\,1\,1\,1 \\ 1\,1\,1\,1\,0\,0\,0\,0 \\ 1\,1\,1\,1\,0\,0\,0\,0 \\ 0\,1\,1\,0\,1\,1\,0\,0 \\ 0\,1\,1\,0\,1\,1\,0\,0 \\ 0\,1\,1\,0\,0\,0\,1\,1 \\ 0\,1\,1\,0\,0\,0\,1\,1 \end{bmatrix} = C.$$

Subcase 1.2.2.2. $\|u_1\| = \|u_2\| = \|u_3\| = 4$.

$$U = \begin{bmatrix} 1\,1\,1\,1\,1\,1\,1\,1 \\ 1\,1\,1\,1\,1\,1\,1\,1 \\ 1\,1\,1\,1\,0\,0\,0\,0 \\ 1\,1\,1\,1\,0\,0\,0\,0 \\ 0\,0\,0\,0 \\ 0\,0\,0\,0 \\ 0\,0\,0\,0 \\ 0\,0\,0\,0 \end{bmatrix} \xrightarrow{Lemma\ 5} \begin{bmatrix} 1\,1\,1\,1\,1\,1\,1\,1 \\ 1\,1\,1\,1\,1\,1\,1\,1 \\ 1\,1\,1\,1\,0\,0\,0\,0 \\ 1\,1\,1\,1\,0\,0\,0\,0 \\ 0\,0\,0\,0\,1 \\ 0\,0\,0\,0\,1 \\ 0\,0\,0\,0\,0 \\ 0\,0\,0\,0\,0 \end{bmatrix} \xrightarrow{Lemma\ 5} \begin{bmatrix} 1\,1\,1\,1\,1\,1\,1\,1 \\ 1\,1\,1\,1\,1\,1\,1\,1 \\ 1\,1\,1\,1\,0\,0\,0\,0 \\ 1\,1\,1\,1\,0\,0\,0\,0 \\ 0\,0\,0\,0\,1\,1\,1\,1 \\ 0\,0\,0\,0\,1\,1\,1\,1 \\ 0\,0\,0\,0\,0\,0\,0\,0 \\ 0\,0\,0\,0\,0\,0\,0\,0 \end{bmatrix} = E.$$

Case 2. $\|u_0^\dagger\| = \|u_1^\dagger\| = 4$.

Subcase 2.1. $\|u_0\| = 8$.

Subcase 2.1.1. $\|u_1\| = 8$.

Subcase 2.1.1.1. $\|u_2\| = 8$, then

$$U = \begin{bmatrix} 1\,1\,1\,1\,0\,0\,0\,0 \\ 1\,1\,1\,1\,0\,0\,0\,0 \\ 1\,1\,1 \\ 1\,1\,1 \\ 1\,1\,1 \\ 1\,1\,1 \\ 1\,1\,1 \\ 1\,1\,1 \end{bmatrix} \xrightarrow{Lemma\ 6} \begin{bmatrix} 1\,1\,1\,1\,0\,0\,0\,0 \\ 1\,1\,1\,1\,0\,0\,0\,0 \\ 1\,1\,1\,1 \\ 1\,1\,1\,1 \\ 1\,1\,1\,1 \\ 1\,1\,1\,1 \\ 1\,1\,1\,1 \\ 1\,1\,1\,1 \end{bmatrix}.$$

Subcase 2.1.1.1.1. $\|u_2^\dagger\| = 8$, then

$$U = \begin{bmatrix} 1\,1\,1\,1\,0\,0\,0\,0 \\ 1\,1\,1\,1\,0\,0\,0\,0 \\ 1\,1\,1\,1\,1\,1\,1\,1 \\ 1\,1\,1\,1 \\ 1\,1\,1\,1 \\ 1\,1\,1\,1 \\ 1\,1\,1\,1 \\ 1\,1\,1\,1 \end{bmatrix} \xrightarrow{\textit{Lemma 5}} \begin{bmatrix} 1\,1\,1\,1\,0\,0\,0\,0 \\ 1\,1\,1\,1\,0\,0\,0\,0 \\ 1\,1\,1\,1\,1\,1\,1\,1 \\ 1\,1\,1\,1\,1 \\ 1\,1\,1\,1\,1 \\ 1\,1\,1\,1\,1 \\ 1\,1\,1\,1\,0 \\ 1\,1\,1\,1\,0 \end{bmatrix} \xrightarrow{\textit{Lemma 5}} \begin{bmatrix} 1\,1\,1\,1\,0\,0\,0\,0 \\ 1\,1\,1\,1\,0\,0\,0\,0 \\ 1\,1\,1\,1\,1\,1\,1\,1 \\ 1\,1\,1\,1\,1\,1\,1\,1 \\ 1\,1\,1\,1\,1\,1\,1\,1 \\ 1\,1\,1\,1\,1\,1\,1\,1 \\ 1\,1\,1\,1\,0\,0\,0\,0 \\ 1\,1\,1\,1\,0\,0\,0\,0 \end{bmatrix} = B.$$

Subcase 2.1.1.1.2. $\|u_2^\dagger\| = 4$. By Lemma 5, there can be two cases: precisely four of $\{u_3^\dagger, u_4^\dagger, u_5^\dagger, u_6^\dagger, u_7^\dagger\}$ have hamming weight 8, or all of $\{u_3^\dagger, u_4^\dagger, u_5^\dagger, u_6^\dagger, u_7^\dagger\}$ have hamming weight 4.

Subcase 2.1.1.1.2.1. Up to row permutation, $\|u_3^\dagger\| = \|u_4^\dagger\| = \|u_5^\dagger\| = \|u_6^\dagger\| = 8$.

$$U = \begin{bmatrix} 1\,1\,1\,1\,0\,0\,0\,0 \\ 1\,1\,1\,1\,0\,0\,0\,0 \\ 1\,1\,1\,1\,0\,0\,0\,0 \\ 1\,1\,1\,1\,1\,1\,1\,1 \\ 1\,1\,1\,1\,1\,1\,1\,1 \\ 1\,1\,1\,1\,1\,1\,1\,1 \\ 1\,1\,1\,1\,1\,1\,1\,1 \\ 1\,1\,1\,1\,0\,0\,0\,0 \end{bmatrix} = B.$$

Subcase 2.1.1.1.2.2. $\|u_3^\dagger\| = \|u_4^\dagger\| = \|u_5^\dagger\| = \|u_6^\dagger\| = \|u_7^\dagger\| = 4$.

$$U = \begin{bmatrix} 1\,1\,1\,1\,0\,0\,0\,0 \\ 1\,1\,1\,1\,0\,0\,0\,0 \\ 1\,1\,1\,1\,0\,0\,0\,0 \\ 1\,1\,1\,1\,0\,0\,0\,0 \\ 1\,1\,1\,1\,0\,0\,0\,0 \\ 1\,1\,1\,1\,0\,0\,0\,0 \\ 1\,1\,1\,1\,0\,0\,0\,0 \\ 1\,1\,1\,1\,0\,0\,0\,0 \end{bmatrix} = K^\mathsf{T}.$$

Subcase 2.1.1.2. $\|u_2\| = 4$. Let (x, y) be a pair of the entries in the i-th column of rows 2 and 3 as shown below, for $3 \le i < 8$. By Lemma 6 with u_3, $x = y$. Hence $u_2^\dagger = u_3^\dagger$.

$$U = \begin{bmatrix} 1\,1\,1\,1\,0\,0\,0\,0 \\ 1\,1\,1\,1\,0\,0\,0\,0 \\ 1\,1\,1 \\ 1\,1\,1 \\ 1\,1\,0 \\ 1\,1\,0 \\ 1\,1\,0 \\ 1\,1\,0 \end{bmatrix} \xrightarrow{\textit{Lemma 6}} \begin{bmatrix} 1\,1\,1\,1\,0\,0\,0\,0 \\ 1\,1\,1\,1\,0\,0\,0\,0 \\ 1\,1\,1\,1\,x \\ 1\,1\,1\,1\,y \\ 1\,1\,0\,0 \\ 1\,1\,0\,0 \\ 1\,1\,0\,0 \\ 1\,1\,0\,0 \end{bmatrix}.$$

Subcase 2.1.1.2.1. $\|u_2^\dagger\| = 8$, then

$$
\begin{bmatrix}
1\,1\,1\,1\,0\,0\,0\,0 \\
1\,1\,1\,1\,0\,0\,0\,0 \\
1\,1\,1\,1\,1\,1\,1\,1 \\
1\,1\,1\,1\,1\,1\,1\,1 \\
1\,1\,0\,0 \\
1\,1\,0\,0 \\
1\,1\,0\,0 \\
1\,1\,0\,0
\end{bmatrix}
\xrightarrow{Lemma\ 5}
\begin{bmatrix}
1\,1\,1\,1\,0\,0\,0\,0 \\
1\,1\,1\,1\,0\,0\,0\,0 \\
1\,1\,1\,1\,1\,1\,1\,1 \\
1\,1\,1\,1\,1\,1\,1\,1 \\
1\,1\,0\,0\,1\,1\,0\,0 \\
1\,1\,0\,0\,1 \\
1\,1\,0\,0\,0 \\
1\,1\,0\,0\,0
\end{bmatrix}
\xrightarrow{Lemma\ 6}
\begin{bmatrix}
1\,1\,1\,1\,0\,0\,0\,0 \\
1\,1\,1\,1\,0\,0\,0\,0 \\
1\,1\,1\,1\,1\,1\,1\,1 \\
1\,1\,1\,1\,1\,1\,1\,1 \\
1\,1\,0\,0\,1\,1\,0\,0 \\
1\,1\,0\,0\,1\,1 \\
1\,1\,0\,0\,0 \\
1\,1\,0\,0\,0
\end{bmatrix}
$$

$$
\xrightarrow{Lemma\ 5}
\begin{bmatrix}
1\,1\,1\,1\,0\,0\,0\,0 \\
1\,1\,1\,1\,0\,0\,0\,0 \\
1\,1\,1\,1\,1\,1\,1\,1 \\
1\,1\,1\,1\,1\,1\,1\,1 \\
1\,1\,0\,0\,1\,1\,0\,0 \\
1\,1\,0\,0\,1\,1\,0\,0 \\
1\,1\,0\,0\,0\,0 \\
1\,1\,0\,0\,0\,0
\end{bmatrix}
\xrightarrow{Lemma\ 5}
\begin{bmatrix}
1\,1\,1\,1\,0\,0\,0\,0 \\
1\,1\,1\,1\,0\,0\,0\,0 \\
1\,1\,1\,1\,1\,1\,1\,1 \\
1\,1\,1\,1\,1\,1\,1\,1 \\
1\,1\,0\,0\,1\,1\,0\,0 \\
1\,1\,0\,0\,1\,1\,0\,0 \\
1\,1\,0\,0\,0\,0\,1\,1 \\
1\,1\,0\,0\,0\,0\,1\,1
\end{bmatrix}
= C.
$$

Subcase 2.1.1.2.2. $\|u_2^\dagger\| = 4$, then

$$
\begin{bmatrix}
1\,1\,1\,1\,0\,0\,0\,0 \\
1\,1\,1\,1\,0\,0\,0\,0 \\
1\,1\,1\,1\,0\,0\,0\,0 \\
1\,1\,1\,1\,0\,0\,0\,0 \\
1\,1\,0\,0 \\
1\,1\,0\,0 \\
1\,1\,0\,0 \\
1\,1\,0\,0
\end{bmatrix}
\xrightarrow{Lemma\ 5}
\begin{bmatrix}
1\,1\,1\,1\,0\,0\,0\,0 \\
1\,1\,1\,1\,0\,0\,0\,0 \\
1\,1\,1\,1\,0\,0\,0\,0 \\
1\,1\,1\,1\,0\,0\,0\,0 \\
1\,1\,0\,0\,1\,1\,0\,0 \\
1\,1\,0\,0\,1\,1\,0\,0 \\
1\,1\,0\,0\,1\,1\,0\,0 \\
1\,1\,0\,0\,1\,1\,0\,0
\end{bmatrix}
= D.
$$

Subcase 2.1.2. $\|u_1\| = 4$. Let x, y, z, w be the entries in U as shown below. By Lemma 6 with row 1, $x = y$ and $z = w$. By Lemma 6 with column 1, $x = z$ and $y = w$. Hence $x = y = z = w$. Moreover, since (x, z) can be any pair of the entries coming from any column i of rows 2 and 3, for $2 \le i < 8$, we have $u_2^\dagger = u_3^\dagger$.

$$
U =
\begin{bmatrix}
1\,1\,1\,1\,0\,0\,0\,0 \\
1\,1\,1\,1\,0\,0\,0\,0 \\
1\,1\,x\,y \\
1\,1\,z\,w \\
1\,0 \\
1\,0 \\
1\,0 \\
1\,0
\end{bmatrix}
$$

Subcase 2.1.2.1. $x = y = z = w = 1$, then

$$U = \begin{bmatrix} 1\,1\,1\,1\,0\,0\,0\,0 \\ 1\,1\,1\,1\,0\,0\,0\,0 \\ 1\,1\,1\,1 \\ 1\,1\,1\,1 \\ 1\,0 \\ 1\,0 \\ 1\,0 \\ 1\,0 \end{bmatrix} \xrightarrow{\textit{Lemma 6}} \begin{bmatrix} 1\,1\,1\,1\,0\,0\,0\,0 \\ 1\,1\,1\,1\,0\,0\,0\,0 \\ 1\,1\,1\,1 \\ 1\,1\,1\,1 \\ 1\,0\,1\,0 \\ 1\,0 \\ 1\,0 \\ 1\,0 \end{bmatrix} \xrightarrow{\textit{Lemma 5}} \begin{bmatrix} 1\,1\,1\,1\,0\,0\,0\,0 \\ 1\,1\,1\,1\,0\,0\,0\,0 \\ 1\,1\,1\,1 \\ 1\,1\,1\,1 \\ 1\,0\,1\,0 \\ 1\,0\,1\,0 \\ 1\,0\,1\,0 \\ 1\,0\,1\,0 \end{bmatrix}$$

Subcase 2.1.2.1.1. $\|u_2^\dagger\| = 8$, then

$$U = \begin{bmatrix} 1\,1\,1\,1\,0\,0\,0\,0 \\ 1\,1\,1\,1\,0\,0\,0\,0 \\ 1\,1\,1\,1\,1\,1\,1\,1 \\ 1\,1\,1\,1\,1\,1\,1\,1 \\ 1\,0\,1\,0 \\ 1\,0\,1\,0 \\ 1\,0\,1\,0 \\ 1\,0\,1\,0 \end{bmatrix} \xrightarrow{\textit{Lemma 5}} \begin{bmatrix} 1\,1\,1\,1\,0\,0\,0\,0 \\ 1\,1\,1\,1\,0\,0\,0\,0 \\ 1\,1\,1\,1\,1\,1\,1\,1 \\ 1\,1\,1\,1\,1\,1\,1\,1 \\ 1\,0\,1\,0\,1\,1\,0\,0 \\ 1\,0\,1\,0\,1 \\ 1\,0\,1\,0\,0 \\ 1\,0\,1\,0\,0 \end{bmatrix} \xrightarrow{\textit{Lemma 6}} \begin{bmatrix} 1\,1\,1\,1\,0\,0\,0\,0 \\ 1\,1\,1\,1\,0\,0\,0\,0 \\ 1\,1\,1\,1\,1\,1\,1\,1 \\ 1\,1\,1\,1\,1\,1\,1\,1 \\ 1\,0\,1\,0\,1\,1\,0\,0 \\ 1\,0\,1\,0\,1\,1 \\ 1\,0\,1\,0\,0 \\ 1\,0\,1\,0\,0 \end{bmatrix}$$

$$\xrightarrow{\textit{Lemma 5}} \begin{bmatrix} 1\,1\,1\,1\,0\,0\,0\,0 \\ 1\,1\,1\,1\,0\,0\,0\,0 \\ 1\,1\,1\,1\,1\,1\,1\,1 \\ 1\,1\,1\,1\,1\,1\,1\,1 \\ 1\,0\,1\,0\,1\,1\,0\,0 \\ 1\,0\,1\,0\,1\,1\,0\,0 \\ 1\,0\,1\,0\,0\,0 \\ 1\,0\,1\,0\,0\,0 \end{bmatrix} \xrightarrow{\textit{Lemma 5}} \begin{bmatrix} 1\,1\,1\,1\,0\,0\,0\,0 \\ 1\,1\,1\,1\,0\,0\,0\,0 \\ 1\,1\,1\,1\,1\,1\,1\,1 \\ 1\,1\,1\,1\,1\,1\,1\,1 \\ 1\,0\,1\,0\,1\,1\,0\,0 \\ 1\,0\,1\,0\,1\,1\,0\,0 \\ 1\,0\,1\,0\,0\,0\,1\,1 \\ 1\,0\,1\,0\,0\,0\,1\,1 \end{bmatrix} = C.$$

Subcase 2.1.2.1.2. $\|u_2^\dagger\| = 4$, then

$$U = \begin{bmatrix} 1\,1\,1\,1\,0\,0\,0\,0 \\ 1\,1\,1\,1\,0\,0\,0\,0 \\ 1\,1\,1\,1\,0\,0\,0\,0 \\ 1\,1\,1\,1\,0\,0\,0\,0 \\ 1\,0\,1\,0 \\ 1\,0\,1\,0 \\ 1\,0\,1\,0 \\ 1\,0\,1\,0 \end{bmatrix} \xrightarrow{\textit{Lemma 5}} \begin{bmatrix} 1\,1\,1\,1\,0\,0\,0\,0 \\ 1\,1\,1\,1\,0\,0\,0\,0 \\ 1\,1\,1\,1\,0\,0\,0\,0 \\ 1\,1\,1\,1\,0\,0\,0\,0 \\ 1\,0\,1\,0\,1\,1\,0\,0 \\ 1\,0\,1\,0\,1 \\ 1\,0\,1\,0\,1 \\ 1\,0\,1\,0\,1 \end{bmatrix} \xrightarrow{\textit{Lemma 6}}$$

$$\begin{bmatrix} 1\,1\,1\,1\,0\,0\,0\,0 \\ 1\,1\,1\,1\,0\,0\,0\,0 \\ 1\,1\,1\,1\,0\,0\,0\,0 \\ 1\,1\,1\,1\,0\,0\,0\,0 \\ 1\,0\,1\,0\,1\,1\,0\,0 \\ 1\,0\,1\,0\,1\,1 \\ 1\,0\,1\,0\,1\,1 \\ 1\,0\,1\,0\,1\,1 \end{bmatrix} \xrightarrow{\;Lemma\;5\;} \begin{bmatrix} 1\,1\,1\,1\,0\,0\,0\,0 \\ 1\,1\,1\,1\,0\,0\,0\,0 \\ 1\,1\,1\,1\,0\,0\,0\,0 \\ 1\,1\,1\,1\,0\,0\,0\,0 \\ 1\,0\,1\,0\,1\,1\,0\,0 \\ 1\,0\,1\,0\,1\,1\,0\,0 \\ 1\,0\,1\,0\,1\,1\,0\,0 \\ 1\,0\,1\,0\,1\,1\,0\,0 \end{bmatrix} = D.$$

Subcase 2.1.2.2. $x = y = z = w = 0$, then we have what follows.

$$U = \begin{bmatrix} 1\,1\,1\,1\,0\,0\,0\,0 \\ 1\,1\,1\,1\,0\,0\,0\,0 \\ 1\,1\,0\,0 \\ 1\,1\,0\,0 \\ 1\,0 \\ 1\,0 \\ 1\,0 \\ 1\,0 \end{bmatrix} \xrightarrow{\;Lemma\;5\;} \begin{bmatrix} 1\,1\,1\,1\,0\,0\,0\,0 \\ 1\,1\,1\,1\,0\,0\,0\,0 \\ 1\,1\,0\,0\,1\,1\,0\,0 \\ 1\,1\,0\,0\,1\,1\,0\,0 \\ 1\,0\,1 \\ 1\,0\,1 \\ 1\,0\,0 \\ 1\,0\,0 \end{bmatrix} \xrightarrow{\;Lemma\;6\;}$$

Let (x, y) be a pair of the entries in the i-th column of rows 4 and 5 as shown below, for $4 \le i < 8$. By Lemma 6 with u_2, $x = y$. Hence $u_4^\dagger = u_5^\dagger$.

$$\begin{bmatrix} 1\,1\,1\,1\,0\,0\,0\,0 \\ 1\,1\,1\,1\,0\,0\,0\,0 \\ 1\,1\,0\,0\,1\,1\,0\,0 \\ 1\,1\,0\,0\,1\,1\,0\,0 \\ 1\,0\,1\,0\,x \\ 1\,0\,1\,0\,y \\ 1\,0\,0\,1 \\ 1\,0\,0\,1 \end{bmatrix} \xrightarrow{\;Lemma\;6\;} \begin{bmatrix} 1\,1\,1\,1\,0\,0\,0\,0 \\ 1\,1\,1\,1\,0\,0\,0\,0 \\ 1\,1\,0\,0\,1\,1\,0\,0 \\ 1\,1\,0\,0\,1\,1\,0\,0 \\ 1\,0\,1\,0\,1\,0\,1\,0 \\ 1\,0\,1\,0\,1\,0\,1\,0 \\ 1\,0\,0\,1 \\ 1\,0\,0\,1 \end{bmatrix} \xrightarrow{\;Lemma\;5\;} \begin{bmatrix} 1\,1\,1\,1\,0\,0\,0\,0 \\ 1\,1\,1\,1\,0\,0\,0\,0 \\ 1\,1\,0\,0\,1\,1\,0\,0 \\ 1\,1\,0\,0\,1\,1\,0\,0 \\ 1\,0\,1\,0\,1\,0\,1\,0 \\ 1\,0\,1\,0\,1\,0\,1\,0 \\ 1\,0\,0\,1\,0\,1\,1\,0 \\ 1\,0\,0\,1\,0\,1\,1\,0 \end{bmatrix} = F.$$

Subcase 2.2. $\|u_0\| = 4$. Let (x, y) be a pair of the entries in the i-th column of rows 2 and 3 as shown below, for $1 \le i < 8$. By Lemma 6 with u_0, $x = y$. Hence $u_2^\dagger = u_3^\dagger$. By Lemma 6 with $u_0^\dagger$, there must be oddly many 1's in $\{x, z, w\}$. Up to column permutation, consider the following two cases: $x = z = w = 1$ or $x = 1$, $z = w = 0$.

$$U = \begin{bmatrix} 1\,1\,1\,1\,0\,0\,0\,0 \\ 1\,1\,1\,1\,0\,0\,0\,0 \\ 1\,x\,z\,w \\ 1\,y \\ 0 \\ 0 \\ 0 \\ 0 \end{bmatrix}.$$

Subcase 2.2.1. $x = z = w = 1$, we have

Subcase 2.2.1.1. $\|u_2^\dagger\| = 8$, then

$$U = \begin{bmatrix} 1\,1\,1\,1\,0\,0\,0\,0 \\ 1\,1\,1\,1\,0\,0\,0\,0 \\ 1\,1\,1\,1\,1\,1\,1\,1 \\ 1\,1\,1\,1\,1\,1\,1\,1 \\ 0 \\ 0 \\ 0 \\ 0 \end{bmatrix}.$$

By Lemma 6 with $u_0^\dagger$, there must be evenly many columns among $\{u_0, u_1, u_2, u_3\}$ that have hamming weight 8. Since $\|u_0\| = 4$, up to column permutation, there can be two cases.

Subcase 2.2.1.1.1. $\|u_1\| = \|u_2\| = 8$ and $\|u_3\| = 4$.

$$U = \begin{bmatrix} 1\,1\,1\,1\,0\,0\,0\,0 \\ 1\,1\,1\,1\,0\,0\,0\,0 \\ 1\,1\,1\,1\,1\,1\,1\,1 \\ 1\,1\,1\,1\,1\,1\,1\,1 \\ 0\,1\,1\,0 \\ 0\,1\,1\,0 \\ 0\,1\,1\,0 \\ 0\,1\,1\,0 \end{bmatrix} \xrightarrow{\textit{Lemma 5}} \begin{bmatrix} 1\,1\,1\,1\,0\,0\,0\,0 \\ 1\,1\,1\,1\,0\,0\,0\,0 \\ 1\,1\,1\,1\,1\,1\,1\,1 \\ 1\,1\,1\,1\,1\,1\,1\,1 \\ 0\,1\,1\,0\,1\,1\,0\,0 \\ 0\,1\,1\,0\,1 \\ 0\,1\,1\,0\,0 \\ 0\,1\,1\,0\,0 \end{bmatrix} \xrightarrow{\textit{Lemma 6}} \begin{bmatrix} 1\,1\,1\,1\,0\,0\,0\,0 \\ 1\,1\,1\,1\,0\,0\,0\,0 \\ 1\,1\,1\,1\,1\,1\,1\,1 \\ 1\,1\,1\,1\,1\,1\,1\,1 \\ 0\,1\,1\,0\,1\,1\,0\,0 \\ 0\,1\,1\,0\,1\,1 \\ 0\,1\,1\,0\,0 \\ 0\,1\,1\,0\,0 \end{bmatrix}$$

$$\xrightarrow{\textit{Lemma 5}} \begin{bmatrix} 1\,1\,1\,1\,0\,0\,0\,0 \\ 1\,1\,1\,1\,0\,0\,0\,0 \\ 1\,1\,1\,1\,1\,1\,1\,1 \\ 1\,1\,1\,1\,1\,1\,1\,1 \\ 0\,1\,1\,0\,1\,1\,0\,0 \\ 0\,1\,1\,0\,1\,1\,0\,0 \\ 0\,1\,1\,0\,0\,0 \\ 0\,1\,1\,0\,0\,0 \end{bmatrix} \xrightarrow{\textit{Lemma 5}} \begin{bmatrix} 1\,1\,1\,1\,0\,0\,0\,0 \\ 1\,1\,1\,1\,0\,0\,0\,0 \\ 1\,1\,1\,1\,1\,1\,1\,1 \\ 1\,1\,1\,1\,1\,1\,1\,1 \\ 0\,1\,1\,0\,1\,1\,0\,0 \\ 0\,1\,1\,0\,1\,1\,0\,0 \\ 0\,1\,1\,0\,0\,0\,1\,1 \\ 0\,1\,1\,0\,0\,0\,1\,1 \end{bmatrix} = C.$$

Subcase 2.2.1.1.2. $\|u_1\| = \|u_2\| = \|u_3\| = 4$.

$$U = \begin{bmatrix} 1\,1\,1\,1\,0\,0\,0\,0 \\ 1\,1\,1\,1\,0\,0\,0\,0 \\ 1\,1\,1\,1\,1\,1\,1\,1 \\ 1\,1\,1\,1\,1\,1\,1\,1 \\ 0\,0\,0\,0 \\ 0\,0\,0\,0 \\ 0\,0\,0\,0 \\ 0\,0\,0\,0 \end{bmatrix} \xrightarrow{\textit{Lemma 5}} \begin{bmatrix} 1\,1\,1\,1\,0\,0\,0\,0 \\ 1\,1\,1\,1\,0\,0\,0\,0 \\ 1\,1\,1\,1\,1\,1\,1\,1 \\ 1\,1\,1\,1\,1\,1\,1\,1 \\ 0\,0\,0\,0\,1\,1\,1\,1 \\ 0\,0\,0\,0\,1\,1\,1\,1 \\ 0\,0\,0\,0\,0\,0\,0\,0 \\ 0\,0\,0\,0\,0\,0\,0\,0 \end{bmatrix} = E.$$

Subcase 2.2.1.2. $\|u_2^\dagger\| = 4$, then

$$U = \begin{bmatrix} 1\,1\,1\,1\,0\,0\,0\,0 \\ 1\,1\,1\,1\,0\,0\,0\,0 \\ 1\,1\,1\,1\,0\,0\,0\,0 \\ 1\,1\,1\,1\,0\,0\,0\,0 \\ 0 \\ 0 \\ 0 \\ 0 \end{bmatrix}.$$

By Lemma 6 with $u_0^\dagger$, there must be evenly many columns among $\{u_0, u_1, u_2, u_3\}$ that have hamming weight 8. Since $\|u_0\| = 4$, up to column permutation, there can be two cases.

Subcase 2.2.1.2.1. $\|u_1\| = \|u_2\| = 8$ and $\|u_3\| = 4$.

$$U = \begin{bmatrix} 1\,1\,1\,1\,0\,0\,0\,0 \\ 1\,1\,1\,1\,0\,0\,0\,0 \\ 1\,1\,1\,1\,0\,0\,0\,0 \\ 1\,1\,1\,1\,0\,0\,0\,0 \\ 0\,1\,1\,0 \\ 0\,1\,1\,0 \\ 0\,1\,1\,0 \\ 0\,1\,1\,0 \end{bmatrix} \xrightarrow{Lemma\ 5} \begin{bmatrix} 1\,1\,1\,1\,0\,0\,0\,0 \\ 1\,1\,1\,1\,0\,0\,0\,0 \\ 1\,1\,1\,1\,0\,0\,0\,0 \\ 1\,1\,1\,1\,0\,0\,0\,0 \\ 0\,1\,1\,0\,1\,1\,0\,0 \\ 0\,1\,1\,0 \\ 0\,1\,1\,0 \\ 0\,1\,1\,0 \end{bmatrix} \xrightarrow{Lemma\ 5} \begin{bmatrix} 1\,1\,1\,1\,0\,0\,0\,0 \\ 1\,1\,1\,1\,0\,0\,0\,0 \\ 1\,1\,1\,1\,0\,0\,0\,0 \\ 1\,1\,1\,1\,0\,0\,0\,0 \\ 0\,1\,1\,0\,1\,1\,0\,0 \\ 0\,1\,1\,0\,1\,1\,0\,0 \\ 0\,1\,1\,0\,1\,1\,0\,0 \\ 0\,1\,1\,0\,1\,1\,0\,0 \end{bmatrix} = D.$$

Subcase 2.2.1.2.2. $\|u_1\| = \|u_2\| = \|u_3\| = 4$. Depending on the hamming weight of $u_4^\dagger$, consider what follows.

Subcase 2.2.1.2.2.1. $\|u_4^\dagger\| = 4$, then

$$U = \begin{bmatrix} 1\,1\,1\,1\,0\,0\,0\,0 \\ 1\,1\,1\,1\,0\,0\,0\,0 \\ 1\,1\,1\,1\,0\,0\,0\,0 \\ 1\,1\,1\,1\,0\,0\,0\,0 \\ 0\,0\,0\,0\,1\,1\,1\,1 \\ 0\,0\,0\,0 \\ 0\,0\,0\,0 \\ 0\,0\,0\,0 \end{bmatrix} \xrightarrow{Lemma\ 5} \begin{bmatrix} 1\,1\,1\,1\,0\,0\,0\,0 \\ 1\,1\,1\,1\,0\,0\,0\,0 \\ 1\,1\,1\,1\,0\,0\,0\,0 \\ 1\,1\,1\,1\,0\,0\,0\,0 \\ 0\,0\,0\,0\,1\,1\,1\,1 \\ 0\,0\,0\,0\,1\,1\,1\,1 \\ 0\,0\,0\,0\,1\,1\,1\,1 \\ 0\,0\,0\,0\,1\,1\,1\,1 \end{bmatrix} = I.$$

Subcase 2.2.1.2.2.2. $\|u_4^\dagger\| = 0$, then

$$
U = \begin{bmatrix} 1\,1\,1\,1\,0\,0\,0\,0 \\ 1\,1\,1\,1\,0\,0\,0\,0 \\ 1\,1\,1\,1\,0\,0\,0\,0 \\ 1\,1\,1\,1\,0\,0\,0\,0 \\ 0\,0\,0\,0\,0\,0\,0\,0 \\ 0\,0\,0\,0 \\ 0\,0\,0\,0 \\ 0\,0\,0\,0 \end{bmatrix} \xrightarrow{\textit{Lemma 5}} \begin{bmatrix} 1\,1\,1\,1\,0\,0\,0\,0 \\ 1\,1\,1\,1\,0\,0\,0\,0 \\ 1\,1\,1\,1\,0\,0\,0\,0 \\ 1\,1\,1\,1\,0\,0\,0\,0 \\ 0\,0\,0\,0\,0\,0\,0\,0 \\ 0\,0\,0\,0\,0\,0\,0\,0 \\ 0\,0\,0\,0\,0\,0\,0\,0 \\ 0\,0\,0\,0\,0\,0\,0\,0 \end{bmatrix} = J.
$$

Subcase 2.2.2. $x = 1$, $z = w = 0$, we have

$$
U = \begin{bmatrix} 1\,1\,1\,1\,0\,0\,0\,0 \\ 1\,1\,1\,1\,0\,0\,0\,0 \\ 1\,1\,0\,0 \\ 1\,1\,0\,0 \\ 0 \\ 0 \\ 0 \\ 0 \end{bmatrix} \xrightarrow{\textit{Lemma 5}} \begin{bmatrix} 1\,1\,1\,1\,0\,0\,0\,0 \\ 1\,1\,1\,1\,0\,0\,0\,0 \\ 1\,1\,0\,0\,1\,1\,0\,0 \\ 1\,1\,0\,0\,1\,1\,0\,0 \\ 0 \\ 0 \\ 0 \\ 0 \end{bmatrix}.
$$

Subcase 2.2.2.1. $\|u_1\| = 8$, then we have what follows.

$$
U = \begin{bmatrix} 1\,1\,1\,1\,0\,0\,0\,0 \\ 1\,1\,1\,1\,0\,0\,0\,0 \\ 1\,1\,0\,0\,1\,1\,0\,0 \\ 1\,1\,0\,0\,1\,1\,0\,0 \\ 0\,1 \\ 0\,1 \\ 0\,1 \\ 0\,1 \end{bmatrix} \xrightarrow{\textit{Lemma 5}} \begin{bmatrix} 1\,1\,1\,1\,0\,0\,0\,0 \\ 1\,1\,1\,1\,0\,0\,0\,0 \\ 1\,1\,0\,0\,1\,1\,0\,0 \\ 1\,1\,0\,0\,1\,1\,0\,0 \\ 0\,1\,1 \\ 0\,1\,1 \\ 0\,1\,0 \\ 0\,1\,0 \end{bmatrix} \xrightarrow{\textit{Lemma 6}} \begin{bmatrix} 1\,1\,1\,1\,0\,0\,0\,0 \\ 1\,1\,1\,1\,0\,0\,0\,0 \\ 1\,1\,0\,0\,1\,1\,0\,0 \\ 1\,1\,0\,0\,1\,1\,0\,0 \\ 0\,1\,1\,0\,x \\ 0\,1\,1\,0\,y \\ 0\,1\,0\,1 \\ 0\,1\,0\,1 \end{bmatrix}.
$$

Let (x, y) be a pair of the entries in the i-th column of rows 4 and 5 as shown above, for $4 \le i < 8$. By Lemma 6 with u_2, $x = y$. Hence $u_4^\dagger = u_5^\dagger$.

$$
\xrightarrow{\textit{Lemma 6}} \begin{bmatrix} 1\,1\,1\,1\,0\,0\,0\,0 \\ 1\,1\,1\,1\,0\,0\,0\,0 \\ 1\,1\,0\,0\,1\,1\,0\,0 \\ 1\,1\,0\,0\,1\,1\,0\,0 \\ 0\,1\,1\,0\,1\,0\,1\,0 \\ 0\,1\,1\,0\,1\,0\,1\,0 \\ 0\,1\,0\,1 \\ 0\,1\,0\,1 \end{bmatrix} \xrightarrow{\textit{Lemma 5}} \begin{bmatrix} 1\,1\,1\,1\,0\,0\,0\,0 \\ 1\,1\,1\,1\,0\,0\,0\,0 \\ 1\,1\,0\,0\,1\,1\,0\,0 \\ 1\,1\,0\,0\,1\,1\,0\,0 \\ 0\,1\,1\,0\,1\,0\,1\,0 \\ 0\,1\,1\,0\,1\,0\,1\,0 \\ 0\,1\,0\,1\,0\,1\,1\,0 \\ 0\,1\,0\,1\,0\,1\,1\,0 \end{bmatrix} = F.
$$

Subcase 2.2.2.2. $\|u_1\| = 4$, then

$$
U = \begin{bmatrix}
1\,1\,1\,1\,0\,0\,0\,0 \\
1\,1\,1\,1\,0\,0\,0\,0 \\
1\,1\,0\,0\,1\,1\,0\,0 \\
1\,1\,0\,0\,1\,1\,0\,0 \\
0\,0 \\
0\,0 \\
0\,0 \\
0\,0
\end{bmatrix}
\xrightarrow{\;Lemma\ 5\;}
\begin{bmatrix}
1\,1\,1\,1\,0\,0\,0\,0 \\
1\,1\,1\,1\,0\,0\,0\,0 \\
1\,1\,0\,0\,1\,1\,0\,0 \\
1\,1\,0\,0\,1\,1\,0\,0 \\
0\,0\,1\,x \\
0\,0\,1\,y \\
0\,0\,0 \\
0\,0\,0
\end{bmatrix} .
$$

Let (x, y) be a pair of the entries in the i-th column of rows 4 and 5 as shown above, for $3 \leq i < 8$. By Lemma 6 with u_2, $x = y$. Hence $u_4^\dagger = u_5^\dagger$. Moreover, by Lemma 6 with $u_0^\dagger$, we have

$$
U = \begin{bmatrix}
1\,1\,1\,1\,0\,0\,0\,0 \\
1\,1\,1\,1\,0\,0\,0\,0 \\
1\,1\,0\,0\,1\,1\,0\,0 \\
1\,1\,0\,0\,1\,1\,0\,0 \\
0\,0\,1\,1 \\
0\,0\,1\,1 \\
0\,0\,0 \\
0\,0\,0
\end{bmatrix}
\xrightarrow{\;Lemma\ 5\;}
\begin{bmatrix}
1\,1\,1\,1\,0\,0\,0\,0 \\
1\,1\,1\,1\,0\,0\,0\,0 \\
1\,1\,0\,0\,1\,1\,0\,0 \\
1\,1\,0\,0\,1\,1\,0\,0 \\
0\,0\,1\,1\,x\,z \\
0\,0\,1\,1\,y\,w \\
0\,0\,0\,0 \\
0\,0\,0\,0
\end{bmatrix} .
$$

By Lemma 6 with $u_2^\dagger$, $x = z$ and $y = w$. Since $x = y$ and $z = w$, $x = y = z = w$.

Subcase 2.2.2.2.1. $x = y = z = w = 1$

$$
U = \begin{bmatrix}
1\,1\,1\,1\,0\,0\,0\,0 \\
1\,1\,1\,1\,0\,0\,0\,0 \\
1\,1\,0\,0\,1\,1\,0\,0 \\
1\,1\,0\,0\,1\,1\,0\,0 \\
0\,0\,1\,1\,1\,1 \\
0\,0\,1\,1\,1\,1 \\
0\,0\,0\,0 \\
0\,0\,0\,0
\end{bmatrix}
\xrightarrow{\;Lemma\ 5\;}
\begin{bmatrix}
1\,1\,1\,1\,0\,0\,0\,0 \\
1\,1\,1\,1\,0\,0\,0\,0 \\
1\,1\,0\,0\,1\,1\,0\,0 \\
1\,1\,0\,0\,1\,1\,0\,0 \\
0\,0\,1\,1\,1\,1\,0\,0 \\
0\,0\,1\,1\,1\,1\,0\,0 \\
0\,0\,0\,0\,0\,0 \\
0\,0\,0\,0\,0\,0
\end{bmatrix}
\xrightarrow{\;Lemma\ 5\;}
\begin{bmatrix}
1\,1\,1\,1\,0\,0\,0\,0 \\
1\,1\,1\,1\,0\,0\,0\,0 \\
1\,1\,0\,0\,1\,1\,0\,0 \\
1\,1\,0\,0\,1\,1\,0\,0 \\
0\,0\,1\,1\,1\,1\,0\,0 \\
0\,0\,1\,1\,1\,1\,0\,0 \\
0\,0\,0\,0\,0\,0\,0\,0 \\
0\,0\,0\,0\,0\,0\,0\,0
\end{bmatrix} = G.
$$

Subcase 2.2.2.2.2. $x = y = z = w = 0$.

$$
U = \begin{bmatrix}
1\,1\,1\,1\,0\,0\,0\,0 \\
1\,1\,1\,1\,0\,0\,0\,0 \\
1\,1\,0\,0\,1\,1\,0\,0 \\
1\,1\,0\,0\,1\,1\,0\,0 \\
0\,0\,1\,1\,0\,0 \\
0\,0\,1\,1\,0\,0 \\
0\,0\,0\,0 \\
0\,0\,0\,0
\end{bmatrix}
\xrightarrow{\;Lemma\ 5\;}
\begin{bmatrix}
1\,1\,1\,1\,0\,0\,0\,0 \\
1\,1\,1\,1\,0\,0\,0\,0 \\
1\,1\,0\,0\,1\,1\,0\,0 \\
1\,1\,0\,0\,1\,1\,0\,0 \\
0\,0\,1\,1\,0\,0\,1\,1 \\
0\,0\,1\,1\,0\,0\,1\,1 \\
0\,0\,0\,0\,1\,1 \\
0\,0\,0\,0\,1\,1
\end{bmatrix}
\xrightarrow{\;Lemma\ 5\;}
\begin{bmatrix}
1\,1\,1\,1\,0\,0\,0\,0 \\
1\,1\,1\,1\,0\,0\,0\,0 \\
1\,1\,0\,0\,1\,1\,0\,0 \\
1\,1\,0\,0\,1\,1\,0\,0 \\
0\,0\,1\,1\,0\,0\,1\,1 \\
0\,0\,1\,1\,0\,0\,1\,1 \\
0\,0\,0\,0\,1\,1\,1\,1 \\
0\,0\,0\,0\,1\,1\,1\,1
\end{bmatrix} = H.
$$

$\square$

A.2   Binary Patterns that are neither Row-paired nor Column-paired

Definition 15. *We define the set $\mathcal{B}_1$ of binary matrices as $\mathcal{B}_1 = \{L, M, N\}$, where*

$$
L = \begin{bmatrix}
1 & 1 & 1 & 1 & 1 & 1 & 1 & 1 \\
1 & 1 & 1 & 1 & 0 & 0 & 0 & 0 \\
1 & 1 & 0 & 0 & 1 & 1 & 0 & 0 \\
1 & 1 & 0 & 0 & 0 & 0 & 1 & 1 \\
1 & 0 & 1 & 0 & 1 & 0 & 1 & 0 \\
1 & 0 & 1 & 0 & 0 & 1 & 0 & 1 \\
1 & 0 & 0 & 1 & 1 & 0 & 0 & 1 \\
1 & 0 & 0 & 1 & 0 & 1 & 1 & 0
\end{bmatrix}, \quad
M = \begin{bmatrix}
1 & 1 & 1 & 1 & 0 & 0 & 0 & 0 \\
1 & 1 & 0 & 0 & 1 & 1 & 0 & 0 \\
1 & 0 & 1 & 0 & 1 & 0 & 1 & 0 \\
1 & 0 & 0 & 1 & 0 & 1 & 1 & 0 \\
0 & 1 & 1 & 0 & 1 & 0 & 0 & 1 \\
0 & 1 & 0 & 1 & 0 & 1 & 0 & 1 \\
0 & 0 & 1 & 1 & 0 & 0 & 1 & 1 \\
0 & 0 & 0 & 0 & 1 & 1 & 1 & 1
\end{bmatrix}, \quad
N = \begin{bmatrix}
1 & 1 & 1 & 1 & 0 & 0 & 0 & 0 \\
1 & 1 & 0 & 0 & 1 & 1 & 0 & 0 \\
1 & 0 & 1 & 0 & 1 & 0 & 1 & 0 \\
1 & 0 & 0 & 1 & 0 & 1 & 1 & 0 \\
0 & 1 & 1 & 0 & 0 & 1 & 1 & 0 \\
0 & 1 & 0 & 1 & 1 & 0 & 1 & 0 \\
0 & 0 & 1 & 1 & 1 & 1 & 0 & 0 \\
0 & 0 & 0 & 0 & 0 & 0 & 0 & 0
\end{bmatrix}.
$$

Proposition 14. *Let $U \in \mathbb{Z}_2^{8 \times 8}$. Suppose U satisfies Lemmas 6 and 5. If there are no identical rows nor columns in U, then $U \in \mathcal{B}_1$ up to permutation and transposition.*

Proof. Let u_i denote the i-th column of U, and $u_i^\dagger$ denote the i-th row of U, $0 \leq i < 8$. Let $\|v\|$ denote the hamming weight of v, where v is a string of binary bits. Since there are no identical rows nor columns in U, we proceed by case distinctions on the maximum hamming weight of a row vector in U.

Case 1. There is a row with hamming weight 8. Up to row permutation, $\|u_0^\dagger\| = 8$.

Subcase 1.1. There is a row with hamming weight 0. Up to row permutation, $\|u_1^\dagger\| = 0$.

$$
U = \begin{bmatrix}
1 & 1 & 1 & 1 & 1 & 1 & 1 & 1 \\
0 & 0 & 0 & 0 & 0 & 0 & 0 & 0 \\
 & & & & & & & \\
 & & & & & & & \\
 & & & & & & & \\
 & & & & & & & \\
 & & & & & & & \\
 & & & & & & &
\end{bmatrix}
\xrightarrow{\text{Case 1}}
\begin{bmatrix}
1 & 1 & 1 & 1 & 1 & 1 & 1 & 1 \\
0 & 0 & 0 & 0 & 0 & 0 & 0 & 0 \\
1 & 1 & 1 & 1 & 0 & 0 & 0 & 0 \\
 & & & & & & & \\
 & & & & & & & \\
 & & & & & & & \\
 & & & & & & & \\
 & & & & & & &
\end{bmatrix}
\xrightarrow{\text{Lemma 5}}
\begin{bmatrix}
1 & 1 & 1 & 1 & 1 & 1 & 1 & 1 \\
0 & 0 & 0 & 0 & 0 & 0 & 0 & 0 \\
1 & 1 & 1 & 1 & 0 & 0 & 0 & 0 \\
1 & & & & & & & \\
1 & & & & & & & \\
0 & & & & & & & \\
0 & & & & & & & \\
0 & & & & & & &
\end{bmatrix}
$$

$$
\xrightarrow{\text{Lemma 6}}
\begin{bmatrix}
1 & 1 & 1 & 1 & 1 & 1 & 1 & 1 \\
0 & 0 & 0 & 0 & 0 & 0 & 0 & 0 \\
1 & 1 & 1 & 1 & 0 & 0 & 0 & 0 \\
1 & 1 & 0 & 0 & 1 & 1 & 0 & 0 \\
1 & & & & & & & \\
0 & & & & & & & \\
0 & & & & & & & \\
0 & & & & & & &
\end{bmatrix}
\xrightarrow{\text{Lemma 6}}
\begin{bmatrix}
1 & 1 & 1 & 1 & 1 & 1 & 1 & 1 \\
0 & 0 & 0 & 0 & 0 & 0 & 0 & 0 \\
1 & 1 & 1 & 1 & 0 & 0 & 0 & 0 \\
1 & 1 & 0 & 0 & 1 & 1 & 0 & 0 \\
1 & 1 & & & & & & \\
0 & & & & & & & \\
0 & & & & & & & \\
0 & & & & & & &
\end{bmatrix}
\xrightarrow{\text{Lemma 5}}
\begin{bmatrix}
1 & 1 & 1 & 1 & 1 & 1 & 1 & 1 \\
0 & 0 & 0 & 0 & 0 & 0 & 0 & 0 \\
1 & 1 & 1 & 1 & 0 & 0 & 0 & 0 \\
1 & 1 & 0 & 0 & 1 & 1 & 0 & 0 \\
1 & 1 & & & & & & \\
0 & 0 & & & & & & \\
0 & 0 & & & & & & \\
0 & 0 & & & & & &
\end{bmatrix}.
$$

Note that $u_0 = u_1$, but it contradicts our assumption that there are no identical columns in U. Thus this case is not possible.

Subcase 1.2. There is no row with hamming weight 0. Up to row and column permutation, consider

$$U = \begin{bmatrix} 1\,1\,1\,1\,1\,1\,1\,1 \\ 1\,1\,1\,1\,0\,0\,0\,0 \\ \\ \\ \\ \\ \\ \\ \end{bmatrix}.$$

Subcase 1.2.1. There is a column with hamming weight 8, consider

$$U = \begin{bmatrix} 1\,1\,1\,1\,1\,1\,1\,1 \\ 1\,1\,1\,1\,0\,0\,0\,0 \\ 1 \\ 1 \\ 1 \\ 1 \\ 1 \\ 1 \end{bmatrix} \xrightarrow{Lemma\ 5} \begin{bmatrix} 1\,1\,1\,1\,1\,1\,1\,1 \\ 1\,1\,1\,1\,0\,0\,0\,0 \\ 1\,1\,0\,0\,1\,1\,0\,0 \\ 1\,1 \\ 1\,0 \\ 1\,0 \\ 1\,0 \\ 1\,0 \end{bmatrix} \xrightarrow{Lemma\ 6} \begin{bmatrix} 1\,1\,1\,1\,1\,1\,1\,1 \\ 1\,1\,1\,1\,0\,0\,0\,0 \\ 1\,1\,0\,0\,1\,1\,0\,0 \\ 1\,1\,0\,0\,0\,0\,1\,1 \\ 1\,0 \\ 1\,0 \\ 1\,0 \\ 1\,0 \end{bmatrix}$$

$$\xrightarrow{Lemma\ 5} \begin{bmatrix} 1\,1\,1\,1\,1\,1\,1\,1 \\ 1\,1\,1\,1\,0\,0\,0\,0 \\ 1\,1\,0\,0\,1\,1\,0\,0 \\ 1\,1\,0\,0\,0\,0\,1\,1 \\ 1\,0\,1 \\ 1\,0\,1 \\ 1\,0\,0 \\ 1\,0\,0 \end{bmatrix} \xrightarrow{Lemma\ 6} \begin{bmatrix} 1\,1\,1\,1\,1\,1\,1\,1 \\ 1\,1\,1\,1\,0\,0\,0\,0 \\ 1\,1\,0\,0\,1\,1\,0\,0 \\ 1\,1\,0\,0\,0\,0\,1\,1 \\ 1\,0\,1\,0 \\ 1\,0\,1\,0 \\ 1\,0\,0\,1 \\ 1\,0\,0\,1 \end{bmatrix} \xrightarrow{Lemma\ 5} \begin{bmatrix} 1\,1\,1\,1\,1\,1\,1\,1 \\ 1\,1\,1\,1\,0\,0\,0\,0 \\ 1\,1\,0\,0\,1\,1\,0\,0 \\ 1\,1\,0\,0\,0\,0\,1\,1 \\ 1\,0\,1\,0\,1\,0\,1\,0 \\ 1\,0\,1\,0 \\ 1\,0\,0\,1 \\ 1\,0\,0\,1 \end{bmatrix}$$

$$\xrightarrow{Lemma\ 6} \begin{bmatrix} 1\,1\,1\,1\,1\,1\,1\,1 \\ 1\,1\,1\,1\,0\,0\,0\,0 \\ 1\,1\,0\,0\,1\,1\,0\,0 \\ 1\,1\,0\,0\,0\,0\,1\,1 \\ 1\,0\,1\,0\,1\,0\,1\,0 \\ 1\,0\,1\,0\,0 \\ 1\,0\,0\,1\,1 \\ 1\,0\,0\,1\,0 \end{bmatrix} \xrightarrow{Lemma\ 6} \begin{bmatrix} 1\,1\,1\,1\,1\,1\,1\,1 \\ 1\,1\,1\,1\,0\,0\,0\,0 \\ 1\,1\,0\,0\,1\,1\,0\,0 \\ 1\,1\,0\,0\,0\,0\,1\,1 \\ 1\,0\,1\,0\,1\,0\,1\,0 \\ 1\,0\,1\,0\,0\,1 \\ 1\,0\,0\,1\,1\,0 \\ 1\,0\,0\,1\,0\,1 \end{bmatrix} \xrightarrow{Lemma\ 6} \begin{bmatrix} 1\,1\,1\,1\,1\,1\,1\,1 \\ 1\,1\,1\,1\,0\,0\,0\,0 \\ 1\,1\,0\,0\,1\,1\,0\,0 \\ 1\,1\,0\,0\,0\,0\,1\,1 \\ 1\,0\,1\,0\,1\,0\,1\,0 \\ 1\,0\,1\,0\,0\,1\,0\,1 \\ 1\,0\,0\,1\,1\,0 \\ 1\,0\,0\,1\,0\,1 \end{bmatrix}$$

$$\xrightarrow{Lemma\ 6} \begin{bmatrix} 1\,1\,1\,1\,1\,1\,1\,1 \\ 1\,1\,1\,1\,0\,0\,0\,0 \\ 1\,1\,0\,0\,1\,1\,0\,0 \\ 1\,1\,0\,0\,0\,0\,1\,1 \\ 1\,0\,1\,0\,1\,0\,1\,0 \\ 1\,0\,1\,0\,0\,1\,0\,1 \\ 1\,0\,0\,1\,1\,0\,0 \\ 1\,0\,0\,1\,0\,1\,1 \end{bmatrix} \xrightarrow{Lemma\ 5} \begin{bmatrix} 1\,1\,1\,1\,1\,1\,1\,1 \\ 1\,1\,1\,1\,0\,0\,0\,0 \\ 1\,1\,0\,0\,1\,1\,0\,0 \\ 1\,1\,0\,0\,0\,0\,1\,1 \\ 1\,0\,1\,0\,1\,0\,1\,0 \\ 1\,0\,1\,0\,0\,1\,0\,1 \\ 1\,0\,0\,1\,1\,0\,0\,1 \\ 1\,0\,0\,1\,0\,1\,1\,0 \end{bmatrix} = L.$$

Subcase 1.2.2. There is no column whose hamming weight is 8. Up to row and column permutation, consider

$$U = \begin{bmatrix} 1\,1\,1\,1\,1\,1\,1\,1 \\ 1\,1\,1\,1\,0\,0\,0\,0 \\ 1 \\ 1 \\ 0 \\ 0 \\ 0 \\ 0 \end{bmatrix} \xrightarrow[\text{Lemma 6}]{\text{Lemma 5}} \begin{bmatrix} 1\,1\,1\,1\,1\,1\,1\,1 \\ 1\,1\,1\,1\,0\,0\,0\,0 \\ 1\,1\,0\,0\,1\,1\,0\,0 \\ 1 \\ 0 \\ 0 \\ 0 \\ 0 \end{bmatrix} \xrightarrow{\text{Lemma 6}} \begin{bmatrix} 1\,1\,1\,1\,1\,1\,1\,1 \\ 1\,1\,1\,1\,0\,0\,0\,0 \\ 1\,1\,0\,0\,1\,1\,0\,0 \\ 1\,1 \\ 0\,0 \\ 0\,0 \\ 0\,0 \\ 0\,0 \end{bmatrix}.$$

Note that $u_0 = u_1$, but it contradicts our assumption that there are no identical columns in U. Thus this case is not possible.

Case 2. There is no row with hamming weight 8. Up to row and column permutation, $\|u_0^\dagger\| = 4$.

Subcase 2.1. There is a column with hamming weight 8, consider

$$U = \begin{bmatrix} 1\,1\,1\,1\,0\,0\,0\,0 \\ 1 \\ 1 \\ 1 \\ 1 \\ 1 \\ 1 \\ 1 \end{bmatrix} \xrightarrow[\text{Lemma 6}]{\text{Lemma 5}} \begin{bmatrix} 1\,1\,1\,1\,0\,0\,0\,0 \\ 1\,1\,0\,0\,1\,1\,0\,0 \\ 1\,1 \\ 1\,1 \\ 1\,0 \\ 1\,0 \\ 1\,0 \\ 1\,0 \end{bmatrix} \xrightarrow[\text{Lemma 6}]{\text{Lemma 5}}$$

$$\begin{bmatrix} 1\,1\,1\,1\,0\,0\,0\,0 \\ 1\,1\,0\,0\,1\,1\,0\,0 \\ 1\,1\,0\,0\,0\,0\,1\,1 \\ 1\,1\,1 \\ 1\,0 \\ 1\,0 \\ 1\,0 \\ 1\,0 \end{bmatrix} \xrightarrow{\text{Lemma 6}} \begin{bmatrix} 1\,1\,1\,1\,0\,0\,0\,0 \\ 1\,1\,0\,0\,1\,1\,0\,0 \\ 1\,1\,0\,0\,0\,0\,1\,1 \\ 1\,1\,1\,1\,0\,0\,0\,0 \\ 1\,0 \\ 1\,0 \\ 1\,0 \\ 1\,0 \end{bmatrix}.$$

Note that $u_0^\dagger = u_3^\dagger$, but it contradicts our assumption that there are no identical rows in U. Thus this case is not possible.

Subcase 2.2. There is no column with hamming weight 8, consider

$$U = \begin{bmatrix} 1\,1\,1\,1\,0\,0\,0\,0 \\ 1 \\ 1 \\ 1 \\ 0 \\ 0 \\ 0 \\ 0 \end{bmatrix} \xrightarrow[\text{Lemma 6}]{\text{Lemma 5}} \begin{bmatrix} 1\,1\,1\,1\,0\,0\,0\,0 \\ 1\,1\,0\,0\,1\,1\,0\,0 \\ 1\,0 \\ 1\,0 \\ 0\,1 \\ 0\,1 \\ 0\,0 \\ 0\,0 \end{bmatrix} \xrightarrow[\text{Lemma 6}]{\text{Lemma 5}} \begin{bmatrix} 1\,1\,1\,1\,0\,0\,0\,0 \\ 1\,1\,0\,0\,1\,1\,0\,0 \\ 1\,0\,1\,0\,1\,0\,1\,0 \\ 1\,0\,0 \\ 0\,1\,1 \\ 0\,1\,0 \\ 0\,0\,1 \\ 0\,0\,0 \end{bmatrix}$$

$$
\xrightarrow[\text{Lemma 6}]{\text{Lemma 5}}
\begin{bmatrix}
1\,1\,1\,1\,0\,0\,0\,0 \\
1\,1\,0\,0\,1\,1\,0\,0 \\
1\,0\,1\,0\,1\,0\,1\,0 \\
1\,0\,0\,1 \\
0\,1\,1\,0 \\
0\,1\,0\,1 \\
0\,0\,1\,1 \\
0\,0\,0\,0
\end{bmatrix}
\xrightarrow{\text{Lemma 6}}
\begin{bmatrix}
1\,1\,1\,1\,0\,0\,0\,0 \\
1\,1\,0\,0\,1\,1\,0\,0 \\
1\,0\,1\,0\,1\,0\,1\,0 \\
1\,0\,0\,1\,0\,1\,1\,0 \\
0\,1\,1\,0\,x \\
0\,1\,0\,1 \\
0\,0\,1\,1 \\
0\,0\,0\,0
\end{bmatrix}.
$$

Subcase 2.2.1. $x = 1$

$$
U =
\begin{bmatrix}
1\,1\,1\,1\,0\,0\,0\,0 \\
1\,1\,0\,0\,1\,1\,0\,0 \\
1\,0\,1\,0\,1\,0\,1\,0 \\
1\,0\,0\,1\,0\,1\,1\,0 \\
0\,1\,1\,0\,1 \\
0\,1\,0\,1 \\
0\,0\,1\,1 \\
0\,0\,0\,0
\end{bmatrix}
\xrightarrow{\text{Lemma 6}}
\begin{bmatrix}
1\,1\,1\,1\,0\,0\,0\,0 \\
1\,1\,0\,0\,1\,1\,0\,0 \\
1\,0\,1\,0\,1\,0\,1\,0 \\
1\,0\,0\,1\,0\,1\,1\,0 \\
0\,1\,1\,0\,1\,0\,0\,1 \\
0\,1\,0\,1\,0 \\
0\,0\,1\,1\,0 \\
0\,0\,0\,0\,1
\end{bmatrix}
\xrightarrow{\text{Lemma 6}}
$$

$$
\begin{bmatrix}
1\,1\,1\,1\,0\,0\,0\,0 \\
1\,1\,0\,0\,1\,1\,0\,0 \\
1\,0\,1\,0\,1\,0\,1\,0 \\
1\,0\,0\,1\,0\,1\,1\,0 \\
0\,1\,1\,0\,1\,0\,0\,1 \\
0\,1\,0\,1\,0\,1\,0\,1 \\
0\,0\,1\,1\,0\,0 \\
0\,0\,0\,0\,1\,1
\end{bmatrix}
\xrightarrow{\text{Lemma 5}}
\begin{bmatrix}
1\,1\,1\,1\,0\,0\,0\,0 \\
1\,1\,0\,0\,1\,1\,0\,0 \\
1\,0\,1\,0\,1\,0\,1\,0 \\
1\,0\,0\,1\,0\,1\,1\,0 \\
0\,1\,1\,0\,1\,0\,0\,1 \\
0\,1\,0\,1\,0\,1\,0\,1 \\
0\,0\,1\,1\,0\,0\,1\,1 \\
0\,0\,0\,0\,1\,1\,1\,1
\end{bmatrix}
= M.
$$

Subcase 2.2.2. $x = 0$

$$
U =
\begin{bmatrix}
1\,1\,1\,1\,0\,0\,0\,0 \\
1\,1\,0\,0\,1\,1\,0\,0 \\
1\,0\,1\,0\,1\,0\,1\,0 \\
1\,0\,0\,1\,0\,1\,1\,0 \\
0\,1\,1\,0\,0 \\
0\,1\,0\,1 \\
0\,0\,1\,1 \\
0\,0\,0\,0
\end{bmatrix}
\xrightarrow{\text{Lemma 6}}
\begin{bmatrix}
1\,1\,1\,1\,0\,0\,0\,0 \\
1\,1\,0\,0\,1\,1\,0\,0 \\
1\,0\,1\,0\,1\,0\,1\,0 \\
1\,0\,0\,1\,0\,1\,1\,0 \\
0\,1\,1\,0\,0\,1\,1\,0 \\
0\,1\,0\,1\,1 \\
0\,0\,1\,1\,1 \\
0\,0\,0\,0\,0
\end{bmatrix}
\xrightarrow[\text{Lemma 6}]{\text{Lemma5}}
$$

$$
\begin{bmatrix}
1\,1\,1\,1\,0\,0\,0\,0 \\
1\,1\,0\,0\,1\,1\,0\,0 \\
1\,0\,1\,0\,1\,0\,1\,0 \\
1\,0\,0\,1\,0\,1\,1\,0 \\
0\,1\,1\,0\,0\,1\,1\,0 \\
0\,1\,0\,1\,1\,0\,1\,0 \\
0\,0\,1\,1\,1\,1 \\
0\,0\,0\,0\,0\,0
\end{bmatrix}
\xrightarrow{\text{Lemma 5}}
\begin{bmatrix}
1\,1\,1\,1\,0\,0\,0\,0 \\
1\,1\,0\,0\,1\,1\,0\,0 \\
1\,0\,1\,0\,1\,0\,1\,0 \\
1\,0\,0\,1\,0\,1\,1\,0 \\
0\,1\,1\,0\,0\,1\,1\,0 \\
0\,1\,0\,1\,1\,0\,1\,0 \\
0\,0\,1\,1\,1\,1\,0\,0 \\
0\,0\,0\,0\,0\,0\,0\,0
\end{bmatrix}
= N.
$$

Hence, when there are no identical rows nor columns in U, $U \in \mathcal{B}_1$ up to permutation. $\square$

References

1. Aharonov, D.: A simple proof that Toffoli and Hadamard are quantum universal. arXiv preprint quant-ph/0301040 (2003)
2. Amy, M., Glaudell, A.N., Ross, N.J.: Number-theoretic characterizations of some restricted Clifford+T circuits. Quantum **4**, 252 (2020)
3. Arute, F., et al.: Quantum supremacy using a programmable superconducting processor. Nature **574**(7779), 505–510 (2019)
4. Cory, D.G., et al.: Experimental quantum error correction. Phys. Rev. Lett. **81**(10), 2152 (1998)
5. Dalla Chiara, M.L., Ledda, A., Sergioli, G., Giuntini, R.: The Toffoli-Hadamard gate system: an algebraic approach. J. Philos. Log. **42**, 467–481 (2013)
6. Fedorov, A., Steffen, L., Baur, M., da Silva, M.P., Wallraff, A.: Implementation of a Toffoli gate with superconducting circuits. Nature **481**(7380), 170–172 (2012)
7. Forest, S., Gosset, D., Kliuchnikov, V., McKinnon, D.: Exact synthesis of single-qubit unitaries over Clifford-cyclotomic gate sets. J. Math. Phys. **56**(8), 082201 (2015)
8. Fredkin, E., Toffoli, T.: Conservative logic. Int. J. Theor. Phys. **21**(3–4), 219–253 (1982)
9. Gajewski, D.C.: Analysis of groups generated by quantum gates. Ph.D. thesis, University of Toledo (2009)
10. Giles, B., Selinger, P.: Exact synthesis of multiqubit Clifford+T circuits. Phys. Rev. A **87**(3), 032332 (2013)
11. Gottesman, D.: Stabilizer codes and quantum error correction. California Institute of Technology (1997)
12. Kay, A.: Tutorial on the quantikz package. arXiv preprint arXiv:1809.03842 (2018)
13. Kliuchnikov, V.: Synthesis of unitaries with Clifford+T circuits. arXiv preprint arXiv:1306.3200 (2013)
14. Kliuchnikov, V., Maslov, D., Mosca, M.: Fast and efficient exact synthesis of single-qubit unitaries generated by Clifford and T gates. Quantum Inf. Comput. **13**(7–8), 607–630 (2013)
15. Kliuchnikov, V., Yard, J.: A framework for exact synthesis. arXiv preprint arXiv:1504.04350 (2015)
16. Li, S.M., Ross, N.J., Selinger, P.: Generators and relations for the group $O_n(\mathbb{Z}[1/2])$. arXiv preprint arXiv:2106.01175 (2021)
17. Nielsen, M.A., Chuang, I.L.: Quantum computation and quantum information. Phys. Today **54**(2), 60 (2001)
18. Niemann, P., Wille, R., Drechsler, R.: Advanced exact synthesis of Clifford+T circuits. Quantum Inf. Process. **19**(9), 1–23 (2020)
19. Paetznick, A., Reichardt, B.W.: Universal fault-tolerant quantum computation with only transversal gates and error correction. Phys. Rev. Lett. **111**(9), 090505 (2013)
20. Reed, M.D., DiCarlo, L., Nigg, S.E., Sun, L., Frunzio, L., Girvin, S.M., Schoelkopf, R.J.: Realization of three-qubit quantum error correction with superconducting circuits. Nature **482**(7385), 382–385 (2012)

21. Russell, T.: The exact synthesis of 1- and 2-qubit Clifford+T circuits. arXiv preprint arXiv:1408.6202 (2014)
22. Shi, Y.: Both Toffoli and controlled-NOT need little help to do universal quantum computing. Quantum Inf. Comput. **3**(1), 84–92 (2003)
23. Vilmart, R.: A ZX-calculus with triangles for Toffoli-Hadamard, Clifford+T, and beyond. In: Chiribella, G., Selinger, P. (eds.) 15th International Conference on Quantum Physics and Logic (QPL 2018), pp. 313–344. Electronic Proceedings in Theoretical Computer Science (EPTCS 287), Halifax, Canada (2018). https://doi.org/10.4204/EPTCS.287.18. arXiv:1804.03084pdf
24. Vilmart, R.: Completeness of sum-over-paths for Toffoli-Hadamard and the dyadic fragments of quantum computation. In: Klin, B., Pimentel, E. (eds.) 31st EACSL Annual Conference on Computer Science Logic (CSL 2023). Leibniz International Proceedings in Informatics (LIPIcs), vol. 252, pp. 36:1–36:17. Schloss Dagstuhl - Leibniz-Zentrum für Informatik, Dagstuhl, Germany (2023). https://doi.org/10.4230/LIPIcs.CSL.2023.36, https://drops.dagstuhl.de/opus/volltexte/2023/17497
25. Yoder, T.J.: Universal fault-tolerant quantum computation with Bacon-Shor codes. arXiv preprint arXiv:1705.01686 (2017)
26. Zhu, Q., et al.: Quantum computational advantage via 60-qubit 24-cycle random circuit sampling. Sci. Bull. **67**(3), 240–245 (2022)

Implementation of a Reversible Distributed Calculus

Clément Aubert[✉] and Peter Browning

School of Computer and Cyber Sciences, Augusta University, Augusta, USA
{caubert,pebrowning}@augusta.edu

Abstract. Process calculi (π-calculus, CCS, ambient calculus, etc.) are an abstraction of concurrent systems useful to study, specify and verify distributed programs and protocols. This project, IRDC, is concerned with the implementation of such an abstraction for *reversible* process calculi. It is, to the best of our knowledge, the first such publicly available tool. We briefly present the current state of this tool, some of its features, and discuss its future developments.

Keywords: Formal semantics · Process algebra and calculi · Reversible Computation · Concurrency · Tool implementation

1 Implementations of (Reversible) Concurrent Calculi

Implementing a process calculus (π-calculus, CCS, etc.) serves overlapping goals:

- It allows to machine-check theorems and definitions [12,14,16] using proof assistants such as Coq [21], resulting sometimes in simplification [12] or the finding of regrettable imprecisions or errors [16].
- It can demonstrate design patterns useful for implementing e.g., safe message passing [22], or to design code optimization for multithreaded systems [17].
- Using it as an actual programming language, it enables the implementation of toy programs [2] that exemplify the purpose and expressivity of the calculus.
- It can also be used as a specification language: typically, the Proverif tool [9], which implements the applied π-calculus [1], has been used to certify and model security protocols in a variety of areas [20].
- Last but not least, it serves a pedagogical purpose. Simply for CCS, projects from the Sapienza Università di Roma, the Università di Bologna, the Università di Pisa or the Aalborg Universitet [13] demonstrate a vivid interest for implementations using a variety of languages (Standard ML, SWI-Prolog or Typescript) and approaches (ability to "play the bisimulation game", focus on program's correctness, etc.).

Reversible process calculi emerged almost 20 years ago with Reversible CCS (RCCS) [11] and CCS with keys (CCSK) [18]. Both calculi evolved over time, and brought many interesting insights on both reversibility and concurrency [3, Sect. 6]. However, aside from SimCCSK [10]—which is not publicly available and

M. Kutrib and U. Meyer (Eds.): RC 2023, LNCS 13960, pp. 210–217, 2023.
https://doi.org/10.1007/978-3-031-38100-3_13

not maintained since 2008 to our knowledge—no implementation of a concurrent, reversible calculus exists. This short note presents the current status of an implementation of CCSK (presented in Sect. 2), called *Implementation of a Reversible Distributed Calculus* (IRDC), that started in February 2022.

2 System Design

We chose to implement CCSK, a variation on CCS that attaches keys to past actions instead of discarding them, and in which every derivation rule has an inverse. Our syntax is faithful to recent papers on the topic [15]:

0	Nil process	a, ..., z	Input channel name
+	Summation operator	'a, ..., 'z	Output channel name
|	Parallel operator	Tau{a}	Silent action on a
\{a, b}	Restriction along a, b	a[k0], ..., 'z[k1]	Label keys

Details can be found in our readme's "Syntax and Precedence of Operators" section. The operational semantics is standard, reminded in our documentation, and can be partially inferred from the following:

```
                      ------| Actionable Labels |------
(((a+b)|'b)|'a)\{a}    [0]  b              [2]  Tau{b}
                       [1]  'b             [3]  Tau{a}
```

After performing e.g., a synchronization on a (action [3]) and performing an output on 'b (action [1]), this process would become

```
(((Tau{a}[k1].0+b)|'b[k3].0)|Tau{a}[k1].0)\{a}
```
from which the actions with keys k1 and k3 could both be undone, in any order. Note that we decided to omit the nil process when preceded by an actionable prefix[1], and that we label the Tau silent action with the name of the complementary channels that synchronized[2].

3 Running and Installing IRDC

Downloading the latest release can done by browsing to https://github.com/CinRC/IRDC-CCSK/releases or by executing this simple one-liner[3]:

```
curl -s https://api.github.com/repos/CinRC/IRDC-CCSK/releases/latest \
| grep browser_download_url | cut -d : -f 2,3 | tr -d \" | wget -qi -
```
Listing 3.1. Fetching the latest release in one command

---

[1] This behavior can be toggled with the **--require-explicit-null** option.

[2] As we illustrate in Sect. 4.3, this does not impact our implementation of simulation, as e.g., Tau{a} and Tau{b} are treated as equivalent. Note that Tau can be used as an action, as long as the channel name is provided, e.g., one would write Tau{a}.b for the process that can synchronize on a and then do a.

[3] The source code is also archived at https://archive.softwareheritage.org/browse/origin/directory/?origin_url=https://github.com/CinRC/IRDC-CCSK.

Instructions on how to build from source are in the readme's "Building" section. The process from Sect. 2 can then be executed "in interactive mode" using

```
java -jar IRDC*.jar --interactive "(((a+b)|'b)|'a)\{a}"
```

Listing 3.2. Launching the command-line interface with a demo process

after which the user can decide on which channel name (for forward transitions) or label key (for backward transitions) they want to act by selecting the corresponding number and hitting ⏎ . Diverse flags can tweak the program's behavior, they can be accessed using the --help flag or by consulting the readme's "Command arguments (flags)" section. We illustrate some of them below.

4   Features

As of now, our tool's primary goal is pedagogical, to raise interest and train in distributed, reversible computation. We illustrate four possible use cases below.

4.1   Understanding the Operational Semantics

The user can interact with a process to get a better understanding of the operators' mechanisms and semantics. They can for instance try to answer the question

> Can the process (a.b.c|('a.'c+'a))\{a} synchronize on c, and if yes, using which reduction sequence?

using a command such as

```
java -jar IRDC*.jar --interactive "(a.b.c|('a.'c+'a))\{a}"
```

Listing 4.1. Process example to understand the operational semantics

that lets them execute (and rewind if needed) the process to find an execution strategy leading to a synchronization on c. It is then possible to check one's answer by removing the --interactive flag (which is equivalent to setting the --enumerate flag on), so that all possible (forward-only) execution sequences are listed, as displayed in Listing 4.2.

```
java -jar IRDC*.jar --enumerate "(a.b.c|('a.'c+'a))\{a}"
(a.b.c|('a.'c+'a))\{a}
└Tau{a}- (Tau{a}[k0].b.c|(Tau{a}[k0].'c+'a))\{a}
  ├b- (Tau{a}[k0].b[k1].c|(Tau{a}[k0].'c+'a))\{a}
  │ ├c- (Tau{a}[k0].b[k1].c[k4].0|(Tau{a}[k0].'c+'a))\{a}
  │ │ └'c- (Tau{a}[k0].b[k1].c[k4].0|(Tau{a}[k0].'c[k6].0+'a))\{a}
  │ ├'c- (Tau{a}[k0].b[k1].c|(Tau{a}[k0].'c[k5].0+'a))\{a}
  │ │ └c- (Tau{a}[k0].b[k1].c[k7].0|(Tau{a}[k0].'c[k5].0+'a))\{a}
  │ └Tau{c}- (Tau{a}[k0].b[k1].Tau{c}[k3].0|(Tau{a}[k0].Tau{c}[k3].0+'a))\{a}
  └'c- (Tau{a}[k0].b.c|(Tau{a}[k0].'c[k2].0+'a))\{a}
    └b- (Tau{a}[k0].b[k8].c|(Tau{a}[k0].'c[k2].0+'a))\{a}
      └c- (Tau{a}[k0].b[k8].c[k9].0|(Tau{a}[k0].'c[k2].0+'a))\{a}
```

Listing 4.2. Demonstrating the --enumerate flag (output abridged)

4.2   Dissociating Temporal and Causal Orders

Our program can also be used to exhibit the difference between temporal and causal orders in reversible systems. For instance, the following execution:

```
java -jar IRDC-*.jar --interactive "a.b | 'b | c"
// Chose 2, 1, 3 and then 1 to obtain the following execution:
// ((a.b|'b)|c) -c-> ((a.b|'b)|c[k0].0)
//               -a-> ((a[k1].b|'b)|c[k0].0)
//               -Tau{b}-> ((a[k1].Tau{b}[k3].0|Tau{b}[k3].0)|c[k0].0)
//               -[k0]-> ((a[k1].Tau{b}[k3].0|Tau{b}[k3].0)|c)
```

Listing 4.3. Illustrating the difference between temporal and causal orders

makes it clear that even if the action on c (to which the key k0 was given) was triggered first when performing forward transitions, it can be undone first. However, since CCSK is causal-consistent, the action on a cannot be undone unless the synchronization between b and 'b is undone first. This example can also serve to observe that b and 'b cannot backtrack independently.

4.3   Testing Forward Equivalences

Traditional (e.g., forward-only) simulation and bisimulation are also implemented, and can be accessed with the --equivalence flag, by inputting any number of processes separated by commas. This will display, if they exist, the simulation and bisimulation relations between given processes:

```
java -jar IRDC*.jar --equivalence "a.b, a|b, a+b"
Simulations and Bisimulations:
------------
a.b ≲ (a|b)
(a+b) ≲ (a|b)


java -jar IRDC*.jar --equivalence "(a|'a)\{a}, Tau{b}"
Simulations and Bisimulations:
------------
(a|'a)\{a} ≈ Tau{b}


java -jar IRDC*.jar --equivalence "a|(b+c)+(a+c)|b,(a|(b+c))+(a|b)+((a+c)|b)"
Simulations and Bisimulations:
------------
((a|(b+c))+((a+c)|b)) ≈ (((a|(b+c))+(a|b))+((a+c)|b))
```

Listing 4.4. Illustrating the --equivalence flag (output abridged).

4.4   Deciding Reachability

IRDC also accepts processes that already started their execution. If they can be obtained by executing forward a process, then our tool will correctly parse them, and display its possible future actions. In interactive mode, the program will offer to undo the actions that have already received keys, and the --regenerate flag can be used to "rewind" the process before it started its execution.

```
java -jar IRDC*.jar --regenerate "((a[k1].b|'b)|c[k4].0)\{b}"
((a.b|'b)|c)\{b}
```

Listing 4.5. Illustrating the `--regenerate` flag (output abridged).

If the process given as input is unreachable (such as `a.b[k1]`), then an exception `Process is unreachable! Keys cannot be prefixed` is thrown.

5   Inner Flow

Our program has two specificities: it uses an object-oriented programming language (Java), and was written entirely from scratch. As a result, tools usually available to e.g., Maude or Redex users had to be programmed, and we did not used parser generators such as ANTLR. This choice was guided by the desire of better understanding CCSK's syntax, and to explore creative solutions to original problems. As most existing implementations use declarative programming languages, our implementation is quite original in that respect.

Our program works in three stages. The `CCSParser` class initially traverses the input and tokenizes each node (i.e., operand) of a process. Each node is then instantiated as an object internally. Then, the program recursively links the nodes together using the appropriate order of binding power of the operators. After the nodes are all linked, only one process is expected to remain: this process is the "ancestor" that can then be acted on.

When generating enumeration trees, we create a custom tree-like data structure in the `LTTNode` class. This structure is similar to a conventional tree, but stores additional information in the parent-child relationship between nodes. In this context, any process in progress would be deemed a child to whichever process acted to have generated said child. The label that was acted on is then stored in the link between the two.

The algorithm we use (`canSimulate` in the `LTTNode` class) to determine equivalences utilizes its own enumeration feature. To determine if two processes P and Q are similar, it essentially proceeds as follows:

```
Class Process P:
  func canSimulate(process Q):
    bool match = false
    for child process Q', action A of process Q:
      for child process P', action B of process P:
        if A == B and P'.can_simulate(Q'):
          match = 1

      if match == 0:
        return false

    return true
```

Listing 5.1. Pseudocode algorithm for determining simulations.

This algorithm iterates through all actionable labels of a process given by argument and the child processes that can be reached by acting on those labels. For each label-process pair, we assert that the process which is hosting this function is capable of acting on every label that the process given through an argument can. If not, we return false and break. Otherwise, we assert that the resulting processes remain in the simulation relation. To determine bisimulation, we simply call the simulation function twice, swapping the order of the processes. If a simulation relation exists both ways, we then say that they are in a bisimulation relation.

Internally, the program does not de-allocate keys when they are freed, so that a process going constantly back-and-forth will always receive different keys:

```
java -jar IRDC*.jar --interactive "Tau{a}[k1].b | Tau{a}[k1]"
// Chose 0 then 2 to obtain the following execution:
// (Tau{a}[k1].b|Tau{a}[k1].0) -[k1]-> (a.b|'a)
//                              -Tau{a}-> (Tau{a}[k2].b|Tau{a}[k2].0)
```

Listing 5.2. Illustrating fresh key generation

This is consistent with CCSK's semantics, that simply requires "fresh" keys to be used. Always opting for new keys also avoids ambiguities when looking at long computations.

6 Software Engineering Best Practices

Our implementation strives to use state-of-the-art technologies and to promote best practices. We decided to use to use the Java Development Kit (17.0.2) for its flexibility, portability and popularity. We use the software project management and comprehension tool Maven (3.6.3) to ease adoption and dependency management, but also to enforce stylistic constraints: our implementation enforces the `google_checks.xml` checkstyle guideline for uniformity and best practises. Our code is versioned using git, publicly available, open source and uses semantic versioning to ease collaboration and adoption.

We also leveraged github's Continuous integration (CI) / Continuous deployment (CD) to remotely compile our source code and automatically offer pre-compiled releases that can be executed directly. Last but not least, our extensive testing suite makes sure that our implementations of action, enumeration (that lists all possible actions) and restriction, but also our parser and simulation implementations, behave as expected.

7 Road Map

Our list of issues highlights some of our challenges and goals. Some of our milestones include:

- Adding a toggle to allow the re-use of freed keys,
- introducing the possibility of infinite behaviours [4],
- implementing one of the "reversible" bisimulation relation [6,15],
- implementing a mechanism to distribute the generation of keys [7],
- formally verifying the correctness of our definition of concurrency [5],
- adding the ability of loading examples from a file,
- and, of course, performing additional tests.

8 Conclusion

The creation of this tool highlighted some interesting components of CCSK as a whole. Acting much like a calculator, our tool had to create multiple algorithms for manipulating and equivocating different processes. One of the most interesting problems raised by the construction of this tool—and that is not solved yet—is to design, for the first time to our knowledge, an algorithm to determine whether two reversible processes are in an history-preserving bisimulations [6,8,19]. As of now, our tool can decide if reversible process are equivalent only *moving forward*:

```
java -jar IRDC*.jar --equivalence "a[k1].b, b"
Simulations and Bisimulations:
------------
a[k1].b ≈ b
```

Listing 8.1. Deciding the (forward) equivalence of reversible processes (output abridged)

Acknowledgments. We would like to thank Brett Williams and John Yalch for their contribution, and Jason Orlosky for his comments. We are also grateful for the reviewers' interesting suggestions, and for the feedback provided by Ivan Lanese. This material is based upon work supported by the National Science Foundation under Grant No. 2242786 (SHF;Small:Concurrency In Reversible Computations).

References

1. Abadi, M., Blanchet, B., Fournet, C.: The applied pi calculus: Mobile values, new names, and secure communication. J. ACM **65**(1), 1:1-1:41 (2018). https://doi.org/10.1145/3127586
2. Affeldt, R., Kobayashi, N.: A coq library for verification of concurrent programs. Electron. Notes Theor. Comput. Sci. **199**, 17–32 (2008). https://doi.org/10.1016/j.entcs.2007.11.010
3. Aman, B., et al.: Foundations of reversible computation. In: Ulidowski, I., Lanese, I., Schultz, U.P., Ferreira, C. (eds.) RC 2020. LNCS, vol. 12070, pp. 1–40. Springer, Cham (2020). https://doi.org/10.1007/978-3-030-47361-7_1
4. Aubert, C.: Replications in reversible concurrent calculi. In: Kutrib, M., Meyer, U. (eds.) RC 2023. LNCS, Springer (2023), to appear
5. Aubert, C.: The correctness of concurrencies in (Reversible) concurrent calculi (Jan 2023). https://hal.science/hal-03950347, under revision for JLAMP
6. Aubert, C., Cristescu, I.: How reversibility can solve traditional questions: the example of hereditary history-preserving bisimulation. In: Konnov, I., Kovács, L. (eds.) CONCUR 2020. LIPIcs, vol. 2017, pp. 13:1–13:24. Schloss Dagstuhl (2020). https://doi.org/10.4230/LIPIcs.CONCUR.2020.13
7. Aubert, C., Medić, D.: Explicit identifiers and contexts in reversible concurrent calculus. In: Yamashita, S., Yokoyama, T. (eds.) RC 2021. LNCS, vol. 12805, pp. 144–162. Springer, Cham (2021). https://doi.org/10.1007/978-3-030-79837-6_9

8. Bednarczyk, M.A.: Hereditary history preserving bisimulations or what is the power of the future perfect in program logics. Tech. rep, Instytut Podstaw Informatyki PAN filia w Gdańsku (1991)

9. Blanchet, B.: Modeling and verifying security protocols with the applied pi calculus and ProVerif. Found. Trends Priv. Secur. 1(1–2), 1–135 (2016). https://doi.org/10.1561/3300000004

10. Cox, G.: SimCCSK: simulation of the reversible process calculi CCSK. Master's thesis, University of Leicester (4 2010). https://leicester.figshare.com/ndownloader/files/18193256

11. Danos, V., Krivine, J.: Reversible communicating systems. In: Gardner, P., Yoshida, N. (eds.) CONCUR 2004. LNCS, vol. 3170, pp. 292–307. Springer, Heidelberg (2004). https://doi.org/10.1007/978-3-540-28644-8_19

12. Despeyroux, J.: A higher-order specification of the π-calculus. In: van Leeuwen, J., Watanabe, O., Hagiya, M., Mosses, P.D., Ito, T. (eds.) TCS 2000. LNCS, vol. 1872, pp. 425–439. Springer, Heidelberg (2000). https://doi.org/10.1007/3-540-44929-9_30

13. Gillet, J.F., Willame, D.: Calculus of communicating systems: a web based tool in scala. Master's thesis, Université de Namur (6 2017). https://researchportal.unamur.be/files/30127909/GILLET_WILLAME_Memoire.pdf

14. Hirschkoff, D.: A full formalisation of π-calculus theory in the calculus of constructions. In: Gunter, E.L., Felty, A. (eds.) TPHOLs 1997. LNCS, vol. 1275, pp. 153–169. Springer, Heidelberg (1997). https://doi.org/10.1007/BFb0028392

15. Lanese, I., Phillips, I.: Forward-reverse observational equivalences in CCSK. In: Yamashita, S., Yokoyama, T. (eds.) RC 2021. LNCS, vol. 12805, pp. 126–143. Springer, Cham (2021). https://doi.org/10.1007/978-3-030-79837-6_8

16. Maksimović, P., Schmitt, A.: HOCore in Coq. In: Urban, C., Zhang, X. (eds.) ITP 2015. LNCS, vol. 9236, pp. 278–293. Springer, Cham (2015). https://doi.org/10.1007/978-3-319-22102-1_19

17. Martins, F., Lopes, L.M.B., Vasconcelos, V.T.: The impact of linearity information on the performance of tyco. In: Barthe, G., Thiemann, P. (eds.) TIP@MPC 2002. Electron. Notes Theor. Comput. Sci., vol. 75, pp. 41–60. Elsevier (2002). https://doi.org/10.1016/S1571-0661(04)80778-3

18. Phillips, I., Ulidowski, I.: Reversing algebraic process calculi. In: Aceto, L., Ingólfsdóttir, A. (eds.) FoSSaCS 2006. LNCS, vol. 3921, pp. 246–260. Springer, Heidelberg (2006). https://doi.org/10.1007/11690634_17

19. Rabinovich, A., Trakhtenbrot, B.A.: Behavior structures and nets. Fund. Inform. 11(4), 357–404 (1988)

20. Ryan, M.D., Smyth, B.: Applied pi calculus. In: Cortier, V., Kremer, S. (eds.) Formal Models and Techniques for Analyzing Security Protocols, Cryptology and Information Security Series, vol. 5, pp. 112–142. IOS Press (2011). https://doi.org/10.3233/978-1-60750-714-7-112

21. The Coq Development Team: the coq proof assistant (2022). https://doi.org/10.5281/zenodo.5846982

22. Wojciechowski, P.T.: Typed first-class communication channels and mobility for concurrent scripting languages. In: Sloane, A., Aßmann, U. (eds.) SLE 2011. LNCS, vol. 6940, pp. 378–387. Springer, Heidelberg (2012). https://doi.org/10.1007/978-3-642-28830-2_22

Improved Cost-Metric for Nearest Neighbor Mapping of Quantum Circuits to 2-Dimensional Hexagonal Architecture

Kamalika Datta[1,2]($\boxtimes$), Abhoy Kole[2] (iD), Indranil Sengupta[3] (iD),
and Rolf Drechsler[1,2] (iD)

[1] Institute of Computer Science, University of Bremen, Bremen, Germany
{kdatta,drechsler}@uni-bremen.de
[2] Cyber-Physical Systems, DFKI GmbH, Bremen, Germany
abhoy.kole@dfki.de
[3] Department of Computer Science and Engineering, Indian Institute of Technology,
Kharagpur, India
isg@iitkgp.ac.in

Abstract. Quantum computing offers substantial speedup over conventional computing in solving certain computationally hard problems. The emergence of quantum computers in recent years has motivated researchers to develop design automation tools to map quantum circuits to such platforms. One major challenge is to limit the noise or computational error during gate operations; in particular, errors are higher when gates operate on non-neighbor qubits. A common approach to tackle this problem is to make the circuits *Nearest-Neighbor* (NN) compliant by inserting either *Swap gates* or *CNOT templates*. Reduction of gate overhead also becomes important as it serves to limit the overall noise and error. In some recent works, mapping of quantum circuits to hexagonal qubit architecture have been investigated. Hexagonal layout of qubits offers extended neighborhood that helps to reduce the number of Swap or additional CNOT gates required for NN-compliance. Existing approaches incur high gate overheads that can be reduced by improved gate mapping strategies with better cost metrics. The present work proposes one such approach using a priority-based cost metric. The proposed cost-metric is general and can be applied to any architectures; however, in this work we show its benefit for hexagonal architecture. Experiments on benchmark circuits confirm that the proposed method reduces gate overhead by 29% over a very recent work based on greedy mapping.

Keywords: Quantum circuits · Architecture-aware decomposition · Qubit mapping · Clean and dirty ancilla

1 Introduction

Quantum computing has been projected to solve some computationally hard problems in appreciably less time as compared to classical computing. Some of

M. Kutrib and U. Meyer (Eds.): RC 2023, LNCS 13960, pp. 218–231, 2023.
https://doi.org/10.1007/978-3-031-38100-3_14

the well-known quantum algorithms include Shor's factorization [18], Grover's database search [9], quantum simulation and annealing [14], etc. Recent developments have allowed industry giants like IBM, Google, Microsoft, etc. to come up with demonstrable quantum computers. Various technologies are used for implementation, like superconducting [8], trapped ion [10], photonic [16], etc.; however, all of them suffer from problems like limited coherence period and noisy gate operations [1].

The architecture of quantum computers can be classified as per the physical layout of the qubits, and also the way they interact among themselves. These generally include regular arrangement of qubits in a wo-dimensional (2-D) plane, on which 1- and 2-qubit gate operations are carried out. One of the major challenges is the noise generated during computation, which often restricts gate operations to neighboring or coupled qubits only. To operate on non-coupled qubits, two broad approaches are followed. In one approach, the states of neighboring qubits are exchanged using *Swap gates*, thereby bringing the states of a pair of interacting qubits to adjacent locations. As an alternative, a sequence of controlled-NOT (CNOT) gates are used to implement the gate operation on non-neighbor qubits, referred to as *CNOT templates* [17]. Both the approaches require the insertion of additional gates in the netlist, which again result in further accumulation of noise. Clearly, we need clever qubit mapping strategies to minimize the number of additional gates required to make a given quantum circuit NN-compliant.

In recent implementations, qubits are arranged in a sparse 2-D grid, with limited coupling between them. In addition, there can be directional constraints between certain pairs of qubits. Recently, the 2-D hexagonal qubit architecture has been explored [12,19], which offers promise due to the extended qubit neighborhood that it supports. However, not much work has been done on the mapping of quantum circuits to such architectures. In a recent work [4], a greedy approach has been proposed for the mapping of qubits to hexagonal architecture based on an axial coordinate system using well-known heuristics like global and local ordering. In another work [7], an evolutionary algorithm is used to generate placement of qubits in hexagonal architecture. The gate overhead in these methods is less as compared to existing methods based on 2-D qubit architectures; however, there are further scopes for improvement.

In this paper, we propose an efficient NN-compliant quantum circuit mapping approach on the hexagonal qubit architecture. The main contributions of the paper are:

a) A new cost estimate has been formulated based on the notion of *priority* of a gate in the quantum circuit, which correlates well with the actual gate overhead for NN-compliant mapping.
b) A gate lookahead approach has been used for optimal insertion of Swap gates in the netlist for NN-compliance.

Though we focus on the hexagonal architecture in this paper, the proposed method is general and can be used for other architectures as well. A wide range of benchmarks of various sizes have been used for experimentation, which shows an average improvement of 29% in terms of gate overhead over [4].

The rest of the paper is organized as follows. Section 2 discusses the general background of the work. Section 3 presents the hexagonal qubit architecture and the coordinate system, and the proposed mapping strategy. Section 4 presents the experimental results, and finally Sect. 5 concludes the paper.

2   Background

In this section, we present a brief introduction to quantum circuits and gates, followed by a brief discussion on emerging quantum computing architectures. Finally, the issue of logical to physical qubit mapping subject to architectural constraints is discussed.

2.1   Quantum Circuits and Gates

In quantum computing, the basic unit of information is the quantum bit or *qubit*. A qubit can exist in one of the basis states, typically denoted as $|0\rangle$ and $|1\rangle$, or in a state of *superposition* denoted as $\psi = \alpha|0\rangle + \beta|1\rangle$, where α and β are complex numbers such that $|\alpha|^2 + |\beta|^2 = 1$. Another important concept in quantum computing is *entanglement*, whereby two or more qubits can exist in entangled states and no such qubit can be measured independently of the others.

A quantum circuit consists of a set of qubits on which a set of 1- and 2-qubit gate operations are carried out in sequence, as shown in Fig. 1. Some of the quantum gate libraries that have been used by researchers include the NCV library [3], Clifford+T library [13], etc. The native gate library that is supported by any quantum computing hardware mainly depends on the technology used to implement and control the qubits. To execute a quantum circuit on a target platform, one of the important steps is to map the circuit qubits (viz., *logical qubits*) to a set of *physical qubits* as supported by the target architecture subject to architectural constraints.

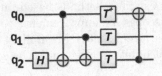

Fig. 1. An example quantum circuit.

2.2   Quantum Computing Architectures

The power and capability of a quantum computer depends on the number of qubits and the coupling constraints between them, which specifies the way the qubits are interconnected. Several initial works have been reported that assume regular arrangement of qubits on 1-, 2- or 3-D grid structures. In recent years, several practical realizations of quantum computers have been reported by IBM, Google, Microsoft, and many others [5]. For instance, the IBM-QX series of quantum computers use a 2-D grid-like structure, with degree of coupling of each qubit as 2 or 3.

To increase the degree of coupling, alternate 2-D structures like the hexagonal architecture has been explored [4,6,7]. Such layout with width w and height h contains $w \times h$ qubits. This allows a maximum qubit coupling of 6, as compared to 4 in standard Cartesian 2-D architecture. This increase in qubit coupling allows added flexibility in performing 2-qubit gate operations. Figure 2 shows an example hexagonal layout of 24 (6×4) qubits.

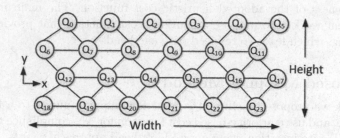

Fig. 2. A 6×4 hexagonal qubit architecture.

In this work, we consider the hexagonal qubit layout for nearest-neighbor mapping of quantum circuits to compare with the other recently introduced works that are discussed next.

2.3 Nearest-Neighbor Mapping of Qubits

When a 2-qubit gate operation is executed, a typical constraint imposed by the target architecture is that the interacting qubits must be neighbors (i.e. coupled). This is referred to as the *nearest-neighbor* (NN) constraint.

Consider a quantum circuit with five 2-qubit gates as shown in Fig. 3(a), with the target architecture shown in Fig. 3(b). In general, the logical qubits are mapped to physical qubits using global (initial) ordering or local ordering of qubits, or a combination of both. For the logical to physical mapping of qubits $(q_0, q_1, q_2, q_3) \xrightarrow{\pi} (Q_0, Q_1, Q_2, Q_3)$, some of the gate operations (viz., $G2$ and $G5$) violate NN-constraints. We typically insert Swap gates[1] as shown in Fig. 3(c) or Remote CNOT (RCNOT) [17] templates to address such violations.

In practical realizations, quantum gate operations are non-ideal, and results in accumulation of errors. It is important to minimize the number of additional gates required for NN-compliance. Since the mapping problem is NP-hard, previous works generally consider heuristics for finding solutions to this problem, e.g. [2,11,15,21,22]. The quality of the obtained solutions directly depends on

---

[1] A Swap gate can be realized using three back-to-back CNOT gates.

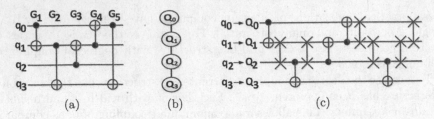

Fig. 3. (a) A quantum circuit, (b) Linear arrangement of physical qubits, (c) Swap gate insertion for NN-compliance.

the effectiveness of the adopted heuristic cost function. The main motivation of the present work is to propose a heuristic cost function that provides better NN-mapping, which leads to reduced gate overhead.

3   Proposed Mapping Method

In this work we propose an efficient scheme for mapping qubits to a hexagonal architecture, and use a priority-based cost function for NN-compliance with Swap and RCNOT gate insertion using a gate lookahead approach.

3.1   Heuristic Cost Function for NN-Mapping

The heuristic cost metric used for logical to physical qubit mapping and subsequent Swap and RCNOT insertion for NN-compliance has a direct impact on gate overhead. There are $n!$ ways (say, $\pi_0, \pi_1, \pi_2, \ldots, \pi_{n!-1}$) to map n logical qubits $\{q_0, q_1, \ldots, q_{n-1}\}$ to equal number of selected physical qubits $\{Q_0, Q_1, \ldots, Q_{n-1}\}$. A poorly selected mapping (π_i) may increase the additional gate overhead.

The cost metric used to evaluate the quality of mapping takes as input: (i) a quantum circuit in the form of a *Qubit Interaction Graph* (QIG), (ii) a *Coupling Graph* (CG) of physical qubits, and (iii) a logical to physical qubit mapping π_k. The cost metric can be expressed as:

$$cost = C \sum_{\substack{q_i, q_j \in QIG \\ \pi_k(q_i), \pi_k(q_j) \in CG}} D\left(\pi_k(q_i), \pi_k(q_j)\right) W(q_i, q_j) \tag{1}$$

where C is a constant, mapping of a logical qubit q_l to a physical qubit Q_p is denoted as $\pi_k(q_l) = Q_p$, the function $D()$ denotes the distance between nodes in CG, and $W(q_i, q_j)$ indicates the edge weight between qubits q_i and q_j in QIG. The value of the constant C gives an overhead estimate in terms of RCNOT templates or Swap gates. We have taken $C = 1$ in our experiments.

For a 2-D arrangement of physical qubits, the CG can be regular or irregular. In case of irregular layout, the distance between each physical qubit pair, $D(Q_i, Q_j)$, can be obtained using *Floyd-Warshall algorithm*. Since the algorithm is computationally expensive (i.e. $\mathcal{O}(n^3)$ for a graph with n vertices), we run it once for each irregular layout to compute a database of the distances for use in future mapping. On the other hand, for regular layout such distance $D(Q_i, Q_j)$ can be computed directly by imposing a co-ordinate system on the layout. On the hexagonal layout, we use the Cartesian co-ordinates of qubits as introduced in [6]. Considering a similar 2-D arrangement of $w \times h$ as shown in Fig. 2, the co-ordinates of a qubit Q_i can be computed as:

$$x_i = (1 - (y_i \bmod 2)) + 2(i \bmod w), \qquad y_i = i/w. \qquad (2)$$

With this co-ordinate system, the distance between a pair of qubits (Q_i, Q_j) can be estimated as:

$$D(Q_i, Q_j) = max \left(|y_i - y_j|, \frac{MD(Q_i, Q_j)}{2} \right) - 1 \qquad (3)$$

where $MD(Q_i, Q_j)$ denotes the *Manhattan Distance* between qubits Q_i and Q_j located at (x_i, y_i) and (x_j, y_j) respectively, i.e.

$$MD(Q_i, Q_j) = |x_i - x_j| + |y_i - y_j|. \qquad (4)$$

The edge weight $W()$ of qubit pairs in QIG plays an important role in discriminating the mapping of qubits using the cost metric defined in Eq. (1). We now explain how the QIG can be exploited to obtain a good qubit mapping.

3.2 Qubit Interaction Graph (QIG)

The *qubit interaction graph* (QIG) captures the degree of interaction among qubit pairs in a given quantum circuit. The vertices of QIG represent logical qubits and edges represent number of 2-qubit gates between qubit pairs.

Consider a quantum circuit with m logical qubits $\{q_0, q_1, \ldots, q_{m-1}\}$ and d gates $\{G_1, G_2, \ldots, G_d\}$. In a previous work [6], the weight of an edge (q_i, q_j) in the QIG has been defined as the number of gate operations between q_i and q_j in the circuit. In other words,

$$W(q_i, q_j) = \sum_{1 \leq k \leq d} GO(q_i, q_j, k) \qquad (5)$$

where $GO(q_i, q_j, k) = 1$, if G_k operates on q_i and q_j
$$= 0, \text{ otherwise.}$$

The main drawback of this measure is that equal weightage is given to all the gates irrespective of their position in the netlist. Intuitively, less weight should be given to gates that are further away from the current position. We propose that all the 2-qubit gates are initially prioritized based on their level in the circuit netlist, such that for a given circuit of depth d, the priority p_i of the gate at level i must satisfy the following criteria:

$$p_i > p_{i+1} + p_{i+2} + \cdots + p_d \tag{6}$$

We have chosen the priority assignment $p_i = M^{d-i}$, for some real number $M \geq 2$, which satisfies Eq. (6). For our evaluation, we have chosen $M = 2$.

In this paper, we propose a priority-based approach to estimate the edge weights in the QIG that specifically addresses this issue. We present the following alternate weight measure based on the above argument:

$$W(q_i, q_j) = \sum_{1 \leq k \leq d} 2^{d-k} \, GO(q_i, q_j, k) \tag{7}$$

$$\text{where } GO(q_i, q_j, k) = 1, \text{ if } G_k \text{ operates on } q_i \text{ and } q_j$$
$$= 0, \text{ otherwise.}$$

Here, the gates that are closer to the point of reference are given higher priority in the weight calculation as compared to those that are further away. We shall refer to the two approaches of weight calculation shown in Eq. (5) and Eq. (7) as *Normal* and *Priority-based* respectively. Once we have the QIG with the weights defined using one of the approaches, the mapping cost is obtained using Eq. (1). The effectiveness of the two cost metrics are analyzed in the following subsection.

3.3   Analysis of Priority-Based Cost Metric

Consider the quantum circuit shown in Fig. 4(a) comprising of four 2-qubit gates, G_1, G_2, G_3, and G_4, operating at level 1, 2, 3, and 4 respectively. Figure 4(b) shows the QIG in which the edge weights are computed using *Normal* approach. Since the 2-qubit gates G_1 and G_4 operate on qubits a and b, the weight of the edge (a, b) is 2. Similarly, the weights of other two edges (a, c) and (b, c) are 1 due to gates G_2 and G_3 respectively.

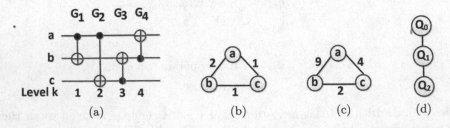

Fig. 4. (a) A quantum circuit of depth $d = 4$, (b) QIG based on Normal approach, (c) QIG based on Priority-based approach, (d) A 3-qubit physical architecture.

Figure 4(c) shows the QIG, where the edge weights are calculated using *Priority-based* approach. The calculation of the edge weights is illustrated below:

$$W(a,b) = p_1 + p_4 = 2^{4-1} + 2^{4-4} = 8 + 1 = 9$$
$$W(b,c) = p_3 = 2^{4-3} = 2$$
$$W(c,a) = p_2 = 2^{4-2} = 4$$

This follows from the fact that between a and b there are two gates at levels 1 and 4, between b and c there is one gate at level 3, and between c and a there is one gate at level 2.

To demonstrate the benefit of the priority-based approach, we consider the mapping of the quantum circuit of Fig. 4(a) to the physical layout shown in Fig. 4(d). We consider two alternate mappings as discussed below.

a) *M1*: We use the mapping $(a,b,c) \rightarrow (Q_0, Q_1, Q_2)$. The total cost using the normal and priority-based methods will be:

$$C_1^N = 0 \times 2 + 0 \times 1 + 1 \times 1 = 1 \tag{8}$$
$$C_1^P = 0 \times 9 + 0 \times 2 + 1 \times 4 = 4 \tag{9}$$

b) *M2*: We use the mapping $(a,b,c) \rightarrow (Q_1, Q_0, Q_2)$. The total cost using the normal and priority-based methods will be:

$$C_2^N = 0 \times 2 + 1 \times 1 + 0 \times 1 = 1 \tag{10}$$
$$C_2^P = 0 \times 9 + 1 \times 2 + 0 \times 4 = 2 \tag{11}$$

The mapping *M1* requires 2 Swap operations for NN-compliance irrespective of the ways swapping is conducted as shown in Figs. 5(a) and (b). On the other hand, *M2* requires only 1 Swap operation for NN-compliance as shown in Fig. 5(c). This indicates that *M2* is better than *M1* in reducing gate overhead. However, the *Normal* approach is unable to discriminate this, as it gives the cost measure of 1 in both the cases as shown in Eqs. (8) and (10). On the other hand, the *Priority-based* approach can distinguish the better mapping between *M1* and *M2* with costs of 4 and 2 respectively, as shown in Eqs. (9) and (11).

3.4   Nearest-Neighbor Mapping

We consider the problem of nearest-neighbor mapping of a given quantum circuit with m logical qubits on a hexagonal qubit architecture with n physical qubits. We assume that the physical qubits are laid out on a $n = w \times h$ 2-D hexagonal structure. The mapping problem is addressed as per the following steps:

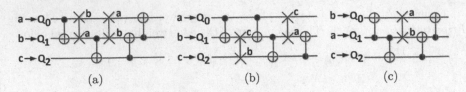

Fig. 5. (a) Swap insertion for qubit mapping *M1*, (b) Alternate Swap insertion for the same mapping, (c) Swap insertion for qubit mapping *M2*.

a) In order to map a m-qubit quantum circuit in a n-qubit layout, the physical qubits can be selected in $\binom{n}{m}$ ways. In doing this, a greedy algorithm is used, that starts with selecting a qubit located at the center of the layout i.e., $Q_c = center(w \times h)$ and the rest of $m-1$ qubits are then picked up from the layout by searching the nearmost un-mapped neighbors of Q_c.

b) There are $m!$ ways in which the m logical qubits can be mapped (π) to selected m physical qubits. We start with a set of k random mappings, $\{\pi_0, \pi_1, \ldots, \pi_{k-1}\}$, and apply an evolutionary approach (i.e. *Genetic algorithm*) over a maximum of N generations. In populating the next generation, 13% best members from the current population are directly copied, while the remaining ones are generated using crossover and mutation operations with probability values of 70% and 10% respectively. The fitness of each member in a population is measured using the cost metric defined in Eq. (1). The best mapping π_i from the Nth generation is considered for further processing.

c) The mapping π_i selected in previous step may not satisfy the NN-constraint for all the 2-qubit gates present in the circuit. The circuit is traversed from left to right, and all such violations identified. For each violation, we insert Swap gates or replace with RCNOT template or use a combination of both that minimizes the NN-violations of subsequent gates in the circuit by looking ahead a further L gates from the current gate position. When Swap gates are inserted, the current mapping π_i is updated accordingly to π_i' and subsequent gates are mapped considering the updated mapping π_i'.

For the present experiment, the parameters are set as follows: population size $K = 30$, number of generations $N = 500$, and lookahead factor $L = 20$.

4   Experimental Evaluation

The proposed approach has been implemented in C++ and run on a computing system with an AMD Ryzen 7 PRO 5850U processor with Radeon Graphics running at 1.90GHz, 48GB RAM, 1TB SSD and Windows 10 Pro operating system. A comprehensive set of benchmark functions available in RevLib [20] is used for the experimentation. The benchmarks are categorized as *tiny, small, medium* and *large* [4]. In this work we have implemented two approaches for NN-compliant mapping, using RCNOT and priority-based cost function respectively. Figure 6 shows the gate overheads in terms of CNOT gates for method [4], RCNOT, and priority-based methods for various benchmarks. It can be seen that the proposed approaches give significant improvements as compared to [4]. Moreover, the priority-based method gives better results as compared to RCNOT-based approach for most of the benchmarks.

The results for *large* benchmarks are summarized in Table 1. In the table, the first four columns respectively denote the name of the benchmarks, number of qubits, number of 2-qubit CNOT gates in the original gate netlist, and the chosen size of the hexagonal array for mapping. The next two columns show the number of additional CNOT gates required and the run time in seconds respectively for the method in [4]. The next four columns shows the number of additional CNOT gates required and the run time in seconds respectively for the RCNOT and priority-based methods. The last three columns shows the % improvements in terms of CNOT gates. R_T is the % improvement of RCNOT method over [4], P_T is the % improvement of priority-based method over [4], and P_R is the % improvement of priority based method over RCNOT based method. Out of total 66 *large* benchmarks, 11 benchmarks gives better results using [4] and the remaining benchmarks provide better results using RCNOT method. Similarly, out of total 66 large benchmarks, 8 benchmarks gives better results using [4] and the remaining benchmarks provide better results using RCNOT method. An average improvement of 23% and 29% are observed for RCNOT and priority-based methods over [4]. This clearly shows the effectiveness of the proposed priority-based cost metric.

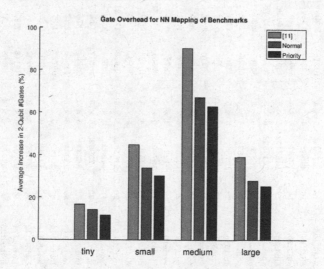

Fig. 6. Gate overhead comparison for the three methods.

Table 1. Analysis of SWAP, RCNOT and Priority cost metrics

Benchmark	Lines	#CNOT	Grid Size	As per [4] SWAP (T)		Proposed Approach RCNOT (R)		Priority (P)		Improvement (%)		
				#CNOT	Time	#CNOT	Time	#CNOT	Time	R_T	P_T	P_R
9symml_195	10	39296	4 × 3	8916	2.72	7099	1.67	6441	1.27	20.38	27.76	9.27
add6_196	19	24745	5 × 4	10218	2.20	6323	4.27	5514	3.00	38.12	46.04	12.79
alu2_199	16	44982	4 × 4	12354	3.38	9065	3.95	9513	3.40	26.62	23.00	-4.94
alu3_200	18	17787	5 × 4	5394	1.40	3823	2.96	3987	1.97	29.12	26.08	-4.29
alu4_201	22	1858472	5 × 5	439200	150.96	446213	238.70	436102	258.70	-1.60	0.71	2.27
apex4_202	28	1249592	6 × 5	467376	117.73	313290	272.64	300590	271.97	32.97	35.69	4.05
apla_203	22	26336	5 × 5	8496	2.30	6310	5.62	6377	4.81	25.73	24.94	-1.06
clip_206	14	39082	4 × 4	11388	2.85	7700	3.00	8237	2.54	32.38	27.67	-6.97
cm151a_211	28	12788	6 × 5	3336	1.24	3459	1.99	2953	5.34	-3.69	11.48	14.63
cm85a_209	14	9558	4 × 4	3522	0.78	2214	1.99	2003	0.90	37.14	43.13	9.53
cmb_214	20	49136	5 × 4	10410	3.97	11206	6.43	10584	5.56	-7.65	-1.67	5.55
co14_215	15	344008	4 × 4	75294	26.05	107222	29.65	84140	23.49	-42.40	-11.75	21.53
cu_219	25	16396	5 × 5	3972	1.27	3256	4.69	3167	3.25	18.03	20.27	2.73
cycle10_2_110	12	9122	4 × 3	1878	0.63	2386	1.47	1764	0.96	-27.05	6.07	26.07
cycle17_3_112	20	1376037	5 × 4	275616	114.71	440948	191.93	381315	216.62	-59.99	-38.35	13.52
dist_223	13	37510	4 × 4	10698	2.79	7493	2.87	8260	2.84	29.96	22.79	-10.24
dk17_224	21	13154	5 × 5	3990	1.08	3336	3.53	2995	2.53	16.39	24.94	10.22
ex1010_230	20	2165828	5 × 4	596298	174.21	496186	223.53	478578	239.60	16.79	19.74	3.55
example2_231	16	44982	4 × 4	12354	3.36	9145	4.75	8675	4.25	25.98	29.78	5.14
f51m_233	22	1759626	5 × 5	406422	139.57	507495	264.59	439626	264.25	-24.87	-8.17	13.37
hwb7_59	7	8423	3 × 3	3126	0.56	1917	0.63	1566	0.23	38.68	49.90	18.31
hwb8_113	8	29034	3 × 3	11856	2.17	7074	1.70	6012	1.23	40.33	49.29	15.01
hwb8_114	8	26169	3 × 3	9972	1.87	6046	1.18	5377	1.09	39.37	46.08	11.07
hwb8_116	8	12245	3 × 3	5310	0.99	3100	0.88	2811	0.39	41.62	47.06	9.32
hwb9_119	9	95787	3 × 3	38202	7.17	22967	3.87	20356	3.01	39.88	46.71	11.37
hwb9_121	9	95703	3 × 3	38118	7.21	23001	3.54	20123	2.97	39.66	47.21	12.51
hwb9_123	9	49777	3 × 3	19668	3.92	12025	2.21	10694	1.80	38.86	45.63	11.07
in0_235	26	1188570	6 × 5	281478	102.30	330120	253.71	295773	285.77	-17.28	-5.08	10.40
in2_236	29	1042525	6 × 5	247038	90.90	262098	257.42	270997	289.05	-6.10	-9.70	-3.40
life_238	10	19936	4 × 3	5364	1.46	3699	1.32	3093	0.77	31.04	42.34	16.38
max46_240	10	22924	4 × 3	5868	1.51	4230	1.49	4000	1.04	27.91	31.83	5.44
misex3c_244	28	5678530	6 × 5	1382388	500.65	1530202	1392.95	1490720	1474.21	-10.69	-7.84	2.58

(continued)

Table 1. (*continued*)

Benchmark	Lines	#CNOT	Grid Size	As per [4] SWAP (T)		Proposed Approach RCNOT (R)		Priority (P)		Improvement (%)		
				#CNOT	Time	#CNOT	Time	#CNOT	Time	R_T	P_T	P_R
mlp4_245	16	16940	4 × 4	5676	1.38	3677	2.91	4018	1.92	35.22	29.21	-9.27
plus127mod8192_162	13	526950	4 × 4	131688	40.66	104848	24.36	101677	23.15	20.38	22.79	3.02
plus63mod4096_163	12	163663	4 × 3	43878	11.81	35368	7.77	32795	6.99	19.39	25.26	7.27
plus63mod8192_164	13	330835	4 × 4	81210	25.42	62713	14.63	65254	14.84	22.78	19.65	-4.05
rd84_253	12	9677	4 × 3	3120	0.76	1871	1.39	2043	0.82	40.03	34.52	-9.19
root_255	13	17103	4 × 4	5190	1.28	3580	1.84	3527	1.24	31.02	32.04	1.48
ryy6_256	17	257389	5 × 4	57648	19.82	70012	25.08	60008	24.62	-21.45	-4.09	14.29
sao2_257	14	76591	4 × 4	18108	5.56	15303	4.80	14954	4.17	15.49	17.42	2.28
sym10_262	11	99332	4 × 3	24108	7.09	18173	3.84	18470	3.54	24.62	23.39	-1.63
sym9_193	10	39296	4 × 3	8916	2.70	7064	1.73	6051	1.18	20.77	32.13	14.34
tial_265	22	1963642	5 × 5	462780	162.31	455134	243.02	454498	275.18	1.65	1.79	0.14
urf1_149	9	69324	3 × 3	56772	8.63	33975	5.21	28436	4.01	40.16	49.91	16.30
urf1_150	9	106039	3 × 3	40968	7.88	25482	4.00	22365	3.38	37.8	45.41	12.23
urf1_151	9	98477	3 × 3	38856	7.25	24156	3.83	21075	3.27	37.83	45.76	12.75
urf1_278	9	24916	3 × 3	22050	3.25	13035	2.36	11324	2.01	40.88	48.64	13.13
urf2_152	8	30180	3 × 3	21582	3.45	13725	2.01	11943	1.65	36.41	44.66	12.98
urf2_153	8	30013	3 × 3	12048	2.24	7167	1.38	6291	0.77	40.51	47.78	12.22
urf2_154	8	28403	3 × 3	11454	2.13	7071	1.46	5901	0.71	38.27	48.48	16.55
urf2_161	8	27460	3 × 3	18642	2.90	11409	1.83	10014	1.42	38.8	46.28	12.23
urf2_277	8	8873	3 × 3	8310	1.22	5132	1.09	4386	0.92	38.24	47.22	14.54
urf3_155	10	158808	4 × 3	134244	20.87	79233	12.28	71287	10.94	40.98	46.90	10.03
urf3_156	10	329500	4 × 3	114342	23.90	71026	11.66	64041	10.10	37.88	43.99	9.83
urf3_157	10	312746	4 × 3	109356	22.64	68380	10.75	60424	9.84	37.47	44.75	11.63
urf3_279	10	66435	4 × 3	51450	8.02	29220	5.08	26803	4.74	43.21	47.9	8.27
urf4_187	11	192024	4 × 3	131454	25.96	95514	16.48	85593	15.03	27.34	34.89	10.39
urf5_158	9	61656	3 × 3	48948	7.47	29976	4.49	25845	3.64	40.19	47.20	11.72
urf5_159	9	56096	3 × 3	18270	3.94	11604	2.15	10512	1.45	36.49	42.46	9.41
urf5_280	9	24200	3 × 3	17736	2.75	10620	2.09	9432	1.73	40.12	46.82	11.19
urf6_160	15	64440	4 × 4	67086	10.95	39401	11.48	36724	10.98	41.27	45.26	6.79
urf6_281	15	176567	4 × 4	57804	14.93	47302	14.5	44717	18.9	18.17	22.64	5.46

5   Conclusion

An improved cost metric for nearest-neighbor mapping of quantum circuits to hexagonal qubit architecture is presented in this paper. A new qubit numbering system has been used, which allows elegant computation of distance between pairs of qubits. To achieve NN-compliance, Swap gates or RCNOT templates are optimally inserted within a window of L gates using a L-gate lookahead approach. A new priority-based measure for estimating the weight of a gate in the netlist has been used, which has good correlation with the actual number of Swap gates required. Experiments on a large number of benchmark circuits show significant reduction in gate overhead over a recently published method. The method is general and can be applied to any other architectures as well.

•

References

1. Ahsan, M., Naqvi, S.A.Z., Anwer, H.: Quantum circuit engineering for correcting coherent noise. Phys. Rev. A **105**, 022428 (2022). https://doi.org/10.1103/PhysRevA.105.022428
2. de Almeida, A.A.A., Dueck, G.W., da Silva, A.C.R.: CNOT gate mappings to Clifford+T circuits in IBM architectures. In: International Symposium on Multiple-Valued Logic, pp. 7–12 (2019)
3. Barenco, A., et al.: Elementary gates for quantum computation. Phys. Rev. A **52**(5), 3457–3467 (1995)
4. Chang, K.Y., Lee, C.Y.: Mapping nearest neighbor compliant quantum circuits onto a 2-D hexagonal architecture. IEEE Trans. CAD Integr. Circuits Syst. **41**(10), 1–14 (2021)
5. Chow, J., Dial, O., Gambetta, J.: IBM Quantum breaks the 100-qubit processor barrier. https://research.ibm.com/blog/127-qubit-quantum-processor-eagle/ (2021). Accessed 16 Nov 2021
6. Datta, K., Kole, A., Sengupta, I., Drechsler, R.: Mapping quantum circuits to 2-dimensional quantum architectures. In: GI-Jahrestagung Workshop 2022, pp. 1109–1120 (2022)
7. Datta, K., Kole, A., Sengupta, I., Drechsler, R.: Nearest neighbor mapping of quantum circuits to two-dimensional hexagonal qubit architecture. In: International Symposium on Multiple-Valued Logic, pp. 35–42 (2022)
8. Delaney, R.D., Urmey, M.D., Mittal, S., et al.: Superconducting-qubit readout via low-backaction electro-optic transduction. Nature **606**(7914), 489–493 (2022). https://doi.org/10.1038/s41586-022-04720-2
9. Grover, L.: A fast quantum mechanical algorithm for database search. In: ACM Symposium on Theory of computing, pp. 212–219 (1996)
10. Hilder, J., Pijn, D., Onishchenko, O., et al.: Fault-tolerant parity readout on a shuttling-based trapped-ion quantum computer. Phys. Rev. X **12**, 011032 (2022). https://doi.org/10.1103/PhysRevX.12.011032
11. Kole, A., Hillmich, S., Datta, K., Wille, R., Sengupta, I.: Improved mapping of quantum circuits to IBM QX architectures. In: IEEE Trans. CAD Integr. Circuits Syst. **39**(10), 2375–2383 (2020)
12. Litinski, D., Kesselring, M.S., Eisert, J., von Oppen, F.: Combining topological hardware and topological software: color-code quantum computing with topological superconductor networks. Phys. Rev. **7**(3), 031048 (2017)

13. Matsumoto, K., Amano, K.: Representation of quantum circuits with Clifford and $\pi/8$ gates. arXiv preprint arXiv:0806.3834 (2008)
14. Nielsen, M., Chuang, I.: Quantum Computation and Quantum Information. Cambridge University Press, New York (2000)
15. Niemann, P., Bandyopadhyay, C., Drechsler, R.: Combining SWAPs and remote Toffoli gates in the mapping to IBM QX architectures. In: Design Automation and Test in Europe, pp. 1–6 (2021)
16. Omkar, S., Lee, S.H., Teo, Y.S., Lee, S.W., Jeong, H.: All-photonic architecture for scalable quantum computing with Greenberger-Horne-Zeilinger states. PRX Quantum **3**, 030309 (2022). https://doi.org/10.1103/PRXQuantum.3.030309
17. Rahman, M., Dueck, G.W.: Synthesis of linear nearest neighbor quantum circuits. In: 10th Internationol Workshop on Boolean Problems, pp. 1–9 (2012)
18. Shor, P.W.: Algorithms for quantum computation: discrete logarithms and factoring. In: Symposium on Foundations of Computer Science, pp. 124–134 (1994)
19. Tang, H., et al.: Experimental quantum fast hitting on hexagonal graphs. Nat. Photonics **12**(12), 754–758 (2018)
20. Wille, R., Große, D., Teuber, L., Dueck, G.W., Drechsler, R.: RevLib: An online resource for reversible functions and reversible circuits. In: Proceedings International Symposium on Multiple-Valued Logic, pp. 220–225. Texas, USA (2008)
21. Zhou, X., Li, S., Feng, Y.: Quantum circuit transformation based on simulated annealing and heuristic search. Trans. Comput. Aided Design Integr. Circuits Syst. **39**(12), 4683–4694 (2020). https://doi.org/10.1109/TCAD.2020.2969647
22. Zulehner, A., Paler, A., Wille, R.: An efficient methodology for mapping quantum circuits to the IBM QX architectures. IEEE Trans. CAD Integr. Circuits Syst. **38**(7), 1226–1236 (2019). http://iic.jku.at/eda/res-earch/ibm_qx_mapping/

Exploiting the Benefits of Clean Ancilla Based Toffoli Gate Decomposition Across Architectures

Abhoy Kole[1], Kamalika Datta[1,3]([✉]), Philipp Niemann[1], Indranil Sengupta[2], and Rolf Drechsler[1,3]

[1] Cyber-Physical Systems, DFKI GmbH, Bremen, Germany
{abhoy.kole,Philipp.Niemann}@dfki.de
[2] Department of Computer Science and Engineering, Indian Institute of Technology, Kharagpur, India
isg@iitkgp.ac.in
[3] Institute of Computer Science, University of Bremen, Bremen, Germany
{kdatta,drechsler}@uni-bremen.de

Abstract. Elementary gate decomposition of larger Toffoli operations is often carried out using additional qubits (ancilla). The number of gates and the circuit depth vary in such transformation depending on the type of ancilla used (clean or dirty). The present *Noisy Intermediate Scale Quantum* (NISQ) devices have limited number of coherent qubits with faulty native operation support. Superconducting devices also have coupling restrictions or *Nearest-Neighbor* (NN) constraints, which require additional gates to map the transformed netlist for execution. While the mapping overhead is correlated with the number of 2-qubit gates and involved qubits, the fidelity of execution is inversely proportional to the number of gates and circuit depth. There is a tradeoff in devising the transpilation (i.e. low-level transformation and mapping) approach — dirty ancilla demands less qubits and overhead at the expense of more gates and depth as compared to clean ancilla, which involves less gates and depth at the expense of more qubits and overhead. This paper analyzes the disparity in gates, depth and qubits between: (i) the low-level transformation approaches without considering device coupling information, and (ii) the mapping schemes based on netlist transformation using a specific type of ancilla. We analyze the benefits of using NN-constraints at the transformation stage, and the impact of distributing clean ancilla across architectures. We have carried out experiments on IBM Q20 and Hexagonal Q20 architectures, which show improvements of 17% and 13% respectively in terms of number of gates.

Keywords: Quantum circuits · Architecture-aware decomposition · Qubit mapping · Clean and dirty ancilla

1 Introduction

We have witnessed rapid developments in quantum computers over the last few years with several prominent physical implementations (viz. by IBM, Google,

M. Kutrib and U. Meyer (Eds.): RC 2023, LNCS 13960, pp. 232–244, 2023.
https://doi.org/10.1007/978-3-031-38100-3_15

DWave and many others). These implementations are often referred to as *Noisy Intermediate Scale Quantum* (NISQ) era devices due to their faulty native operations within a small number of limited coherent qubits. Additionally, the coupling restrictions or *Nearest-Neighbor* (NN) constraints between qubits, built using technologies like superconducting elements, require additional gates to perform 2-qubit operations on any pair of uncoupled qubits. While the number of operations (gates) and latency (circuit depth) of a computation pose a threat to its reliability, the overhead further leads to the accumulation of noise.

The transpilation of quantum circuits for a NN-architecture is typically a two-step process. Initially, a given netlist realized using multi-qubit operations like *Multiple-Control Toffoli* (MCT) gates is transformed into a low-level description using 1- and 2-qubit elementary gates from a specific library, e.g. the Clifford+T. The gates are then mapped satisfying the NN-constraints of the target architecture. For such low-level description of MCT operations, the use of additional qubits (ancilla) is very effective in reducing the gates and depth of the netlist [7]. While the use of *dirty ancilla* reduces the qubit requirement by reusing circuit qubits, the gates and depth can be further minimized when qubits not used in the circuit are used as *clean ancilla* in the transformation [11]. During the final stage of transpilation, NN-compliance is achieved by introducing more gates to satisfy the NN-constraints.

There exist several works for transforming MCT operations into elementary gate netlists [4,14] with varying gates, depth and qubits. The mapping overhead (i.e. number of 2-qubit gates and required qubits) is inversely related to the computational reliability. Most of the mapping methods have used generated netlists obtained from standard transformations without considering the device constraints [9,18]. For quantum devices with NN-constraints [1,15], it is important to consider architectural information at the transformation stage to reduce gates and depth of the transpiled netlist. In a recent work Baker et al. [5] have shown decomposition of Toffoli gate with arbitrary number of clean and dirty ancilla qubits. In another related work, Balauca et al. [6] have proposed efficient construction of multi-control quantum gates. However, no specific analyses considering the architectural information to map these decomposed netlists have been carried out so far.

One of the recent works [12] combine *Swap* gates and *Remote-CNOT* templates to generate a database of MCT operations transpiled using dirty ancilla for the IBM Q20 architecture. With the gradual increase in the number of qubits, more number of qubits can be used for transpilation. To this end, in this paper we exploit clean ancilla based transpilation of MCT gate netlists with NN-compliance. We show that the use of clean ancilla outperforms the approach that uses dirty ancilla, and analyze the impact of clean ancilla distribution on two architectures, viz. 20-qubit IBM Q20 and Hexagonal Q20. Experimental results confirm that clean ancilla based approach is beneficial in reducing the gate overhead. Overall improvements of up to 17% and 13% respectively are obtained for IBM Q20 and Hexagonal Q20 architectures.

Rest of the paper is organized as follows. Section 2 provides the necessary background and motivation for the work. Section 3 presents the proposed database-driven architecture-aware decomposition approach. Section 4 presents the experimental results, and finally the conclusion is provided in Sect. 5.

2   Background and Motivation

In this section we discuss about quantum gates and architectures, and some of the cost metrics used for decomposition.

2.1   Quantum Gates and Quantum Circuits

In quantum computing, the basic unit of information is quantum bits or *qubits*. The state of a qubit can be represented as $|\psi\rangle = \alpha|0\rangle + \beta|1\rangle$, where α and β are complex amplitudes such that $|\alpha|^2 + |\beta|^2 = 1$. A qubit can be in a state of superposition, and also a set of qubits can exist in states of entanglement. Quantum gates operate on qubits and change their states; typically, we have 1- and 2-qubit primitive gate operations. A quantum circuit consists of a sequence of quantum gates, where each m-qubit quantum gate can be represented by a $2^m \times 2^m$ unitary matrix. Also, every quantum gate operation is inherently reversible.

A Toffoli gate $T(\{c_1, c_2\}; t)$ is a 3-input reversible gate that has two controls c_1 and c_2 and a target t. If the values of c_1 and c_2 are both 1, then the target t changes to $c_1 c_2 \oplus t$. Figure 1 shows a Toffoli gate and its realization using Clifford+T gate library. Another gate library that has been used by many researchers is known as NCV [7].

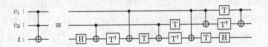

Fig. 1. Toffoli gate and its Clifford+T realization.

2.2   Quantum Architecture

Several implementations of quantum computers have emerged in the last five years [2, 3, 8, 10, 15]. Most of these devices are built using superconducting qubits. Recently photonic technologies have also been explored to realize qubits [15]. Figure 2 shows two different NN architectures each comprising of 20 qubits and having maximum degree of qubit coupling of six.

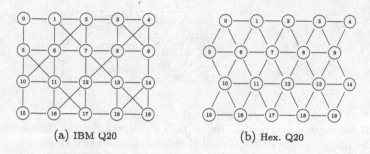

(a) IBM Q20   (b) Hex. Q20

Fig. 2. Qubit coupling layout for two 20-qubit architectures.

For mapping quantum circuits, additional gates are required to comply with the architectural limitations or NN-constraints [10]. Typically, Swap gates [17] or remote-CNOT templates [13] are inserted in the netlist for compliance. As the gate operations are noisy, the inclusion of extra gates accumulate more errors in the final results. Hence reducing the number of gates has a direct bearing in controlling the error. Most of the existing works in the literature consider netlists consisting of 1- and 2-qubit gates that are generated using existing transformation methods. However, by exploiting information about the architecture (viz. number of qubits, inter-qubit coupling, error statistics, etc.), we can suitably select the ancilla lines so as to minimize the gate overhead. One recent work [12] has considered the IBM Q20 architecture to generate a complete database for MCT gates using dirty ancilla; however, the possibility of clean ancilla usage is unexplored. In this paper we explore the benefits of using clean ancilla during gate decomposition, and show how MCT gate networks can be mapped to various architectures efficiently.

2.3 Cost Metric and WCOST

To execute quantum gates with NN-compliance, two broad approaches exist, both of which incur the use of additional CNOT gates in the netlist. The first approach tries to bring the states of a pair of interacting qubits to adjacent locations by adding Swap gates [17]. As an alternative, a 2-qubit gate operation on non-adjacent qubits can be carried out as a cascade of NN-compliant CNOT operations, called remote-CNOT template [13]. In the latter case, the number of additional gates required is $4d$, where d is the distance between the pair of physical qubits. The cost is estimated as the number of additional CNOT gates.

For the netlist of Fig. 1, the *Qubit Interaction Graph* (QIG) is shown in Fig. 3(a). The edge weights represent the number of 2-qubit operations between qubit pairs. We calculate the total cost (WCOST) for mapping the netlist to IBM Q20 and Hexagonal Q20 architectures. With respect to the QIG and a layout mapping, $\pi : q_i \rightarrow Q_k$, let E denote the set of edges, w_{ij} the edge weight between qubits q_i and q_j, and d_{ij} the number of qubits in the shortest coupling path between $\pi(q_i)$ and $\pi(q_j)$. The total cost can be estimated as:

Qubit Mapping				
c_1	c_2	t	Architecture	WCOST
Q_0	Q_2	Q_1	IBM Q20	12
Q_8	Q_{14}	Q_{11}		32
Q_0	Q_2	Q_1	Hex. Q20	12
Q_8	Q_{16}	Q_{11}		26

(a)   (b)

Fig. 3. (a) Interaction graph of a Toffoli gate $T(\{c_1, c_2\}; t)$, and (b) corresponding WCOST for mapping into IBM Q20 and Hexagonal Q20 architectures.

$$WCOST = \sum_{(i,j) \in E} C_{ij} \text{ where } C_{ij} = \begin{cases} w_{ij} & \text{if } d_{ij} = 0 \\ 4d_{ij}w_{ij} & \text{otherwise.} \end{cases} \quad (1)$$

Figure 3(b) shows the WCOST for four different mappings for the two architectures.

3   Proposed Method

In this work we show how clean ancilla is beneficial as compared to dirty ancilla for MCT gate decomposition. We first analyze ancilla usage in realizing Toffoli gates using primitive quantum gates. The mapping overhead on two specific architectures, viz. IBM Q20 and 20-qubit regular hexagonal, are presented next. Finally, the effects of clean ancilla distribution on given qubit layout are examined.

3.1   Realization of MCT Netlist

The transformation of an $(m+1)$-qubit MCT gate requires $m-2$ ancilla qubits for $m > 2$. The number of gates in the transformed netlist may vary depending on whether clean or dirty ancilla are used. A $(m+1)$-qubit MCT gate (for $m > 2$) requires $4(m-2)$ 3-qubit Toffoli gates when $m-2$ dirty ancilla are used [7], and $(2m-3)$ Toffoli gates when $m-2$ clean ancilla are used [11].

Example 1. Figure 4 shows the realization of a 5-qubit MCT gate, $T(\{c_1, \ldots, c_4\}, t, \{a_1, a_2\})$ decomposed using 8 and 5 Toffoli gates considering a_1 and a_2 as dirty and clean ancilla qubits, respectively.

The number of gates can be further reduced by performing some optimization. In general, the operation of a Toffoli gate can be realized as a sequence of 3-qubit $C^2(-iZ)$ $(C^2(iZ))$ and CS $(CS^\dagger)$ operations. For such Toffoli gate pairs operating on same set of qubits in presence of an intermediate gate, the component CS $(CS^\dagger)$ gate pair can be removed completely (partially) depending on the intermediate gate operation. This is illustrated by the following example.

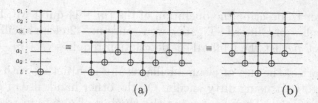

Fig. 4. Decomposition of a 4-controlled MCT gate as a netlist of Toffoli gates using (a) 2 dirty ancilla, (b) 2 clean ancilla.

Fig. 5. A pair of Toffoli gates and a intermediate CNOT gate operating on the (a) target and (b) control qubits of the Toffoli gates.

Example 2. Figure 5 shows the netlists comprising of pair of 3-qubit Toffoli gate, $T(\{q_1, q_2\}; q_3)$, with an intermediate CNOT gate, $CX(q_c, q_t)$. The component CS ($CS^\dagger$) from the netlist can be removed completely, if the control, q_c is q_3 and target, $q_t \notin \{q_1, q_2\}$ (see Fig. 5a). Similarly, for the netlist shown in Fig. 5b, one CNOT operation from each of the CS ($CS^\dagger$) realization can be removed, when the q_2 (or q_1) becomes q_t.

Considering such cancellation, the number of CNOT operations to realize a $(m+1)$-qubit MCT gate (for $m > 2$) gets reduced to $(20m - 42)$ when $m - 2$ dirty ancilla are used. Similarly, for $m - 2$ clean ancilla, the required number of CNOT operations is reduced to $(8m - 10)$. However, it may be noted that the ability to reuse circuit qubit as ancilla leads to a final netlist with fewer qubits when dirty ancilla are used for decomposition instead of clean ancilla.

Lemma 1. *A r-qubit MCT network can be described optimally using 1- and 2-qubit Clifford+T gates and r qubits, when only dirty ancilla qubits are used and the largest MCT gate in the network is of size $(m+1)$-qubit where $m \leqslant \frac{r+1}{2}$.*

Proof. In order to describe the operation of an $(m+1)$-qubit MCT gate using minimum number of Clifford+T gates, we require $m - 2$ dirty ancilla qubits. Thus, for a r-qubit MCT network, the Clifford+T description does not require any additional qubits, when the largest MCT gate in the netlist is of size $(m+1)$-qubit, and it satisfies the condition, $(m+1) + (m-2) \leqslant r$ i.e., $m \leqslant \frac{r+1}{2}$.

The Clifford+T description of an MCT gate netlist requires additional qubits other than circuit when clean ancilla are used.

Lemma 2. *A r-qubit MCT network can be described optimally using $r + m - 2$ qubits and 1- and 2-qubit Clifford+T gates when only clean ancilla are used and the largest MCT gate is of size $(m+1)$-qubit.*

238   A. Kole et al.

Proof. In order to describe the operation of the $(m+1)$-qubit MCT gate using minimum number of Clifford+T gates, we require $m-2$ clean ancilla. Thus, for a r-qubit MCT netlist the Clifford+T description requires $(r+m-2)$ qubits.

To summarize, the use of clean ancilla results in a netlist with fewer gates as compared to that using dirty ancilla. On the other hand, use of dirty ancilla requires fewer qubits. Thus, increasing the number of qubits in re-describing a MCT netlist can reduce the number of gates in the final netlist as illustrated by the following example.

Example 3. Figure 6 shows two equivalent descriptions of a 5-qubit MCT netlist using clean and dirty ancilla qubits. The use of dirty ancilla requires 5 Toffoli gates with no additional qubits (vide Lemma 1). The use of clean ancilla requires one additional qubit (q_a) and 4 Toffoli gates (vide Lemma 2).

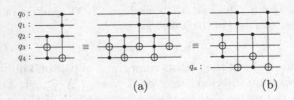

(a)   (b)

Fig. 6. Decomposition of a MCT netlist using (a) dirty ancilla, (b) clean ancilla.

Clearly, there is a tradeoff in using either clean or dirty ancilla qubits for decomposition. In addition, while mapping the gate operations to some physical architecture, the NN-constraints must be taken into account. This is discussed in the next subsection.

3.2 Architectural Mapping of MCT Netlist

Current NISQ architectures have limited number of qubits, and mapping a r-qubit MCT netlist requires re-describing it in terms of native 1- and 2-qubit gates. Of course, the number of qubits in the final netlist cannot exceed the available number of physical qubits. The number of qubits in the decomposed netlist depends on two factors: (i) size of the largest MCT gate in the netlist, and (ii) the type of ancilla used in decomposition. This limits the size of the MCT netlist that can be mapped to n physical qubits.

Lemma 3. *In an n-qubit target architecture, an n-qubit MCT netlist can be mapped if the largest MCT gate present in the network never occupies more than 50% (or $\lfloor \frac{n+1}{2} \rfloor +1$) of n qubits, where dirty ancilla are used in the decomposition.*

Proof. Decomposing an $(m+1)$-qubit MCT gate requires $m-2$ ancilla qubits, where $m>2$. To map the decomposed netlist on an n-qubit architecture, it must satisfy the inequality: $m+m-2+1 \leqslant n$. That is, $n \geqslant 2m-1$. Thus the largest MCT gate can occupy $\frac{m+1}{2m-1} \times 100 \approx 50\%$ (for large m) of the n physical qubits.

As the supported gate operations on current NISQ architectures are noisy, and requires additional gates to satisfy the underlying NN-constraints, it is essential to describe the the netlist using minimal number of primitive gates. We have already discussed that clean ancilla based decomposition requires less gates but more physical qubits.

Lemma 4. *In an n-qubit architecture, a r-qubit MCT netlist containing r-qubit MCT gates can be mapped if the MCT network never occupies more than 50% (or $\lfloor \frac{n+3}{2} \rfloor$) of n qubits, where clean ancilla are used in the decomposition.*

Proof. The decomposition of a r-qubit MCT gate requires $r - 3$ clean ancilla with the constraint, $r + r - 3 \leqslant n$. That is, $2r - 3 \leqslant n$. Thus the MCT netlist containing largest MCT gate can occupy, $\frac{r}{2r-3} \times 100 \approx 50\%$ (for large r) of the n physical qubits.

It may be noted that while mapping a MCT netlist to a target architecture, dirty ancilla based decomposition imposes restriction on the largest MCT gate, whereas clean ancilla based approach restricts the number of qubits. The following example illustrates the mapping of the largest MCT netlist described at primitive gate level using both clean and dirty ancilla.

Example 4. Consider the 5-qubit MCT netlist shown in Fig. 6. On the 5-qubit IBM QX2 architecture shown in Fig. 7a, the netlist can only be mapped if it is decomposed using dirty ancilla qubits (vide Lemma 3). However, on the 7-qubit IBM Falcon architecture (see Fig. 7b), such 5-qubit MCT netlists described using clean ancilla can be mapped (vide Lemma 4).

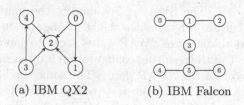

(a) IBM QX2   (b) IBM Falcon

Fig. 7. IBM quantum architectures with 5 and 7 qubits.

For an n-qubit architecture, the mapping of r-qubit MCT netlist can be done by describing the network using clean ancilla if it satisfies Lemma 4; otherwise dirty ancilla should be used, provided it does not violate Lemma 3. In such cases when Lemma 4 is applicable, clean ancilla based description provides mapping with less overhead as illustrated by the following example.

Example 5. Consider the mapping of the MCT netlist shown in Fig. 6 on an IBM 7-qubit Falcon processor (see Fig. 7b). For the dirty ancilla based decomposed network, a mapping $\pi : (q_0, q_1, q_2, q_3, q_4) \rightarrow (Q_0, Q_2, Q_5, Q_1, Q_3)$ incurs a WCOST of 60. In contrast, for the clean ancilla based decomposed network, a mapping $\pi : (q_0, q_1, q_2, q_3, q_4, q_a) \rightarrow (Q_0, Q_2, Q_5, Q_6, Q_3, Q_1)$ leads to a WCOST of 48.

The choice of physical qubits as clean ancilla also plays a major role during NN-mapping to reduce gate overhead. A viable approach for effective selection of physical qubits is presented next.

3.3   Clean Ancilla Based MCT Netlist Mapping

The clean ancilla based low-level transformation of MCT netlists almost doubles the number of required physical qubits. In fact, for an n-qubit architecture, the largest MCT gate of size n_r $(= \lfloor (n+3)/2 \rfloor)$ qubits can be realized in this way by selecting required ancilla from n_a $(= n_r - 3)$ qubits. There are $\binom{n}{n_a}$ ways these n_a ancilla can be distributed among the n physical qubits.

For each ancilla configuration there exists $(n - n_a) \times \binom{n-n_a-1}{m}$ number of $(m + 1)$-qubit MCT gate configurations, where each MCT configuration in turn can have $\binom{n_a}{m-2}$ ancilla configurations.

For a given MCT configuration $T(C; t; A)$ where A denotes the set of ancilla qubits, the optimal remote MCT template is determined by considering $T(\pi_{min}(C); \pi_{min}(t); \pi_{min}(A))$, where π_{min} denotes mapping to physical architectural qubits, $\pi_{min} : q_i \rightarrow Q_k$ that provides minimum WCOST. By exploring all such configurations for $(m + 1)$-qubit MCT gates where $3 \leqslant m + 1 \leqslant n_r$, a complete database of optimal remote MCT realizations is created for mapping purpose.

The MCT circuit is then processed gate-wise and each MCT gate is realized by an optimal remote MCT gate. As it has been observed in the case of dirty ancilla based decomposition [12], it is often beneficial not to directly realize an MCT gate via the corresponding remote MCT realization, but rather to apply SWAP gates first. The SWAP gates modify the mapping of logical to physical qubits, which also changes the MCT configuration of the next gate to be realized. Even though the SWAP gates seem to increase the mapping overhead, the WCOST of the resulting configuration is often significantly smaller and outweighs the cost of the SWAP gates. The same methodology as in [12] (i.e., formulation as a single source shortest path problem) is used to determine optimal combinations of SWAPs and remote MCT realization. However, in order to reduce the search space, the position of the clean ancilla qubits is fixed and those qubits will not change their position at all.

Example 6. Figure 8 shows a clean ancilla based MCT gate, $T(\{c_1, c_2, c_3\}; t; a_1)$, realized using 3 Toffoli gates. and its corresponding QIG for the final netlist. Considering the set of clean ancilla $A = \{Q_1, Q_3, Q_6, Q_8, Q_{11}, Q_{13}, Q_{16}, Q_{18}\}$ on IBM Q20 architecture (see Fig. 2a), the π_{min} of the remote MCT realization, $T(\{Q_2, Q_{12}, Q_{15}\}; Q_0; Q_{11})$ has WCOST of 44. Swapping the target Q_0 to Q_7 (through the shortest coupling path $Q_0 \rightarrow Q_1 \rightarrow Q_7$) as well as swapping the control Q_{15} to Q_{10} (having direct coupling $Q_{15} \rightarrow Q_{10}$) require 3 SWAPs (i.e., 9 CNOTs), but the π_{min} WCOST of the resulting configuration $T(\{Q_2, Q_{10}, Q_{12}\}; Q_7; Q_6)$ is only 20, such that the overall realization of the gate requires only $20 + 9 = 29$ CNOTs.

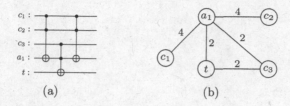

(a)   (b)

Fig. 8. (a) Clean ancilla based decomposition of a 4-qubit MCT gate using 3 Toffoli gates, and (b) corresponding interaction graph.

4 Experimental Evaluation.

The proposed gate decomposition approach using clean ancilla qubits has been implemented in C++, and run on a number of reversible benchmark circuits available in RevLib [16]. For evaluation, two distinct 20-qubit architectures are considered, viz. IBM Q20 and Hexagonal Q20. We need to block 8 physical qubits for clean ancilla based decomposition; the remaining qubits can support 12-qubit MCT networks with largest MCT gate of size 11-qubits. There are $\binom{20}{8}$ possible ways in which the ancilla can be selected. For experimentation, we consider the following three clean ancilla distributions:

$$\text{Dist.1} = \{Q_1, Q_3, Q_6, Q_8, Q_{11}, Q_{13}, Q_{16}, Q_{18}\}$$
$$\text{Dist.2} = \{Q_2, Q_6, Q_7, Q_8, Q_{12}, Q_{16}, Q_{17}, Q_{18}\}$$
$$\text{Dist.3} = \{Q_1, Q_2, Q_6, Q_7, Q_{11}, Q_{12}, Q_{16}, Q_{17}\}$$

For each distribution, we generate the complete database for all n-qubit MCT gate configurations, where $3 \leqslant n \leqslant 11$. We also generate a similar dirty ancilla database for the same MCT gate configurations. For each clean ancilla distribution, database creation took under one hour whereas for dirty ancilla it took 4 hours for both the architectures. The mapping algorithm [12] took few seconds for both the architectures.

4.1 Dirty vs Clean Ancilla Based Decomposition

For comparing the mapping overheads for clean and dirty ancilla based approaches, we consider the clean ancilla distribution *Dist.1*. The results of the experiments are presented in Table 1. The first three columns give the serial no. (Sl.), the benchmark names and the number of qubits in the original netlist respectively. The next three columns respectively show the number of CNOT gates required for dirty and clean ancilla based decomposition, and the percentage improvement in using clean ancilla. Columns 6-8 show the additional CNOT gate overheads for mapping these dirty and clean ancilla based decomposed netlists on IBM Q20 architecture, and the percentage improvements respectively. Columns 9-11 show similar data for the Hexagonal Q20 architecture. The last two columns show the overall improvement percentage, calculated based on the

Table 1. Results of clean and dirty ancilla based decomposition for IBM and Hexagonal architectures

Sl.	Benchmark	n	MCT decomposition			IBM Q20 Mapping Ovrd.			Hex. Q20 Mapping Ovrd.			Overall Imp.(%)	
			dirty	clean	Imp.(%)	dirty	clean	Imp.(%)	dirty	clean	Imp.(%)	IBM	HEX
1	9symml_195	10	6792	3152	53.59	1380	954	30.87	1026	1002	2.34	49.76	46.87
2	alu-v2_30	5	146	114	21.92	30	84	-180.00	27	90	-233.33	-12.50	-17.92
3	cm152a_212	12	358	218	39.11	27	66	-144.44	27	87	-222.22	26.23	20.78
4	con1_216	9	284	180	36.62	45	98	-117.78	45	118	-162.22	15.50	9.42
5	cycle10_2_110	12	1264	616	51.27	261	283	-8.43	267	335	-25.47	41.05	37.88
6	dc1_220	11	570	390	31.58	105	354	-237.14	105	373	-255.24	-10.22	-13.04
7	dc1_221	11	570	390	31.58	111	368	-231.53	99	368	-271.72	-11.31	-13.30
8	f2_232	8	358	222	37.99	39	99	-153.85	36	123	-241.67	19.14	12.44
9	rd73_252	10	1468	876	40.33	306	922	-201.31	273	1008	-269.23	-1.35	-8.21
10	sym10_262	11	12034	5514	54.18	2742	2103	23.30	2358	2205	6.49	48.45	46.37
11	sym6_145	7	1008	600	40.48	129	252	-95.35	117	285	-143.59	25.07	21.33
12	sym9_148	10	6300	3948	37.33	576	2750	-377.43	489	3080	-529.86	2.59	-3.52
13	sym9_193	10	6792	3152	53.59	1398	957	31.55	1041	1023	1.73	49.83	46.70
14	urf1_150	9	59133	33461	43.41	11323	22044	-94.68	10230	23588	-130.58	21.22	17.75
15	urf1_151	9	56583	32187	43.12	10929	21911	-100.48	10040	22861	-127.70	19.87	17.37
16	urf2_153	8	19951	11899	40.36	3784	5747	-51.88	3471	6539	-88.39	25.65	21.28
17	urf2_154	8	18857	11289	40.13	3733	5717	-53.15	3485	6334	-81.75	24.72	21.12
18	wim_266	11	290	202	30.34	48	172	-258.33	51	181	-254.90	-10.65	-12.32
19	z4_268	11	920	560	39.13	108	402	-272.22	150	437	-191.33	6.42	6.82

CNOT gate overhead that includes both decomposition and mapping for clean ancilla based approach over dirty ancilla based approach for the two architectures.

The results show that clean ancilla based approach outperforms dirty ancilla based approach for most of the benchmarks. Although the mapping overhead is better for dirty ancilla based approach for many of the benchmarks, the overall improvement is better for clean ancilla based approach. Since any circuit qubits can be reused as the basis for dirty ancilla based decomposition, it is possible to have better qubit selection leading to reduced mapping overhead. On the other hand for clean ancilla based approach, distribution of ancilla greatly influences the mapping overheads across architectures.

4.2   Effect of Clean Ancilla Distribution

The overall improvements for all the three clean ancilla distributions over dirty ancilla for both the architectures are shown in Fig. 9. For both the architectures, *Dist.1* outperforms *Dist.2* and *Dist.3* in most of the cases. It is found that no single ancilla distribution across the architectures provide better results for all the benchmarks. For example, the benchmark *9symml_195* gives best result with *Dist.1*. On the other hand, for the benchmark *z4_268*, *Dist.2* provides the best result. But, *Dist.3* does not give the best result for any of the benchmarks. This clearly shows that the distribution of clean ancilla has a significant impact on the mapping overhead.

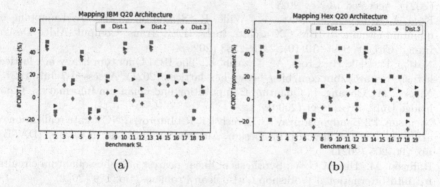

(a)   (b)

Fig. 9. Effects of ancilla distribution across architectures.

5   Conclusion

In this work we critically analyze two alternate decomposition schemes for realizing MCT netlists using Clifford+T gates based on (i) dirty ancilla, and (ii) clean ancilla. With the increasing power of modern-day quantum computers we can use clean ancilla based decomposition that reduces the overall gates in the transpilled netlist, which in turn increases operation fidelity. Two alternate 20-qubit architectures have been used for transpilation, the IBM Q20 and the

20-qubit hexagonal architectures. We show that although dirty ancilla help in reducing the total number of required qubits, the use of clean ancilla can significantly reduce the number of gate operations and hence the accumulated errors. In addition, using a database-driven approach the impact of distributing clean ancilla for NN-mapping of logical qubits has been analyzed across architectures.

References

1. Ibm, Q.: https://www.research.ibm.com/ibm-q. Accessed 20 Mar 2019
2. IBM Quantum Processor Types. https://quantum-computing.ibm.com/services/d-ocs/services/manage/systems/processors/ (2017)
3. The IBM Hummingbird Architecture. https://quantum-computing.ibm.com/services/docs/services/manage/systems/processors#hummingbird/ (2021). Accessed 1 Dec 2021
4. Amy, M., Maslov, D., Mosca, M., Roetteler, M.: A meet-in-the-middle algorithm for fast synthesis of depth-optimal quantum circuits. IEEE Trans. Comput.-Aided Design Integrated Circ. Syst. **32**(6), 818–830 (2013)
5. Baker, J.M., Duckering, C., Hoover, A., Chong, F.T.: Decomposing quantum generalized Toffoli with an arbitrary number of ancilla. ArXiv abs/1904.01671 (2019)
6. Balauca, S., Arusoaie, A.: Efficient constructions for simulating multi controlled quantum gates. In: Computational Science - ICCS 2022, pp. 1–14 (2022)
7. Barenco, A., et al.: Elementary gates for quantum computation. Phys. Rev. A **52**(5), 3457–3467 (1995)
8. Chow, J., Dial, O., Gambetta, J.: IBM Quantum breaks the 100-qubit processor barrier. https://research.ibm.com/blog/127-qubit-quantum-processor-eagle/ (2021). Accessed 16 Nov 2021
9. Kole, A., Hillmich, S., Datta, K., Wille, R., Sengupta, I.: Improved mapping of quantum circuits to IBM QX architectures. IEEE Trans. Comput.-Aided Design Integr. Circuit. Syst. **39**(10), 2375–2383 (2020)
10. Nation, P., Paik, H., Cross, A., Nazario, Z.: The IBM Quantum heavy hex lattice. https://research.ibm.com/blog/heavy-hex-lattice/ (2021). Accessed 7 July 2021
11. Nielsen, M., Chuang, I.: Quantum Computation and Quantum Information. Cambridge Univ, Press (Oct (2000)
12. Niemann, P., Bandyopadhyay, C., Drechsler, R.: Improved NCV gate realization of arbitrary size Toffoli gates. In: Design, Automation and Test in Europe (DATE), pp. 200–205 (2021)
13. Rahman, M., Dueck, G.W.: Synthesis of linear nearest neighbor quantum circuits. In: 10th International Workshop on Boolean Problems, pp. 1–9 (2012)
14. Selinger, P.: Quantum circuits of t-depth one. Phys. Rev. A **87**(4), 042302 (2013)
15. Tang, H., et al.: Experimental quantum fast hitting on hexagonal graphs. Nat. Photonics **12**(12), 754–758 (2018)
16. Wille, R., Große, D., Teuber, L., Dueck, G., Drechsler, R.: RevLib: an online resource for reversible functions and reversible circuits. In: International Symposium on Multi-Valued Logic, pp. 220–225 (2008). http://www.revlib.org
17. Wille, R., Lye, A., Drechsler, R.: Optimal SWAP gate insertion for nearest neighbor quantum circuits. In: Proceedings Design Automation Conference (DAC), pp. 489–494. IEEE, Suntec, Singapore (2014)
18. Zulehner, A., Paler, A., Wille, R.: An efficient methodology for mapping quantum circuits to the IBM QX architectures. EEE Transactions on Computer-Aided Design of Integrated Circuits and Systems **38**(7), 1226–1236 (2019)

Author Index

M. Kutrib and U. Meyer (Eds.): RC 2023, LNCS 13960, p. 245, 2023.
https://doi.org/10.1007/978-3-031-38100-3

Printed in the United States
by Baker & Taylor Publisher Services